What Can We Know?

AN INTRODUCTION TO THE THEORY OF KNOWLEDGE

SECOND EDITION

Louis P. Pojman

UNITED STATES MILITARY ACADEMY

Wadsworth
Thomson Learning™

Australia • Canada • Mexico • Singapore • Spain • United Kingdom • United States

PHILOSOPHY EDITOR: Peter Adams
EDITORIAL ASSISTANT: Mark Andrews
MARKETING MANAGER: Dave Garrison
PERMISSIONS EDITOR: Bob Kauser
PRODUCTION SERVICES: Proof Positive/
Farrowlyne Associates, Inc.

TEXT DESIGNER: Luba Yudovich
COVER DESIGN: Annabelle Ison
COVER PRINTER: Webcom, Limited
COMPOSITOR: Black Dot Group
PRINTER: Webcom, Limited

Thomson Learning Academic Learning Center
1-800-423-0563
http://www.wadsworth.com

Wadsworth/Thomson Learning
10 Davis Drive
Belmont, CA 94002-3098
USA

International Headquarters
Thomson Learning
International Division
290 Harbor Drive, 2nd Floor
Stamford, CT 06902-7477
USA

UK/Europe/Middle East/South Africa
Thomson Learning
Berkshire House
168-173 High Holborn
London WC1V 7AA
United Kingdom

Asia
Thomson Learning
60 Albert Street #15-01
Albert Complex
Singapore 189969

Canada
Nelson Thomson Learning
1120 Birchmount Road
Toronto, Ontario M1K 5G4
Canada

Library of Congress Cataloging-in-Publication Data
Pojman, Louis P.
    What can we know?: an introduction to the theory of knowledge/
    Louis P. Pojman—2nd ed.
        p.cm.
    Includes bibliographical references and index.
    ISBN 0-534-52417-6 (alk. paper)
    1. Knowledge, Theory of. I. Title.
BD161 .P68 2000
    121—dc21   00-029007

THIS BOOK PRINTED ON ACID-FREE RECYCLED PAPER

Dedicated to the cadets in my Epistemology class
Brian Betts
Kerry Burzynski
Sally Carlson
Raina Chesser
Tom Dowd
Robert Falzone
Tom Grywalski
Gabe Kimble
Michael Lang
Juris Matusevics
John Nakata
Tim Peterman
Michael Piro
Michael Rosol
Scott Ross
who exemplify the Platonic tradition of developing philosopher-leaders from the Guardian class and the West Point tradition of the soldier-scholar.

If God held the complete Truth in His right hand, and in His left hand the passionate, lifelong pursuit of Truth, howbeit with the addition that I would forever risk being in error; and if God said to me, "Choose!", I would touch His left hand and say, "Give me this, Father, the pure Truth is for Thee alone."

G. E. Lessing, 1729–1781

There are two ways of looking at our duty in the matter of opinion—ways entirely different, and yet ways about whose difference the theory of knowledge seems hitherto to have shown very little concern. We *must know the truth:* and we *must avoid error*—these are our first and great commandments as would-be knowers; but they are two separable laws.

William James, 1842–1910

Why should we, as cognitive beings, *care* whether our beliefs are epistemically justified? What makes us cognitive beings at all is our capacity for belief, and the goal of our distinctively cognitive endeavors is *truth:* we want our beliefs to correctly and accurately depict the world.

Laurence BonJour

Contents

PREFACE

I have tried to write a textbook that will both analyze the central concerns in epistemology and at the same time be interesting to students who have taken no more than an introductory course in philosophy. I have tried to be fair to the positions discussed, though doubtless in many places my own preferences will be apparent. This book has been written in such a way that it can be used either as a single text or as a supplement to my anthology, *The Theory of Knowledge* (published by Wadsworth in 1993 2nd ed., 1999). Most of the readings in that work are discussed in this one. There are study questions at the end of each chapter to help students come to terms with the salient points.

Altogether, this book is more comprehensive than other textbooks in epistemology. It covers the standard material, such as skepticism, perception, the analysis of knowledge, a priori knowledge, the foundationalism–coherentism debate, and the internalist–externalist debate; it treats neglected material, such as memory, other minds, the nature of belief, belief and will, and the ethics of belief; and it discusses newer material, such as Plantinga's theory of warrant and proper function and naturalized epistemology. Questions for discussion and a short reading list conclude each chapter.

Chapter 2 on the skeptical tradition endeavors to show students something of the powerful role that skepticism has played in the history of philosophy. Chapter 9 offers a critical analysis of Alvin Plantinga's recent theory of warrant and proper function. Chapter 11 takes a brief look at the latest epistemic theory, virtue epistemology. One of the longest chapters in the book, chapter 13, discusses memory, a topic that I was not able to include in my anthology, but which I find fascinating. This topic deserves more attention than it gets in contemporary epistemology. Chapter 15 discusses the nature of belief; chapter 16 discusses the relationship of belief to will; chapter 17 discusses whether ethical evaluations may be attributed to beliefs; and chapter 18 compares belief with acceptance of propositions. In chapter 19 I apply epistemological categories to the topic of religious beliefs, developing a notion of rationality that includes nonrule-governing reason. I suggest that my analysis of religious theories is applicable to all theoretical beliefs: scientific, political, and moral.

Some of the material from the introductions to the various sections in the anthology are included in this work.

Here is a list of the topics, numbered according to their appearance as chapters:

1. What Can We Know? Introduction
2. The Skeptical Tradition
3. Modern Skepticism
4. Perception: Our Knowledge of the External World
5. What Is Knowledge? An Analysis
6. Theories of Justification (I): Foundationalism
7. Theories of Justification (II): Coherentism and Modest Foundationalism
8. Theories of Justification (III): Internalism and Externalism
9. New Externalism: Plantinga's Theory of Warrant and Proper Function
10. Naturalized Epistemology
11. Virtue Epistemology
12. A Priori Knowledge
13. Memory
14. Other Minds
15. The Nature of Belief
16. Belief and Will
17. The Ethics of Belief
18. Belief and Acceptance
19. Epistemology and Religious Belief

Glossary

There is more material here than can normally be covered in one course. I usually spend eight or nine weeks on the first eight chapters (one session is sufficient for chapter 3, and some may want to skip it). Then I choose from the remaining topics, depending on what I perceive the needs and interests of the students to be. Each of us has his or her specialties. There is, of course, no need to follow the chapter sequence used in this book. Most of the chapters (the exceptions are chapters 6 through 8 and 15 through 18) can be examined in any order one desires.

A couple of years ago when the philosophy editor at Wadsworth asked me what I'd most like to write a textbook on, I said epistemology. "It's my favorite subject. I love to teach it, but I'm not satisfied with any of the textbooks or anthologies." A few weeks later a contract for the anthology *The Theory of Knowledge* was at my door. After that came out I started to work on the present textbook.

Epistemology is at the very center of philosophy. Its problems and puzzles have haunted the best minds for centuries, sometimes inspiring bold and imaginative systems, sometimes resulting in despair. What could be more important for intellectual development, the ramifications of which spread out to all areas of life, than understanding what knowledge is; what are its structure, scope, and limits; what is it to have justified beliefs?

Perhaps my appreciation of this subject is due to the resistance of my graduate school teachers. At Oxford University in the early 1970s epistemology was considered moribund, having been displaced by philosophy of language. I, however, had gone into philosophy in order to understand better whether I could justify my religious and moral beliefs. I never actually had a course in epistemology. But in 1976 Alvin Plantinga came to Oxford as a visiting professor and through him I began to study contemporary epistemology, especially the work of Roderick Chisholm and Keith Lehrer. In 1981 I was a participant in Robert Audi's summer seminar "Reason, Justification, and Knowledge" sponsored by the National Endowment for the Humanities at the University of Nebraska. That seminar is one of the highlights of my academic career, for it was there that I began to see how various aspects of the theory of knowledge could fit into a coherent pattern.

Precisely because I have never had a formal course in epistemology but had to learn most of its material through my own reading, I am especially sensitive to the difficulties of understanding some of its more technical matters. I can only hope that this shows through in this book. Nothing would please me more than that this work would stir a renewed interest in the subject, which I regard as the central focus of philosophy.

Like any credible philosopher I have endeavored to justify (at least to myself) every assertion put forth in this book, and only wish that I could guarantee that every such statement is true. Indeed, I believe that every individual assertion is true, yet given my fallibility, I also believe that some false statements are contained herein. That is, I believe that some (I hope very few) of the propositions that I believe are true are false. I shall not tell you which ones they are, but I'd be grateful to have you identify them and bring them to my attention.

Several people have read through preliminary drafts of the various chapters in this work. Robert Audi, Jonathan Kvanvig, Jim Landesman, Michael Levin, Tom Senor, and Wallace Matson provided helpful comments on previous drafts of different chapters. Earl Conee, University of Rochester; Peter Hutcheson, Southwest Texas State University; Eric Kraemer, University of Wisconsin, La Crosse; and Mark A. Michael, Austin Peay State University offered many helpful suggestions on the entire work. I am also indebted to those epistemologists who have influenced me during my studies (in addition to some of those already named): Alvin Goldman, Alvin Plantinga, and Ernest Sosa. Their influence will be apparent to the perceptive reader. This book was written in three places. It was begun in spring 1993 at the University of Mississippi. Chapters 5 through 9 were written during the NEH Summer Institute in Naturalism under the direction of Robert Audi at the University of Nebraska. The rest, including the two chapters on skepticism, was written at the University of California, Berkeley, where Wallace Matson graciously allowed me to use his office. This second, revised edition was written at the United States Military Academy at West Point. Peter Adams, the philosophy editor for Wadsworth, facilitated this project nicely, saving me all sorts of inconveniences. I have made the following revisions for this edition: added a section on theories of truth to chapter 1, reversed the order of the two chapters on skepticism (chapters 2 and 3), revised the arguments in chapters 5 and 7 on (coherentism), on externalism in chapter 8, and on naturalism in chapter 10. I have also added an introductory *Word to the Student*. I trust and believe these and other minor improvements have resulted in a better book.

Thanks is due to Peter Adams, the philosophy editor at Wadsworth Publishing Company, and to Gail Savage, who did an excellent job bringing this book to publication.

The book is dedicated to the cadets in my Epistemology class, whose participation greatly improved the content of this book.

Louis P. Pojman
The United States Military Academy
West Point, NY
March 28, 2000

A Personal Word to You, The Student

To love the truth for truth's sake is the principal part of human perfection in this world and the seed-plot of all other virtues.

(John Locke)

Epistemology is as important for philosophy as it is difficult sometimes to understand. However, the rewards are enormous for those who persevere. The subject often seems boring, but for those who have thought deeply about life and its problems, it can be liberating. In order to give this book a personal dimension, I have included this prefatory word for your consideration.

When I was a child I was taught that my religion, a form of Christianity, was the one and only true religion and that all other religions were false; that the theory of Creationism was true and Evolutionary Theory false; that the U.S. Government always acted justly.

Sometime later I began to doubt each of these assertions. I met people from other religious faiths who were as convinced that their religion was the only true religion as my friends were that Christianity was the only true religion. Yet, since these religions made mutually exclusive claims they couldn't both be true! I noticed that people had opposing political convictions. I read in my biology textbook about Darwinian Evolution, which made good sense. Could my religious authorities be wrong about evolution? As the War in Vietnam developed, I began to question the premise that America was always right in its actions. I met Marxists who claimed that Capitalism would soon topple under its own oppressive weight and Capitalists who asserted that Capitalism was the only Economic theory that could promote freedom, prosperity, and responsibility. All of my teachers taught, and my peers confirmed, the proposition that all humans were of equal and positive value. But is this really so? I wondered. People looked of differing value to me. Some are highly moral, some of middle morality, and some of low morality or even immoral. Similarly with intelligence, talents, and wisdom. People seemed radically different and unequal in worth. Furthermore, while traveling to the West, I noticed that I was sometimes mistaken about appearances, erroneously thinking that I saw a lake in the Mojave Desert. Working with my chemistry set at the age of 12, I noticed that the idea of causal connection pervaded every experiment. Every event seemed to have a cause. But, I asked, if this was true of the natural world, could it also be true of the world of human actions? Could all of our acts be caused (fully determined) by antecedent events? In my physics class I was assured that sub-atomic particles underlay all matter, yet no one had really observed these sub-atomic particles. Could the scientists be mistaken about these alleged entities? I queried: Why do we submit to scientists without protest? Because they have Ph.D.s? Sometimes I even wondered whether there was an external world or whether everything was a figment of my imagination. Perturbed by such questions and uncertainties, I wrote a poem for my high school literary magazine.

> I wonder as I wander here,
> What came before, What comes after.
> Who can say and who can know,
> What is Truth and Why tis so?

What is the truth and what can we really know? How can we be certain that we have the truth? How can we be sure that we can know anything at all? What is knowledge and why is it important? Is knowledge a unique state of mind or is it simply a type of belief? If we know something, must we know that we know it?

I thought that these questions were so important that I decided to dedicate my life, cost what it may, to pursue the truth of these and other metaphysical matters.

This book is about the quest for knowledge and truth. It is an invitation addressed to you personally to join the Voyage of Epistemology in order to attain a better understanding of your own belief systems, making progress in the quest for truth. My deepest hope is that this book enables you to make progress improving your belief system.

First, let us examine the nature of the various types of knowledge.

CHAPTER 1

What Can We Know?

What can we really know? How can we be certain that we have the truth? How can we be certain that we know anything at all? What is knowledge, and how is it different from belief? If we know something, must we *know* that we know it? Is it possible to have genuine knowledge of the external world, or must we be content with mere appearances?

Knowledge and Its Types

The theory of knowledge, or *epistemology*—from the Greek *episteme,* or "knowledge," and *logos,* or "science" i.e. the science of knowing—inquires into the nature of knowledge and justification of belief. Many philosophers, I among them, believe that it is the central area of philosophy, for if philosophy is the quest for truth and wisdom, then we need to know how we are to obtain the truth and justify our beliefs. We need to know how to distinguish the true from the false and justified beliefs from unwarranted beliefs.

If we consult the *Oxford English Dictionary,* we will find the following definition of the verb *know:* "to recognize, to identify, to distinguish, to be acquainted with, to apprehend or comprehend as a fact or truth." This definition puts us in the ballpark in terms of understanding the word, but it is too broad for philosophical purposes. So let us note some typical uses of the verb "know."

1. "I know my friend John very well."
2. "I know how to speak English."

3. "I know that Washington, D.C., is the capital of the United States."

These three sentences illustrate three different types of knowledge: knowledge by acquaintance, competence knowledge, and descriptive or propositional knowledge. We may characterize each of them this way:

1. *Knowledge by Acquaintance* Person S knows something or someone *x*, where *x* is the direct object of the sentence. We have personal and direct experience with the objects in the world, our thoughts, and sensations. I know my friend Robert. I know Chicago (i.e., I am acquainted with it). I know the answer to that question. We know our headache pain, our personal strengths and weaknesses, and our own bodies and sense experiences; for example, I am acquainted with the white computer screen appearing before me. We also have direct acquaintance knowledge of our introspective states: our loves and hates, desires, hopes, memory states, beliefs, and doubts. One version of acquaintance knowledge is sometimes called *objectual knowledge,* where the object of knowledge is not a proposition but a particular object or thing. *Perceptual knowledge* is often of this kind: we see a blue spot in front of us or hear a sound. Animals and small children, who do not think in propositions, have this kind of belief and knowledge.

2. *Competence Knowledge* (sometimes called skill knowledge) Person S knows how to D (where D stands for an infinitive). This is *know-how.* You know how to speak English and get around campus, or at least your room, when it isn't too cluttered. You may know how to ride a bicycle, drive a car, use a computer, speak a foreign language as well as your native one, play the piano, or swim. Competence knowledge involves an ability to perform a skill and may be done consciously or unconsciously. You may not be able to explain how you accomplish your feat to others. We will look at this type of knowledge in the last chapter of the book.

3. *Propositional Knowledge* (or descriptive knowledge) Person S knows that *p* (where *p* is some statement or proposition). Propositions have truth value; that is, they are true or false. They are the objects of propositional knowledge. When we claim to know that *p* is the case, we are claiming that *p* is true. Examples of the use of propositional knowledge are "I know that the sun will rise tomorrow," "I know that Sacramento is the capital of California," "I know that I have a mind," and "I know that Columbus discovered America in 1492."

Many philosophers believe that only reflective beings, such as human beings and perhaps some adult primates and cetaceans (e.g., dolphins and porpoises), are able to have this kind of knowledge. An interesting question is whether all propositional knowledge is based on acquaintance knowledge. The model used by those who assert that this relation holds true is perceptual knowledge. To know that the tree in front of me is green entails having experienced the properties "green" and "tree." Those who deny such dependence argue that the structures of our mind are such that we can have knowledge (or justified beliefs) of some universal propositions that are not dependent on experience. Examples of such propositions are "Every event has a cause," "All events take place in time," and "A contradiction cannot be true."

Although a lot more needs to be said about these three kinds of knowledge, I think that the central distinctions will be a good beginning point. Epistemology is primarily interested in propositional knowledge, and it is this kind of knowledge we shall mainly be examining in the following chapters. But this only scratches the surface of what we are concerned with in the theory of knowledge.

The field of epistemology seeks to throw light upon the following kinds of questions.

1. What is knowledge? That is, what are its essential characteristics? What are its necessary and sufficient conditions?

2. What is truth? Since truth is the desideratum or goal of cognitive processes, how shall we define this vital concept?

3. Can we know anything at all? Or are we doomed to ignorance about the most important subjects in life?

4. How do we obtain knowledge? Is it through the use of our senses, our intellect, or both?

Let us briefly examine each of these questions.

What Is Knowledge?

Can you know something that is really false? Consider these propositions: "The people in the Middle Ages knew that the earth was flat, but they were wrong," "I know that the U.S. Declaration of Independence was signed in 1945, but it was not," and "I used to know that Chicago was the capital of the United States, but now I know that Washington, D.C., is." Does it strike you that these are odd statements? Normally, when we use the word "know" or "knowledge," we are making a claim that we possess the truth. Statements like "I know the answer to that question" or "I know that Germany started World War II and not England" assert that we have access to the truth about "that question" or the cause of World War II. So first of all, knowledge entails truth.

Theories of Truth

> "What is the truth?" Pontius Pilate to Jesus, just before he delivered him up to be crucified. (John 18:38)

What is the truth? Religions like Christianity, Judism, Hinduism, Buddhism, and Islam claim to have the truth. Ideologies like libertarianism, Marxism, liberal democracy, socialism, and fascism all claim to be the truth about how society should be governed. Freudians, Jungians, behaviorists, and existentialists debate about which theory of human nature is true. Does empirical science offer the truth, or something close to it, about human nature and the world in general, or do art, literature, and religion approach more nearly to that ideal? What is truth?

Throughout this work we will make reference to the idea of truth. We have noted that it is one of the conditions of knowledge and a desideratum of our cognitive processes. Here I want briefly to consider the meaning of the concept of truth from a philosophical perspective. There have been three main theories of truth in the history of philosophy: the correspondence theory, the coherence theory, and the pragmatic theory. Each has present-day advocates. We want to examine each of these.

The Correspondence Theory of Truth

The correspondence theory of truth is the theory that truth consists in the *relationship between the proposition (or sentence) and the facts or states of affairs that verify or confirm the propositions.* A belief is true if it asserts a proposition that corresponds to facts. This is probably the oldest general theory of truth, going back at least as far as Plato, who wrote:

> The true [sentence] states facts as they are . . . and the false one states things that are other than the facts. . . . In other words, it speaks of things that are not as if they were.[1]

Aristotle refined Plato's definition.

> To say that what is, is not, or that what is not is, is false; but to say that what is, is, and what is not is not, is true; and therefore also he who says that a thing is or is not will say either what is true or what is false.[2]

The correspondence theory captures our common-sense intuition that truth depends on something objective (or mind-independent) in the world that makes it true. Beliefs are not made true by mere wishful thinking or imagination, but have an objective basis in reality. Ludwig Wittgenstein said that "A proposition is a picture of reality. A proposition is a model of reality as we imagine it."[3]

Consider the following:

1. The book is on the table.
2. The colors in the flag of the United States of America are red, white, and blue.
3. _____ is the true religion. (Fill in the blank any way you wish.)
4. One ought not cause unnecessary suffering.
5. The law of gravity is a true law.

According to this "common sense" or picture theory, we judge the sentence "The book is on the table" to be true if we perceive that the book is on the table and false if it is not. We can test the sentence and what it asserts for its truth value by observation. Likewise, we can look and see whether U.S. flags have the colors claimed in sentence (2). Regarding (3), if all of the assertions of that religion turn out to be true, then the religion as a whole is true. In sentence (4) "One ought not cause unnecessary suffering," the picture theory doesn't seem to do justice to this universal normative statement, and it isn't easy to analyze via the correspondence method. Similarly (5) "The law of gravity is a true law" fails to fit the picture theory. But they may still represent a wider version of the correspondence theory (see below).

Truth adheres to propositions (or statements), not facts. The locution "These are the true facts," sometimes heard in law courts, is a malapropism. For *facts* are not true or false, but just are. They are what propositions are about. We might now ask what is a *proposition?* It is a thought, the meaning of a sentence. For instance, the two sentences "Happy Dancer is a good horse," and "Happy Dancer is a good steed" express the same proposition since the word "steed" means "horse." They are synonyms. Likewise, the sentences "Es ist heisst," "Il fait chaud," "Det er warm," and "It is warm" all express the same proposition, even though they are sentences in four different languages (German, French, Danish, and English). We speak of propositions as *bearers of truth,* since a proposition is *either* true or false. They purport to assert the truth. In this way, propositions differ from questions and imperatives, which make no assertions (but question or command). Compare:

The book is on the table.

Is the book on the table?

Put that book back on the table!

The second term in our formula, "facts" (or "states of affairs"), points to reality itself: the book on the table, the flag with three colors, the number of planets in the solar system. We need not have knowledge of reality for the facts to exist. For example, we may not know the facts about the origin of the universe, but if the universe did have an origin (and is not simply eternal), then it originated the way it did whether anyone knows it or not. We may not know whether God exists, but there is a fact about the matter. Either God does or does not exist, but not both.

The third term of the formula, "correspondence," seems most problematic. Is the correspondence between the proposition and the fact one of identity, close resemblance, or simply rough correlation? The proposition "The turkey is in the oven" only stands for the fact that the turkey is in the oven. Unlike the turkey, the proposition cannot be weighed, seen, eaten, or savored. Do all the parts of the sentence have to correspond with items in the world? As mentioned above, Wittgenstein thought of true proposition as accurate pictures of facts in the world, but whereas my picture of the American flag resembles a real flag, the sentence "The colors in the flag of the United States of America are red, white, and blue" neither resembles the flag nor is colored like the flag. No one has successfully shown how to get an exact one-to-one correspondence between the elements in propositions and the elements of the states of affairs to which they correspond. But interpreting *correspondence* too literally may be unnecessary.

Contemporary versions of the correspondence theory attempt to get around the vagueness involved in the idea of correspondence by confining their definition to a simple logical formula such as:

(C) The proposition p is true if and only if p;

or, if you don't like the notion of a proposition, then:

(S) The sentence s is true in language L if and only if s.

For example, the sentence "Snow is white" is true in English if and only if snow is white.[4]

Perhaps the best way to view beliefs (as the bearers of propositions) and propositions from the point of view of correspondence
theory is to see them as maps. They are conventions that locate relationships in reality. Our beliefs are maps by which we steer our way
through life. True beliefs will direct us to our goals, whereas false beliefs will not get us to our goals but will get us lost.

Or we may resort to Aristotle's simple definition.

> To say that what is, is not, or that what is not is, is false; but to say that
> what is, is, and what is not is not, is true; and therefore also he who says
> that a thing is or is not will say either what is true or what is false.

So (4) "One ought not cause unnecessary suffering" is true just in case
it is morally wrong to cause unnecessary suffering and (5) "The statement the law of gravity is a valid law" is true just in case it is always the
case that objects fall at the required velocity. Otherwise it is false.

The Coherence Theory of Truth

The coherence theory of truth states that to say a proposition or belief is true is to say it coheres with a system of other propositions or
beliefs. A true proposition is true by virtue of its legitimate member-
ship in the system whose individual parts are related to each other by
logical necessity. Truth is the whole whose parts are harmoniously
conjoined.

Often a corollary thesis is connected to the coherence theory, resulting in the doctrine of internal relations. This doctrine signifies that
each member of the system necessarily implies every other member.
Hence the truth test will be whether the statement is consistent with
every other (known) part of the system. At least it must not contradict
what is already known. This doctrine is illustrated by the sorts of internal relationships present in mathematical and logical systems.
However, the adherent of the coherence theory claims that these sciences are models for all reality. In G. W. Hegel's words, "The real is
the rational and the rational is the real."

A further feature of coherence theories is the doctrine of the degrees of truth. If the truth is essentially the whole, then the individual
parts will not be the complete truth but only contextually true, or
true to a certain degree. As finite beings, we can never know the
whole truth, but only partial, fragmented truth. Some sets of beliefs
will cohere better than other sets of beliefs, but no one will have a
perfectly coherent set. In a sense all our beliefs are false because we

only have the truth when we know it as a whole, knowing all the individual parts and their interrelationships.

Hegel's dialectical method is one result of such a doctrine. According to Hegel, the individual parts must be viewed as segments of a dialectical process, the way of truth in the world, and must be interpreted teleologically, from the perspective of the end result. The truths of any one period of history are only relatively true, demanding an opposite truth and finding its meaning only in the absolute truth, which subsumes all relative truths within itself.

Søren Kierkegaard pointed out that a coherence system like Hegel's was nicely suited to God, who could see the whole from a perspective from a point beyond time (*sub specie aeternitatis*), but it was useless for humans who had to live their lives with partial knowledge and limited information. There may be a grand scheme of things, a total truth, but it is presumptive to claim that we are close to such a system.

The opponents of the coherence theory point out that there can be two incompatible coherent systems and that even fairy tales and big lies are coherent—that is, consistent and mutually supportive—and this fact would seem to undermine it as a definition of truth. They argue that coherence or consistency between propositions is a *necessary* condition for the truth of the propositions in question but not a sufficient condition. The propositions must somehow correspond to the facts. When we ask the question "Is the coherence theory of truth true," it seems we want an answer in terms of broad correspondence, not coherence. This is not to dismiss the criterion of coherence altogether, for it may be the relevant criterion for justification, which will be examined in chapter 7.

The Pragmatic Theory of Truth

The pragmatic theory of truth, as propounded by William James, states that a belief is true if it is useful or expedient. "The true is only the expedient in the way of our behaving, expedient in almost any fashion, and expedient in the long run and on the whole course."[5]

Truth seems synonymous with practical success. It is action-oriented, aimed at reaching future goals. "Grant an idea or belief to be true, what concrete difference will its being true make in anyone's actual life? . . . What, in short, is the truth's cash value in experiential terms?"

James used this conception of truth to justify religious belief where the objective evidence was insufficient to prove the belief. Our passional nature has a right to choose whether we believe in God or in whatever will make us happy. One religion may be true for you, but a contradictory one true for me. As such, the pragmatic theory is a form of cognitive relativism, denying any objective, interest-independent reality, as the proponents of the correspondence theory and the coherence theory would maintain. Later in this chapter, we will examine the contemporary rendition of this theory in the work of Richard Rorty, who characterizes truth as that which one can defend against all comers.

Bertrand Russell argued against the pragmatic theory that practical "success" is a dubious criterion for truth. By such a criterion, Nazism would have been true if it had succeeded in leading Germany to win World War II. James's proviso "in the long run and on the whole of the course" seems too vague to help his definition, since we can never know whether our beliefs are true (that is, successful). For example, we would not be able to know whether our belief that love is better than hate were true until the whole course of history had finished. Likewise, we could not know whether analytic truths were true until we had made an exhaustive investigation into their utility. On the other hand, erroneous beliefs such as medieval beliefs in Aristotle's four elements (cold, hot, wet, and dry) could be said to be true as long as they gave successful results. Such a belief might be said to have been true for millions of people for over 2000 years until John Dalton showed decisively that it was false.

Even if we decided to use the term *true* in the pragmatic sense, we would still need to distinguish it from a more objective kind of truth. Suppose Jim believes against all evidence that he is the smartest person alive, a genius. Suppose his wife and friends all humor him by pretending that he is correct. For Jim, who does not know he is only of average intelligence, this belief in his genius is what gives meaning to his life. Because he is so self-confident, he usually performs to his optimum level. He is happy. Still, although he has a "true" belief from the point of view of pragmatism, we still want to say that there is a misrelationship between his belief and the facts. He doesn't have a true belief as far as the *facts* are concerned, but he does have what constitutes a pragmatically successful belief.

Or suppose Christy believes in astrology. Because the astrological forecasts are so general, she always manages to find something helpful in consulting the daily astrology columns. Astrology is what gives her life meaning, and she functions well. Without her astrological faith, her life would be miserable. Granting that she may very well live better because of her beliefs, those of us who believe that astrology is a false worldview (as I believe it is) cannot allow that Christy has a *true* belief. Perhaps we need to distinguish *true-P* (P = pragmatic) from *true-C* (C = correspondence or coherence). When someone says "This is true for me, though it may not be true for you," they may have a pragmatic view of truth.

Pragmatic notions of truth seem to interpret it either as (1) what a subject *believes* to be true (judged by correspondence criteria) or (2) what a subject can be *justified* in believing. Interpretation (1) reduces truth to belief and (2) to justification, but we still need a concept that points to facts or the way things are independent of our beliefs or justifications. And so the Pragmatic Theory seems to miss the objective or mind-independent feature of the notion of truth.

At this point we must distinguish between what makes a proposition true and how we determine that it is true. The former is a semantic/metaphysical notion, having to do with how we define or characterize the concept "truth," while the latter is an epistemic notion, having to do with interpreting evidence, justifying beliefs, and the like. Some philosophers conflate these two notions. The pragmatist Richard Rorty says that "true" means roughly "what you can defend against all comers, . . . what our peers will . . . let us get away with saying." He goes on to say that the line "between a belief's being justified and its being true is very thin" and that alternate definitions are "what it is better for us to believe" and "warranted assertibility."[6] Similarly, Hilary Putnam speaks of "internal realism," that which we are justified in believing, as a characterization of truth.

But it seems a mistake to conflate truth with justification. First of all, Rorty's definition seems self-refuting. I for one don't think that he has defended the definition against all comers, so if it's true, then it's false.

a. Truth = df "What one can defend against all comers."

b. Rorty hasn't adequately defended (a) against many people, including me.

If you insist that Rorty has defended (a) against all comers, only we do not realize it, then are you not that appealing to an objective standard of truth, one that says that something is true whether anyone realizes it or not? If so, then Rorty's definition is mistaken.

To Rorty's claim that truth is "what our peers allow us to get away with saying," why can't we respond "As one of Rorty's peers, I won't let him get away with saying that"?

Similarly, we may indicate a self-referential problem with Rorty's second definition of truth as "what it is better for us to believe."

c. Truth = df. A proposition that "it is better for us to believe."
d. But I don't think it is better to believe (c) than some other definition of "truth."

Since we have a conflict over (c), we need an objective standard to decide whether it really is better to believe (c) or not, but what could that be but an objective idea of *truth*. We want to know whether it is objectively true that it is better to believe (c) than not.

But in case you are dissatisfied with these kinds of arguments, here is a concrete example of the distinction between truth and justification. Suppose that it is the final inning of the final game of the World Series between the Oakland A's and the New York Mets. Each team has won three games. Now in the last of the ninth there are two out and your team is winning 3 to 2, but the bases are loaded and the count is 3 and 2 on the batter. The pitch is a curve ball and just makes the inside lower corner of the strike zone. But just as you are about to throw your glove in the air to celebrate the championship, the umpire calls "Ball four!" The tying run comes in. You protest, but to no avail. Your team protests on principle, but no one but you really believes that the ball was within the strike zone. When the commotion dies down, the next batter comes to the plate and singles in the winning run. Protest as you do, it is to no avail. The umpire's word is final and is successfully defended to all but you, because no one really believes you.

Suppose that you are correct and the ball really was within the strike zone. That you can't successfully defend your position is unfortunate, even deplorable, considering the stakes involved, but it has nothing to do with your lacking the fact of the matter. It is true that the ball was within the strike zone, regardless of what others believe. There can be true beliefs and propositions that can't be successfully defended (or justified) "against all comers," but so what? Justification is not the same thing as truth. Nor is it relevant to ask which proposition it is "better to believe," for it could turn out that going along with the umpire's decision in these kinds of cases has positive utilitarian consequences. But, again, this has nothing to do with the truth itself. Perhaps we can speak of "social truth" as that which a consensus of your peers believes at any time, but then we need to point out that from an objective perspective *social truth* can be false. It would be better to reserve the term "truth" for that which communicates or corresponds to the facts.

Let us sum up our discussion of theories of truth. Three classical theories of truth are the correspondence theory of truth, which views truth as an appropriate relationship between a statement and the facts it represents; the coherence theory of truth, which views truth holistically, as a mutually supportive set of statements that together depict reality; and the pragmatic theory of truth, which equates truth with usefulness, that which works "in the long run and on the whole course." We noted strengths and weaknesses in each theory.

In this work I follow J.L. Mackie in holding to the commonsense notion of truth first articulated by Aristotle. This notion is compatible with Alfred Tarski's disquotational, or semantic, theory and the classical correspondence theory of Thomas Aquinas, Bertrand Russell, and others. Although I accept the idea of correspondence, I don't interpret correspondence as isomorphic between statements and facts. Rather, the sentence adequately represents the way things are.

Of course, we may be wrong about our knowledge claims. The drunk claims to know that there are pink elephants in the room with him, the child claims to know that Santa Claus exists, and two witnesses may make contradictory knowledge claims in reporting an accident. I may have good evidence that I will inherit a fortune, so that I claim to know it but, alas, be mistaken. We often falsely believe that we know. Sometimes the evidence on which our knowledge claim is based is inadequate or misleading, or we misremember or misperceive. Sometimes our knowledge claims are contradicted by those of others, as when two people of different religious faiths each claims that his or hers is the only true religion, or when one person claims with certainty that abortion is morally wrong and the other person claims with equal certainty that it is morally permissible.

Knowledge and Belief

Knowledge involves possessing the truth, but *how* does it possess it? When you know something, must you be in a special psychological state? Or is knowing just a special kind of correct believing? Plato and Descartes held that knowledge was different from believing, involving an infallible state of mind, so that if you found yourself in that knowledge state of mind, you would be guaranteed to possess the truth. Belief, on the other hand, was a kind of uncertainty, an "opinion." Whereas knowledge implied absolute certainty, belief only implied high probability. No doubt there are self-evident truths, such as knowledge of your own existence, simple mathematical truths, and possibly some psychological states (e.g., "I know that I'm surprised"), but it seems doubtful that a sharp line of demarcation can be drawn. People often feel absolutely certain about all sorts of things. Mary is absolutely certain that the Catholic Church is the one and only true religion, whereas Hussein is just as certain that Islam alone deserves that distinction. A person in the Middle Ages might have been absolutely certain that the earth was flat and that the sun revolved around the earth, whereas we may be absolutely certain of just the opposite.

It seems wiser to see the state of knowledge as a type of believing what is true. Perhaps it is a type of true believing where *certainty* is required. How much certainty? Absolute certainty? This seems too strong. Some philosophers like John Pollock and A. Phillips Griffiths argue that knowledge does not require belief. You may know the truth of proposition *p* without believing it. Phillips Griffiths suggests that it is possible for a person to know that *p* even where he doubts *p*. He asks us to consider a child who is terrorized by a brutal teacher. "He may be so put off by fear that he makes mistakes or hesitates about things that he knows perfectly well. As a well-informed, conscientious, intelligent boy he really does know the answers; yet on particularly tense occasions, he really does doubt that the correct answer that springs to his lips is correct."[7]

Is Phillips Griffiths correct about disbelieving what you know? I think that these borderline cases are difficult to be sure about and that before we can be confident of our answers, we need a full-blown epistemology. Nevertheless, let me make an important distinction that may throw light on this problem by suggesting that, in a way, the terrorized boy does not know the answer—and in a way he does. We may divide beliefs into two varieties: *occurrent* and *dispositional*. An occurrent belief is one that you are conscious of at the moment. If I ask you "How are you feeling now?" you will probably find yourself believing something about your present state of mind. Right now I believe that I have five fingers on each hand, and that it is raining outside. Those are occurrent beliefs.

But there is also a different type of belief, one that I would become conscious of under suitable conditions. I have not thought about my late younger brother, Everett, for days, but suddenly I realize that today is the tenth anniversary of his tragic death. Even though I had not thought about this fact for days, I believed it every day for the past ten years. You too have dispositional beliefs. You probably haven't thought about Venus or Jupiter lately, but you probably have had the dispositional belief that each of them is a planet and that they are a long distance from Earth. You have dispositional beliefs about love being better than hate, happiness better than sadness, and peace better than violence, and about getting A's in courses being a lot more satisfying than failing them. While we are stocked full of dispositional beliefs, we can only handle a few occurrent beliefs at any one time. We will discuss the concept of belief in chapter 15.

Let us return to our terrorized, conscientious, intelligent boy. We may surmise that *dispositionally* he knew the answer to the question because he believed it in the right way, but we may also say that when it came to consciousness, he did so under emotionally stressful conditions so that he lacked the normal psychological certainty that usually accompanies such beliefs. The *occurrent* aspect of believing was not completely successful, but he possessed his data as surely as he possessed his gender, size, and name. The lesson of this example is that one need not always *know that one knows* in order to have knowledge.

Illustrations of knowing without knowing that you know abound. Children know who their mother is and gradually come to learn that the building block they have placed behind them will still be there when they go for it in a couple of minutes, without being self-conscious about their knowledge. I believe that many of my memory reports are knowledge, but I may not be able to give these second-order beliefs (about my memory claims) the kind of backing that knowledge would require. You probably knew that you were reading this paragraph before you realized that you knew that you knew that you were. But now that you think about it, you probably do know that you know this. Well, you could doubt it. We'll come to that possibility in a moment.

Knowledge and Justification

So far we have concluded that knowledge is a type of true belief. But it is more than just believing truly. Imagine that I am holding up four cards so that I can see their faces but you can only see their backs. I ask you to guess what types of cards I am holding. You feel a hunch or a weak belief that I am holding four aces and correctly announce "You are holding four aces in your hands." Although we both possess the truth, I have something you don't—an adequate justification for my belief that there are four aces in my hand. You, accidentally, have guessed the right answer, whereas I have ascertained it so by a more reliable process. But even a stopped clock is accidentally right twice a day. So knowledge differs from mere true belief in that the knower has nonaccidental grounds or, in normal philosophical parlance, an adequate "justification" for claiming to have true beliefs.

Now the question shifts to the nature of justification. What is *justification*? In general, justification is a normative term, indicating meeting an acceptable standard or doing the right thing. Examples of the use of justification language in ethics are "The end doesn't justify the means" and "President Truman's decision to bomb Hiroshima in 1945 was (or was not) justified, all things considered." There is also a pragmatic or prudential use of justification, as in "Linda's decision to get an MBA was justified since she would thereby increase her chances of getting a promotion."

Epistemic justification signifies meeting acceptable epistemic standards and having positive epistemic status. As reason-giving creatures, we seek to support our beliefs and knowledge claims in ways similar to the way we support moral and prudential claims. If someone asks you "Why do you believe x will win the election," you cite the grounds or evidence for your belief "Because the polls show x to have a significant lead over the other candidates." Likewise, we seek to support our moral, religious, political, and philosophical beliefs with good evidence. A general assumption is that, all things being equal, the more evidence you have or the better justified you are regarding a given belief, the more likely it is that your belief is true. But can we justify that assumption?

Guessing that I had four aces in my hands was not an example of knowledge. Hunches, guesses, conjectures, and wishful thinking do not yield cases of knowledge, even if they are true, for they are not the kinds of things that justify beliefs. But what kinds of things *do* justify beliefs? Must evidence be undeniable, such as when we believe that $2 + 2 = 4$ or when we feel pain and cannot help believe that we are in pain? Can we have sufficient evidence to justify belief in physical objects? Our belief in other minds? Beliefs about metaphysical propositions such as the existence of God or freedom of the will? How much evidence must one have before he or she can claim to know a belief is true? We will examine the problem of justification in chapters 6 through 9 and analyze the concept of knowledge in more detail in chapter 5.

Can We Know Anything at All?

Let us turn to our third question: *Can we know anything at all?* Or are we doomed to ignorance about the most important subjects in life? Could it be that our most treasured beliefs are merely unjustified biases, that even our sense of being a self is an illusion? Could it be that we really know nothing at all? If knowledge entails being completely justified in our beliefs, do we ever possess complete justification for a belief? Could we be systematically deceived by nature or an evil demon? *Skepticism* is the theory that we do not have any knowledge or at least that we do not know most of the things we claim to know. Moderate skepticism claims that we cannot be completely justified regarding any of our beliefs. A weak skepticism holds that we can know some obvious truths, such as mathematical and logical truths, but not metaphysical or empirical truths. Radical skepticism goes even further and claims that we cannot even be certain of the belief that we cannot be completely certain that any of our beliefs are true. We cannot even know that we cannot have knowledge!

Can you defeat the skeptic? We will examine arguments for and against skepticism, as well as the historical significance of skepticism in chapters 2 and 3.

How Do We Obtain Knowledge?

We turn to our fourth question: *How do we obtain knowledge?* Is it through use of our senses or our intellect, or both? There are two classic theories on the acquisition of knowledge, *rationalism* and *empiricism*. "Rationalism" may be a misleading name for the first theory since according to both theories we use reason in acquiring knowledge. It is simply that rationalists believe that reason is sufficient to discover truth whereas empiricists hold that all knowledge originates through sense perception (that is, through seeing, hearing, touching, tasting, and smelling).

The first comprehensive rationalist theory was put forth by Plato (427–347 B.C.), who distinguishes between two approaches to knowledge: sense perception and reason.[8] Sense perception cannot be adequate for possessing the truth because its objects are subject to change and decay. All one gets in this way of apprehending things is beliefs about particular objects. Knowledge, on the other hand, goes beyond the particular and grasps universal *ideas* or *forms*. Plato argues that all knowing is the knowing of objects, so that these ideas must exist in the really real world, the world of being. The philosopher is a person who works his way through the world of becoming—the empirical world—to this higher reality. Plato uses the allegory of the cave to illustrate his doctrine.

> Imagine a group of prisoners who from infancy have had their necks and legs chained to posts within a dark cave. Behind them is a raised walkway where people and animals travel to and fro, bearing diverse objects.

Behind the walkway is a large fire which projects the shadows of the people, animals, and objects onto the wall in front of the prisoners. The shadows on the wall grow and diminish, and move up and down and around as the fire behind the objects wafts and wanes. But the prisoners do not know that the shadows are merely appearances of real objects. They take the shadows for reality, talk about them as though they were real, name them, reidentify them, and incorporate their knowledge of the various forms into their social life. Their lives are centered on the shadows.

Now imagine that someone tries to liberate one of the prisoners from the cave. At first, the prisoner kicks and screams as he is forcibly moved from the only home and social milieu he has ever known. Being dragged through the cave against his will, he is at last taken outside, where the dazzling bright sunlight blinds him. Our prisoner begs to be allowed to be returned to his safe shelter in the cave but the way is closed. Gradually, his eyes adjust to the sunlight, and he is able to see the beautifully colored flowers and wide spreading branches of oak trees and hear the songs of birds and watch the play of animals. Delighted, his powers of sight increase until at last he is able to look at the bright sun itself and not be harmed.

But now his liberator, who has become his friend and teacher, instructs him to return to the cave to teach the other prisoners about the real world and to get them to give up their chains and journey upward to the sunlight. But our hero quakes with fear at such an ordeal for he wants no part of that dark, dismal existence, preferring the light of day to the dark of the abyss.

He is told that it is his duty to go so he makes his way into the cave again. Returning to his chained mates, he tells them that the shadows are merely illusions and that a real world of sunlight and beauty exists above, outside the cave. While he is proclaiming this gospel, his former mates grab him, beat him for impugning their belief and value system, and put him to death.

But every now and then the liberator comes back, drags one or two prisoners out of the cave against their will, and teaches them to enjoy the light. Such is the process of educating the soul to perceive the Truth, the form of the Good. What is Plato saying in this allegory?

The bridge between the world of being and the world of becoming is *innate ideas*. Plato held that learning is really a recollecting of what we learned in a previous existence. He believed in reincarnation, that in a previous existence we saw all essential truths but have lost awareness of them through birth. The educator should be a spiritual midwife who stimulates the labors of the soul so that a person recalls what he or she really possesses but has forgotten. In the *Meno*, Socrates (Plato's mouthpiece) claims to demonstrate this doctrine of recollection of innate ideas by teaching geometry to an uneducated slave. Drawing a square in the sand, Socrates asks the boy to try to double the area of the figure. Through a process of question and answer, in which the boy consults his own unschooled understanding, he eventually performs this feat. He seems to have "brought up knowledge from within." Likewise, Socrates argues, we can teach virtue only by causing our auditors to recollect what they have forgotten about the Good.

Types of Knowledge

Plato thought that all knowledge was *a priori* (that which is prior) knowledge that one possesses independently of sense experience as opposed to *a posteriori* (that which is posterior) knowledge—contingent, empirical knowledge, which comes to us from experience through the five senses. Unless they are related to the Forms, ordinary empirical beliefs, according to Plato, are not knowledge but simply unstable appearance. Examples of candidates for a priori knowledge are the mathematical equation $2 + 2 = 4$, the statement "nothing that is green all over is red," and the statement "not both p and not-p." You don't have to appeal to experience in order to see that these propositions are true. As Immanuel Kant (1724–1804) said, "Though all our knowledge begins with experience, it does not follow that it all arises out of experience. For it may well be that even our empirical knowledge is made up of what we receive through impressions and of what our own faculty of knowledge supplies from itself."[9]

Kant refined these notions, making a posteriori knowledge refer to judgments that depend on empirical experience and a priori knowledge refer to those judgments that do not depend on empirical experience.[10] But he went further. He took the linguistic or semantic notions *analytic* and *synthetic* statements and combined them with a priori and a posteriori knowledge. Analytic statements are those in which the predicate is already contained in the subject (e.g., "All mothers are women," in which the subject term "mother" already contains the idea of "woman," so we learn nothing new in our statement). Synthetic statements are just the opposite; the predicate term adds something new about the subject. For example, "Mary is now a mother" is a sentence in which we learn something new about Mary.

The empiricists John Locke (1632–1704) and David Hume (1711–1776) argued that at birth our minds are an empty slate, a *tabula rasa,* on which the world via our sense organs makes impressions which in turn produce ideas.[11] All knowledge of the world is a posteriori knowledge and knowledge of logic and mathematics purely analytic and a priori.

A classification of the relevant concepts is as follows:

EPISTEMOLOGICAL CATEGORIES

1. A priori knowledge does not depend on evidence from sense experience (Plato's Innate Ideas and Leibniz's "Truths of Reason"; e.g., mathematics and logic).
2. A posteriori knowledge depends on evidence from sense experience (Plato's Appearance and Leibniz's "Truths of Fact"; e.g., empirical knowledge).

SEMANTICAL CATEGORIES

1. *Analytic.* The predicate is *contained* in the subject (explicative, not ampliative; e.g., "All mothers are women").
2. *Synthetic.* The predicate is not contained in the subject but adds something to the subject (ampliative, not explicative; e.g., "Mary is now a mother").

Kant rejected the theory that there were only two kinds of knowledge: a priori and a posteriori. Combining a priori knowledge with synthetic propositions, he argued that we have a third kind of knowledge, *synthetic a priori knowledge*—knowledge that may begin with experience but does not arise from experience, but is nevertheless known directly.

The essential claim of those who hold to synthetic a priori knowledge is that the mind is able to grasp connections between ideas (concepts) that are not strictly analytically related. For example, we simply know upon reflection that all events have causes or that time and space are real without having an empirical proof or logical argument. Kant thought that our knowledge of mathematical truths was really synthetic a priori, rather than analytic. Likewise, the moral law—that we ought to act in such a way that we could will the maxims of our actions into universal laws—is known without appeal to experience. Other philosophers, such as Descartes and Søren Kierkegaard, believed that we have synthetic a priori knowledge of God's existence and the immortality of the soul. We will examine the notion of a priori knowledge in chapter 12.

Let us turn to empiricism. Empiricism, the classic rival of rationalism, is the doctrine that all knowledge originates in the senses. John Locke systematically attacked the notions of innate ideas and a priori knowledge, arguing that if our claims to knowledge are to make sense they must be derived from the world of sense experience.

> "Let us then suppose the mind to be, as we say, white paper, void of all characters, without any ideas; how comes it by that vast store, which the busy and boundless fancy of man has painted on it with an almost endless variety? Whence has it all the materials of reason and knowledge? To this I answer, in one word, from experience: in that all our knowledge is founded."[12]

All knowledge comes through sensory experience. Our ideas are a product of sensory impressions and from simple ideas, like brown and hard and square, we construct complicated ideas like "a hard brown square." If an idea or belief cannot be analyzed in terms of these basic foundational ideas, it is unworthy of belief.

Locke goes on to set forth a representational theory of knowledge, which claims that the core of what we know is caused by the world itself, though some qualities are the products of the way our perceptual mechanisms are affected by the world. The former qualities, called *primary qualities,* such as motion, size, shape, and number are the true building blocks of knowledge because these qualities are accurate representatives of the objective features of the world. On the other hand, the *secondary qualities* are modes of apprehending the primary qualities. Examples of these qualities are taste, color, odor, and sound. Because the color or taste of the same object can appear differently to different people or to the same person at different times, secondary qualities are subjective, even though they are caused by the objective primary qualities. We will examine these concepts further in chapter 4 when we treat the problem of perception.

Book Outline

We have described the basic concepts and questions of epistemology, to be analyzed in greater detail in the rest of this work. After looking at the question of skepticism in the next two chapters, we will discuss perception, our knowledge (or claims to knowledge) of the external world. In chapter 5 we will attempt to analyze the concept of knowledge as true, justified belief, noting that this conception is fraught with problems (most of them based on "the Gettier problem" after the philosopher Edmund Gettier, who first revealed problems with the standard definition).

Chapters 6 through 9 deal with theories of justification or substitutions for that concept. In chapters 6 and 7 on foundationalism and coherentism respectively, we ask whether the justificatory process is more like building a house on a foundation or like a spider web, which holistically links the essential components in a broad network. Chapter 8 examines the question of whether justification is internal to the knower—something he or she must be able to access—or whether it is external—something that need not be accessed by the knower, as long as it is produced by a reliable process. Chapter 9 looks at one of the most sophisticated versions of externalism, Alvin Plantinga's "Warrant and Proper Function," in which he substitutes a concept of *warrant* for the more traditional concept of *justification*. In chapter 10 we examine the attempts of W. V. Quine and others to do away with the need for justification of one's knowledge claims by subsuming epistemology under the domain of psychology, and in chapter 11 we will take a glance at the idea of virtue epistemology.

Chapter 12 discusses the concept of a priori knowledge, knowledge that does not depend on perception, including innate ideas and synthetic a priori knowledge. Chapter 13 examines the concept of memory. How do these experiences function in our evidential base? Chapter 14 looks at a difficult puzzle: How do you know that there are other minds, that those around you are persons with pains and feelings and other mental experiences? You've only experienced your own mental states, so why should you suppose those other bodies are having mental experiences?

The last few chapters take us back to the idea of belief. Chapter 15 analyzes the nature of belief, examining Hume's occurrentist theory and more recent dispositionalist theories. Chapter 16 examines the relationship between believing and willing. Do we have some direct control over our belief formations, as Descartes, Kierkegaard, Pieper, and Chisholm suggest we do, or is belief formation involuntary? Chapter 17 asks whether an ethical dimension attaches to some or all of our belief states. Is it immoral to believe against the evidence—or unjustified? If people will be happier not knowing the truth, should we keep it from them or do we have an obligation to provide full disclosure where possible? Chapter 18 compares believing with accepting propositions. Through analyzing recent work by L. J. Cohen, some critical distinctions are set forth. Chapter 19 shows how one might apply epistemological considerations to other domains. It takes religious beliefs as a case study and analyzes how one might justify those beliefs.

I hope that you will enjoy the quest for understanding what epistemology is all about. If I have been successful, by the time you have gone through this book, you will have come to appreciate the nature of the theory of knowledge and understand why every rational person should be interested in it.

QUESTIONS FOR DISCUSSION

1. Distinguish three ways we use the verb *know*. Which way is most important from the view of the theory of knowledge?

2. Some people believe that we should concentrate on competence knowledge more than we do—and even make it the basic epistemic type (Michael Polanyi seems to do this sometimes; see "Further Reading"). Knowledge is a result of a holistic competence, an ability to perceive, reflect, *and* act correctly. Take riding a bicycle. One cannot easily separate the propositional knowledge, acquaintance knowledge, and competence knowledge in such a process. One acts holistically, integrating all of these types, and the process involves personal interest, concentration, and even emotions—thus going against the standard model of detached, impartial reasoning. Do you find this more existential type of knowledge appealing? Explain your answer.

3. Can there be false knowledge? Why or why not?

4. Can there be false beliefs? Can you name any of your false beliefs? Why or why not? Try to define the concept "belief."

5. What is the best definition of truth? Critically examine the three theories of truth discussed in this chapter. What do people mean when they say "This is true for me, though not necessarily for you"? Can (some) truth be mind-dependent? Consider ideas in the imagination. Explain.

6. Discuss the relation of justification to knowledge. What do we mean by the justification of a belief? Does this imply that we are irresponsible if we believe propositions without being able to give our evidence? Laurence BonJour writes:

   We cannot, in most cases at least, bring it about directly that our beliefs are true, but we can presumably bring it about directly . . . that they are epistemically justified.

   It follows that one's cognitive endeavors are epistemically justified only if and to the extent that they are aimed at this goal, which means very roughly that one accepts all and only those beliefs which one has good reason to think are true. To accept a belief in the absence of such a reason . . . is to neglect the pursuit of truth; such acceptance is, one might say, *epistemically irresponsible*. My contention here is that the idea of avoiding such irresponsibility, of being epistemically responsible in one's believings, is the core of the notion of epistemic justification. (*The Structure of Empirical Knowledge*, 8)

Evaluate BonJour's claims as best you can. The question, one to which we shall return throughout this book, especially in chapters 9, 16, and 17, is whether we have epistemic duties. In what sense can we be said to be responsible for the beliefs we have? Can we be held accountable for our beliefs? Take an example of a prejudicial belief. Is the prejudiced person responsible for his or her prejudiced beliefs?

7. Read the three quotations by G. E. Lessing, William James, and Laurence BonJour (page iv) having to do with truth and justification, and analyze them. What differences do you see between them? Do these differences reflect fundamental differences or are they compatible reflections, mere differences in emphasis?

8. The skeptic asks how it is possible to know anything at all. Does the skeptic's question make sense to you? What could he or she mean by "total skepticism"? We will get to this problem in the next chapter, so it would be helpful if you formulated your initial response before you read the text.

9. What is the difference between rationalism and empiricism?

10. Distinguish between a priori and a posteriori knowledge. Then go over Kant's notion of synthetic a priori knowledge. Do you agree with his view that we cannot think about the world apart from such concepts? Do you agree that time, space, causality, and arithmetic are examples of such knowledge?

11. Why do empiricists reject the notion of synthetic a priori knowledge?

NOTES

1. Plato, *Sophist*, 263 (author trans.).
2. Aristotle, *Metaphysics* IV:7, 1011b.
3. Ludwig Wittgenstein, *Tractatus Logico-Philosophicus* (London: Routledge & Kegan Paul, 1921), 4.01.
4. This version of the correspondence theory of truth was first put forth by Alfred Tarski and is usually called the semantic theory of truth.

5. William James, *Essays in Pragmatism* (New York: Hafner Publishing Co, 1948), 170.

6. Richard Rorty, *Philosophy and the Mirror of Nature* (Princeton, NJ: Princeton University Press, 1979), 176, 308. He opposes the metaphysical/semantical notion of truth as representation, saying "The aim of all such [representational] explanation is to make truth more than what Dewey calls 'warranted assertibility': more than what our peers will, *ceteris paribus,* let us get away with saying. Such explanation, when ontological, usually takes the form of a redescription of the object of knowledge so as to bridge the gap between it and the knowing subject. To choose between the approaches is to choose between truth as 'what is good for us to believe' and truth as 'contact with reality' (176). Dewey's term "warranted assertibility," signifies what a speaker in a given social context is justified in asserting. The idea is that the social context, rather than some eternal perspective, defines justification and is the closest we can come to the truth. See also Hilary Putnam, *Meaning and the Moral Sciences* (London: Routledge & Kegan Paul, 1978) and *Reason, Truth and History* (Cambridge: Cambridge University Press, 1981).

7. A. Phillips Griffiths, *Knowledge and Belief* (Oxford: Oxford University Press, 1967), 10.

8. Plato, "The Republic." In *Plato: The Collected Dialogues,* ed. Edith Hamilton and Huntington Cairns (Princeton, NJ: Princeton University Press, 1982). See especially Books VI and VII.

9. Kant, *Critique of Pure Reason,* trans. Norman Kemp Smith (New York: St. Martin's Press, 1969), 41.

10. Ibid., 41–44.

11. John Locke, *An Essay Concerning Human Understanding* (Oxford: Oxford University Press, 1924), Book II, Chapter 1, 121.

12. Ibid.

FOR FURTHER READING

Audi, Robert. *Belief, Justification and Knowledge.* Belmont, CA: Wadsworth, 1988. An excellent short introduction to the subject.

Audi, Robert. *Epistemology.* London: Routledge and Kegan Paul, 1998. A thorough, penetrating contemporary introduction to epistemology.

Blanshard, Brand. *The Nature of Thought.* Vol. 2. London: Allen & Unwin, 1939.

BonJour, Laurence. *The Structure of Empirical Knowledge.* Cambridge, MA: Harvard University Press, 1985. A comprehensive treatment. Advanced but well written.

Capaldi, Nicholas. *Human Knowledge.* New York: Pegasus, 1969. A helpful, accessible introduction to the subject.

Chisholm, Roderick. *Theory of Knowledge.* 3rd ed. Englewood Cliffs, NJ: Prentice Hall, 1988. A rich exposition of the major problems.

Dancy, Jonathan. *Contemporary Epistemology.* New York: Basil Blackwell, 1985. This book defends a coherentist position against foundationalism.

Dancy, Jonathan, and Ernest Sosa, eds. *A Companion to Epistemology.* London: Basil Blackball, 1992. An excellent comprehensive encyclopedia of epistemology

Davidson, Donald. *Truth and Interpretation.* Oxford: Clarendon Press, 1984.

Horwich, Paul. *Truth.* London: Basil Blackwell, 1990.

James, William. *The Meaning of Truth.* London: Longmans Green, 1909.

Lehrer, Keith. *Theory of Knowledge.* Boulder, CO: Westview, 1990. A thorough and thoughtful survey of the subject.

Moser, Paul, Dwayne H. Mulder, and J. D. Trout, *The Theory of Knowledge.* New York: Oxford University Press, 1998.

O'Connor, D. J., and Brian Carr. *Introduction to the Theory of Knowledge.* Minneapolis: University of Minnesota Press, 1982. A good survey of the basic issues.

Plantinga, Alvin. *Warrant and Proper Function.* Oxford: Oxford University Press, 1993. A penetrating and comprehensive work in contemporary epistemology.

Plantinga, Alvin. *Warrant: The Current Debate.* Oxford: Oxford University Press, 1993. A thorough critique of contemporary epistemology. An advanced but clearly written text, so that a beginning philosopher can understand most of it without too much trouble.

Pojman, Louis. *The Theory of Knowledge: Classical and Contemporary Readings.* 2nd ed. Belmont, CA: Wadsworth, 1993. A comprehensive anthology containing many of the authors referred to and works used in this part of our book.

Polanyi, Michael. *Personal Knowledge.* Chicago: University of Chicago Press, 1958. An important work on nonstandard accounts of knowledge, especially competence knowledge.

Pollock, John. *Contemporary Theories of Knowledge.* Totowa, NJ: Rowman & Littlefield, 1986. A lively, challenging study that focuses primarily on epistemic justification.

Rorty, Richard. *Philosophy and the Mirror of Nature.* Princeton, NJ: Princeton University Press, 1979. A critique of the whole enterprise of epistemology, aiming to replace it with "social knowledge" and intellectual conversation.

Russell, Bertrand. *The Problems of Philosophy.* Oxford: Oxford University Press, 1912. A classic—pithy, succinct, and engaging. Contains a classic treatment of the correspondence theory of truth.

Steup, Matthias, *Contemporary Epistemology.* Prentice Hall, 1996.

Wittgenstein, Ludwig. *Tractatus Logico-Philosophicus.* London: Routledge and Kegan Paul, 1922.

CHAPTER 2

The Skeptical Tradition

Socrates began by seeking to find a wise man and ended up identifying human wisdom with skepticism. At his defense, set forth by Plato (427–347 B.C.) in the *Apology*, Socrates tells how Chaerephon brought back the message from the Oracle at Delphi that Socrates was the wisest man alive. Socrates, determined to disprove the Oracle, went into the marketplace to seek a man wiser than himself. He questioned the politicians, poets, and artisans, reducing them to silent confusion, and discovered that while they all thought of themselves as wise, they knew precious little. So he concluded that both they and he were essentially ignorant, but while they knew nothing and were ignorant of their lack of knowledge, he both knew nothing and knew that he knew nothing. So he knew one more thing than they. That was sufficient to constitute wisdom.

The term *skeptic* (Greek "to inquire or investigate") got its impetus from Socrates' frequent refrain, "We ought to investigate this," something he said of every philosophically interesting subject. To him no subject was too sacred for rational inquiry. The greater the system the greater the challenge for the skeptic. And in the ancient world, during the first and second century B.C., no greater system existed than Stoicism. Skepticism was the worm that nibbled at this giant until it toppled over.

The Ancient School of Skepticism

Largely in opposition to the Stoics, who held a dogmatic metaphysic, Plato's Academy gradually evolved into the School of Skepticism, deemphasizing Plato's positive metaphysics and taking Socratic agnosticism (agnoia) as its model. Its successive leaders, Arcesilaus (ca. 315–240 B.C.) and Carneades (ca. 214–129 B.C.), opposed the Stoics' notion of self-evident perceptual knowledge. Quoting Socrates, Arcesilaus would contend that "there is only one thing I know and that is that I know nothing," adding, "and I don't even know that." Carneades must have been a remarkable dialectician. In 155 B.C. he was sent on a diplomatic mission to Rome. In his spare time he gave two lectures. On the first day he eulogized justice, making a profound impression on his audience. To their amazement on the second day he gave a diatribe against justice, arguing that there were equally good reasons for not adopting it. For one thing, it would cause the Romans to give up all their conquests and return to living in huts. This balancing of arguments on both sides of an issue struck the Romans as sophistry, and not long after, a law was passed against philosophers. Because these skeptics arose within Plato's Academy, they were called "Academic Skeptics."

In the same century the philosopher Pyrrho of Elis (ca. 360–270 B.C.) developed a more radical form of skepticism. Whereas the Academics claimed to know one thing (that they didn't have any knowledge), the Pyrrhonians denied that we could even know that. The Greek Pyrrhonist Sextus Empiricus (second century A.D.) described Pyrrhonism as a purge that eliminated everything, including itself. But these two schools were not always distinguished in the ancient world. I'll say more about their differences later.

Stoic Epistemology

Skepticism arose as a counterforce to the most prominent and dogmatic philosophy of its day, Stoicism. The Stoics held a position that may appear to be an oxymoron; they were spiritual materialists. On the one hand, they held to a materialist world view. Everything that exists is material substance and operates by deterministic laws. On the other hand, they believed in a providential God, who ruled the world for human good. God had a material body, consisting of fire, and it was from this active fire that all cruder material objects derive. Within each person dwelt a lesser fire, a divine spark, or reason, and it was this seed of God that gave us inherent worth, making all people equal citizens of a universal commonwealth. The Stoics were the first cosmopolitans, citizens of the world.

A rich, optimistic metaphysic resulted in a confident, rationalist, "dogmatic" epistemology. The idea of "dogma" (opinion or belief) was a positive one, conveying inner certainty in one's beliefs. All the positive philosophies of the ancient world were dogmatic in this sense.

The Stoics were simply more self-consciously so, justifying their sense of certainty on a comprehensive, coherent set of arguments, which they saw as deriving from God himself. The law by which God governed the universe was reason, the Logos, the very fire of God's nature. Immanent within every person resided a portion of that reason, a divine spark (*logos spermatikos,* "rational sperm"). Reason, rightly used, leads us to knowledge of all essential truths, including the existence and nature of God, the soul, providence, and other metaphysical and moral truths.

This rich metaphysical Stoic epistemology centered around the notion of certainty, or "certain representations." In perception the object perceived physically communicates itself on the mind like a seal on wax. As long as we pay attention we will not be deceived about these basic appearances. We could, in fact, have certainty about physical reality from the smallest object to the greatest, God himself. A criterion was constructed based on the idea of clear and distinct ideas, similar to that of Descartes's criterion years later.[1]

Whatever appears to us as definitely clear and distinct is self-evidently true. From this criterion, arguments were constructed to convince people, not only of the existence, but of the nature of God. A theory of perception afforded self-evident representations of external objects. Stoic epistemology thus confirmed the rich, confident, comprehensive Stoic metaphysic.

It was this criterion of self-evident truth that led to certainty and dogmatism that drew the Skeptics' fire and turned even the followers of Plato into doubters. The Skeptics argued that we were not only fallible, but that we could know virtually nothing about the things of which the Stoics were so confident: the inner nature of things, God, the soul, morality, causality, determinism, and the nature of the physical world. Even if a perception fulfilled Stoic ideal conditions (the sense organs are functioning properly, the environment is cooperative, the object is in close proximity, and so forth), we could still make mistakes in our judgments. We could still mistake Socrates' identical twin for Socrates. The Stoics replied that no two things were identical, so that one could always discern some difference. The Skeptics responded that this very doctrine of distinguishable nonidenticality was a metaphysical dogma.

The Skeptical Position   Sextus Empiricus, a Greek Skeptic and physician who gives us the most complete outline of the Skeptical position, defines "skepticism" this way. "Scepticism is an ability to place in antithesis, in any manner whatever, appearances and judgements, and thus—because of the equality of force in the objects and arguments opposed—to come first of all to a suspension of judgement and then to mental tranquillity."[2]

The Skeptic accepts appearances but not positive beliefs. Appearances of the way the world exists are passive aspects of perception. One is forced, involuntarily, to see the world the way one does, but the skeptic *actively* refuses to draw conclusions from this regarding real existence. "While living undogmatically, we pay due respect to appearances" (40).

Using a device called "tropes" (modes of balancing arguments), Skeptics like Aenesidemus (ca. 90 B.C.) called attention to the relativity and undecidability of beliefs and explanations. They said that for every physical or nonphysical state of affairs, there were innumerable possibilities for its explanation, and there is no reason to suppose that we can know which is the correct explanation. While skeptics conceded similarities in some appearances, they doubted whether these led to essential knowledge. "It appears to us that honey is sweet. This we concede, for we experience sweetness through sensation. We doubt, however, whether it is sweet by reason of its essence, which is not a question of the appearance, but of that which is asserted of the appearance" (40). They pointed out that animals and humans perceived things differently and that among humans, enormous differences existed in judgment, evaluation, taste, ability, and habits. "Different men take delight in different deeds" and "If fair and wise meant both the same to all, Dispute and strife would be no more" (55).

Different philosophies and religions offer equally dogmatic accounts of the origin of life and the nature of reality. There is relativity of knowledge and custom, so that it is impossible to decide the truth of any matter. This inherent undecidability leads to a state of confusion. Here the Skeptics advised withholding assent or dissent regarding any opinion. The term they coined for this suspension of judgment was *epoche,* a state of purposefully refusing to have an opinion on metaphysical matters. It was not that they denied the gods or the soul, but they refused to assent either to their existence or nonexistence. They espoused a deliberate agnosticism. Doubt all! Maintain an inner *aphasia* (silence) on metaphysical matters! Doubt, thus characterized as the purgation or laxative of the soul, cleanses the soul of the excrescences that befoul it.

Not only did the Skeptics use epoche to undermine the senses. They attacked the citadel of philosophy, reason. Carneades argued that the intellect is no more trustworthy than the senses and that equally good reasons could be found on either side of an issue (illustrated by his two speeches on justice in Rome). Even the sacred method of syllogistic reasoning came under the scrutiny of epoche. Take the classical syllogism:

1. All men are mortal.
2. Socrates is a man.
3. Therefore, Socrates is mortal.

How do we establish the first premise, that all men are mortal? We have to know that every individual man, including Socrates, is mortal. But knowing that Socrates is mortal is exactly what we are trying to prove. The argument clearly begs the question. Carneades argues that all deductive reasoning is either circular (question begging) or involves an infinite regress of "proofs." Using this argument, he claimed to reduce the Stoic sacred oracle, reason, found as the essence of God, to the demise of doubt.

But doubt was not seen as an end in itself. Like the Stoics, Epicureans, Platonists, and Aristotelians of the ancient world, the Skeptics sought happiness. Doubt was the means to that end. Through this attitude of epoche, by grace the end product, *Ataraxia* (tranquillity or imperturbability—a skeptical version of happiness), would be attained. One would be led by doubt to cease to worry about metaphysical issues and thus rest, content in the commonsensical and everyday world. It is fear of the gods and of what may happen to one in another life that causes perturbations in the soul. Once one notices that different religions enjoin different beliefs to mutually exclusive gods and suspends judgment on the whole enterprise of religion, one is liberated from the deep but unnecessary worries. Here is how Sextus Empiricus puts it.

> The Sceptic, in fact, had the same experience as that related in the story of Apelles the artist. They say that when Apelles was painting a horse, he wished to represent the horse's foam in the painting. His attempt was so unsuccessful that he gave up and at the same time flung at the picture his sponge, with which he had wiped the paints off his brush. As it struck the picture, the sponge produced an image of horse's foam. So it was with the Sceptics. They were in hopes of attaining mental tranquillity, thinking that they could do this by arriving at some rational judgement which would dispel the inconsistencies involved in both appearances and thoughts. When they found this impossible, they withheld judgement. While they were in this state, they made a chance discovery. They found that they were attended by mental tranquillity as surely as a body by its shadow. (41–42)

Attaining tranquillity is a six-step process.

1. The philosopher seeks knowledge and tranquillity.

2. He inevitably discovers that knowledge is impossible and that therefore it cannot bring tranquillity.

3. All attempts to find knowledge, let alone to base tranquillity on it, lead to frustration and suffering.

4. When this truth sinks in, the philosopher accepts the impossibility of knowledge.

5. This leads to the further step of withholding judgment (epoche), thus preventing further frustration.

6. As a chance discovery, the philosopher attains a state of tranquillity, the very thing that he sought through pursuing knowledge.

Skeptics and Belief   Does the skeptic have beliefs? Here Sextus Empiricus points out an ambiguity in the word *belief.* The word *believe* has several senses.

> It has the meaning, first, of not resisting but simply following, without strong inclination or attachment, as a boy is said to "mind" his tutor. But sometimes it means to assent to something by choice and with a kind of affinity that comes from desiring it strongly, as the profligate believes the man who advocates extravagant living. Now, Caneades and Clitomachus and their followers affirm that both when they believe a thing and when they assert its probability their action is accompanied by a strong inclination to do so. We, on the other hand, do so as a matter of simple yielding, without attachment. Therefore our position would be different from theirs in this respect as well. (95)

While both the Academic and the Pyrrhonian skeptics reject full-blown beliefs, or those beliefs claiming knowledge, the Academic skeptic accepts the idea of probability. Certain propositions are more probable than not and should be considered more action guiding. The Pyrrhonian skeptic, on the other hand, rejects the idea of probability in believing but accepts some kind of living "as if" a proposition were true. The Pyrrhonian skeptic would assert that he believed it "without strong inclination" or "without attachment."

The question arises whether the skeptic can live life without a stronger notion of belief, without at least the Academic's notion of probability. When a dog said to have rabies is about to bite Pyrrho's child, would he not take action to protect the child? Isn't it more rational to eat fruits and vegetables than mushrooms, which have apparently caused the deaths of your neighbors? Doesn't the skeptic have to believe that his version of skepticism is really more accurate than his rivals?

To these questions the Pyrrhonian skeptic is likely to respond that, of course, he is inclined to do what common sense advises, but that he withholds any strong conviction about these things and refuses even to treat these practices with any sense of probability.

To this response the critic might reply, "Yes, but in doing what common sense advises, you are behaving exactly as if those practices were probable. The difference between you and the Academic is vanishingly slim."

You may decide for yourself how the conversation would continue.

Ancient Skepticism: Academics and Pyrrhonians

What is the relationship between classical and modern or contemporary Skepticism? Modern Skepticism denies knowledge—not belief. The major difference between ancient Skepticism and modern or contemporary Skepticism is that whereas modern Skepticism denies knowledge but allows belief, ancient Skepticism disallows belief, especially metaphysical belief. Contemporary Skepticism points out that while our beliefs may be justified in part, they are inadequately justified, lacking the complete justification necessary for knowledge.

Here we may distinguish the Academic Skepticism (originating in Plato's Academy) of Socrates, Arcesilaus, and Carneades from the Pyrrhonian Skepticism of Pyrrho, Aenesidemus, and Sextus Empiricus. Academic Skepticism, founded in Socrates' denial of knowledge, was not as radical as Pyrrhonism. It denied that we had any knowledge of reality itself or metaphysical truth, but claimed that we could know that we didn't have such knowledge ("I know one thing, that I don't know anything . . ."). Furthermore, it embraced a notion of probabilism, the idea that while we cannot know anything, some things are more probable than others, and we must let probability be the guide of life.

Pyrrhonian Skepticism seems to derive more from the pre-Socratic philosopher Heraclitus, who taught that everything is in flux and that we cannot even step into the same river twice, signifying human inability to discover any stable, immutable truths about reality. The Pyrrhonists accused the Academic of being "negative dogmatists," only half-skeptics. Aenesidemus, who came to the conclusion that this bastardized Skepticism was too close to its enemy, Stoicism, converted from Academic Skepticism to the Pyrrhonian camp. Under his leadership Pyrrhonism had a rebirth in the first century B.C. Rejecting the doctrine of Probabilism, he refused to grant assent to the deliverances of inductive reason, though he continued to follow it as an informal guide to life. Aenesidemus advocated the suspension of all judgment. We don't know even that we don't know anything, but what is more important is that we voluntarily suspend all judgment on metaphysical matters.

Secondly, whereas modern Skepticism is purely formal and wholly negative, describing our absence of knowledge but leaving us with nothing to put in its place, ancient Skepticism was substantive, advocated a way of life, leading to imperturbability. It produced skeptical "saints," models of how to live, Socrates, Pyrrho, Aenesidemus, and Carneades. True, they were not saints in the modern religious or moral sense, but they were looked upon as models of the way to live. A look at Pyrrho of Elis is instructive in this regard.

Pyrrho of Elis   Pyrrho of Elis (ca. 360–270 B.C.), who is sometimes said to be the founder of Skepticism, was known for his exemplary way of life, his *agoge*. To be a Pyrrhonist was to live the simple, non-speculative, tranquil way, apathetic to pleasures and pains, oblivious to dangers. The ancient writer Diogenes Laertius tells us that Pyrrho would not look where he was going, and that only the solicitous care of his devoted friends kept him alive in his total disregard for "carts, precipices, dogs or what not."[3]

Another story relates how one day Pyrrho was attacked by a wild dog. He fled and climbed a tree. After being rescued, he apologized to his friends for his terror, announcing that it is hard for a man to strip himself of his humanity.

But a second tradition held by Aenesidemus (ca. 90 B.C.), the philosopher who revived Pyrrhonism in the first century B.C., holds that Pyrrho was in fact a man of common sense who valued life and health. He avoided carts, precipices, and dogs; helped his friends; and lived a practical life, but eschewed all metaphysical dogma and fanaticism about anything. He lived a practical life of moderation, demonstrating Ataraxia in the face of temptation and social upheaval.

In one story related by Diogenes, Pyrrho was a passenger on a ship caught up in a violent storm. The passengers were panic-stricken, wailing and crying with horror. Pyrrho calmly observed the storm and the panic of the passengers. When the storm grew worse, and the cries of the passengers crescendoed, Pyrrho pointed to a little pig standing before them on the deck calmly munching its food. He told them that the unperturbedness of that pig was the mark of wisdom. "According to this second tradition, Pyrrho did not strip himself, or try to do so, of his sensibilities; he was solicitous of the feelings of his fellow passengers enough to give them a little demonstration, and he advocated a life imitative of a pig calmly eating rather than imitative of an ascetic trying to act as if he had no body."[4]

Consider the following: Three men are engaged in building houses, a carpenter, a roofer, and a bricklayer. They work together happily and with good humor, solve disagreements by commonsense procedures, share their bread as well as their profits. Their business is successful. Now one day the subject of religion surfaces. It turns out that the carpenter is an evangelical Christian, the roofer an orthodox Jew, and the bricklayer an atheist. They soon begin quarrelling about the existence of God and the true religion. The Christian declares that he is absolutely certain that Jesus Christ is the Messiah, the Son of God, the second person of the Trinity, and that apart from faith in Christ there is no salvation. The Jew objects and states that the Jews are the chosen people, that the Messiah has not yet come, and that Christians are heretics, enemies of the truth. They agree only on one thing, the bricklaying atheist is damned. The bricklayer argues, just as fervently as his co-workers, that there is no God, that they are fools and are wasting their energy with superstitious myths of the past. The argument continues, and soon they come to blows. The next days are difficult. They find that they cannot work together in harmony for they no longer see each other as co-workers in a common cause, but as enemies, holding incompatible world views. The joy has gone out of the partnership. It is doomed.

One way to interpret classical Skepticism is to see it as the rejection of the kinds of dogmatism illustrated in this story. The three people need not be religious for the point to be made. They could be three teachers working with children—one a radical feminist, one a Marxist, and the other a political conservative—who together destroy their school over ideology. The hallmark of classical Skepticism was the rejection of dogmatism and the commitment to commonsensical, practical living; to moderation; to keeping the passions under control even when confronted with forces that are beyond our control. Indeed, Skepticism resembles the original goal of Stoicism before it became encumbered with an inflationary metaphysic.

QUESTIONS FOR DISCUSSION

1. The Christian existentialist Søren Kierkegaard was deeply influenced by the Greek skeptics. He followed them in placing the deliverances of the senses and reason, especially the "rationalism"

of Hegel's philosophy, under the domain of epoche, and so neutralizing the Greek skeptics in order to make way for religious faith. Fideism (see the glossary) seems to get a clean bill of health in this process. Is this a valid way of using Skepticism?

2. Kierkegaard wrote,

> "Greek skepticism was a withdrawing skepticism (epoche); they doubted not by virtue of knowledge but by virtue of will (deny assent) . . . This implies that doubt can be terminated only in freedom, by an act of will, something every Greek skeptic would understand, inasmuch as he understood himself, but he would not terminate his skepticism precisely because he *willed* to doubt. . . . It is now readily apparent that belief is not a knowledge but an act of freedom, an expression of will." (*Philosophical Fragments,* trans. Howard V. Hong and Edna H. Hong (Princeton: Princeton University Press, 1985), 82–83)

Two questions arise: (a) Is this a correct interpretation of the Skeptics? From what you know of them, did they believe that we could will to suspend judgment and thus be successful? (b) Is this really possible? Are doubt and belief acts of the will or propositional attitudes that are forced upon us?

3. Is it possible for humans to live like the Pyrrhonian skeptics advise us to live? Explain your answer.

4. Review the story of Pyrrho on board a ship during a storm who points to the imperturbable pig as the example of correct living. Compare this with John Stuart Mill's dictum "better to be a human being dissatisfied than a pig satisfied; better to be Socrates dissatisfied than a fool satisfied" (*Utilitarianism,* (1863)). Discuss these two outlooks on life.

5. Note the description of Pyhrronian Skepticism given in this chapter. "They espoused a deliberate agnosticism. Doubt all! Maintain an inner *aphasia* (silence) on metaphysical matters! Doubt, thus characterized as the purgation or laxative of the soul, cleanses the soul of the excrescences that befoul it." If you know something about Eastern religions (e.g., some forms of Buddhism), compare the two views.

NOTES

1. For a helpful discussion of this point, see Michael Frede, "Stoics and Skeptics on Clear and Distinct Impressions." In *The Skeptical Tradition,* ed. Myles Burnyeat (Berkeley: University of California Press, 1983). Henceforth, page references to this are found in parentheses in the text.

2. Sextus Empiricus, *Selections from the Major Writings on Scepticism, Man and God,* trans. Sanford G. Etheridge, ed. Philip P. Hallie (Indianapolis: Hackett Publishing Co., 1968), 32.

3. My description of Pyrrho and much of Skepticism is indebted to Philip P. Hallie's "Introduction" to *Sextus Empiricus: Selections from the Major Writings on Scepticism, Man and God* (Indianapolis: Hackett Publishing Co., 1985) and to the writings of Sextus Empiricus therein.

4. Philip P. Hallie, "Introduction" to *Sextus Empiricus,* ibid., 12–13.

FOR FURTHER READING

Annas, Julia, and Jonathan Barnes, eds. *The Modes of Scepticism: Ancient Texts and Modern Interpretations.* Cambridge: Cambridge University Press, 1985.

Burnyeat, Myles, ed. *The Skeptical Tradition.* Berkeley: University of California Press, 1983. Contains an excellent set of articles, especially on the Greek skeptics.

Diogenes Laertius. *Lives of Eminent Philosophers.* Vol. 2, trans. by R. D. Hicks. Cambridge, MA: Harvard University Press, 1925. Contains a sketch of the lives of two skeptics, Pyrrho and Timon.

Frede, Michael. *Essays in Ancient Philosophy.* Minneapolis: University of Minnesota Press, 1987. An important collection of essays, including three on ancient skepticism.

Matson, Wallace. "Certainty Made Simple." In *Certainty and Surface in Epistemology and Philosophical Method: Essays in Honor of Avrum Stroll,* edited by A. P. Martinich and Michael J. White. Lewiston, NY: Edwin Mellen Press, 1991.

Sextus Empiricus. *Selections from the Major Writings on Scepticism, Man and God,* trans. by Sanford G. Etheridge, edited by Philip P. Hallie. Indianapolis: Hackett Publishing Co., 1968. A good selection at an affordable price. Hallie's introduction is outstanding.

Stough, Charlotte. *Greek Skepticism: A Study in Epistemology.* Berkeley: University of California Press, 1969.

CHAPTER 3

Modern Skepticism

Can we know anything at all? Can we ever be certain that we have the truth? If we know something, must we know that we know it? If so, can we know that we have knowledge? Are any truths so certain as to exclude all reasonable doubt? Is some knowledge infallible, or is everything subject to some legitimate doubt? Can we know that there is an external world, that we are truly perceiving the objects we seem to be perceiving? Or could we be systematically deceived, so that none of the things we seem to be seeing, hearing, feeling, and so forth are what they appear to be? Could we be wrong about all our empirical beliefs? How do we know that the future will be like the past or, even, that the past existed at all, let alone as we seem to have remembered it. Can we have knowledge of other minds, or could it be that other people are simply robots or figments of our imagination? What can we know and how can we be sure that we have knowledge?

The Challenge of Skepticism

Skepticism is the theory that we do not have any (or almost no) knowledge. We cannot be completely certain that practically any of our beliefs are true. More precisely, two types of skeptics exist. The *global* skeptic asserts and generally argues that we can know nothing or next to nothing. The *local*, or mitigated, skeptic argues that while we can have knowledge of some general and specific truths, we have no knowledge about the external world, induction, other minds, the self, immortality, free will, and other metaphysical truths. Traditionally, one who rejects skepticism and claims that we do have knowledge is a "dogmatist," from the Greek word *dogma*, meaning opinion or belief. I will use the term dogmatist in its original epistemological sense.

I am in my study (at least I strongly believe I am) in a house in Berkeley, California. I see a white wall with a brown shelf before me. On the left-hand side of the shelf are six Russian dolls (which successively fit into the next largest). How do I know that I am really in my study or that the house I am in is in Berkeley? Can I be sure that the wall in front of me is white or that there really are six Russian dolls on the shelf projecting from the wall? Like most people, I sometimes dream. Like many people, my dreams are so vivid that while I am dreaming I believe the events in my dream to be occurring. I have even had dreams within my dreams. Could I be dreaming now? How would I prove that I was not dreaming?

Or could I be hallucinating? My mother claims that after my twenty-year-old brother died in an automobile accident, he appeared to her two or three times while she was sitting alone in her bedroom. I think she was hallucinating. Could I be hallucinating now? How do you know that you are not hallucinating now?

Or suppose that a malevolent demon exists who is causing you to have all the appearances that you're now having. Do you know for sure that such a demon is not affecting you, causing you to have the kinds of sense experiences that you're having?

Or you could be a brain suspended in a large vat full of chemical solution in a neuroscientist's laboratory, and wired to a computer that is causing you to have the simulated experiences of what you now seem to be experiencing. The neuroscientist has programmed your brain to "feel", "touch", "see", and "hear" the very appearances you are now having. Could you tell the difference between these appearances and reality? Can you demonstrate that you are not a brain in a vat, being manipulated by a neuroscientist (or a whole team of them)? Even your attempt to prove that you are not a brain in a vat has been programmed into you by the neuroscientist. Even your comparison of your beliefs with your perceptions has been caused by this superprogram. Your vat is your destiny.

How do you know that you are not the only person who exists and that everyone else is not a robot programmed to "listen" to a robot teacher; to speak, ask questions, and smile; to sit in class and take notes and write exams; to stand up after class and walk out the door? Can you prove that other people have consciousness? Have you ever felt their consciousness, their pain, or their sense of the color blue? How do you know that other persons really exist?

Do you have any answers to these questions? Do you have an argument establishing that you have some knowledge? Can you refute the skeptic?

Descartes

The classic work on global skepticism is *Meditations* in which René Descartes (1596–1650) places all his previous knowledge in doubt in order to build a secure house of knowledge.

> It is now some years since I detected how many were the false beliefs that I had from my earliest youth admitted as true, and how doubtful was everything I had since constructed on this basis; and from that time I was convinced that I must once and for all seriously undertake to rid myself of all the opinions which I had formerly accepted, and commence to build anew from the foundation, if I wanted to establish any firm and permanent structure in the sciences.

He begins by showing that sensory experience is unstable.

> All that up to the present time I have accepted as most true and certain I have learned either from the senses or through the senses; but it is sometimes proved to me that these senses are deceptive, and it is wiser not to trust entirely to any thing by which we have once been deceived. . . . Reason persuades me that I ought to withhold my assent from matters which are not entirely certain and indubitable.[1]

Certainty demands reliable sources, but the senses are fickle and fallible—are unreliable—and wisdom teaches that unreliable witnesses are not to be completely trusted, so I should withhold assent from them.[2] The unreliable witness argument can be formulated like this:

1. Whatever has been found to be an unreliable witness should (prudentially) never again be trusted, since I can never be sure that it is not presently deceiving me.
2. The senses have sometimes been found to be unreliable witnesses.
3. Therefore, the senses should not be trusted.

Is this a sound argument? No. From the fact that someone or something sometimes deceives me, I cannot infer that it may always deceive me—at least not without supplementary reasons. I may have evidence that the senses or witnesses sometimes do not deceive me. Descartes recognizes that there are some experiences that only a lunatic would doubt, such as this body is mine, and I have two hands and feet. All the unreliable witness argument does is make us aware of our fallibility, that we are sometimes mistaken about what we take ourselves to be perceiving or remembering. Fallibility does not entail universal skepticism, but it may cause us to become aware of the possibility of skeptical situations. It checks the dogmatist, the person who is certain of his or her beliefs, and forces him or her to consider the possibility of the skeptical hypothesis.

I said that Descartes recognizes that there are some experiences that only a lunatic would doubt, such as this body is mine, and I have two hands and feet. But on deeper reflection these beliefs should also be called into question. For I sometimes sleep and therein dream.

> How often has it happened to me that in the night I dreamt that I found myself in this particular place, that I was dressed and seated near the fire, whilst in reality I was lying undressed in bed! At this moment it does indeed seem to me that it is with eyes awake that I am looking at this paper; that this head which I move is not asleep, that it is deliberately and of set purpose that I extend my hand and perceive it; what happens in sleep does not appear so clear nor so distinct as does all this. But in thinking over this I remind myself that on many occasions I have in sleep been deceived by similar illusions, and in dwelling carefully on this reflection I see so manifestly that there are no certain indications by which we may clearly distinguish wakefulness from sleep that I am lost in astonishment. And my astonishment is such that it is almost capable of persuading me that I now dream.[3]

Barry Stroud comments on this passage.

> With this thought, if he is right, Descartes has lost the whole world. He knows what he is experiencing, he knows how things appear to him, but he does not know whether he is in fact sitting by the fire with a piece of paper in his hand. It is, for him, exactly as if he were sitting by the fire with a piece of paper in his hand, but he does not know whether there really is a fire or a piece of paper there or not; he does not know what is really happening in the world around him. He realizes that if everything he can ever learn about what is happening in the world around him comes to him through the senses, but he cannot tell by means of the senses whether or not he is dreaming, then all the sensory experiences he is having are compatible with his merely dreaming of a world around him while in fact that world is very different from the way he takes it to be. That is why he thinks he must find some way to tell that he is not dreaming. . . . He thinks it is eminently reasonable to insist that if he is to know that he is sitting by the fire he must know that he is not dreaming that he is sitting by the fire.[4]

I could be dreaming or hallucinating or a demon could be deceiving me about my experiences. The essential point is that we do not have a criterion to distinguish illusory experience from veridical perception. The argument may be formulated in this way:

1. In order to have knowledge we need to be able to tell the difference between a hallucination (deception) and a perception. (Where there is no relevant difference, no epistemological distinction can be made.)

2. It is impossible to distinguish between a hallucination (or deception) and a normal perception.

3. Therefore, we do not know whether any of our perceptual beliefs are true.

If this is so, then we do not have any knowledge of the external world. All our experiences could be illusory. Not only Descartes, but all of us have "lost the whole world."

But Descartes goes on to doubt even our mathematical judgments. He imagines that an ingenious demon is deceiving him about everything, even about the most secure mathematical sums, so that it is possible that he is mistaken about adding 2 + 2.

This seems preposterous. Surely we know that 2 + 2 = 4 and many other logical and mathematical truths as well. Surely we know that a contradiction cannot be true, that the laws of logic are valid, and that nothing that is black is at the same time white. Perhaps, but the skeptic's challenge is for you to give a cogent reason defeating his or her challenge. If you cannot demonstrate or give a cogent reason to show that you are not dreaming or a brain in a vat, how can you be sure you know anything that you seem to know?

Descartes himself thought he could defeat the skeptic. First, he reasoned that if he was doubting everything, he could be sure of one thing: that he existed. For if I am doubting, I must exist in order to doubt. Doubting is a form of thinking, so I must exist in order to think. *"Cogito ergo sum"*; I think; therefore I exist.

> [Suppose] that there is some deceiver or other, very powerful and very cunning, who ever employs his ingenuity in deceiving me. Then without doubt I exist also if he deceives me, and let him deceive me as much as he will, he can never cause me to be nothing so long as I think that I am something. So that after having reflected well and carefully examined all things, we must come to the definite conclusion that this proposition: I am, I exist, is necessarily true each time that I pronounce it, or that I mentally conceive it.[5]

While I think that I am thinking, I cannot doubt that I exist. I have certain, indubitable knowledge of my own existence.

From this one item of certain knowledge, he derives a criterion of certainty. Self-knowledge is self-authenticating. It is clear and distinct, self-evident. Generalizing from this, Descartes concludes that whatever is clear and distinct is true and cannot be doubted. It is knowledge. He thinks that the existence of God is such a clear and distinct idea, or is deduced from ideas that are clear and distinct. When the question arises, "How do you know that a demon is not deceiving you into thinking that whatever is clear and distinct is always true?" Descartes answers that God, being good and all powerful, would not allow us to be so deceived. It has been noticed that Descartes is reasoning in a circle here. From the premise that clear and distinct ideas are true, he infers the existence of God, but to infer the truth of the premise that clear and distinct ideas are always true, he appeals to the premise that God exists and is not a deceiver. So Descartes's argument does not establish that whatever is clear and distinct is true. Something could appear to be clear and distinct and yet be false. It could also appear to be clear and distinct and not be clear and distinct. Besides, as many critiques have pointed out, the notions "clear" and "distinct" themselves are not clear or distinct but somewhat vague and indistinct. Descartes never defines these characteristics, but they seem to signify self-evidence, obviousness, and distinguishability from other things. But, again, these qualities seem contextually conditioned. What is self-evident to a computer engineer about my computer may be incomprehensible to me.

Descartes's justification of the thesis that we have knowledge of the external world rests ultimately on the idea that God exists and is not a deceiver. If the world did not exist as our critical perceptions (our best science) says it does, God would be a deceiver. Since this is not so, the best explanation of our belief in the reality of the external world is that the world really does exist. Unless you think that Descartes has established the existence of God, which almost all inquirers agree he has not, his argument for the reality of the external world fails. He has not defeated skepticism about the external world.

But I think that Descartes's ingenious argument has established at least one bit of knowledge: If I am thinking, then I must exist—and the same goes for you. If you are thinking, then you must exist. (This is a good reason to exercise your thought about your existence.) Strictly speaking it doesn't prove that "I" exist, for the "I" is still undefined. But it shows that *something* exists that is conscious and thinking, and we may identify with this something, whatever it is. But apart from this, Descartes hasn't really defeated the skeptic.

Hume

David Hume (1711–1776), the next great skeptic, was both narrower and deeper than Descartes. He was deeper or more authentic (in the sense of putting forth the skeptical hypothesis as a plausible option) in that while Descartes was only a *methodological* skeptic, Hume was a *substantive* skeptic. Descartes sought to use skepticism to filter out error and so arrive at indubitable knowledge of metaphysical truth. Hume believed metaphysics was doomed by the skeptical hypothesis. On the other hand, Hume was narrower in scope than his French counterpart, for he conceded that we can know the truths of mathematics and logic as well as common-sense truths (e.g., memory reports and reports about our impressions). There is no equivalent to the Cartesian demon operating systematically to deceive us. Simplifying a bit, we may call Descartes a global but methodological skeptic and Hume a local or mitigated, but substantive, skeptic.

Hume's epistemology is grounded in the experience of having sense impressions—having appearance of sights, sounds, smells, and so forth. He supposes that all our beliefs (or ideas) are caused by both internal and external impressions—the passions and the perceptions. But we cannot get behind the impressions to check whether the world is really like what we are experiencing, so we can never know to what extent our impressions and ideas resemble the world (supposing there is a world behind the impressions). Hume goes on to argue that since all our beliefs are founded on these insecure impressions, we can have no metaphysical knowledge. We cannot even trace our belief in cause and effect, induction, matter, the self, the existence of God, or free will to impressions. Hence, they lack justification and we lack knowledge of them. Here is a brief summary of Hume's skeptical musings on these subjects.

Cause and effect Hume points out that the inferences we make about causality are not logical ones but arise out of experience. Going against the standard view of his day that the connection between cause and effect is necessary, like the connection between triangularity and three-sidedness, Hume attributed our belief in causality to the observation of regular conjunctions of events. "When many uniform instances appear, and the same object is always followed by the same event; we then begin to entertain the notion of cause and connexion. We then *feel* a new sentiment or impression, to wit, a customary connexion in the thought or imagination between one object and its usual attendant."[6] We cannot prove that every event has a cause nor that the same cause will always have a like effect, but we see two events in constant conjunction and *unjustifiably* infer a necessary connection. But there is no *necessity* about this connection. We do not have a priori knowledge of such a connection, nor can we infer it from other truths. Our belief that every event has a cause is simply a psychologically habitual inference derived from our experience. We know nothing about how things are in themselves.[7]

Modern quantum physics comes to a similar conclusion as Hume about our notion of *omnicausality* (that every event has a cause). It posits that at a subatomic level noncausal events occur. Chance is at the heart of reality. But if chance is at the heart of physics, why should we hold on to the idea of omnicausality on the macroscopic level of the world?

Induction Hume argues that we have no good reason to believe in induction. What follows is a quotation from his *Enquiry Concerning Human Understanding* (1748):

> This proposition, that causes and effects are discoverable, not by reason but by experience, will readily be admitted with regard to such objects, as we remember to have once been altogether unknown to us; since we must be conscious of the utter inability, which we then lay under, of foretelling, what would arise from them. Present two smooth pieces of marble to a man, who has no tincture of natural philosophy; he will never discover, that they will adhere together, in such a manner as to require great force to separate them in a direct line, while they make so small a resistance to a lateral pressure. Such events, as bear little analogy to the common course of nature, are also readily confessed to be known only by experience; nor does any man imagine that the explosion of gunpowder, or the attraction of a loadstone, could ever be discovered by arguments a priori. In like manner, when an effect is supposed to depend upon an intricate machinery or secret structure of parts, we make no difficulty in attributing all our knowledge of it to experience. Who will assert, that he can give the ultimate reason, why milk or bread is proper nourishment for a man, not for a lion or a tiger?
>
> But the same truth may not appear, at first sight, to have the same evidence with regard to events, which have become familiar to us from our first appearance in the world, which bear a close analogy to the whole course of nature, and which are supposed to depend on the simple qualities of objects, without any secret structure of parts. We are apt to imagine, that we could discover these effects by the mere operation of our reason, without experience. We fancy, that were we brought, on a sudden, into this world, we could at first have inferred, that one Billiard-ball would communicate motion to another upon impulse; and that we needed not to have waited for the event, in order to pronounce with

certainty concerning it. Such is the influence of custom, that, where it is strongest, it not only covers our natural ignorance, but even conceals itself, and seems not to take place, merely because it is found in the highest degree.

But to convince us, that all the laws of nature, and all the operations of bodies without exception, are known only by experience, the following reflections may, perhaps, suffice. Were any object presented to us, and were we required to pronounce concerning the effect, which will result from it, without consulting past observation; after what manner, I beseech you, must the mind proceed in this operation? It must invent or imagine some event, which it ascribes to the object as its effect; and it is plain that this invention must be entirely arbitrary. The mind can never possibly find the effect in the supposed cause, by the most accurate scrutiny and examination. For the effect is totally different from the cause, and consequently can never be discovered in it. Motion in the second Billiard-ball is a quite distinct event from motion in the first; nor is there any thing in the one to suggest the smallest hint of the other. A stone or piece of metal raised into the air, and left without any support, immediately falls: But to consider the matter a priori, is there any thing we discover in this situation, which can beget the idea of a downward, rather than an upward, or any other motion, in the stone or metal?

In reality, all arguments from experience are founded on the similarity, which we discover among natural objects, and by which we are induced to expect effects similar to those, which we have found to follow from such objects. And though none but a fool or madman will ever pretend to dispute the authority of experience, or to reject that great guide of human life; it may surely be allowed a philosopher to have so much curiosity at least, as to examine the principle of human nature, which gives this mighty authority to experience, and makes us draw advantage from that similarity, which nature has placed among different objects. From causes, which appear similar, we expect similar effects. This is the sum of all our experimental conclusions. Now it seems evident, that, if this conclusion were formed by reason, it would be as perfect at first, and upon one instance, as after ever so long a course of experience. But the case is far otherwise. Nothing so like as eggs; yet no one, on account of this appearing similarity, expects the same taste and relish in all of them. It is only after a long course of uniform experiments in any kind, that we attain a firm reliance and security with regard to a particular event. Now where is that process of reasoning, which, from one instance, draws a conclusion, so different from that which it infers from a hundred instances, that are nowise different from that single one? This question I propose as much for the sake of information, as with an intention of raising difficulties. I cannot find, I cannot imagine any such reasoning. But I keep my mind still open to instruction, if any one will vouchsafe to bestow it on me.

Hume, while agreeing that we cannot live without supposing the validity of inductive reasoning, argues that we cannot give a rational justification for our belief in this supposition. He points out that there is no contradiction in denying induction or the uniformity of nature. We cannot reason that the sun will rise tomorrow because it has always done so in the past, for that assumes that the future will be like the past, which in turn assumes the uniformity of nature. We may formulate the argument like this:

1. The sun has risen every day of my life.
2. Therefore the sun will rise tomorrow.

But something seems missing. We need a premise linking the past to future behavior. We need the proposition: 1* The future will be like the past. But, Hume asks, how do we know 1*? It's not a necessary truth. We appeal to all past futures which have been like past pasts. In other words, we appeal to the uniformity of nature's laws: 1**nature's laws will be the same tomorrow or in the future as in the past. But how do we know this? What reason is there to believe in the uniformity of nature? "Well, these laws have always functioned in the past," someone says. But this is circular reasoning, boiling down to the tautology that the future will be like the past because the future has been like the past. In fact the future is not always like the past. As Bertrand Russell once pointed out, the chicken who comes to the farmer each day to be fed one day finds herself the object of feeding. Similarly, in last Saturday's game the tight end caught a ball thrown just in front of him, but this Saturday he dropped the ball.

Take a moment to see whether you can construct an argument to show that we are justified in believing that the future will resemble the past.

The Self   Even the reality of the *self* and personal identity are called into question. If all knowledge about reality comes through impressions, where is the impression that produces the notion of a self which exists over time?

> From what impression could [the idea of the self] be derived? . . . It must be some one impression, that gives rise to every real idea. But self or person is not any one impression, but that to which our several impressions and ideas are supposed to have a reference. If any impression

gives rise to the idea of self, that impression must continue invariably the same, through the whole course of our lives; since self is supposed to exist after that manner. But there is no impression constant and invariable. . . . For my part, when I enter most intimately into what I call *myself*, I always stumble on some particular perception or other, of heat or cold, light or shade, love or hatred, pain or pleasure. I never can catch *myself* at any time without a perception, and never can observe any thing but the perception. . . . If any one upon serious and unprejudiced reflection, thinks he has a different notion of *himself*, I must confess I can reason no longer with him. All I can allow him is, that he may be in the right as well as I, and that we are essentially different in this particular. . . . But setting aside some metaphysicians of this kind, I may venture to affirm of the rest of mankind, that they are nothing but a bundle or collection of different perceptions, which succeed each other with an inconceivable rapidity, and are in a perceptual flux and movement.[9]

The self is a fiction, what our imagination projects on the basis of various perceptions and a need for coherence and constancy. The mind is simply a "kind of theater, where several perceptions successively make their appearances; pass, re-pass, glide away, and mingle in an infinite variety of postures and situations."[10] Of course, we may ask who is the "our" whose imagination manufactures a self out of particular perceptions?

Existence of God   Hume claims that the classic proofs, the cosmological and teleological arguments, fail to establish the existence of an omnipotent, omnibenevolent designer of the universe. Since all our ideas derive from initial impressions, the idea of God must be an imaginative construction from simple ideas (power, knowledge, goodness, and so forth) based originally on impressions.

Free will   Perhaps all our actions are determined by antecedent states of affairs so that we are not free. To suppose that an action, such as deciding to raise my hand in order to vote for a candidate, is deliberate is to suppose that I could have done otherwise and that I am fully responsible for my act. But if something caused me to raise my hand, libertarian free will is a fiction and responsibility boils down to nothing more than being the locus of causal processes.

So, it seems that nature systemically deceives us. We cannot help believing that we are free when acting, but, on reflection, the notion of free will does not even seem to make sense. It does not make sense, not only because it contrasts with a notion of causal determination (which Hume doubts anyway), but because the notion of chance does not give us a notion of freedom and responsibility either. If my behavior is produced not by determinate causes but by random events, then that behavior is arbitrary and capricious, not rationally grounded. So either my actions are caused in a lawlike manner and I am not free, or my actions are the product of chance and they are not really *my* acts, but the irrational product of a randomizing nature. Either way I am not free. Nevertheless, when I act I feel that I am in control, that I could have done otherwise if I had willed to do otherwise (and I could have willed to do otherwise).

According to Humean reason, this feeling is unsupported by reflection. Nonetheless, Hume is not a hard determinist, but a compatibilist (trying to reconcile determinism and freedom of the will). He believes that we must be held accountable for our voluntary actions, because we *chose* to do them—even though we were caused to choose to do them.

But if we cannot help believing in causation, induction, matter, the identity of the self, freedom of the will (at least while acting), and possibly the existence of a higher being, in spite of their absence of rational justification, the skeptic has a firm basis for his or her contention that we know very little and that we may be systematically misled by nature (perhaps for our own good).

> As long as our attention is bent upon the subject, the philosophical and studied principle may prevail; but the moment we relax our thoughts, nature will display herself, and draw us back to our former opinion. . . . The skeptical doubt, both with respect to reason and the senses, is a malady, which can never be radically cured, but must return upon us every moment, however we may chance it away. . . . As the skeptical doubt arises naturally from a profound and intense reflection on those subjects, it always increases, the farther we carry our reflections, when in opposition or conformity to it. *Carelessness and inattention alone can afford us any remedy.*[11]

Fortunately, Hume concludes,

> It happens that since reason is incapable of dispelling these clouds, nature herself suffices to that purpose, and cures me of this philosophical melancholy and delirium, either by relaxing this bent of mind, or by some avocation, and lively impression of my senses, which obliterate all these chimeras. I dine, I play a game of backgammon, I converse, and am merry with my friends; and when after three or four hours' amusement, I would return to these speculations, they appear so cold, and strained, and ridiculous, that I cannot find in my heart to enter into them any farther.[12]

A natural propensity prohibits perseverance in skepticism and forces us to act as though the deliberations of reason were chimeras. But when we come back to philosophical reflection, we must suspect, if not profoundly conclude, that we know very little indeed.

Do We Have Knowledge of the External World?

Suppose that we follow Hume and allow that we do know mathematical and logical truths. The question now is whether we can know anything else. For example, do we have knowledge of the external world? Are the particular things we seem to perceive really what they seem to be? Suppose we are looking at a lush red McIntosh apple. We take it in our hands, feel its firmness, bring it to our mouths, bite into it, and experience its luscious taste. Our senses work in harmony, it seems, conveying powerful experiences about the McIntosh apple. But could we not be deceived about all of this? Could not the taste be due to our taste buds—lusciousness not being a property of the apple but of our taste mechanisms; redness not being a property in the world but an effect manufactured in our minds; firmness being likewise a property in us, not the apple (which physics tells us is made up of mostly space and microphysical particles)? Or could we not be hallucinating or be brains in a vat?

We might set forth the argument this way.

1. If I know that I have a McIntosh apple in my hand, then I know that I am not hallucinating or dreaming this.
2. But I do not *know* that I am not hallucinating or dreaming this, since knowledge entails having a complete justification for what is known and I have no complete justification that I am not hallucinating.
3. Therefore, I do not know that I have a McIntosh apple in my hand.

What can we make of this argument? It seems valid. Premise (1) seems true. If I really do have a McIntosh apple in my hand, then I am not simply hallucinating that I do (of course, I could be hallucinating and still have a McIntosh apple in my hand, but let us ignore that complication for the moment).

Premise (2) seems true also. I cannot prove that I am not hallucinating or dreaming, for even if I am not hallucinating or dreaming, I wouldn't know the difference if I were. My experiences would be relevantly similar to what they are now.

So the argument seems sound. If I don't know that I'm not hallucinating or dreaming all this, how can I know that I really do have a McIntosh apple in my hand? If I can't prove or don't know that I am not hallucinating at any particular moment of my life, how can I know anything about the external world—even if I'm not hallucinating?

The force of the argument is not that we don't have *justified* beliefs or even true justified beliefs. We're doing the best we can, and perhaps that's enough to give us truth. But it's not enough, claims the skeptic, to give us knowledge or justified certainty about the truth of our experiences. We could be wrong about any of our appearances. So we don't have knowledge.

Of course the antiskeptic will try to counter the skeptic's argument. He or she will claim that it is unsound. I can know that I have a McIntosh apple in front of me even if I cannot know that I am not hallucinating. This is based on the premise *H:* If I know that a McIntosh apple is in front of me and I know that if a McIntosh apple is in front of me, then I am not hallucinating, so then I know that I am not hallucinating. Let K stand for "I know," p for the proposition "a McIntosh apple is in front of me," q for the proposition "that I am not hallucinating," and "$\rightarrow$" for "entails." We get the following modus ponens formal argument.

1. Kp & $K(p \rightarrow q) \rightarrow Kq$ (formulation of proposition *H*).
2. Kp (statement of knowledge based on my commonsense perception).
3. $K(p \rightarrow q)$ (analytic statement about the knowing relationship: I know that if p, then q, and I know this because, given the p and q in question, the conditional $p \rightarrow q$ is analytic).
4. Therefore, Kq (I know that I'm not hallucinating).

Of course, the skeptic uses modus tollens to argue just the reverse.

1. Kp & $K(p \rightarrow q) \rightarrow Kq$ (formulation of *H*).
2. Not-Kq (I do not know that I am not hallucinating, for I cannot refute the skeptic).
3. $K(p \rightarrow q)$ (analytic truth as above: I know that if a McIntosh apple is in front of me, then I am not hallucinating).
4. Therefore, not-Kp (I do not know that a McIntosh apple is in front of me).

So we seem to come to a standoff. It's all a matter of quickness—who can draw his logical pistol first? Can the believer draw his modus ponens before the skeptic draws his modus tollens? Obviously something is wrong here. Either the antiskeptic must find a way around this standoff, or the skeptic wins by default because the skeptic is claiming not that we don't have true beliefs but that we do not have complete justification or certainty—knowledge.

Tracking Truth

Robert Nozick has challenged this argument,[13] claiming that the antiskeptic argument can be shown to work. His argument is based on a denial of premise (1) in *H*: Kp & $K(p \rightarrow q) \rightarrow Kq$.

I can know that a McIntosh apple is in front of me, and I can know that if such an apple is in front of me I am not hallucinating, but knowing all this does not entail that I know that I am not hallucinating. That is, knowledge is not closed under known entailment. I don't have to refute the skeptic in order to know that I am truly perceiving.

How can this be? It has to do with Nozick's theory that knowledge *tracks truth*. According to Nozick, a person *S* knows that *p* if and only if

1. *p* is true.
2. *S* believes that *p*.
3. If *p* were not true, *S* would not believe that *p*.
4. If *p* were true (in slightly altered circumstances), *S* would still believe that *p*.

Conditions (3) and (4) consist of subjunctive conditionals which are left vague, but depend on the idea of "close possible worlds." A close possible world is a situation very much like the actual situation, but with some small change. To say that I would do something in a close possible world is to say that even in a situation slightly different from this one, I would still do it. So Nozick's condition (4) means that even if things were slightly different, I would still believe that *p*. We can illustrate condition (4) this way. Suppose you believe that a McIntosh apple is before you. In one situation such a lone McIntosh apple is before you, but in a second situation the single genuine McIntosh apple is in a bushel of wax imitation McIntosh apples. If you would have mistaken the wax apple for a real McIntosh, then you cannot be said to know that the genuine McIntosh apple is really a McIntosh apple. In order to meet condition (4), we must be able to make relevant discriminations.

According to this theory, conditions (3) and (4) take the place of the standard condition that S must be justified in believing p (see chapter 5). Since knowledge is defined as truth-tracking, it only matters whether the belief in question is true, would not have been believed if it weren't true, and would remain true in slightly altered circumstances.

The question arises: What would lead Nozick to say that you can know p and know $p \rightarrow q$, but not know q? It's this sort of consideration. Suppose I know I'm eating an apple. If I weren't eating it, I wouldn't believe I was, and if I were eating it in slightly different circumstances, I would still believe I was. Also, I know that if I'm eating an apple, I'm not being deceived by a demon. But now, let's run the tracking test on whether I'm being deceived by one. Suppose I *were* being deceived by a demon. If I were being so deceived, one of his deceptions, presumably, would be to make me believe I wasn't being deceived by a demon. So, if I were being deceived by a demon, I would not believe I was being deceived by one. Hence, my belief that I am not demon-deceived fails to track truth. I don't know that I'm not being deceived by a demon.

Attractive as Nozick's solution is at first sight, we should hesitate to give up the idea of knowledge being closed under known entailment. Normally, we do suppose that it is. Note the difference between

a. $Kp \,\&\, K(p \rightarrow q) \rightarrow Kq$

and

b. $Kp \,\&\, (p \rightarrow q) \rightarrow Kq$

(b) says that if I know p (e.g., that the sun is a star) and if p entails q (e.g., the sun being a star entails that it is made up of molecules), then I know q (that the sun is made up of molecules). But I may not even understand the concept of a molecule (as most people before the nineteenth century did not), let alone believe that the sun is made up of them. Knowledge is not closed under entailment.

But (a) adds a K operator to the second conjunct. If I know that the sun is a star and *know* that the sun being a star entails that it is made up of molecules, then I know that the sun is made up of molecules. If Nozick's argument needed only (b) as a premise, it would be a sound argument, but since it needs (a) it seems unsound. For normally we do hold that knowledge under *known* entailment is closed. If I believe that you went to the baseball game yesterday, and believe that if you went you enjoyed yourself, then I believe that you enjoyed yourself. The main reason for giving up the notion that knowledge is closed under known entailment is that it would provide a way to refute the skeptic. But I doubt that it is a successful refutation. Here is a counterexample to Nozick's proposal. It strikes at condition (3)—if *p* were not true, *S* would not believe that *p*. Let *p* be the proposition: "I know that I have a head" and *S* stand for myself (I). Then (3) becomes: If the proposition "I know that I have a head" were false, I would not believe "I know that I have a head."

But this is clearly false. If a demon were deceiving me or I were hallucinating, I would still believe that I knew that I had a head even if I didn't. So unless Nozick can repair condition (3), it cannot stand for a necessary condition for knowledge, and so it cannot be used to defeat skepticism. Knowledge seems to be closed under known entailment. The skeptic escapes Nozick's truth-tracking strategy.

The Relevant Alternatives Model

A similar attempt to solve the problem of skepticism is the relevant alternatives model set forth by Fred Dretske.[14] Dretske asks you to imagine taking your son to a zoo where you see several zebras. When questioned by your son, you tell him that the animals in the pen before you are zebras. Do you know that they are zebras? Most of us would say without hesitation that we do, for we have a pretty good idea what zebras look like, the pen is marked "Zebras," and the like. "Yet," says Dretske, "something's being a zebra implies that it is not a mule and, in particular, not a mule cleverly disguised by the zoo authorities to look like a zebra. Do you know that these animals are not mules cleverly disguised by the zoo authorities to look like zebras?" No, you don't. If they were cleverly disguised mules, you wouldn't know the difference.

> Have you checked with the authorities? Did you examine the animals closely enough to detect such a fraud? You might do this, of course, but in most cases you do nothing of the kind. You have some general uniformities on which you rely, regularities to which you give expression by such remarks as "That isn't very likely." . . . Granted, the hypothesis [that the "zebras" are disguised mules] is not very plausible, given what we know about people and zoos. But the question here is not whether this alternative is plausible, not whether it is more or less plausible than that there are real zebras in the pen, but whether *you know* that this alternative hypothesis is false. I don't think you do.[15]

But does this mean that you and your son don't know that zebras are in front of you? No, you do know (we're assuming that they're zebras). The point is simply that you need not rule out the possibility of implausible alternatives in order to be said to have knowledge. "To know that *x* is *A* is to know that *x* is *A* within a framework of relevant alternatives, *B, C,* and *D.*" As long as you can pick out a zebra from a horse or an elephant or an elm tree and correctly identify it, you may be said to know that you're seeing a zebra—even if you can't rule out the possibility that it is a painted mule or a weird hologram or a robot from a Steven Spielberg epic.

Dretske's argument emphasizes that knowledge has a contextual aspect. What you know about the external world depends to some extent on your discriminating ability in various contexts—your ability to distinguish between genuine objects and relevant alternatives—but our knowledge does not depend on being able to discriminate between real objects and all logically possible appearances. Knowledge is a practical affair and must only be able to meet real objections and actual possibilities.

Contextual theories We will examine contextual theories of knowledge in chapter 5, but here we should point out that contextual theories have three problems.

1. It is unclear what a relevant alternative is. The notion of relevance is vague. How do we know whether the possibility of a mule being painted to look like a zebra is relevant to picking out zebras? If I believe in demons who intervene in human affairs, does the possibility of a demon causing these animals to look like zebras become a relevant alternative? This leads to a second problem.

2. Contextualism relativizes knowledge in a way that may be unduly subjective. What you know may depend on whether or not you have certain background beliefs. I may be said to know that the zebra in front of us is truly a zebra because I can just barely distinguish it from painted mules and because I don't believe in demons. You, however, may not be said to know that the same zebra in front of us is a zebra even though you can distinguish it from painted mules even better than I can. You, we may suppose, believe in demons who could disguise mules as zebras, hence your added belief robs you of knowledge—even though your perceptual mechanisms are more discriminating than mine.

Or, while I am out in the garage building a table or repairing a chair, I may be said to know that there is an external world, but in my study or in an epistemology class, where the possibility arises that I may be systematically mistaken about my experiences, that knowledge is suddenly withdrawn—since the possibility of systematic error is now a relevant alternative. Usually, we think that the more we reflect and find evidence for our beliefs, the closer to certainty and knowledge we come. But paradoxically the idea of relevant alternatives seems to take knowledge away from us. The more I seem to know about or reflect on a subject, the less I can be said to know it. As Bernard Williams puts it "reflection destroys knowledge."[16]

At first glance, tying our attributions of knowledge to such vague and relativized notions with such paradoxical results seems to make knowledge an extremely unstable entity. But if it is this unstable, doesn't the skeptic win the day?

3. A third criticism of the theory of relevant alternatives concerns whether knowledge is externalist or internalist and works if knowledge is externalist. There are two radically different theories of justification and/or knowledge (to be examined in detail in chapter 8): internalism and externalism. The internalist says that one must have or be able to give the reasons for one's belief in order to have knowledge of the proposition in question, but the externalist says that one need not have reasons for a belief in order to have knowledge of that proposition. All that is necessary is that the true belief has been brought about by a reliable (nonaccidental) process.

If internalism is correct and we accept the closure argument (i.e., If Kp & $K(p \rightarrow q) \rightarrow Kq$; not-$Kq$; therefore, not-$\overline{K}p$), the statement "if you don't know that the animal before you is not a painted mule, then you don't know that it is not a zebra" tends toward a skeptical conclusion. You don't know that the animal before you is a zebra.

But if externalism is correct, as long as your belief that a zebra is before you has been caused in the right way, you don't have to be able to rule out all the alternatives. You know that the animal in front of you is a zebra because that knowledge has been caused in the right way. Since you know that if it is a zebra it is not a painted mule, a hologram of a zebra, an illusion caused by a malicious demon, and so forth, you can be said to know that it is not a painted mule, a hologram of a zebra, an illusion, and so forth. Of course, this antiskeptical argument only works if a form of externalism is true.

For all its problems, the idea of relevant alternatives may play a role in defeating the skeptic. Not all doubts are rational ones or justified. And the burden of proof does seem to be on the shoulders of the skeptic at least to give us positive reasons for doubting self-evident, commonsense beliefs about the external world.

Moore's Defense of Common Sense

Can you defeat the skeptic? Two other related refutations of skepticism have been attempted.

G. E. Moore (1873–1958) claims that we can know that there is an external world, because we can know we have bodies. I can know that my body was born at a certain time in the past and has existed continuously ever since.

> It was much smaller when it was born, and for some time afterwards, than it is now. Ever since it was born, it has been either in contact with or not far from the surface of the earth; and, at every moment since it was born, there have also existed many other things, having shape and size in three dimensions, from which it has been at various distances.[17]

In a famous lecture, Moore claimed that he would then and there prove two things: that he had two hands. How? Here is Moore's proof.

> I can prove now . . . that two human hands exist. How? By holding up my two hands, and saying, as I make a certain gesture with the right hand, "Here is one hand," and adding, as I make a certain gesture with the left, "and here is another." But now I am perfectly well aware that, in spite of all that I have said, many philosophers will still feel that I have not given any satisfactory proof of the point in question. . . . If I had proved the proposition which I used as *premises* in my two proofs, then they would perhaps admit that I had proved the existence of external things. . . . They want a proof of what I assert *now* when I hold up my hands and say "Here's one hand and here's another." . . . They think that, if I cannot give such extra proofs, then the proofs that I have given are not conclusive proofs at all. . . . Such a view, though it has been very common among philosophers, can, I think, be shown to be wrong. . . . I can know things which I cannot prove; and among things which I certainly did know were the premises of my two proofs. I should say, therefore, that those, if any, who are dissatisfied with these proofs merely on the grounds that I did not know their premises, have no good reasons for their dissatisfaction.[18]

Moore claimed that we do not need to be able to prove all the premises of our argument in order to end up with a sound argument. If our premises are self-evident, we may consider them innocent until proven guilty. Accordingly, Moore claimed to have thereby given a rigorous proof that there was an external world, because the premises are known to be true (even though we can't prove them), and the conclusion follows by valid inference from these premises.

The general form of Moore's strategy is

1. If skepticism is true, we do not have knowledge of the external world.
2. But we do have knowledge of the external world (the examples given).
3. Therefore, skepticism is false.

Accordingly, we do not have to provide a complete explanation of the difference between dream states (or hallucination states) and veridical experiences in order to know that some of my self-evident perceptions are veridical. Common sense is innocent until proven guilty.

Skeptics have not taken kindly to Moore's refutation, claiming that it has all the virtues of "theft over honest toil" (in Bertrand Russell's phrase). Moore, they claim, is begging the question against the skeptic, for the question of whether Moore—or those "watching" him— are dreaming or hallucinating cannot be so easily ruled out.

Can We Justify Induction Against Hume's Criticism?

We must return to Hume's problem of induction. As you will recall from our discussion earlier, Hume argued that neither deductive nor inductive reasoning could establish the principle of induction. Since Hume, there have been many attempts to justify induction. There is a consensus that we cannot construct a deductive proof for induction but there are other justification strategies. Hans Reichenbach argues that we have a pragmatic justification for induction. It works. It is the only game in town. Its alternative is to live as though the future will not resemble the past.[19] Yesterday, a man jumped out of a skyscraper and fell to his death, his motion conforming to the law of gravity. The anti-inductivist would have us suppose that today the laws of nature will be reversed so that if you wish to fly, you should jump out of a skyscraper. Although we cannot prove that we will fail to fly simply by jumping out of a tall building, it seems prudent to act as though these laws were unexceptional. We make predictions that the law of gravity will govern physical objects. In the past we have always been correct. Since all past futures have turned out to be governed by inductive reasoning, we should bet that all future futures will too. Hume, of course, doesn't deny that it's practical to live by probability. Only a fool or madman would think otherwise. So, in a way, Hume's point still stands. Where Hume may be criticized is in supposing that a pragmatic justification is inadequate for a philosophical justification. Indeed, our very notion of justification or evidential support itself seems to presuppose the idea of induction. If I ask John to justify his belief that the New York Yankees won the 1999 World Series, he will likely produce evidence: newspaper articles, the testimony of others and perhaps, if pressed, a video of the games, showing the Yankee victory. He will use inductive methods to show that we have good grounds for believing that the Yankees won the World Series. But if pressed far enough on what justifies his trust in good inductive evidence, I suppose John will have to fall back on the pragmatic argument. It just works and there is no alternative available.

Weak vs. Strong Knowledge

In the second attempt to refute skepticism, related to the first and set forth by the American philosopher Norman Malcolm (1911–1990), two types of knowledge are distinguished: *weak* and *strong*.[20] There are some knowledge claims about which, on being challenged, I would be wise to admit I could be wrong; these are "weak" knowledge. For example, I believe that the sun is about 90 million miles from the earth, but if someone were to challenge me on this, I might well admit that I'm not certain about it. Likewise, I claim to know that I was born in Chicago, Illinois, to Louis and Helen Pojman, but if someone challenged me, claiming that there was evidence that I was adopted at six months of age or not born in Chicago but in Madison, Wisconsin, I might well retract my knowledge claim.

But there are other kinds of knowledge claims that are so certain that no conceivable challenges could cause me to give them up; "strong knowledge" is the kind that Moore was so adamant about. For example: I have a body; I have two hands; my dog is called Caesar; I am now reading a philosophy book; I am now sitting on a chair; I am not sleeping or dreaming.

So while we are willing to let further investigation determine whether we really have knowledge in the instances of weak knowledge, we do not concede that anything whatsoever could prove us mistaken in the cases of strong knowledge.

Malcolm's argument is really an elaboration of Moore's, but the distinction is important. There are experiences about which we cannot imagine being wrong. We want to say that the burden of proof is on the skeptic to tell us why we should doubt these things.

If this is so, then while the skeptic cannot be refuted, he or she can be *rebutted*. We can accept our claims to knowledge as working hypotheses, challenging the skeptic to show us what is wrong with any specific knowledge claim. If we are at least prima facie justified in making claims to knowledge, if we cannot in good faith discover defeaters to these claims, then we may have knowledge after all.

Of course, the skeptic is not going to be convinced about this sort of claim to knowledge. The skeptic's point is that we are not completely justified in our knowledge claims. Since we could be wrong, we should hold back claims to knowledge.

Whatever the truth of the matter is on making knowledge claims, at least one value of skepticism is to make us modest about our pretensions to knowledge. It is harder than most of us imagine to justify our claims to knowledge, and much of what we claim to know turns out to be mistaken. Such lessons in humility are steps toward wisdom. Mark Twain once said, "The real trouble isn't in what we believe, but in what we know that ain't so."

Summary

Skepticism is the theory that we do not have any knowledge at all. One of the goals of epistemology is to come to terms with skepticism—either defeating it or conceding its force. Global skepticism denies that we can know anything at all—except *perhaps* mathematical and simple logical truths. Local skepticism admits that we can have empirical knowledge but denies that we can have metaphysical knowledge. René Descartes represents the global skeptic, arguing that a demon could be deceiving us about even simple mathematical statements. David Hume, while denying that we can have empirical *knowledge,* admits that we are justified in our empirical *beliefs,* but denies metaphysical knowledge. We are systematically deceived by nature about causation, induction, the identity of the self, the reality of matter, free will, and the existence of God. Philosophical reflection informs us that we have no metaphysical knowledge, but we must act as though we do. We cannot live as skeptics.

Robert Nozick and Fred Dretske seek to break the hold of skepticism by denying that knowledge is closed under known entailment and that only relevant alternatives should be taken into consideration when evaluating knowledge claims. Both of these attempts are fraught with difficulties, among them the question of whether it makes sense to say that knowledge is not closed under known entailment.

G. E. Moore and Norman Malcolm have each tried to undermine the skeptic's arguments by shifting the burden of proof back to the skeptic, demanding that he or she tell us why we should not trust our commonsense judgments where no specific defeater is forthcoming.

They claim that while the skeptic cannot be refuted, he or she can be rebutted.

Perhaps it is helpful to see the three main positions discussed in this chapter as responses to the following proposition: If you know that *p* and know that *p* entails *q*, then you know that *q* (e.g., if I know that I have a body and know that if I have a body, then I am not a brain in a vat, then I know that I am not a brain in a vat).

$$Kp \ \& \ K(p \rightarrow q) \rightarrow Kq$$

The standard dogmatists, Moore and Malcolm, directly assert that we have knowledge. So they simply assert the antecedent:

$$Kp \ \& \ K(p \rightarrow q)$$

I do know that I have a body and know that if I have a body I am not a brain in a vat. Therefore, by modus ponens, *Kq:* I know that I am not a brain in a vat.

The nonclosurists, Nozick and Dretske, deny the entailment between the antecedent and consequent: $Kp \ \& \ K(p \rightarrow q) \rightarrow Kq$.

They accept Kp and $K(p \rightarrow q)$ but deny that I know that I am not a brain in a vat. They hold not-Kq.

The skeptic responds to the proposition, $Kp \ \& \ K(p \rightarrow q) \rightarrow Kq$, by denying the consequent and so, by modus tollens, denying the antecedent, $Kp \ \& \ K(p \rightarrow q)$. They accept the second conjunct, but deny the first Kp. I do not know that I have a body.

It seems then that the question of skepticism hangs on whether or not one accepts closure under known entailment and if one does, whether one is inclined to draw a modus ponens or a modus tollens argument. Perhaps we need to understand the various characterizations of knowledge, perception, and justification before we can fully appreciate this issue. So you will want to come back to the question of skepticism after you have worked through the rest of this book.

QUESTIONS FOR DISCUSSION

1. Go over the various types of skepticism. Distinguish Descartes's methodological skepticism from Humean substantive skepticism. Which are the strongest types?

2. Can you refute the skeptic? Which arguments against skepticism seem most plausible?

3. Descartes says that wisdom teaches us that we should never entirely trust a witness who deceived us. He uses this idea to cast

doubt on the deliverances of the senses. But doesn't this assertion presuppose that we (or Descartes) know that our senses have sometimes deceived us?

4. Hume noted that skeptical arguments "admit of no answer and produce no conviction." What do you think Hume meant by this?

5. What is the difference between global and local skepticism? Which do you find more plausible or cogent?

6. What is the strength of Nozick's method of truth tracking? What are the main problems with it?

7. Consider Dretske's relevant alternative scheme for knowledge. Explain its strengths and weaknesses.

8. Do you think that Moore's strategy is convincing? Why can't the skeptic accuse Moore of begging the question against skepticism? Can the skeptic simply argue that Moore has not provided a justification for why he believes he has two hands?

9. Evaluate Malcolm's notion of weak and strong knowledge.

10. Can the skeptic live by his or her skepticism? Examine this passage from Hume's *Treatise.*

> A Stoic or Epicurean displays principles, which may not only be durable, but which have an effect on conduct and behavior. But a Pyrrhonian [skeptic] cannot expect, that his philosophy will have any constant influence on the mind: or if it had, that its influence would be beneficial to society. On the contrary, he must acknowledge, if he will acknowledge anything, that all human life must perish, were his principles universally and steadily to prevail. All discourse, all action would immediately cease; and men remain in a total lethargy, till the necessities of nature, unsatisfied, put an end to their miserable existence. It is true; so fatal an event is very little to be dreaded. Nature is always too strong for principle. And though a Pyrrhonian may throw himself or others into a momentary amazement and confusion by his profound reasonings; the first and most trivial event in life will put to flight all his doubts and scruples, and leave him the same, in every point of action and speculation, with the philosophers of every other sect, or with those who never concerned themselves in any philosophical researches. When he awakes from his dream, he will be the first to join in the laugh against himself, and to confess, that all his objections are mere amusement, and can have no other tendency than to show the whimsical condition of mankind, who must act and reason and believe; though they are not able, by their most diligent enquiry, to satisfy themselves concerning the foundation of these operations, or to remove the objections, which may be raised against

them. (David Hume, *An Enquiry Concerning Human Understanding,* Sec. XII)

Do you agree with Hume that we cannot live as skeptics? What then is the lesson, if any, of skepticism?

NOTES

1. René Descartes, *Meditations on First Philosophy,* trans. Elizabeth Haldane and G. Ross (Cambridge: Cambridge University Press, 1931), 145.
2. Note that Descartes's argument seems to assume that we *know* that our senses have sometimes deceived us.
3. Descartes, 148.
4. Barry Stroud, *The Significance of Philosophical Scepticism* (Oxford: Oxford University Press, 1984), 12.
5. Descartes, 150.
6. David Hume, *Enquiry Concerning Human Understanding* (Oxford: Clarendon Press, 1748), 78.
7. Michael Levin has pointed out (in correspondence) that when Hume speaks of beliefs about the future being derived from experience, he seems to be assuming causation himself.
8. Hume, 15.
9. Hume, *Treatise of Human Nature* (Oxford: Clarendon Press, 1739), 252.
10. Ibid.
11. Ibid., 218. Hume's conclusion regarding metaphysics is worth quoting:

    When we run over libraries, persuaded of these principles [of empiricism], what havoc must we make? If we take in our hands any volume of divinity or school metaphysics, for instance, let us ask, Does it contain any abstract reasoning concerning quantity or number? No. Does it contain any experimental reasoning concerning matter of fact and existence? No. Commit it to the flames, for it can contain nothing but sophistry and illusion. (*Enquiry,* 165)

12. Ibid., 269.
13. Robert Nozick, *Philosphical Explanations* (Cambridge, MA: Harvard University Press, 1981), 166–247. See *The Possibility of Knowledge,* ed. Steven Luper-Foy (Totowa, NJ: Rowman & Littlefield, 1987) for a collection of critical articles on Nozick's epistemology.
14. Fred Dretske, "Epistemic Operators," *Journal of Philosophy* (December 24, 1970); Gail Stine, "Dretske on Knowing the Logical Consequences," *Journal of Philosophy* (May 6, 1971). For a critique of the relevant alternatives approach, see Palle Yourgrau, "Knowledge and Relevant Alternatives," *Synthese* 55 (1983).
15. Ibid., 1016.
16. Bernard Williams, *Ethics and the Limits of Philosophy* (Cambridge, MA: Harvard University Press, 1985), 167.
17. G. E. Moore, "A Defense of Common Sense," *Philosophical Papers* (London: Allen & Unwin, 1959).

18. Ibid., 144f.
19. Hans Reichebach, "The Pragmatic Justification of Induction" in L. Pojman, ed., *The Theory of Knowledge* (Wadsworth, 1999), 497–501.
20. Norman Malcolm, *Knowledge and Certainty* (Englewood Cliffs, NJ: Prentice Hall, 1963).

FOR FURTHER READING

Burnyeat, Myles, ed. *The Skeptical Tradition*. Berkeley: University of California Press, 1983. A set of scholarly essays on the skeptical tradition from the Greeks to Kant.

Descartes, René. *The Philosophical Works of Descartes,* trans. by Elizabeth Haldane and G. Ross. Cambridge: Cambridge University Press, 1931. Especially Descartes's classic *Meditations on First Philosophy*.

Hookway, Christopher, *Scepticism*. London: Routledge & Kegan Paul, 1990. Contains both an important historical survey, especially of Pyrrhonism, Descartes, and Hume, and a philosophical analysis of the problem of skepticism.

Hume, David. *A Treatise of Human Nature*, ed. by L. A. Selby-Bigge. Oxford: Clarendon Press, 1896.

Hume, David. *Enquiries Concerning the Human Understanding and Concerning the Principles of Morals*, edited by L. A. Selby-Bigge. Oxford: Clarendon Press, 1902.

Klein, Peter. *Certainty: A Refutation of Scepticism*. Minneapolis: University of Minnesota Press, 1981. A clear and cogent argument against skepticism.

Pojman, Louis, ed. *The Theory of Knowledge*. Belmont, CA: Wadsworth, 1999. 2nd ed. Part II contains several relevant essays.

Sextus Empiricus. *Selections from the Major Writings on Scepticism, Man & God*, trans. by Sanford G. Etheridge; ed. by Philip Hallie. Indianapolis: Hackett Publishing Co., 1985.

Stroud, Barry. *The Significance of Philosophical Skepticism*. Oxford: Oxford University Press, 1984. A sympathetic exposition of the major skeptical arguments.

CHAPTER 4

Perception: Our Knowledge of the External World

In daily life, we assume as certain many things which, on a closer scrutiny, are found to be so full of apparent contradictions that only a great amount of thought enables us to know what it is that we really may believe. In the search for certainty, it is natural to begin with our present experiences, and in some sense, no doubt, knowledge is to be derived from them. But any statement as to what it is that our immediate experience makes us know is very likely to be wrong. It seems to me that I am now sitting in a chair, at a table of a certain shape, on which I see sheets of paper with writing or print. . . . I believe that, if any other normal person comes into my room, he will see the same chairs and tables and books as I see, and that the table which I see is the same as the table which I feel pressing against my arm. All this seems to be so evident as to be hardly worth stating, except in answer to a man who doubts whether I know anything. Yet all this may be reasonably doubted, and all of it requires much careful discussion before we can be sure that we have stated it in a form that is wholly true.[1]

Appearance and Reality

Appearance is different from reality. An object may look, sound, feel, taste, or smell differently from the way it actually is. We see two parallel railroad tracks as if they converge in the distance. We hear the sound of an ambulance gradually increase in loudness as it approaches us and gradually diminish as it recedes into the distance, even though the sound remains constant to those in the ambulance. Place one hand on a warm stove and the other in a bowl of ice cubes and then place both hands in a bowl of lukewarm water. What happens? The hand that was in the warm place feels as though the water is cold, while the other hand feels as though the water is hot, yet the temperature of the water remains constant. Mirages of oases appear in the desert or on a road during a sunny summer day. A coin looks elliptical when viewed from a certain angle and stars that are several times larger than our sun appear as tiny sparks in the heavens. We never see these gigantic objects as they really are. (What size would that be? How close would we have to be to see a star in its actual size?) A straight stick placed halfway in water looks bent. White shirts, walls, and paper appear red in red lighting and blue in blue lighting. When we put on sunglasses, the colors around us appear different from what they are. Pineapples and yogurt taste different before and after we have brushed our teeth with a pungent toothpaste or when we have a fever.

In more serious cases, in hallucinations, we see ghosts and people who are not present. Remember Shakespeare's *Macbeth:*

> Is this a dagger which I see before me,
> The handle toward my hand? Come, let me clutch thee:
> I have thee not, and yet I see thee still.
> Art thou not, fatal vision, sensible
> To feeling as to sight? or art thou but
> A dagger of the mind, a false creation,
> Proceeding from the heat-oppressed brain? (II. 1. 41–47)

We want to distinguish these appearances from veridical perceptions. It is clear that these illusory appearances are not the way the world really is. They are images in our mind, caused by the world but not in the world. Philosophers call these images or appearances "sense data" or "sense impressions."

So far, so good, but now the real problem arises. How do we know that we ever do have veridical appearances of the world? How do we know that what we take for nonillusory appearances really are such? For there doesn't seem to be any intrinsic difference between illusions and veridical appearances. We see a "white table" as blue in blue lighting and red in red lighting, but the only reason we see it as white is because of the way light waves reflect off the surfaces of the table onto our retina, which sends information to the visual center at the back of our brain. The table is not really colored at all. And sounds are simply wave frequencies in the atmosphere picked up by our eardrums and translated in the auditory centers of our brains.

So the question is forced upon us. What exactly do we know of the external world?

Theories of Perception

What is the direct object of awareness when we perceive? Traditionally, three answers have been given to this question: (1) Direct Realism (sometimes referred to as "Naive Realism" or "Commonsense Realism"), (2) Representationalism, and (3) Phenomenalism. Direct realism claims that the immediate object of perception is a physical object that exists independently of our awareness of it. Representationalism and phenomenalism answer that the immediate object of perception is a *sense datum* (or *sense impression*), an object that cannot exist apart from our awareness of it. Sense data, according to these two theories, are internal presentations, for example the colors, shapes, and sizes of appearances in our minds.

But representationalism and phenomenalism divide over the relationship of sense data to the physical world. For the representationalist the physical world exists independently of and is the cause of our perceptions. Physical objects give rise to the sense data we perceive, so we only have mediate knowledge of the external world. For phenomenalism, on the other hand, physical objects are simply constructions of sense data. They do not exist independently of sense impressions. Both theories agree that all our experience is confined to sense data, except that representationalism claims that there really is a physical world independent of us, whereas phenomenalism claims that there is nothing besides sense data in the world.

Common sense rejects both representationalism and phenomenalism and tells us that we, through our five senses—sight, hearing, touch, taste, and smell—do directly perceive the *real* world. Common sense tells us that the physical world exists independently of our awareness of it, and that the things we perceive are pretty much the way we perceive them. They exist here and now. Common sense supports naive or direct realism.

Unfortunately for common sense, science casts doubt on this simple picture of our relationship to the world. As Bertrand Russell succinctly says, "Naive realism leads to physics, and physics, if true, shows that naive realism is false. Therefore, naive realism, if true, is false; therefore, it is false."[2] Science tells us that the physical objects we perceive are not what they seem to be nor do we ever see things in the present. Colors are not in the objects but are the way objects appear as they reflect light. Since light travels at 186,000 miles per second, it takes time to reach our eyes. All that we see really existed in the past. It takes 8 minutes for the light from the sun to reach us, over 8 years for it to reach us from the distant and brightest star, Sirius, and 650 years for the light from the distant star, Rigel, to reach us. So when we look up into the heavens at the stars, we do not see any of them as they now are, but as they existed in the near or distant past. Indeed, some of these stars may no longer exist. In fact, since it takes light time to reach us, we never see anything as it is in the present. Even near objects are not seen as they presently exist. All sight is of the past.

Likewise, science tells us that the sounds we hear, the flavors we taste, the sensations we feel, and the odors we smell are not what they seem to be. They are mediated through our ways of perceiving, so that we seldom or never experience them as they really are in themselves.

So representationalism seems to succeed in giving an explanation of perception that is more faithful to science than direct realism. Representationalism holds that the real world causes our appearances or perceptions by representing the physical world through sense data, mental entities that are private to individual perceivers.

Locke's Representationalism

John Locke (1632–1704) set forth the classic expression of this view. Attacking the notion that we have innate knowledge of metaphysical truths, Locke argued that all our knowledge derives ultimately from sense experience. "Let us then suppose the mind to be, as we say, white paper, void of all characters, without any ideas; how comes it by that vast store, which the busy and boundless fancy of man has painted on it with an almost endless variety? Whence has it all the materials of reason and knowledge? To this I answer, in one word, from experience: in that all our knowledge is founded."[3]

Locke held a causal theory of perception in which processes in the external world impinge on the perceiver's sense organs, which in turn send messages to the brain where they are transformed into mental events. We may diagram Locke's Causal Theory of Perception this way:

Objects and Events in the Real World
   | (Energy coming to sense organs: insensible particles reflected
   | from the object onto the sense organ or coming into contact
  ↓ with the sense organ)
Sense Organs
  ↓ (Signals to brain)

Brain Event
  ↓ (Transformation from physical to mental event)
Perceptual Experience
  ↓ (Mechanical input yields the nonmechanical *idea* in the Mind)

Although the process is physical and mechanistic, it yields a non-physical result, a mental event—the perceptual experience, which subsequent philosophers described as a *percept* (sense datum or sense impression).

We are aware of not the thing in itself, the object that is perceived and causes the idea to arise in our mind, but only the idea or *representation* of the object. We are directly aware of the idea but in as much as the object is the *cause* of the idea, we may be said to be indirectly aware of the object.

Now a problem arises. Do these ideas that occur in the mind faithfully, accurately represent the external world taken to be their cause?

Locke said yes and no. His answer has to do with two types of qualities of physical objects. Let me explain.

Locke divides the qualities of physical objects into two basic classes: *primary qualities* and *secondary qualities*. Here is Locke's classic passage.

> Qualities thus considered in bodies are, First, such as are utterly inseparable from bodies, in what estate soever it be; such as, in all the alterations and changes it suffers, all the force can be used upon it, it constantly keeps; and such as sense constantly finds in every particle of matter which has bulk enough to be perceived, and the mind finds inseparable from every particle of matter, though less than to make itself singly be perceived by our senses; e.g., take a grain of wheat, divide it into two parts, each part has still *solidity, extension, figure,* and *mobility;* divide it again, and it retains still the same qualities: and so divide it on till the parts become insensible. They must retain still each of them all those qualities. For, division . . . can never take away either solidity, extension, figure, or mobility from any body, but only makes two or more distinct separate masses of matter of that which was but one before; all which distinct masses, reckoned as so many distinct bodies, after division, make a certain number. These I call *original* or *primary* qualities of body, . . . solidity, extension, figure, motion, or rest, and number.[4]

Primary qualities are really in their objects and inseparable from their objects, and so our ideas of them truly represent the objects. Such qualities are solidity (or bulk), extension, figure, movement (and rest), and number. These are the true building blocks of knowledge because they accurately represent features in the world. Ultimately, the world is made up of indivisible, minute atoms, which underlie physical objects. Secondary qualities are not in the things themselves but are powers to cause various sensations in us. The powers themselves are in the object. What is not in the object is the quality that our secondary quality idea represents as being in the object.

For example, an object's color is its power to cause color ideas in us. It does this by reflecting certain kinds of light and not others. It reflects certain kinds of light because its surface has a certain structure. That surface structure is a primary quality. When under normal circumstances we look at an object it looks a certain color, say, red. The redness with which we are acquainted is not in the object itself, but it is the light reflecting off the object into our eye, which is then communicated to our brain. The primary quality (the surface structure) is what gives the object the power to reflect some kinds of light and so cause some kinds of sensation (idea), but it doesn't really cause the secondary quality. All there really is to objects are their primary qualities. Because of their primary qualities, those same objects have the power to cause certain kinds of sensations (ideas). They really have that power. The power is in the object. However, some of those ideas represent the object as having qualities—color, smell, sound, taste, and the like—that aren't really in the object. These secondary qualities are types of powers, or potentialities or *dispositions,* that reside in a physical object.

Locke adds a third quality, disposition, which has the power to cause changes in the external world. For example, fire has the power to change liquids into gases, sugar is soluble in warm water, and glass is fragile. Solubility, flammability, and fragility are dispositional qualities in bodies.

Locke's Dualism   There is a problem with Locke's theory of representationalism; it is difficult to see how we could justify any knowledge claim regarding the external world if we are never directly aware of anything except the ideas in our mind. Locke, aware of this problem, said that we have as much certainty as our condition needs but, in reality, we can't know very much. Our senses only represent large objects and not their smaller particles, so that the mysteries of the natural world are forever hidden from our view.

But the critic can press the point, making a criticism that has been labeled the "permanent picture gallery" objection. Ordinarily, we check a picture of a landscape against the scene pictured, but in perception, if Locke is right, we never get a look at the scene itself. So how can we know if the picture faithfully represents the landscape?

No comparison seems possible, so we pause to wonder whether Locke's theory doesn't really lead to skepticism, or if not skepticism, immaterialism.

Locke thought that it was incoherent to speak of qualities existing in their own right, so he relied on the Aristotelian notion of substance as that which underlies all other properties, the foundation of matter itself. Substance is an unknown "something I know not what."

Being a devout Christian, Locke inferred that this mechanistic materialism could not be the last word on the subject of substance, so he posited a second, spiritual substance with nonmaterial properties, including the soul, consciousness, and sensations. Locke was aware that he had no philosophical grounds for this distinction. Faith dictated dualism.

Berkeley's Idealist Attack on Representationalism

Locke thought that he had done justice to both science and faith with this dualism, but his theory soon came under attack as being dangerous, repugnant, and absurd. The philosopher who led the attack was an Irish bishop, George Berkeley (1685–1753), who was unsparing in his zeal to demolish the damned doctrine of mechanistic materialism. In its place, Berkeley erected an ingenious idealism called Immaterialism. First, let us note Berkeley's criticisms of Locke's representationalism.

1. Locke's ideas are *dangerous,* because they made religion (and God) unnecessary, reducing all to a Newtonian mechanistic model of the universe, under physical causation. All is matter in motion, with bodies interacting in accordance with rigorously formulated mechanical laws. If this is true, where does God fit in?

Locke's God is reduced to a prime mover (or the "Big Push"), largely superfluous for daily purposes.

Furthermore, Locke's notion of atomism and his vague concept of substance really was a thinly disguised materialism (not that he thought Locke realized this), for Locke made it possible that the world was exclusively material, and that there were no souls or spirits, but that consciousness was merely a property of matter. So, the mind would cease to exist at death.

Berkeley, being a devout Christian and a bishop, felt it his duty to combat this incipient materialism, secularism, and atheism. Locke, though a Christian himself, had played right into the enemy's hands: yielding either skepticism or materialism.

2. Locke's ideas are *loathsome* because they took away the beauty of the physical world. Common sense was outraged in supposing, as Locke's theory did, that the visible beauty of creation was no more than "a false imaginary glare" (e.g., the flowers in our garden are not really colored and have no fragrant aroma).

3. Locke's ideas yield *absurd consequences.* First, Berkeley noted that Locke's primary/secondary qualities distinction was very weak. The primary qualities are no more "in" the objects of perception than the secondary ones. Both types or qualities are relative to the perceiving mind.

It is said that heat and cold are affections only in the mind, and not at all patterns of real beings existing in the corporeal substances which excite them, for that the same body which appears cold to one hand seems warm to another. Now, why may we not as well argue that figure and extension are not patterns or resemblances of qualities existing in matter, because to the same eye at different stations, or eyes of a different texture at the same station, they appear various and cannot, therefore, be the images of anything settled and determined without the mind.[5]

Second, he argued that there were logical problems in the theory that our perceptions resembled physical objects ("an idea can be like nothing but an idea"). Locke's theory led to skepticism because it offered no basis for comparing representations with their objects. Recall our permament picture gallery objection. Third, Berkeley undermined the whole notion of substance, which Locke needed to maintain his theory. What is the difference, Berkeley rhetorically asked, between a "something I know not what" (Locke's notion of substance) and nothing at all? Ultimately, Locke's causal theory really supports materialism.

4. Finally, Berkeley charged that Locke's system was an *explanatory failure.* Locke asserted that ideas in the mind were caused by mechanical actions upon our sense organs and brains. But Berkeley pointed out that this fails to explain mental events both in detail and in principle: in *detail* because it was impossible to explain why a certain physical event should produce certain but quite different (in character) mental states (e.g., light waves producing the color red); in *principle* because the whole notion of dualistic interactionism was incoherent, misusing the notion of "cause." A cause makes something happen, but for this you need a notion of a will, or agency—all causation is agent causation. But events in nature do not make other events happen; one only sees two events in temporal succession—with regularity. But this only signals the reality of a cause; it is not the cause because it is not an agent and exerts no will. If Locke's model for the world was a clock, Berkeley's was an agent with radical free will.

What was Berkeley's own solution to the problem of how we know the external world? It was incredibly simple: to deny matter. In one fell swoop the intractable problems of substance, dualist interactionism, causation, and knowledge of the external world are swept away in the supposition that material substance doesn't exist.[6]

Berkeley held that there were only two realities: minds and mental events. Ideas exist in the mind alone. All qualities are essentially secondary and attain their reality by being perceived (*esse est percipi*—"To be is to be perceived."). There is no material world. Physical objects are simply mental events. "The table I write on exists, that is, I see and feel it; and if I were out of my study I should say it existed— meaning thereby that if I was in my study I might perceive it, or that some other spirit actually perceives it."[7] All physical objects are mental phenomena that would cease to exist if they were not perceived. Why do physical objects continue to exist when no one is perceiving them? What happens to them when we are not looking at trees or mountains? Do they cease to be? No, someone is always perceiving them. God's eye keeps the world from dissolving.

> There was a young man who said, "God
> Must think it exceedingly odd
> If he finds that this tree
> Continues to be
> When there's no one about in the quad."
> Dear Sir, your astonishment's odd
> I'm always about in the quad,
> And that's why the tree
> Will continue to be
> since observed by,
> Yours faithfully, God

Hence, we bring God back into philosophy and science as the necessary being that keeps our world intact. This thought frees us from mechanism, skepticism, and atheism all at once and offers us dignity—for we are not mere machines but infinitely valuable souls, finite and infinite spirits.

God communicates directly with our finite minds by the mediation of ideas—the orderly, regular, and admirable connection of which forms the rational discourse of the infinite Creator with finite spirits.

Berkeley sought to stave off the charge that his theory eliminated the need for scientific investigation. He argued that his theory reduces science to general rules (instrumentalism). The atomistic theory is a useful myth (serviceable fiction).

Phenomenalism

Contemporary phenomenalism differs with Berkeley but only with his theological moorings. It doesn't posit God as necessary to hold the physical world in existence. Instead, it views the physical world as a construct of ideas. In John Stuart Mill's words, objects are "permanent possibilities of sensation," meaning that if one were to get into the appropriate condition, one would experience the sense data. Philosophers like W. T. Stace (1886–1967) argue that the realist's view of the world as containing material objects behind the perceived world is an unjustified faith. The world of scientific discourse (e.g., "atoms," "gravity," and "conservation of energy") is not to be taken literally, but instrumentally, as providing useful fictions that help us to predict experiences. Consider his argument.

> So far as I know scientists still talk about electrons, protons, neutrons, and so on. We never directly perceive these, hence, if we ask how we know of their existence the only possible answer seems to be that they are an inference from what we do directly perceive. What sort of an inference? Apparently a causal inference. The atomic entities in some way impinge upon the sense of the animal organism and cause [it] to perceive the familiar world of tables, chairs, and the rest.
>
> But is it not clear that such a concept of causation, however interpreted, is invalid? The only reason we have for believing in the law of causation is that we *observe* certain regularities or sequences. We observe that, in certain conditions, A is always followed by B. We call A the cause, B the effect. And the sequence A-B becomes a causal law. It follows that all *observed* causal sequences are between sensed objects in the familiar world of perception, and that all known causal laws apply solely to the world of sense and not to anything beyond or behind it. And this in turn means that we have not got, and never could have, one jot of evidence for believing that the law of causation can be applied *outside* the realm of perception, or that the realm can have any causes (such as the supposed physical objects) which are not themselves perceived.[8]

Strictly speaking, Stace continues, "*Nothing exists except sensations* (and the minds which perceive them). The rest is mental construction or fiction." All that the so-called laws of science do is enable us to organize our experiences and predict future sensations.

Bertrand Russell (1872–1970) has defended representational realism, developing Locke's causal theory of perception in the light of contemporary science. According to Russell our knowledge of physical objects is inferred from percepts (sense data) in our brain. One may ask why Russell does not simply accept phenomenalism since he makes percepts primary to our knowledge. Russell concedes that phenomenalism is not impossible. But there are deeper reasons for rejecting it. Let me mention three of them, together with the phenomenalist response.[9]

1. *Appearance and Reality* The stick in water appears bent, and we all agree that this is an illusion, but the phenomenalist can find no essential difference between this and our visual perception of the stick out of water (or our tactile perception of the straightness of the stick even while in water) as the way it really is shaped, for the phenomenalist can admit no difference between appearance and reality. The real-unreal and genuine-counterfeit distinctions vanish. Material things consist of sense data and nothing else.

But the phenomenalist responds that the everyday distinctions between reality and appearance are not metaphysical ones but practical, enabling us to deal with the experiences we encounter.

What causes us to condemn an experience as an "illusion" is that it leads us astray. A mirage is an illusion because it causes us to make a mistake. But what kind of mistake? Surely, not the mistake of thinking that we now see trees and water, but the mistake of expecting that we shall soon be able to have a drink and sit down in the shade. The mistake consists in the false expectation of certain other sense data. Thus, the illusoriness is not in the sense data itself, but in the expectation which we form when we sense it.[10]

The bent stick in the water is an illusion too because sticks that "look bent" usually "feel bent" as well, and so we are surprised to find that it feels straight.

2. *The Permanency of Material Things* Sensations are flighty, intermittent, depending on our sense organs, but material objects, we intuitively suppose, are permanent things, enduring uninterruptedly for long periods of time (and are not mind dependent).

I don't annihilate this room and all of you every time I close my eyes. On a phenomenalist account it would seem that we could not say this stone has existed ten years or one million years without it having a rotation shift of nurse-watchers to keep it in existence.

The phenomenalist replies with Mill that sense data are "permanent possibilities of sensation," so we may distinguish between an actual or possible sense datum. To say that there is a table in my office now is to say that if there were anyone in the room he would be having the kind of experience that we call seeing a table. "There is a table" means "Go and look and you will see a table."

Still, we might ask what sense can be given to the directive, "Go and look and you will see a table"? Does it mean that you will have experiences as if you were going to look and you will have experiences as if you were seeing a table? The problem is that you could have such experiences in a dream or hallucination.

3. *Causal Activity*   Causal interaction in nature seems undermined by phenomenalism. As C. H. Whiteley says, "Surely, the room cannot be warmed by my visual sense datum of a fire! Still less can it be warmed by the possibility of a visual sense datum of a fire during my absence, when I am not looking at the fire, but the room gets warmed all the same." Ideas are inert and can do nothing.

The phenomenalist responds, as Stace does in the earlier quotation that we should reinterpret the concept of causality. We never see "causes," but only regular succession of events.

I think that this response is inadequate, for we generally believe that a cause is something that actually exists and that something that does not actually exist or occur can have no effects. Phenomenalism implausibly makes causality a relation between something and nothing, since most of the causes are unperceived.

Representationalism, we saw, led to phenomenalism, and phenomenalism seems to take the world away from us, landing us, if not completely back into skepticism, then into solipsism, the view that no one else exists besides me. If I can only have sense experiences of my own, then how can I take other people's experiences into account?

A Return to Direct Realism   So where does that leave us? Perhaps you will choose between phenomenalism and representationalism, but some philosophers like D. M. Armstrong, John Searle, and William Alston have returned to direct realism, though not a "naive" variety, but one chastened by the long history of the problem. Armstrong defines perception as the acquiring of beliefs (true or false) about the current state of our bodies or environment. In perceiving, we do encounter the world directly, though always through the interpretive powers of our mind.

One reason Armstrong rejects representationalism and phenomenalism is the problematic notion of sense data. These intermediary things seem unnecessary and even paradoxical. They are unnecessary because we can give an account of our perceptions as taking in objects in the world directly. They are paradoxical in two ways.

The first is the nontransitivity of perception. Take three pieces of red colored paper. Suppose that we cannot distinguish between samples *A* and *B*. They seem exactly the same color. Likewise, samples *B* and *C* are indistinguishable. But we can distinguish between *A* and *C!* Given the notion of sense data this is puzzling, since we should be able to distinguish our sense data from one another. The second puzzle is indeterminateness. Suppose we see a speckled hen. How many speckles does our sense datum hold? If we say that it is indeterminate, we seem to have a paradox between the indeterminate sense datum and the determinate objects that are supposed to be represented.[11]

Adverbial Perception Many philosophers have sought to avoid taking a strong stand on the philosophy of perception by simply using adverbial language. For example, when seeing a red book, I state my perception in appearance language, "I am appeared to redly and bookishly," or when seeing a red ball, "I am appeared to redly and ballishly." This is known as the "adverbial theory of perception," and it receives its fullest expression in the work of Roderick Chisholm (1916–) and Robert Audi.[12] The theory has the advantage of doing without the troublesome notion of sense data and being compatible with direct realism. Indeed, the adverbial theory claims to be a more coherent version of direct realism, claiming that we are in direct contact with objects in the external world. This theory points to the fact that we experience things in particular ways. But it's hard to see that the adverbial theory solves anything, for the question arises about these *appearings:* Are they veridical or illusory? Are we being appeared to the way the object is just now or the way light waves (or sound waves) are revealing aspects of the near past? If it takes time for light waves to reach the retina and pass along "the optic nerve before they reach the back of the brain where they are interpreted by consciousness, then aren't we back where we started from in rejecting direct realism for representationalism? These two problems, the need to distinguish veridical from unveridical (illusory) appearances and the facts of light and sound waves taking time to travel to our brains, seem to drive us either to representationalism or phenomenalism. Perhaps it is wiser to admit how little we know about the nature of perception, to choose the least objectionable theory, and to interpret ordinary language accordingly.

Summary

The problem of perception concerns our knowledge of the external world. Three theories have been advanced to solve that problem: (1) direct realism, which holds that we know the world directly and pretty much as it is; (2) representationalism, which holds that we know the world indirectly pretty much as it is—at least regarding the primary qualities; and (3) idealism or phenomenalism, which holds that all we really know are sense data. Locke set forth the classical rendition of representationalism, distinguishing between primary and secondary qualities. Berkeley, criticizing Locke's theory as dangerous, loathsome, and absurd, put forth the classic version of idealism, whose motto was "to be is to be perceived." The fact that God is always perceiving us and the world insures our continued existence. Modern phenomenalists follow Berkeley, but subtract the notion of God from the epistemic domain. There has been a move by contemporary epistemologists like Armstrong and Searle back to direct realism, but the issue is one of lively debate.

QUESTIONS FOR DISCUSSION

1. Why is the subject of perception a philosophical problem? Do you think that science has decided on the answer? Explain.

2. Explain the theory of direct realism. What are the objections to it? Can you defend a version of direct realism against criticisms? Explain the adverbial theory of perception.

3. Examine Locke's theory of indirect realism (representationalism). What are its strengths and weaknesses? Do you agree with Berkeley's criticisms?

4. What are sense data? What are the objections to their existence?

5. Examine phenomenalism. What are its strengths and weaknesses?

6. Having worked through the problem of perception, which theory makes the most sense?

NOTES

1. Bertrand Russell, *Problems of Philosophy* (Oxford: Oxford University Press, 1912), 7, 8.

2. Bertrand Russell, *Inquiry into Meaning and Truth* (London: Allen & Unwin, 1940), 15.

3. John Locke, *An Essay Concerning Human Understanding* vol. II (London: Awsham & John Churchill, 1689), 104.

4. Ibid., II. viii. 9.

5. George Berkeley, *A Treatise Concerning the Principles of Human Knowledge* (Oxford: Oxford University Press, n.d.), par. 14.

6. Berkeley wrote in his notebook, "I wonder not at my sagacity in discovering the obvious though amazing truth, I rather wonder at my stupid inadvertency in not finding it out before." He was astonished at the strong reaction against his position.

7. Berkeley.

8. W. T. Stace, "Science and the Physical World," *Man Against Darkness and Other Essays* (Pittsburgh: University of Pittsburgh Press, 1967).

9. I am indebted to C. H. Whiteley, *An Introduction to Metaphysics* (London: Methuen & Co., 1950), who points out three advantages of phenomenalism. It removes doubt and skepticism. We can't really doubt that there is a table before us, but the representationalist program would lead us to doubt it. The sense data are all there is, so there is no cause to doubt—unless we suspect that there are pseudosense data. It also answers the problem of deception, but does it solve the problem of Descartes's demon or dream hypothesis? It also saves us from worrying about involvement with unobservable matter. We can preserve our empiricism. Science becomes "the recording, ordering, and forecasting of human experience."

10. Ibid. See also A. J. Ayer, *Central Questions of Philosophy* (New York: Holt, Rinehart and Winston, 1973), 106.

11. D. M. Armstrong, *Perception and the Physical World* (London: Routledge & Kegan Paul, 1961). See also John Searle, *Intentionality* (Oxford: Oxford University Press, 1983) and William Alston, *Epistemic Justification* (Ithaca, NY: Cornell University Press, 1989).

12. Roderick Chisholm, *Perceiving: A Philosophical Study* (Ithaca, NY: Cornell University Press, 1957) and *Theory of Knowledge* (Englewood Cliffs, NJ: Prentice Hall, 1989). Robert Audi has a good discussion of this theory in *Belief, Justification, and Knowledge* (Belmont, CA: Wadsworth, 1988), 21–24.

FOR FURTHER READING

Alston, William. *The Reliability of Sense Perception*. Ithaca, NY: Cornell University Press, 1993. Alston argues that we must rely on circular arguments to defend the view that sense perception is a reliable source of beliefs.

Armstrong, D. M. *Perception and the Physical World*. London: Routledge & Kegan Paul, 1961. A thorough defense of direct realism. Advanced.

Audi, Robert, *Belief, Justification, and Knowledge*. Belmont, CA: Wadsworth, 1988.

Audi, Robert, *Epistemology*. Oxford: Blackwell, 1998.

Berkeley, George. *Three Dialogues Between Hylas and Philonous*. Oxford: Oxford University Press, 1713. The classic defense of idealism.

Heil, John. *Perception and Cognition.* Berkeley: University of California Press, 1983. A clear, thoughtful presentation.

Landesman, Charles. *Color and Consciousness.* Philadelphia: Temple University Press, 1989. A provocative defense of representationalism.

Locke, John. *An Essay Concerning Human Understanding.* London: Awsham & John Churchill, 1689. The classic defense of representationalism.

Pojman, Louis, ed. *The Theory of Knowledge.* 2nd ed. Belmont, CA: Wadsworth, 1999. Contains several relevant essays on the topics discussed in this chapter.

Price, H. H. *Perception.* London: Methuen & Co., 1932. A classic study of the topic.

CHAPTER 5

What Is Knowledge?
An Analysis

What are the criteria of knowledge? Can we give an adequate analysis of *knowledge*? That is, can we state exactly what the necessary and sufficient conditions of knowledge are? Does knowing entail having absolute certainty? Must we be aware of the evidence on which our knowledge is based in order to know?

Jack sees Jill get on flight 101 for Miami and believes correctly that Jill is now in Miami, but unbeknown to Jack, flight 101 has been hijacked and diverted to Havana. However, Jill has fortunately taken a boat back to Miami, and two days after her original flight, has just arrived in Miami. Under these circumstances does Jack know that Jill is in Miami? Many would argue that he merely has a true, justified belief of this fact. His belief that Jill is in Miami is justified since normally a flight bound to Miami will land in Miami. However, while Jack's belief that Jill is in Miami is true and justified, the reason on which his belief is based is false.

Jane truly believes that George Washington was the first president of the United States of America. However, she received this information from her brother John, who guessed it on a multiple-choice test and, without believing one way or another, told Jane what his answer was. Jane, falsely believing that John knows what he is talking about (John is usually a reliable witness about such matters), truly believes John's testimony, but does she know that George Washington was the first president of the United States?

Joe has read in two separate newspapers that the Boston Celtics beat the Los Angeles Lakers last night by a score of 100 to 99, so Joe believes that the Celtics won the game last night. The Celtics did win the game last night, but they beat the Detroit Pistons, not the Lakers. A drunken sports reporter made a mistake and wrote down the losing team as the Lakers rather than the Pistons, and the score was 101 to 99. A second newspaper simply copied his official report. Does Joe know that the Celtics won last night?

On the basis of these reports Joe also believes that the Lakers didn't win last night. He is right about that, because the Lakers didn't have a game, but does Joe know that the Lakers didn't win last night or does he merely have a justified true belief?

When I was about nine or ten, a day or two before Christmas, I told my brother Vincent that I had snuck into my father's workroom, something forbidden, and had discovered Vincent's Christmas present, a railroad train set. I actually had not gone into my father's room but had made up the story to mislead my brother. But, I had guessed correctly; Vincent was indeed to be given a railroad set that Christmas. Vincent told my father that he knew what he was getting for Christmas, and my father, who regarded knowledge of Christmas presents as tantamount to the Oracle of Delphi and his workroom as Delphi itself, angrily spanked me for my sacrilege. While I was being spanked, I pled that I had not gone into my father's room and did not see the Christmas presents. "How did you know that Vincent was getting a railroad train set?" he asked. "I didn't know it. I just made up the story," I responded. The question is, Did Vincent know that he was going to get a railroad train set on believing my lie two days before Christmas?

Tripartite Analysis

Before 1963 the concept of knowledge was either left unanalyzed or defined more or less as *true, justified belief.* Plato was the first to suggest a tripartite analysis of knowledge, defining it as true belief with a rational explanation or justification (Greek *logos*). Citations can be found in C. I. Lewis, Roderick Chisholm, and A. J. Ayer with similar definitions. Roughly, *S* knows that *p* if and only if:

1. *S* believes that *p*.
2. *p* is true.
3. *S*'s belief that *p* is justified.

These three conditions constitute the *necessary* and *sufficient* conditions of the standard account of knowledge. If one of them is missing, *S* does not know that *p*. If all of them are present, *S* cannot fail to know that *p*. Let us call this the "tripartite analysis" of knowledge.

Alvin Plantinga reports the following anecdote. In 1962 he was drinking a cup of coffee in the cafeteria of Wayne State University with his colleague Edmund Gettier, when Gettier mentioned that he was concerned that he would be coming up for tenure the next year without having a lot of material published. He did have an idea of setting forth and publishing a few minor counterexamples to the traditional definition of knowledge, but he considered that a minor matter. The next year, Gettier's article on the definition of knowledge, which was less than three pages, was published in *Analysis,* and epistemology has never been the same.

Gettier's analysis was based on two counterexamples to the tripartite analysis. The first is as follows: (G) Smith and Jones have applied for a certain job, and Smith has strong evidence for the conjunctive proposition *d,* "Jones is the man who will get the job, and Jones has ten coins in his pocket."

Proposition *d* entails *e,* "The man who will get the job has ten coins in his pocket." We may suppose that Smith sees the entailment and believes *e*.

But unbeknown to Smith, he will get the job and happens to have ten coins in his pocket. So, while *d* is false, *e* is true, and Smith truly and justifiably believes *e,* but we would not say that Smith *knows* that the man who will get the job has ten coins in his pocket.

So the tripartite analysis fails, for he neither knows that he will get the job nor that he has ten coins in his pocket.

Keith Lehrer offers the following variation of Gettier's second counterexample. (L) A pupil in *S*'s office, Mr. Nogot, has given *S* evidence, *e,* that justifies *S* in believing "Mr. Nogot, who is in the office, owns a Ford," from which *S* deduces *p:* "Someone in the office owns a Ford." But unsuspected by *S*, Mr. Nogot has been shamming and *p* is only true because another person in the office, Mr. Havit, owns a Ford.[1] Again, the tripartite analysis seems to fail since the true, justified belief is based on a false proposition.

Gettier's counterexamples have the following form:

1. *S* believes that *p*.
2. *p* is true.
3. *S*'s belief that *p* is justified.
4. *p* is entailed by or probabilistically inferred from some proposition *q*.

5. *S* is justified in believing *q*.

6. *q* is false.

Therefore,

7. *S* doesn't know that *p*.

Note that Gettier is not arguing that the tripartite analysis is wholly wrong. The thrust of his counterexamples is simply that the tripartite analysis, while perhaps necessary, is not sufficient for knowledge.

Quartet Solutions

Several proposals have been offered to meet the Gettier-type counterexamples. Most of them accept the tripartite analysis as part of the full account of knowledge but include a necessary fourth condition. Together the four conditions would provide the complete analysis of knowledge, containing both its necessary and sufficient conditions. We may refer to these as *quartet solutions*. Let me describe four such attempts to save the tripartite account by supplementing it with a fourth condition. After this analysis, I'll turn to a suggestion that we abandon the tripartite analysis altogether. The four strategies are: (1) the no false-belief condition; (2) the conclusive reasons condition; (3) the causal condition; and (4) the defeasibility condition.

The No False-Belief Condition

Early on it was thought that the Gettier counterexamples could be defeated by simply stipulating that the belief that *p* must not be caused by or based on a false belief. In the preceding examples the belief that *p* is based on a false belief *q*. In (G), Smith falsely believes that Jones will get the job, and in (L), *S* falsely believes that Nogot owns a Ford. However, this attempt at a solution was soon found to be both too *strong* and too *weak*.

It was too strong because we can think of instances of knowing where a false belief is present. For example, I believe *h*, that Joan will be elected president of the student body because I justifiably believe: *a*, all the fraternity members, constituting 30 percent of the student body, are committed to Joan; *b*, all the sorority members, constituting 30 percent of the student body, are committed to Joan; and *c*, all the on-campus independents, constituting 30 percent of the student body, are committed to Joan. I believe *d*, that only the off-campus independent students, constituting only 10 percent of the student body, are against Joan. But I may be wrong about *c*. A last-minute change causes the independents to switch their vote. Nevertheless, I may still know Joan will win the election based on my justified true belief. If my belief in *h* is based on evidence *a*, *b*, and *c*, where any combination of two will justify *h*, I may hold a false belief and still be said to know *h*. We may call such cases as this one, cases of *overdetermination*, where more than one course of evidence justifies a belief.

Marshall Swain offers another example of justification including a false belief.[2] Suppose that you are attending your friends', Jack and Jill's, church wedding. You carefully note that the ceremony has been performed without a single error by the officiant. On the basis of this evidence, you come to believe that Jack and Jill were married in the ceremony, and so you conclude that they are married. However, unknown to you, your friends were married a month ago in a civil ceremony, and hence were not married in the ceremony you witnessed. You still know that they are married even though your belief is based partly on the false belief that they were married in the church wedding that you witnessed. This is a case of overdetermination because if they hadn't already been married, the church ceremony would have tied the marital knot.

The no false-belief condition was also shown to be too weak, and examples in which no false belief was present were offered. One of the most famous was set forth by Carl Ginet (and developed by Alvin Goldman). Henry is driving in the country and correctly identifies a red barn in the distance. Unknown to Henry, someone has set up a series of red barn facades in this vicinity, so that Henry cannot distinguish the real barn from the facades. Hence, Henry cannot be said to know that he is seeing a red barn even though he has a justified true belief. But, Henry's failure to know is not attributed to any false proposition on which his belief is based. So, the no false-belief condition does not succeed in saving the tripartite analysis.

The Conclusive Reasons Condition   In 1971 Fred Dretske pointed out that the tripartite analysis allowed beliefs that were only accidentally true to count as knowledge. An additional condition was needed that guaranteed the truth of the belief in question. He then set forth an ingenious solution to the Gettier puzzle by offering an account that argued that *S knows that p* if *S* has a reason, *R*, for *p*, such that if *p* were not the case, *S* would not have *R*.[3] Such a reason supported by the counterfactual ("if *p* were not the case, *S* would not have *R*") guarantees the truth of *S*'s belief that *p*. It is a conclusive reason for believing *p*. In counterexample (G), Smith's believing that the man who will get the job has ten coins in his pocket is not based on a conclusive reason, for Smith would still have the same reason for believing *p* even if he (Smith) didn't have ten coins in his pocket. In (L), *S*'s believing that someone in the room owns a Ford is not based on a conclusive reason, for *S* would have believed that someone in the room owned a Ford even if Mr. Havit had not been in the room.

But, there are problems with the conclusive reasons condition. George Pappas and Marshall Swain argued that it was too weak. Suppose *S* were looking at a table on which there was a cup.[4] *S* truly and justifiably believes that a cup is before him on the table, but unknown to him what he is seeing is not the cup itself but a hologram caused by rays given off by the cup. So the conclusive reasons account fails, for *S* would not have the reason he does for believing *p* if *p* were not the case, but we would not want to say that *S* knows that a cup is on the table.

Or you truly believe that you are speaking to your friend on the telephone, but a world-class prankster has arranged that after ten minutes of speaking with your friend, he will cause that line to go dead and speak to you impersonating your friend. You will not know the difference. However, exactly as the line goes dead, a repairer installs a new line between you and your friend, so that the prankster doesn't get a chance to fool you. Nevertheless, if he had, you wouldn't have known it. So on Dretske's analysis you don't know that you are speaking with your friend.

How would Dretske reply to these counterexamples? He could argue that having a conclusive reason doesn't logically guarantee the truth of a belief, but rather the belief must be reliably tied into one's reason for it. The two counterexamples fail because the resulting beliefs are not tied in, in a reliable way, to the reasons for them. We will come back to this issue in chapter 8 when we discuss reliabilism.

Even if Dretske can (via reliabilism) find a way out of the hologram and telephone counterexamples, we may still conclude his solution to be too strong. We often apply knowledge ascriptions to situations where we may not have the kind of conclusive reasons that Dretske demands. We claim to know that we have hearts and kidneys, that there are other minds, that water boils at 100 degrees Celsius at sea level, that we will die, and that some memory and testimony beliefs are true. Dretske's play-it-safe condition would exclude these and confine knowledge to the set of ironclad guaranteed beliefs. If nothing better is forthcoming, perhaps we should be thankful for this, but such a confining thesis seems counterintuitive. I suggest that we agree that Dretske has at least shown that we have some knowledge, call it "guaranteed knowledge" or "knowledge$_G$". But we are in search of a wider domain of knowledge.

The Causal Condition In a watershed article, "A Causal Theory of Knowledge" (1967), Goldman offered the hypothesis that the justification of a belief depends on the way it was caused.[5] If S knows that p, then S's belief that p must be caused by the state of affairs corresponding to p. Recurring to the Gettier example (G), Smith does not know that the person who will get the job has ten coins in his pocket because that belief is not caused in the right way. Likewise, in (L), S's belief that someone in the room owns a Ford has not been caused in the right way. For someone to know something there must be proper causal connections between the evidence and the belief.

Take first a perceptual belief. Suppose that you see a glass on the table before you and that this perception causes you to believe that a glass is on the table before you. Let p represent the state of affairs that the glass is on the table and let q represent the intermediate state of the light reflected from the glass to your eye, and that the message is transmitted by the optic nerve to the appropriate place in the back of your brain. Let S represent the believer (in this case you) and b represent the state of believing. Then your believing that the glass is on the table, Sbp, is a case of knowledge because it was caused in the right way.

Similarly, Goldman argued that testimony beliefs constituted knowledge if and only if they adhered to a proper causal pattern. Suppose p, Mary sees Jack kill Jill. If q, Mary tells Sam what she has witnessed, and Sam, knowing that Mary is generally trustworthy, believes her, then Sam's belief, Sbp, is a case of knowing. The simplest pattern may be represented this way:

State of affairs $\to$ Intermediate stage(s) $\to$ Resulting belief

p $\qquad\qquad\qquad$ q $\qquad\qquad\qquad\qquad\qquad$ Sbp

Our two examples would be represented this way:

A. Perception

p The glass is on $\to$ q Light causes the $\to$ Sbp You believe that
the table. $\qquad$ image on the glass $\qquad$ the glass is on
$\qquad\qquad\qquad$ on the table to reach $\qquad$ the table.
$\qquad\qquad\qquad$ your retina, etc.

B. Testimony

p Mary sees Jack $\to$ q Mary tells Sam what $\to$ Sbp Sam believes
kill Jill. $\qquad\qquad$ she has witnessed. $\qquad\qquad$ that Jack
$\qquad\qquad\qquad\qquad\qquad\qquad\qquad\qquad\qquad\qquad$ killed Jill.

This seems promising and perhaps it can ultimately be refined to do the work Goldman intended, but it was quickly pointed out that the notion of causality is very vague here, and that explaining knowledge via causality is an explanation *obscurum per obscurius* (explaining the obscure by what is more obscure). For example, it is not clear how the numbers 2 and 3 cause us to believe that they make 5, or how the future fact that I will die causes me to know this fact, or how the universal proposition that all humans are mortal causes me to know that truth.

Furthermore, it is hard to separate highly probable beliefs from knowledge. Suppose you have bought 1 of 1,000 lottery tickets. I believe that you will not win the lottery and am justified in that belief, given the odds. Suppose that I am right and you don't win. Many would say I knew that you would lose (given the remote possibility of your winning). If I do know this, it's hard to see how the fact of your not winning causes me to have that correct belief. It's my knowledge of probabilities that causes me to have the belief. Perhaps you demur and contend that I don't have knowledge that you won't win—I only have .999 certainty regarding it. But if we are this fastidious about knowledge, won't we have to give up knowledge of all future events—even ones that science and experience overwhelmingly support? By these rigorous requirements I don't know that I will be alive one second from now or that I will ever die or that anything will happen in the future (or that there will be a future). And, what's even more alarming, you don't know these things either. Such a path leads toward skepticism.

For all these reasons, most epistemologists were dissatisfied with the causal theory of knowledge. Gilbert Harman, in his book *Thought* (1973), sought to save the essence of the causal theory by proposing a near relative, *inference to the best explanation*.[6] The theory goes like this: We do not need to be able to reconstruct the causal chain that led to event X in order to know X.

Consider, says Harman, the case of the mad fiend. Omar suffers a fatal heart attack in the street. An hour later a mad fiend comes down the street and sees Omar lying in the gutter. He cuts off Omar's head. You walk down the street an hour later, see Omar lying there with his head detached and immediately infer from that state of affairs that Omar is dead. Harman points out that there is no causal connection between Omar's having died and his head being cut off. Having his head cut off did not cause Omar's death, the heart attack did. Hence, knowledge cannot be based on any causal connection between the belief and the event. You know that Omar is dead not because of any connection between the cause of his death and your belief, but because of a correct explanatory inference, "Normally, if someone's head is cut off, that person is dead." Incidentally, this also serves as a

counterexample to the no false-belief condition; you may believe that
Omar is dead because someone cut off his head, but in fact his head
was cut off because he was dead. Even though you are mistaken about
the cause of Omar's death, you still know that he is dead.

Harman sees his explanatory account of knowledge as an enlarge-
ment of Goldman's causal account. Inference to the best explanation
is the general theory of knowledge within which the causal account
functions as a special case. It is not clear, however, how one arrives at
the *best* explanation in many situations. What are the criteria involved?
Coherence, simplicity, predictability, comprehensiveness? Are these
concepts any less elusive than the concept of knowledge? In what order do we rank these criteria when they conflict?

Take, for example, the classical metaphysical question, What is the
best explanation of the universe? God, the eternity of matter, or
something else? How does an appeal to the best explanation grant us
knowledge here? Furthermore, unless we are begging the question, it
may not always be the case that the "best" explanation in terms of evidence is the correct explanation (some highly irregular events may
actually account for the event in question). So while we do try to
meet the criteria in explaining events, it's not clear that Harman's theory saves or improves the causal theory of knowledge.

The Defeasibility Condition   The defeasibility requirement, set forth
by Lehrer and Thomas Paxson, states that if there is no other truth, *q*
such that *S*'s believing it would have destroyed his justification for
believing that *p*, then this condition, along with the tripartite conditions, entails that *S* knows that *p*.[7] Lehrer and Paxson set forth the following illustration of defeasibility. *S* sees a man named Tom Grabit
steal a book. However, unknown to *S*, Tom's deranged mother lies
and testifies that Tom is a thousand miles away, so that it must have
been his twin brother John who stole the book. If *S* had known that
Mrs. Grabit had testified the way she did, he would not have been justified in believing that Tom stole the book. The statement, "Mrs.
Grabit testified that Tom was a thousand miles away at the time in
question," would have defeated *S*'s knowledge. However, one can
imagine a defeater to the defeater here. If *S* knew that Mrs. Grabit was
a deranged liar, he would have warrant to dismiss her testimony, and
continue to hold to his original belief about Tom.

One problem with the defeasibility criterion is that it may be just a
matter of luck that there is no true proposition, which, if known,
would defeat your justification. It is just a matter of luck that Tom
doesn't have a twin brother in the vicinity of the library because if he

did, then *S* would not be able to distinguish between them. If being able to discriminate between objects is necessary for knowledge, then virtually every perception will have a possible defeater—some exactly similar perception.

It seems that the defeasibility criterion must assume a notion of relevant alternatives. Only alternatives that are relevant to the actual situation may count as defeaters. Since Tom really doesn't have a twin brother, the fact that *S* would not be able to distinguish between them if he did is irrelevant to *S*'s knowing that Tom stole the book. Likewise, in the case of Henry and the red barns, the fact that Henry couldn't discriminate between a red barn and a red barn facade is irrelevant to Henry's knowing that he sees a red barn—if there really are no red barn facades in the neighborhood.

These considerations show that the defeasibility criterion is vague and open-ended. Harman argues that for any inductive belief there will always be some true proposition such that if the person knew of it, his or her justification would be defeated. For a large number of knowledge claims we can imagine some true proposition which, if we believed it, would defeat our claim to knowledge. But then we can think of some further true belief that would defeat the defeater, and some other true belief that would defeat the antidefeater, and so on. One may suspect that this condition is really appealing to omniscience. Only an omniscient being, say God, could sort out all the defeaters in the right order. Nonetheless, many epistemologists, like Lehrer and Paxson, believe that we can distinguish between defeating and nondefeating conditions. Others like Harman hold that the best we can do is set forth as a requirement that if a person is justified in inferring that there is no defeating counterevidence to a true, justified belief, then that person knows the proposition in question.

Other Attempts to Solve the Gettier Problem

Other solutions to the Gettier problem, that do not depend on a fourth condition, have been advanced. In 1981 Dretske put forth a *contextual* account of knowledge wherein justification is held to be relative to a given context.[8] Dretske argues that knowledge is *absolute* and admits of no degrees. However, whether we have sufficient justification for a belief to count as knowledge depends on the context or subject matter in question. First, he asks us to consider other concepts.

Take, for example, the concept "flatness." Something is flat only if it is not bumpy or irregular. If we take this literally, nothing is flat, for all surfaces will be found to have irregularities under a magnifying glass or microscope. Absolute flatness doesn't exist. But Dretske argues that we only need a relative notion. What counts as a bump or irregularity depends on the type of surface in question. A road with minor irregularities may be genuinely flat relative to our standards for roads even though a mirror or lens with the same irregularities would not be considered flat. Dretske calls this a *relationally absolute* concept.

The same discussion could be applied to the concepts "straight," "round," "good," "accurate," "rich," and many others. A rich person in a Third World country may be considered middle class or less in Europe or in the United States.

Dretske applies this relativity to justification for knowledge. What makes a belief adequately justified so that it counts as knowledge is that we can eliminate all the relevant alternatives. In (G), Smith must be able to rule out the relevant alternative that Jones will get the job. In (L), *S* must be able to eliminate the alternative that Nogot owns a Ford. In the case of *S*'s seeing Tom Grabit steal the book, *S* would have to be able to rule out the testimony of Mrs. Grabit. Henry would have to be able to distinguish facade barns from real barns when believing that the barn in question is really such. Dretske gives the example of Henry and his son seeing a zebra at the zoo. The son asks his father if the animal could be a mule painted with stripes. Before the son asks, Henry knows he is seeing a zebra but is now forced to distinguish a zebra from a painted mule. Since Henry acknowledges that he can't do that, he doesn't have knowledge. Before he considered the relevant alternative, he had knowledge. But after he considered the relevant alternative, he didn't. Now you know *p*, but in a new context, you don't. How can knowledge be so relative and circumstantial?

One need not be able to rule out all the evidence or alternatives for which one has evidence that are inconsistent with his or her belief, but only the *relevant* alternatives. These are alternatives based on evidence that is available to the believer in question. For example, *S* need not be able to rule out Mrs. Grabit's testimony if he doesn't know that Mrs. Grabit has testified that it wasn't Tom who stole the book. Only when he is challenged with that news does Mrs. Grabit's testimony become relevant. So, although knowledge is absolute, it is dependent on the relativity of the context and challenges. As long as my true, justified belief that *p* is not challenged, I may be said to know that *p*. But, once it is challenged, I lose that knowledge unless I can eliminate any relevant challenge.

Dretske's contextualism has the virtue of providing a solution to the Gettier problem by showing that what counts as knowledge may depend on the circumstances, and that the standards for justification may change depending on the issue and what is wanted. For example, an undergraduate, asked to give an account of the immune system, may arrive at an answer that satisfies his physiology course, but be inadequate (lacking justification) in a medical school oral exam. But, it seems, contextualism is too vague and relative to serve our purposes. Vagueness is sometimes appropriate to the subject matter (e.g., the concepts of "baldness" or "wealth"), but here it seems to exceed the vagueness inherent in the subject matter. If contextualism is true, might we not obtain some absurd conclusions? How would a contextualist respond to this puzzle: If a clever mathematician sets forth an elaborate "proof" that $1 + 1 = 3$, and you cannot show his or her proof to be fallacious, would you cease to know that $1 + 1 = 2$? Or if an honest person testified against one of your memory beliefs (and said that you ate in a certain restaurant last year), would you suddenly cease to *know* whether you ate in that restaurant last year? Does contextualism put too much in doubt? Does contextualism itself have to be contextualized? While a core of common sense remains, as a theory, contextualism may be too vague to serve as a complete theory of knowledge.

Recently Keith DeRose has sought to make sense of a constrained contextualism. Responding to the criticism put forth by Peter Unger and Palle Yourgrau, that the context takes knowledge away: "Now you know it, now you don't," DeRose distinguishes between *low* contexts and *high* contexts.[9] Less is needed for justification or knowledge to satisfy a low context than a high one. (Think of the student describing the workings of the immune system or the case of Henry and the zebra—both mentioned above.) In the low context we can attribute knowledge to the student or Henry, which would not count as such in the high context. Whether contextualism can meet all possible criticisms and constitute an adequate theory, I must leave you to decide.

Many epistemologists, dissatisfied with these proposed solutions, threw up their hands in despair at the attempts to solve the Gettier problem. Still, over thirty years after Gettier first set forth his three-page article, nothing close to a consensus is in sight. The tortuous reasoning through labyrinthine paths and the record of counterexample upon counterexample is recorded in Robert Shope's *The Analysis of Knowing*. A large number of epistemologists have concluded that no solution to the Gettier problem exists because the wrong model is being used. Instead of making knowledge depend on the reasons one has for a given true belief, some epistemologists contend that knowledge depends on being produced by a reliable process. The knower need not be able to say why he or she believes that *p* in order to have knowledge that *p*. All one has to do is come to the belief via a right kind of procedure. We postpone a critical discussion of *reliabilism* (or *externalism*, as it is often called, in opposition to *internalism*, in which the subject needs to be able to come up with reasons) until chapter 8.

The Pluralistic Right Way My own suggestion is that there may not be a neat set of necessary and sufficient conditions that will encompass all cases of "knowledge." Knowledge is a multifaceted or family-resemblance term covering our relations to different types of situations of knowledge (there is some truth in contextualism—justification will vary given the situation). There may be a core meaning that captures the paradigm cases—though there will be some cases that don't quite fit and borderline cases where we could decide in either direction. Following this line of thought would lead us to adopt a general rule that does not offer a single criterion. I suggest that we accept the tripartite analysis (i.e., knowledge is true, justified belief) as essentially correct, at least, for the core idea of knowledge, adding the stipulation that the justification of the true belief must have been formed or grounded in the *right way,* where the context enables us to understand the right kind of way. Sometimes this will mean that, following Goldman, the belief was caused by the proper state of affairs. This is the case with perceptual knowledge, memory knowledge, and testimony knowledge. At other times, knowledge may include something like Harman's "best [correct] explanation" account, wherein we can be said to know because we have made a correct inference even though we haven't gotten the causal chain quite right (e.g., the case of Omar). At still other times, it will mean that we reasoned logically (as in the case of $1 + 1 = 2$ or a deductive argument). Descartes's *cogito,* knowledge that I (or a thinking thing) exists, will be justified as a self-evident intuition. If you agree that inferring is a causal mechanism (as I do), then we may conclude that my analysis is simply a broader version of Goldman's original causal theory of knowledge.

This pluralistic right way account will solve the Gettier counterexamples, showing that in (G), Smith does not know that "someone with ten coins in his pocket will get the job" and in (L), *S* will not be said to know that someone in the room owns a Ford, because of the kinds of reasons the causal account offers. The true, justified beliefs weren't caused in the right way.

This account has the benefit of answering the main objection to the causal account of knowledge. It can handle knowledge of future events, such as our death. We may arrive at the conclusion that "I will die" through a combination of inductive and deductive reasoning. Understanding the nature of life, that it involves a dying process and, eventually, death, and having observed no instance of a living thing live beyond a limited time, we generalize the conclusion: All living things die. The argument reads thus:

1. All living things die.
2. I am a living thing.
3. Therefore, I will die.

If it somehow turns out to be false that all living things die, it might still be the case that all mammals (or even human beings) die, in which case we would have to substitute "mammals" (or "human beings") for "living things." We would still know that we will die, since we arrive at the first true premise through a legitimate means. If it were only 99 percent probable that all things die (or that we would die), we could not use this argument to make a genuine knowledge claim.

Now, here is a counterexample that gives my account difficulties. Return to the example of Mary seeing Jack kill Jill. Mary, a reliable witness, tells you about the murder and on the basis of her testimony you believe that Jack killed Jill. Normally, we would say that you knew that Jack killed Jill. But suppose, a few hours later, nineteen other people whom you know to be reliable people also tell you that they saw Jack somewhere else during the time of the crime. We may suppose that they have different reasons for their falsehood. Some are trying to protect Jack. Others forgot to change their clocks forward, not knowing that the time changed last night. Others have confused Jack with his twin brother John, and so forth. You, however, have no knowledge of these deviant occurrences.

What effect does the testimony of nineteen normally reliable people have on your claim to know that Jack killed Jill? Normally, such recalcitrant evidence would cause us to doubt or deny that Jack killed Jill and thus take away any knowledge we might have had. But suppose you maintain your belief that Jack killed Jill. Is it a rational belief? One that you are justified in believing? The answer to this question may depend on whether you accept an internalist or externalist account of knowledge and justification. An internalist, one who believes that justification depends on being able to access the grounds of one's belief, may conclude that your belief is not justified. The externalist, one who says that as long as the belief was caused by a reliable process it is justified, may conclude that it is justified. The case is difficult, borderline, but perhaps both internalists and externalists agree that the weight of nineteen testimonies prohibits one from being justified. If so, you don't have knowledge that Jack killed Jill.

An even more difficult case is this. The nineteen witnesses are going around telling their stories exonerating Jack. The evidence is public, but you haven't heard it. Since there is powerful evidence against your belief that Jack killed Jill, are you nevertheless justified in that belief? Do you still *know* that Jack killed Jill in spite of all this evidence?

Whatever you decide on these hard cases, my account can accommodate special cases of knowing, such as the case of forgotten knowledge. Suppose that many years ago you made an in-depth study of the First World War and learned the details of the war, including the fact that Germany lost the war. Now you have forgotten virtually all of the evidence, including the evidence for the conclusion that Germany lost the war. Do you still know those facts? Some epistemologists would say, "No, since you can't access your evidence, you don't know those facts any more." Others say, "Yes, but this just shows that not all knowledge needs justification." On my account you know the facts and are justified in believing them, since they were caused in the right way and you have no reason to give up the conclusions. Knowing and being justified do not depend on knowing that you know or knowing that you are justified.

A second difficult problem is the famous lottery paradox. Suppose the lottery consists of 1,000 tickets and you have one of them. Do you know that you won't win? You know that someone will win, but the probability of your winning is vanishingly small. Normally, we would say regarding inductive evidence that 999 out of 1,000 chances of being right constitutes knowledge. If 999 out of 1,000 people who jumped off the Empire State Building died, many of us would be inclined to say that we know the next person to jump will die. Even though there is a logical possibility that a catastrophe might falsify our claim, most of us would say that we know that the sun will rise tomorrow. The difference in the lottery case is that we know that someone will win, so we might be inclined to say, "I don't know that I won't win, only that I have only a 1/1,000 chance of winning."

We hesitate to say that we know or even believe of any given person that he or she will not win the lottery because we know that someone will win it, thus involving ourselves in a contradiction. We believe both that someone among these 1,000 people will win, but for each one person in 1,000 we believe that he or she will not win. It seems that we can have inconsistent beliefs and perhaps have knowledge without certainty.

This same point is made in the paradox cited in the preface to this book. I wrote that I believe every claim I make in the book (when I am reporting my own views) is true, but then I went on to say that given my fallibility, "I also believe that some false statements are contained herein," meaning that at least one of my claims in this book is false (though, of course, I won't tell you which one is false). Why won't I tell you which is false? Because if I knew, it wouldn't be one of my beliefs. So, I have contradictory beliefs. If my claim to fallibility is justified, do I *know* that I have some false beliefs (stated in this book)?

Can we have knowledge without complete certainty? Can we know without knowing that we know? Remember the distinction between *strong* and *weak* knowledge. Strong knowledge is that which we know we know, such as I know that I know that I exist, or that 2 + 2 = 4, or that the law of noncontradiction is a universally valid logical principle. I have complete certainty about these things. They are indubitable, self-evident. But, I am not as certain about my memory beliefs; they are weak knowledge. I believe that I know that I was in Lincoln, Nebraska, in July 1993 when I wrote the first draft of this chapter, but I could be misremembering, in which case, I don't know that I was in Lincoln, Nebraska. I could be wrong about many of the things I claim to know, and so could you. Nevertheless, if they have been formed and are sustained in the right way, we do know them. Unless we admit these two kinds of knowledge (perhaps there are other kinds), the concept of knowledge reduces to what Dretske called "guaranteed knowledge." Earlier we gave reasons for doubting whether that was a broad enough account.

It may be troubling to some that we cannot say exactly all the possible conditions that must be fulfilled in all possible cases of knowledge, but why should we have to do that? We have a good intuitive idea of how evidence supports our beliefs. That may be sufficient for our purposes. But I leave it to you to decide whether the "right way" analysis is sufficient to satisfy our quest for necessary and sufficient conditions for knowledge.

Summary

The standard conception of knowledge from Plato until the mid-twentieth century has been that it is *true, justified belief.* Gettier's counterexamples show problems with this definition. Several theories have tried to meet Gettier's challenge. Internalist theories hold that justification depends on the reasons one has for a true belief. Internalists typically specify a fourth condition that defuses the problematic counterexamples: a causal condition, defeasibility, and the like. We saw that difficulties haunt each attempt to solve the

Gettier counterexamples and suggested a general "right way" analysis, which accepts the tripartite analysis as essentially correct but also takes into account the relativity that is inherent in our concept of knowledge.

QUESTIONS FOR DISCUSSION

1. Go over the Gettier counterexamples. What is their general format? Why did they cause such a revolution in epistemology?

2. How effective are these counterexamples in attacking the standard account of knowledge? Which of the four strategies discussed best solves the Gettier counterexamples?

3. One could save a lot of time and effort by simply accepting one of the accounts discussed in this chapter and biting the bullet with regard to alleged counterexamples. For example, suppose I simply maintain that knowledge is true belief caused by the fact in question. I could then simply dismiss the counterexamples offered. Which counterexamples would I have to dismiss? How appealing is such a move?

4. Evaluate Dretske's contextualism. What are its strengths and weaknesses?

5. Examine Harman's idea of inference to the best explanation and the criticisms of it. How might Harman respond to my criticism that the best explanation that we have is not necessarily the correct one? Could he contend that this is not a reason for dismissing it since it only shows that under certain circumstances the truth is unknowable?

6. Is the "right way" analysis, which I suggest as a general strategy to the Gettier cases, a helpful way of looking at the problem or does it merely ignore the problem?

7. Can we have inductive knowledge? Go over the lottery paradox and discuss the problems inherent in it. Suppose that you know (by divine authority or by a clear new law of science) that a "freak" genetic event will cause at least one, but no more than two, people now alive (the earth's population is presently estimated at 6.0 billion) not to die in the next 1,000 years. No one knows who this person is. Would you say of any person (not terminally ill) that you know that he or she will die before he or she lives to be 1,000? Would you know that you would die before 1,000 years were up?

8. One problem you may have noticed is that virtually every definition of the concept of knowledge depends on an appeal to certain
intuitions, but that there can always be found some other intuition to serve as a counterexample to any given theory. What does
this tell us about the relation of intuitions to theory?

9. Examine contextualism as a solution to the Gettier problem.
What are its strengths and weaknesses?

NOTES

1. Keith Lehrer, "Knowledge, Truth and Evidence," *Analysis* 25, 5 (1965), 169.
(Ithaca, NY: Cornell University Press, 1981), 149f.

2. Marshall Swain, *Reasons and Knowledge* (Ithaca, NY: Cornell University Press,
1981), 149f.

3. Fred Dretske, "Conclusive Reasons," *Australasian Journal of Philosophy* 49
(1971). Reprinted in *Essays on Knowledge and Justification,* eds. George Pappas
and Marshall Swain. (Ithaca, NY: Cornell University Press, 1978).

4. George Pappas and Marshall Swain, "Some Conclusive Reasons Against 'Conclusive Reasons.' " In Pappas and Swain.

5. Alvin Goldman, "A Causal Theory of Knowing," *The Journal of Philosophy* 64,
12 (1967). Reprinted in *The Theory of Knowledge* 2nd ed., IV.2, ed. Louis Pojman. I have simplified Goldman's diagram, leaving out the important element of
background knowledge.

6. Gilbert Harman, *Thought* (Princeton: Princeton University Press, 1973). The
relevant section is reprinted in Pojman IV.4.

7. Keith Lehrer and Thomas Paxson, "Knowledge: Undefeated Justified True Belief." In Pappas and Swain. Reprinted in Pojman IV.3.

8. Fred Dretske, "The Pragmatic Dimension of Knowledge," *Philosophical Studies*
40 (1981), 363–378.

9. Palle Yourgrau, "Knowledge and Relevant Alternatives" *Synthese* 55 (1983); Peter Unger, *Philosophical Relativity* (Minneapolis: University of Minnesota Press,
1984); Keith DeRose, "Contextualism and Knowledge Attributions," *Philosophy
and Phenomenological Research* (1992) and "Now You Know It, Now You
Don't" (unpublished manuscript, 1999).

FOR FURTHER READING

Audi, Robert, *Belief, Justification, and Knowledge.* Belmont, CA: Wadsworth, 1988.

BonJour, Laurence. *The Structure of Empirical Knowledge.* Cambridge, MA: Harvard
University Press, 1985. A strong internalist account of knowledge.

Carrier, L. S. "The Causal Theory of Knowledge," *Philosophia* (1976).

Fumerton, Richard. *Metaphysical and Epistemological Problems in Perception.* Lincoln:
University of Nebraska Press, 1973.

Moser, Paul. *Knowledge and Evidence*. Cambridge: Cambridge University Press, 1989. A clear comprehensive defense of a foundational theory of knowledge.

Nozick, Robert. *Philosophical Explanations*. Cambridge, MA: Harvard University Press, 1981, 167–290. A defense of a conditional theory of knowledge similar to Dretske's account of conclusive reasons.

Pappas, George, and Marshall Swain, eds. *Essays on Knowledge and Justification*. Ithaca, NY: Cornell University Press, 1978. Contains excellent articles on the analysis of knowledge.

Pojman, Louis, ed. *The Theory of Knowledge*. Belmont, CA: Wadsworth, 1993. Parts IV and VI contain important papers by Gettier, Goldman, Lehrer, Paxson, Harman, Quine, Kim, Pollock, Plantinga, and others.

Pollock, John, *Contemporary Theories of Knowledge*. Totowa, NJ: Rowman & Littlefield, 1986. A provocative, original study of most of the issues discussed in this chapter.

Shope, Robert. *The Analysis of Knowledge*. Princeton, NJ: Princeton University Press, 1983. Contains a helpful history of the Gettier problem.

Swain, Marshall. *Reasons and Knowledge*. Ithaca, NY: Cornell University Press, 1981. A careful, detailed advancement of the position that knowledge is indefeasibly true, justified belief.

CHAPTER 6

Theories of Justification (I): Foundationalism

Now of the thinking states by which we grasp truth, some are unfailingly true; others admit of error—opinion, for example, and calculation, whereas scientific knowledge and intuition are always true; further, no other kind of thought except intuition is more accurate than scientific knowledge, whereas primary premises are more knowable than demonstrations, and all scientific knowledge is discursive. From these considerations it follows that there will be no scientific knowledge of the primary, and since, except intuition, nothing can be truer than scientific knowledge, it will be intuition that apprehends the primary premises. (Aristotle, Posterior Analytics vol. II, par. 19)

Classical Foundationalism

Until recently, most epistemologists have held that there are self-evident first principles, which are immediately known to the understanding and sufficient to build a complete system of knowledge. For Plato, these principles were the Forms, the knowledge of which was latent as Innate Ideas within us. We were born with Innate Ideas of *equality, redness, triangularity, goodness, justice,* and so forth. For Aristotle, as the opening quotation indicates, self-evident first principles, such as the axioms of mathematics and logic, may be grasped immediately by the understanding, and from them all other knowledge is inferred. They are unfailingly true, and form the basis of all scientific knowledge. Following Aristotle, Thomas Aquinas (1225–1274) wrote,

Now a truth can come into the mind in two ways, namely, as known in itself, and as known through another. What is known in itself is like a principle, and is perceived immediately by the mind. And so the habit which perfects the intellect in considering such a truth is called *understanding;* it is a firm and easy quality of mind which sees into principles. A truth, however, which is known through another is understood by the intellect, not immediately, but through an inquiry of reason of which it is the terminus.[1]

For Aquinas, the understanding can use these first principles to deduce knowledge of metaphysical truths, including the existence and attributes of God.

René Descartes further developed the foundational doctrine, asserting that knowledge of the existence and mental nature of the self is grasped noninferentially by the understanding. Furthermore, we can have infallible knowledge of our psychological states, that is, our beliefs and desires. I can know infallibly that I am in pain, that I am thinking, that I believe that I have a body, and that I seem to see a tree in front of me. In addition, Descartes thought we had immediate knowledge of certain metaphysical truths. That there must be as much reality in the total cause as in the effectual proposition enabled him to deduce the existence of a perfect divine being, who in turn guaranteed the veracity of our empirical beliefs. Self-evident truths were clear and distinct, having a luminous aura about them that the intuition could not fail to grasp as obvious truth, and *indubitable,* beyond the possibility of doubt. I may know with certainty that I *seem* to see a tree in front of me, but I cannot know *directly* that there really is a tree in front of me, since empirical beliefs are subject to error and knowledge must be indubitable.

According to Descartes only two methods guarantee arriving at knowledge: intuition and deductive reasoning.

By *intuition* I understand, not the fluctuating testimony of the senses, nor the misleading judgment that proceeds from the blundering constructs of imagination, but the conception which an unclouded and attentive mind gives us so readily and distinctly that we are wholly freed from doubt about that which we understand. Or, what comes to the same thing, *intuition* is the undoubting conception of an unclouded and attentive mind, and springs from the light of reason alone; it is more certain than deduction itself, in that it is simpler. . . . Thus each individual can mentally have intuition of the fact that he exists, and that he thinks; that the triangle is bounded by three lines only, the sphere by a single superficies.[2]

Intuition, the natural light of reason, provided the only noninferential, infallible beliefs possible, whereas deductive reason served to transmit knowledge from the intuitions to the derived entailments of our intuitions. Deductive reason preserved truth. No other methods guaranteed knowledge. Certainly not fallible induction!

Empiricists like John Locke and, before him, Thomas Aquinas, extended the scope of knowledge to include perceptual beliefs. Although not as certain as intuitive, self-evident truths (mathematics, logic, the existence of God), empirical knowledge is still knowledge. David Hume held a similar position, based on the certainty of sense impressions but not extending to metaphysical beliefs.

What all of these philosophers have in common is the theory that we can have immediate and infallible knowledge of first principles or basic propositions, from which we can deduce further truths. Building on the infallible foundations of indubitable first principles or intuitions, we can construct via a process of deductive reasoning a solid house of knowledge.

There are two related ideas in this notion of immediate and infallible, or indubitable, knowledge: *self-evidence* and *incorrigibility*. A proposition is self-evident when, if one understands and considers it, one cannot help but believe and know it. It is obvious, luminous, certain.[3] Examples of such propositions are the law of noncontradiction or basic truths of arithmetic such as $1 + 1 = 2$. A belief is incorrigible for someone S if and only if it's not possible to show that person that he or she is mistaken.[4] Examples of this would be appearance statements such as "I seem to see a red object," "I am in pain," and "I exist." All of these notions have been considered certain, but only propositions are self-evident. Incorrigibility is primarily a property of beliefs, but these terms often overlap. I interpret Descartes' use of *indubitable* to include the notions of self-evidence, incorrigibility, and infallibility, but this is not one of my incorrigible beliefs. There is no clear consensus on the definitions of these notions, and the reader will find that epistemologists use them slightly differently.

We call the traditional view—that we may have infallible noninferential knowledge upon which all other knowledge is based—*classical foundationalism*. Note the architectural metaphor *foundation*. Descartes spoke of tearing down the superstructure and destroying the foundations of our epistemically unjustified house and of laying a new, infallible foundation with indubitable propositions and thereupon erecting a solid and certain superstructure, a house of knowledge.

Basic and Nonbasic Beliefs

We may divide all beliefs into two kinds: basic beliefs and inferred beliefs. We may define the primary epistemic unit *properly basic beliefs* this way:

> A belief that *p* is properly basic for a person *S* if and only if it is (1) basic (noninferential) for *S* and (2) properly so (justified noninferentially).

A nonbasic justified belief is one that is inferentially based on one or more properly basic beliefs.

The relationship is asymmetrical in that the basic beliefs *transfer* (or *transmit*) justification and knowledge to the derived belief but not vice versa. In classical foundationalism, truth is preserved in the transmission process from the infallible first principles to the superstructure in a treelike relationship:

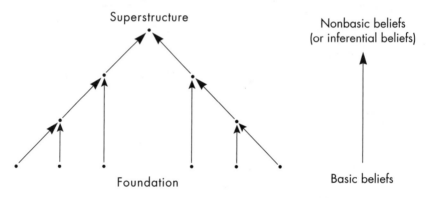

A more accurate diagram would place more items and connections in the superstructure. We may call this the complex treelike relationship:

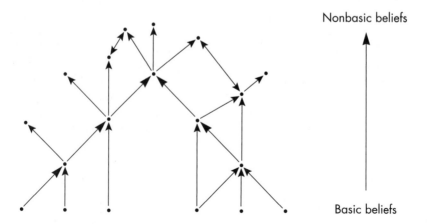

From indubitable first premises Descartes deduced the existence of God as an omnibenevolent being whose nature excluded deception. One of his arguments depended on the premise that there must be at least as much reality in the efficient and total cause as in its effect.[5] From this clear and distinct idea he reasoned the existence of a superior being, the cause of all reality. Because God implanted our perceptual mechanisms within us, it follows that we can know that we are not being deceived when we believe things about objects in the world. Normally, if I seem to see a tree I really do see one. Only under abnormal circumstances will I be deceived about such matters. Yet, because I can be deceived, I should withhold the attribution of knowledge to such empirical judgments. Induction can never be a means of knowledge, but only of belief.

We may define Descartes foundational notion of a properly basic belief this way:

> **(D)** Belief B is properly basic for person P if and only if B is indubitable or self-evidently true for S.

For other classical foundationalists who were empiricists, such as Aquinas, Locke, Hume, and Clifford, we must add the notion of an empirical deliverance being evident to the senses:

> **(E)** Belief B is properly basic for person P if and only if B is indubitable or self-evident or evident to the senses.

Contemporary philosophers have found problems with both of these theses. They point to problems with Descartes' (1) arguments for the existence of God, (2) his notion that "there must be at least as much reality in the total cause as in the effect," (3) his notion of clear and distinct ideas, and (4) his notion of infallibility (or incorrigibility). It is generally conceded that Descartes fails to establish (1), (2), and (3).[6] Notion (4) is held by many philosophers but denied by others. Whether our appearance beliefs, for example, "I am in pain," "I seem to see a red object," and "I have a hot sensation," are really infallible (or incorrigible) is a matter of debate.

Consider the statement, "I am in pain." If I believe that I am in pain, is it necessarily so? Do I infallibly know that I am in pain when I believe that I am? Consider this counterexample adapted from Keith Lehrer. A gullible woman who is having shoulder pains sees her physician, who, believing the woman to be a hypochondriac, informs her that she is mistaken about these pains. "They really are acute tickles," he avers. "Acute tickles sometimes resemble pains, but they are really more pleasurable." The gullible woman believes the physician and the next day tells her husband that she is having tickling sensations in her left shoulder.

Consider the statement "I am having a hot sensation," uttered by one who believes it with infallible certainty. Plausible counterexamples are available to this belief too. I once heard the following story about a fraternity initiation. The pledge was told that he was to be branded on his rear end with a branding iron containing the Greek letters of his fraternity. The inductee saw the red hot iron pulled from the stove and heard it sizzling. He removed his pants and bared his backside to the fraternity members in anticipation of the branding iron. Then an ice cold metal bar was applied to his backside. The pledge reported that for several seconds he felt an incredibly hot sensation.

Likewise, we may ask whether the appearance belief "I seem to see a red object" is infallible or incorrigible. Could I be confused about colors so that I am really having an orange sensation? Or is seeming to see X sufficient to make such a belief incorrigible?

But there is an even more fundamental problem with classical foundationalism. The formulations (**D**) and (**E**) do not pass their own test. Consider (**D**): Belief B is properly basic for person P if and only if B is indubitable or self-evidently true for S.

Is (**D**) indubitable or self-evident to you? Do you fully grasp it and have no doubt that all and only indubitable or self-evident beliefs are so certain as to guarantee truth? I for one think that perceptual and memory beliefs can also bring us knowledge. I remember that I saw my dog and heard it bark ten minutes ago. So I claim to know now that I saw and heard her a short while ago. That seems to constitute knowledge. If so, then I will doubt (D). So (D) fails its own test. It is self-referentially incoherent.

Likewise, (**E**)—*Belief* B *is properly basic for person* P *if and only if* B *is indubitable or self-evident or evident to the senses*—is itself neither indubitable, self-evident, or evident to the senses. So, it fails to live up to its own standards. It is self-referentially incoherent.

Fallibilism

Most contemporary foundationalists, persuaded by the force of these and similar counterexamples and considerations, have dropped the thesis that all of our properly basic beliefs need to be infallible, incorrigible, self-evident, or evident to the senses. That is, most contemporary foundationalists are not of the classical variety. They tend to relativize the idea of self-evidence or proper basicality to individuals. What is self-evident to you may not be self-evident to me. You may see immediately that $13 \times 13 = 169$ or even that $69 \times 69 = 4,761$, while I may have to work these sums out from simpler self-evident truths (e.g., that $3 \times 3 = 9$; $3 \times 10 = 30$; $10 \times 13 = 130$; and the like).

Perhaps there are some self-evident, incorrigible truths, such as simple mathematical statements and the truths of logic, as well as the *cogito* (I think, therefore I am), but this doesn't give us enough of a foundation to build a sturdy superstructure. It doesn't even include empirical beliefs, and so fails to afford infallible knowledge of the external world.

It must be admitted that classical foundationalism has proved a disappointing failure. But we would all like to have the kind of absolute certainty that it attempted to procure: solid proof for the existence of God, immortality, free will, other minds, and the moral order.

So the trend has been for foundationalists to become more moderate, dropping the requirement that properly basic beliefs must be infallible or incorrigible. Instead they have adopted *fallibilism,* the thesis that almost any of our basic beliefs could turn out to be false. What the moderate foundationalist continues to hold is the essential structure of properly basic (that is, unmoved movers but not unmovable movers) beliefs that support all other nonbasic beliefs. Why do they continue to maintain this essential structure? The main reason is the *regress problem*. We now turn to it.

The Regress Problem

A driving force behind contemporary foundationalists is the problem of stopping the regress of inferential justification. Suppose that you believe that eating vegetables will promote your health. I ask you why you believe that. You answer that your belief is based on your beliefs about nutrition. Vegetables have the kind of vitamins necessary for the proper maintenance of the human body. But suppose I ask you why you believe that vegetables contain the kind of vitamins necessary for the proper maintenance of the human body. Well, you'd either appeal to common knowledge or start discussing chemistry and physiology. Where would the demand for a justification stop? Does it matter?

Structurally, your belief A, that vegetables promote health, is based on your belief B, that vegetables contain necessary vitamins, which in turn is based on belief C, having to do with chemistry and physiology. Need you go further and base C, your beliefs about chemistry and physiology, on D, beliefs about physics?

Another way of putting the matter is to say that we infer belief A from belief B, and B from C, and so on. Four kinds of such inference chains may be identified.

1. Belief *A* is itself inferred directly from a belief *B*, which is unjustified.
2. Belief *A* owes its justification to belief *B*, which is based on belief *C* and so on *ad infinitum*.
3. Belief *A* owes its justification to belief *B*, which is based on belief *C*, which is based on belief *A*, doubling back in a circle.
4. Belief *A* owes its justification to belief *B*, which is based on a foundational or noninferential belief that needs no further justification.

There are problems with each type of chain.

Ludwig Wittgenstein seems to have held the first option when he enigmatically remarked that at the foundation of well-founded beliefs lies belief that is not founded. Perhaps contextualism (see chapter 8 or the glossary) fits this category, but without more qualifications, it is hard to see how unjustified beliefs can yield a justified belief. If all our beliefs end in unjustified beliefs, we seem caught forever in skepticism.

The second option identifies an infinite regress chain. It is difficult to believe that creatures like us have an infinite set of beliefs, and, even if we did, it would be impossible to ever show that such a justified belief was justified. Some people argue that we have an infinite set of mathematical beliefs:

1. 2 is larger than 1,
2. 3 is larger than 2,
3. 4 is larger than 3,

and so on forever.

However, if beliefs are defined as corresponding to discrete propositions or sentences, then it is doubtful that we have such an infinite set. It is even more doubtful that we have an infinite set of empirical beliefs. How could the finite human mind contain such an infinite set of beliefs? We have no evidence that we have (or could have) an infinite set of beliefs. Furthermore, if all our beliefs are justified by appeal to other mediate beliefs, we never arrive at what is required for justification, a nonmediate belief. The notion of an infinite set (or infinite sets of all our justified beliefs) has little to commend it. No one has given a good argument in support of the infinite regress chain, though it hasn't been disproved either.

Turning to the third pattern of inference chains, the circular scheme, we may say that it seems to beg the question. If belief *A* is justified by belief *B*, which in turn is justified by belief *C*, which in turn is justified by belief *A*, we seem to have gone around in a circle.

For example, suppose you ask me why I believe in the Bible and I say, "Because it is inspired by God." Then you ask me why I believe in God, and I say, "I believe in God because the Bible says God exists." Arguing in a circle can be done by any fool and proves nothing. However, as we shall see, if the circle is big enough and the interrelations are intricate enough, many philosophers will accept something like the circular scheme. It is called *coherentism*. We will examine this doctrine in the next chapter.

The final pattern, which posits self-justified beliefs (*unmoved movers*, to use Chisholm's phrase) are the base of every inferential chain, is the one that foundationalists choose. Every justified belief is either a properly basic (justified) belief or ends in a chain of beliefs, the last of which is self-justified. On the face of it, foundationalism seems the most satisfactory solution to the regress problem. It stops the chain of justification and does so in a nonquestion-begging way.

A Critique of Foundationalism

In spite of its initial structural attractiveness, there are several problems with foundationalism. First, as we have already noted, classical or strong foundationalism, with its demand for infallible knowledge, allows us too little content to sustain the edifice of knowledge, or what our reflective judgment takes to be the edifice of knowledge. The appeal to infallible knowledge doesn't seem adequate to yield much inferred knowledge or justified belief but tends toward skepticism about the external world, perception, memory beliefs, other minds, induction, and the like. On the other hand, the critic continues, moderate foundationalism doesn't give us the strong justification, let alone knowledge, that we would like to have. In fact, because it compromises and accepts coherence constraints, it tends to become indistinguishable from moderate coherentism. So foundationalism seems to lead to the option of either skepticism or coherentism.

Second, the Epistemic Ascent Argument set forth by Wilfred Sellars and Laurence BonJour maintains that without appealing to an unwarranted stipulation, foundationalism cannot explain how an empirical justification terminates. Let A represent the property of being a properly basic belief, then for a belief B to qualify as properly basic, the premises of the following justificatory argument S (standing for Sellars) must themselves be justified.

THE ASCENT ARGUMENT (S)

1. S's belief B has property A.
2. Beliefs having property A are highly likely to be true.
3. Therefore, S's belief B is highly likely to be true.
4. Therefore, S's belief B is epistemically justified (by the meaning of epistemically justified).[7]

BonJour argues that for the foundationalist to be justified in believing that B is properly basic, he must depend on argument S, so that his justification is not immediate or basic but inferential.

Let us look more closely at this argument. Keep in mind that we are discussing empirical beliefs, that is, beliefs about the external world but including perceptual beliefs, memory beliefs, and introspective beliefs (beliefs about one's present state of mind). BonJour claims that if B were basic, premise (1) would have to be justified as well, and if it is reasonable to accept B, one must grasp the relationship between premises (1) and (2), inferring (3). That is, in order to be justified in accepting B as properly basic, S must be in cognitive possession of the reasons for accepting B, in which case B is not basic but justified by other beliefs. We get the disturbing result that B is not basic after all, since its justification depends on that of at least one other empirical belief. It would follow that moderate foundationalism is untenable as a solution to the regress problem.[8] BonJour next develops these basic ideas into a fuller antifoundationalist argument we will call J (for BonJour).

ANTI-FOUNDATIONALIST ARGUMENT (J)

1. Suppose that there are *basic empirical beliefs*, that is, empirical beliefs (a) that are epistemically justified and (b) whose justification does not depend on that of any further empirical beliefs.
2. For a belief to be epistemically justified requires that there be a reason why it is likely to be true.
3. For a belief to be epistemically justified for a particular person requires that this person be himself in cognitive possession of such a reason.
4. The only way to be in cognitive possession of such a reason is to believe *with justification* the premises from which it follows that the belief is likely to be true.
5. The premises of such a justifying argument for an empirical belief cannot be entirely *a priori*; at least one such premise must be empirical.

6. Therefore, the justification of a supposed basic empirical belief must depend on the justification of at least one other empirical belief, which contradicts (1); it follows that there can be no basic empirical beliefs.

Premise (1) simply states the basic foundationalist thesis. Premise (2) says that every belief must be justified by a reason even if that reason is self-evident or inherent in the basic belief in question. Premise (5) states that empirical beliefs must have some empirical input, otherwise they wouldn't be empirical. So BonJour thinks that the foundationalist must find a way to reject either (3) or (4).

The Externalist Response

Regarding (3), the foundationalist may object that it is not necessary that the person for whom a belief is basic be able to know, let alone show to another person, that the basic belief is justified. This may be called the *externalist* (or *reliabilist*) ploy. In this externalist version, as long as the belief is caused in the right way, it doesn't matter whether the subject is aware of the belief, let alone can explain how it serves as a basic belief. So the thesis that one must be in cognitive possession of the justifying reason is to be rejected. Proponents of this position are D. M. Armstrong, Alvin Goldman, William Alston, and Fred Dretske. We will briefly consider this position here but deal more fully with it in chapter 8.

There are weaknesses in externalism. First, exactly what counts as a reliable belief-forming process or mechanism is vague. Specifying the necessary and sufficient conditions for a reliable process has throttled the project. Furthermore, we can imagine reliable processes that yield true beliefs where we would not want to say the subject was justified. Alvin Plantinga gives the example of a brain lesion that causes havoc in one's noetic structure, producing mostly false beliefs, except for the notable exception that it causes the subject to believe that he has a brain lesion. The subject is not warranted in believing he has a brain tumor, even though it has been reliably produced. Other counterexamples have been offered as well. We will examine the doctrine of reliabilism, or externalism, in chapters 8 through 10. Meanwhile, let's look at another response of the foundationalist.

The Internalist Response

The second way to save foundationalism would be to reject premise (4). This is a common internalist response, which agrees with BonJour that the subject must be *in some sense* in cognitive possession of the appropriate justification. However, continues the foundationalist, this awareness of the reason for the basic belief is an immediate awareness or self-evident intuition, which needs no further justification. This is sometimes called the idea of the *given*, that empirically basic beliefs are simply given or presented and cannot have (or need not have) any further justification. Internalists Roderick Chisholm and Paul Moser hold this view and have attempted to defend the thesis against critics like BonJour. They argue that the argument from ascent is not decisive against them.[9]

The concept of the *given* refers to an immediate apprehension of the contents of one's sense experience. It is always expressed in the first person, present tense, reporting direct appearances, as in "I seem to see a red tomato in front of me," "I am appeared to redly," or "I feel a throbbing pain just above my left eye." Classical foundationalists held that such apprehensions are absolutely certain, infallible, and incorrigible, so that if the subject believes he or she is so appeared to, he or she is and can be said to know this.

As we mentioned earlier in this chapter, the thesis dates back to Descartes, who argued in *Meditations* (II) that it was beyond all possible doubt and error that he seemed to see light, hear sounds, have sweet tastes, and feel the texture of objects. The empiricists, Locke and Hume, went even further in building their systems entirely on such foundational impressions. In the twentieth century, C. I. Lewis, H. H. Price, and A. J. Ayer, among others, appealed to the given as self-justifying and as offering a secure basis for empirical knowledge.[10]

The idea of the given was first challenged by Kant in his *Critique of Pure Reason* (1781). He argued that thoughts without content are empty, percepts without concepts are blind. Being noncognitive, percepts or sensations cannot serve as epistemic foundations. As Alan Goldman comments, once we recognize that we must apply concepts of properties to appearances and that we must formulate beliefs utilizing those concepts before the appearances can play any epistemic role, it becomes more plausible that such beliefs are fallible.[11] Kant's insight was developed by Wilfred Sellars, who first called it the Myth of the Given in 1963. Sellars argued that the doctrine of the given involves a confusion between (1) sensing particulars (mere percepts or sense impressions), which are nonepistemic, and (2) having noninferential knowledge of propositions referring to appearances. Sensing impressions are necessary for acquiring perceptual knowledge, but impressions are not themselves a kind of knowing. The same quality that renders them immune from error—their immediate, precontent-laden aspect— also makes them unsuitable for epistemological foundations. Noninferential perceptual knowledge, on the other hand, is fallible and requires the acquisition of concepts mediated through a public language. As such, there is no independent given in experience. What we take as the given is the result of trained responses to public physical objects. Here is Alan Goldman's version of the critique (or myth) of the given.

> The contention that even reports of appearances are fallible can be supported from several directions. First, it seems doubtful that we can look beyond our beliefs to compare them with an unconceptualized reality, whether mental or physical. Second, to judge that anything, including an appearance, is *F*, we must remember which property *F* is, and memory is admitted by all to be fallible. Our ascribing *F* is normally not explicitly comparative, but its correctness requires memory nevertheless, at least if we intend to ascribe the concept *F* consistently, and it seems always at least logically possible to apply it inconsistently. If the latter is not possible, if, e.g., I intend in referring to an appearance merely to pick out demonstratively whatever property appears, then I seem not to be expressing a genuine belief. My apprehension of the appearance will not justify any other beliefs. Once more it will be unsuitable as an epistemic foundation.[12]

Whether you think that the given is a myth or a valid basis for foundationalism will depend on whether you believe that sensations can themselves provide sufficient content to ground knowledge or that nondoxastic states (e.g., percepts) are adequate to ground perceptual knowledge.

Before we decide whether the idea of the given is salvageable, let us look in the next chapter at the main rival to foundationalism, coherentism.

Summary

Foundationalism provides an appealing answer to the regress problem. Its structure seems to mirror our conscious experience in inferring some beliefs from more basic or more certain others. However, classical foundationalism, with its requirements of self-evidence and incorrigibility, has severe problems. Contemporary foundationalists have opted for fallibilist versions of foundationalism. In this chapter we have noted two cogent criticisms of foundationalism: the epistemic ascent argument and the argument based on the myth of the given. In the next chapter, after examining coherentist accounts of justification, we will return to foundationalism.

QUESTIONS FOR DISCUSSION

1. Analyze the notions of self-evidence and incorrigibility. Are they clear notions? Or should they be replaced by more adequate concepts?

2. What is the key difference between classical and contemporary foundationalists? Why have contemporary foundationalists modified the classical position?

3. What is the regress problem? Discuss how various theories try to solve it.

4. Go over the critique of foundationalism. What is the ascent argument? Assess its merits.

5. Explain the so-called myth of the given. How does it bear on foundationalist claims? How might foundationalists respond to it?

6. Crispin Sartwell claims that it is inconsistent to hold that epistemic justification is only of instrumental value to knowledge and yet is logically necessary for knowledge.

   > It is inconsistent to build a specification of something regarded *merely* as a means of achieving some goal into the description of the goal itself; in such circumstances the goal can be described independently of the means. So, if justification is demanded because it is instrumental to true belief, it cannot also be maintained that knowledge is justified true belief. (Sartwell, "Why Knowledge Is Merely True Belief," *Journal of Philosophy* 89 (1992), 167–180)

   Is Sartwell correct? Discuss this criticism of the idea that knowledge entails justification.

NOTES

1. St. Thomas Aquinas, *Summa Theologica* (London: Benziger Brothers, 1911), I2ae, Q57, a2.
2. René Descartes, *Rules for the Direction of the Mind* (1644). In *The Philosophical Works of Descartes,* trans. by G. Ross and Elizabeth Haldane (Cambridge: Cambridge University Press, 1911), vol. 1:7.
3. J. Dancy and E. Sosa ed., *A Companion to Epistemology* (Oxford: Blackwell, 1992). Here is how *A Companion to Epistemology* defines *self-evidence:*
   Self-evident propositions are those evident in themselves or known independently of all other propositions and evidence. To comprehend such a proposition is to be fully justified in believing it, or to know it. Such propositions might include first, some necessary truths of logic, for example laws of noncontradiction and identity; second, analytically true propositions, such as *all*

bachelors are unmarried; and third, some contingent propositions, such *as I exist* or *I am appeared to redly.* (Alan Goldman, 466)

4. *A Companion to Epistemology* gives this definition of *incorrigibility:*
   Incorrigible impossibility of one's being refuted, corrected, shown to be mistaken, in a belief, though there is a persistent misuse of the term for the impossibility of being mistaken (infallibility). As with infallibility, incorrigibility is most often asserted of one's beliefs about ocurrent states of consciousness. It is plausible to think that a person is the final authority on what he is thinking, feeling, or sensing at the moment, and that his sincere report will always prevail against any counter-evidence. On the other hand, it seems plausible to suppose that physiological psychology could develop to the point that we would be justified in preferring neutral readings to the subject's report where they conflicted. (William Alston, 195).

5. Descartes, *The Philosophical Works of Descartes* vol. 1: 162.

6. For a discussion of these points see the articles by A. K. Stout, Harry Frankfurt, Emile Brehier, Anthony Kenny, and Alan Gewirth in *Descartes: A Collection of Essays,* ed. Willis Doney (London: Macmillan, 1968).

7. Laurence BonJour, *The Structure of Empirical Knowledge* (Cambridge, MA: Harvard University Press, 1985), 31–32. I have altered the argument slightly to bring out its fuller implications.

8. Ibid.

9. See Roderick Chisholm, *Theory of Knowledge,* 3d ed. (Englewood Cliffs, NJ: Prentice Hall, 1985) and Paul Moser, *Epistemic Justification* (Dordrecht, Holland: D. Reidel, 1985), Chapter IV. My discussion is indebted to Alan Goldman's article in *A Companion to Epistemology,* ed. J. Dancy and E. Sosa (Oxford: Blackwell, 1992), 159–162.

10. H. H. Price, *Perception* (London: Allen & Unwin, 1932); C. I. Lewis, *An Analysis of Knowledge and Valuation* (LaSalle, IL: Open Court, 1946); A. J. Ayer, *The Foundations of Empirical Knowledge* (London: Macmillan, 1969).

11. Goldman, in *Companion A.*

12. Goldman's own attempt to save the given is to use the strategy of arguing to the best explanation.
    A better strategy is to tie an account of self-justification to a broader exposition of epistemic warrant. One such account sees justification as a kind of inference to the best explanation. A belief is shown to be justified if its truth is shown to be part of the best explanation for why it is held. A belief is self-justified if the best explanation for it is its truth alone. The best explanation for my belief that I am appeared to redly may be that I am. Such accounts seek to ground knowledge in perceptual experience without appealing to an infallible given, now universally dismissed. (Goldman, 159–161)

FOR FURTHER READING

Alston, William. "Two Types of Foundationalism." *Journal of Philosophy* 73 (1976). Reprinted in his book *Epistemic Justification: Essays in the Theory of Knowledge* (Ithaca, N.Y.: Cornell University Press, 1990).

——. "Concepts of Epistemic Justification" *The Monist 68* (1985). Also in *Epistemic Justification.*

Ayer, A. J. *The Foundations of Empirical Knowledge.* New York: St. Martin's Press, 1955.

BonJour, Laurence. *The Structure of Empirical Knowledge.* Cambridge, MA: Harvard University Press, 1985.

Butchvarov, Panayot. *The Concept of Knowledge.* Evanston, IL: Northwestern University Press, 1970.

Chisholm, Roderick. *The Foundations of Knowing.* Minneapolis: University of Minnesota Press, 1982.

Chisholm, Roderick, and Robert Schwartz, eds. *Empirical Knowledge.* Englewood Cliffs, NJ: Prentice Hall, 1973.

Foley, Richard. *The Theory of Epistemic Rationality.* Cambridge, MA: Harvard University Press, 1987.

Goldman, Alvin. *Epistemology and Cognition.* Cambridge, MA: Harvard University Press, 1986.

Lehrer, Keith. *Knowledge.* Oxford: Clarendon Press, 1974.

——. *Theory of Knowledge.* Boulder, CO: Westview, 1990.

Lewis, C. I. *An Analysis of Knowledge and Valuation.* LaSalle, IL: Open Court, 1946.

Moser, Paul. *Empirical Justification.* Boston: D. Reidel, 1985.

Moser, Paul, ed. *Empirical Knowledge.* Totowa, NJ: Rowman & Littlefield, 1986.

Pappas, George, ed. *Justification and Knowledge.* Dordrecht, Holland: D. Reidel, 1979.

Pappas, George, and Marshall Swain, eds. *Essays on Knowledge and Justification.* Ithaca, NY: Cornell University Press, 1978.

Pollock, John. *Contemporary Theories of Knowledge.* Totowa, NJ: Rowman & Littlefield, 1986.

Sosa, Ernest. "The Foundations of Foundationalism," *Nous* 14 (1980).

Van Cleve, James. "Foundationalism, Epistemic Principles and the Cartesian Circle," *Philosophical Review* 88 (1979).

CHAPTER 7

Theories of Justification (II): Coherentism and Modest Foundationalism

The totality of our so-called knowledge or beliefs, from the most casual matters of geography and history to the profoundest laws of atomic physics or even of our mathematics and logic, is a man-made fabric which impinges on experience only along the edges. Or, to change the figure, total science is like a field of force whose boundary conditions are experience. A conflict with experience at the periphery occasions readjustments in the interior field. Truth values have to be redistributed over some of our statements. Reevaluation of some statements entails reevaluation of others, because of their logical interconnections—the logical laws being in turn simply certain further statements of the system, certain further elements of the field. Having reevaluated one statement we must reevaluate some others, which may be statements logically connected to the first or may be the statements of logical connections themselves. But the total field is so underdetermined by its boundary conditions, experience, that there is much latitude of choice as to what statements to reevaluate in the light of any single contrary experience. No particular experiences are linked with any particular statements in the interior of the field, except indirectly through considerations of equilibrium affecting the field as a whole.

If this view is correct, it is misleading to speak of the empirical content of an individual statement—especially if it is a statement at all remote from the experiential periphery of the field. Furthermore, it becomes folly to seek a boundary between synthetic statements, which hold come what may. Any statement can be held true come what may, if we make drastic enough adjustments elsewhere in the system. Even a statement very close to the periphery can be held true in the face of recalcitrant evidence by pleading hallucination or by amending certain statements of the kind called logical laws. Conversely, by the same token, no statement is immune to revision. Revision even of the logical law of the excluded middle has been proposed as a means of simplifying quantum mechanics; and what difference is there in principle between such a shift and the shift whereby Kepler superceded Ptolemy, or Einstein Newton, or Darwin Aristotle? (W. V. Quine)[1]

Varieties of Coherentism

There have always been coherence theories of truth, theories that state that the truth resides in the Absolute System of knowledge. Plato's theory of the Real could be interpreted as an absolute system of truth, wherein the forms cohere in a grand unified design. In more recent times Georg W. F. Hegel (1770–1831), Francis H. Bradley (1846–1924), and Brand Blanshard (1892–1987) held the view that truth was defined not as the correspondence of propositions with facts but as integrated and absolute wholes in which individual propositions received justification and relative truth credentials.[2] In its strong version, every true belief is entailed by every other belief or proposition in the coherent system. Absolute Truth, which no mortal possesses, consists in knowing All, every true proposition in the universe. Our finite knowledge only approximates this Absolute Truth. In a sense, we don't know anything, since all our beliefs are incomplete, but we can be said to know in part, in degrees, and by increasing our understanding, we can increase the degrees of knowledge. We have already examined the coherence theory of truth along with its rivals in chapter 1 of this book.

However, most contemporary coherentists, like W. V. Quine, Wilfred Sellars, Gilbert Harman, Keith Lehrer, and Laurence BonJour, reject the coherence theory of truth as an implausible metaphysical doctrine and adhere instead to a coherentist theory of justification.[3] Individual beliefs are justified by the entire system of beliefs in which they cohere. All justification is inferential, so the notion of proper basicality is a contradiction in terms.

There are several versions of coherentism. The most basic two are *linear* and *holistic* coherentism. In linear coherentism, a belief B_1 gets its justification from belief B_2, which in turn gets its support from $B_3 \ldots$, B_{n1}, which gets its support from B_n, which finally gets its support from B_1. The process is an example of the circular scheme discussed in chapter 6. We found it to be an implausible attempt at escaping the regress problem, since it does not explain how simply moving in a circle can justify anything. If B_1 doesn't have any positive epistemic warrant in its own and B_2, . . . do not have any warrant in their own rights, how can the whole receive positive epistemic status?

Holistic Coherentism is nonlinear. A belief does not receive positive epistemic status merely from other beliefs, but by playing an important role in a total system of beliefs. Picture a three-dimensional web, such as a bee's nest or spider web, in which each belief is a connecting node, held together by other beliefs. Most contemporary coherentists reject the simple linear mode of inference, instead accepting this holistic model, wherein a target belief may receive support from many different kinds of propositions. Unlike foundationalism, support is symmetrical and reciprocal. That is, belief *A* may support *B*, and in a complex way *B* may support *A*. Coherentism is a theory that requires that our belief system functions as a whole, is more or less consistent, and provides the best explanation of the relevant facts.

Consider your belief that you are seeing a certain object before you. Say it is a red tomato. The coherentist avers that what seems like a simple perception is really a very complicated process. In the first place, to understand what *red* and *tomato* mean involves a rich conceptual scheme, consisting in understanding (to some adequate degree) the idea of colors, vegetables, food, and physical objects. A baby lacks all of these concepts, and most animals probably do too. Your belief must be consistent with other beliefs, such as that you are awake and not hallucinating, that the tomato is not simply a wax replica, that the lighting is normal, and that you are at a proper distance from the tomato to discern it as such, distinguishing it from a red pepper (for instance).

A more theoretical example of a coherent justification would be Sherlock Holmes' solving a murder. He takes disparate clues—the various footprints, the print type of the newsprint left at the scene of the crime, the motives, and methods of execution—and he somehow puts them together, arguing to the best explanation, arriving at a sound judgment as to who, why, and how regarding the murder.

Or consider: You are awakened in the middle of the night by noise in the hallway. Your first thought is that an intruder is in your house. But then you remember that your cat has a rubber ball tied to a string with which he loves to play. You reflect that an intruder would probably make a different kind of noise, perhaps more regular and heavier. Your neighborhood has always been free from burglary. These beliefs make it more likely that it is the cat rather than a burglar who is making the noise outside your room. If suddenly you should hear heavy footsteps coming toward your room, this would disconfirm the cat hypothesis. If you heard meowing, that would confirm the cat hypothesis.

This illustration features several characteristics of Coherentism. First, the belief that the cat is making the noise is not a foundational or basic belief, nor is it derived from one. Second, the belief is the outcome of a complex set of relevant beliefs, including the ruling out of the intruder hypothesis. Third, accepting the cat hypothesis confirms the beliefs that supported it, namely, my belief that cats like to play with balls and that they can see in poor lighting; my antecedent belief that intruders and burglars don't haunt our neighborhood; and my belief that they could not perform so quietly in my house. Finally, coherentism states that justification is a matter of degrees. If I heard meowing, the degree of justification would be increased. If I heard a lamp fall over and crash against the floor, my degree of justification would probably diminish.

Objections to Coherentism

The question is whether coherence is a necessary and sufficient condition for justification. Three classic criticisms have been offered to coherence as a sufficient condition: the isolation, or alternative systems, objection; the lack of input objection; and the infinite regress objection. We will examine each of these as well as a fourth, more general objection. We will offer two objections to coherence as a necessary condition: the lottery objection and the countercoherence objection. Let us turn to the criticisms of the sufficiency condition.

The Alternative Systems Objection

The alternative systems (or worlds) objection states that the coherence of a theory is inadequate as a theory of justification since by itself it doesn't tell us how to *distinguish* between alternative, mutually incompatible coherent belief systems. It is true that an infinite number of belief systems can be consistent and mutually supportive, but how may we decide which one is true or closest to the truth? Each individual explanation or theory simply has too many competitors. Fairy tales may sometimes be coherent, as may dreams and hallucinations. Astrology may be as coherent as astronomy or Ptolemaic physics, or perhaps as coherent as Einsteinian physics. But surely, the objection runs, if we can't determine which of these internally consistent systems is more likely to be true, we are not justified in believing one over another. We are left with skepticism. Consistency may, in general, be a necessary condition for justification (though see a later discussion), but it is not a sufficient condition for justification.

Bruce Russell illustrates this objection this way.

> [Coherence is] not sufficient because one can imagine situations in which one's beliefs remain coherent, but fixed as one's experiences change. Suppose I hike up Skyline Ridge near Mt. Baker in Washington and form the beliefs typically produced by the experiences associated with hiking in mountainous terrain. I believe, for instance, that I am walking briskly along a trail through some woods, that the air is cool, and that the sun is shining at an oblique angle through the trees. Suppose, now, that I am riding home in the backseat of an automobile and my experiences are those one typically has when traveling along. But suppose, also, for some odd reason, that my beliefs remain those coherent ones I had while hiking down the mountain trail. Despite having the experience of seeing the paved road, the fences, the grassland besides the road, of smelling the cigar smoke in the car, and so on, I still believe that I am hiking down the shaded trail in the open air. Although my beliefs form a coherent set, the ones about my hiking down the shaded trail would not be justified and not properly basic. Hence, coherence is not sufficient for a belief to be justified for some one.[4]

Alternative, mutually incompatible coherent systems of belief are equally justified on the holistic coherentist account. But this must either be false or leave us with skepticism. Surely something—namely a criterion for distinguishing the veracity of belief systems—is missing. Can the coherentist provide an additional criterion for distinguishing valid and invalid systems? If not, then how can we decide between them? Perhaps the coherentist is forced to accept a set of foundational beliefs or an a priori core, but then this is no longer pure Coherentism. It is a mixed system of foundationalism and coherentism. This leads to the second objection.

The Input Objection

Coherence consists *wholly* in a set of mutually supportive internal connections between beliefs. As such, coherence lacks criteria connecting it with the external world. As we saw in considering the alternative systems objection, this leads to absurd consequences. What is lacking is input from the world. Our empirical beliefs must be caused in the right way by the external world in order to be true. Otherwise, they are detached from reality. Observational beliefs that are *noninferential* in character play this causal role. They must be the foundations of an adequate belief system.

The Infinite Regress Objection

One of the most rigorous, and to my mind, cogent versions of holistic coherentism is that of BonJour. Like most recent versions of coherentism, it is internalist. That is, it requires that the believer have *access* to those beliefs that justify his or her beliefs. We saw how this worked in BonJour's epistemic ascent argument against foundationalism. The believer must be able to justify the inference process that links the foundational belief to the justification result. But the ascent argument can be used to undermine coherentism as well, as Paul Moser points out.[5]

Recall that holistic internal coherentism holds that one's entire system of beliefs is the source of empirical justification. So any particular belief must derive its individual justification from its cohering with the holistic system. As BonJour says, when criticizing foundationalism, "If a particular belief B is to be justified for a particular person by virtue of possessing [a certain] property, then (if externalism is to be avoided) that person must believe with justification that B does in fact have this property."[6] But given the access requirement, the individual must also be able to access one's overall belief system or at least show that a given belief B_1 coheres with the set of beliefs S. We may call this third belief A. But we must go on to justify A by appealing to its being justified in coherent system S. Call this new belief A_1. But A_1 must also be justified within set S and so on.

A: My belief set is S and B_1 coheres with S.

A_1: My belief set is S and A coheres with S.

A_2: My belief set is S and A_1 coheres with S.

    . . .

Some Coherentist Replies to Criticisms

The coherentist has replies to all of these objections. To the *infinite regress* objection, the coherentist might reply that the objection confuses the process of discovering whether a belief is justified with the status of actually being justified. I may never finish the job of completely justifying all my beliefs to myself or anyone else. As finite beings with finite capacities living in time, we must stop the justification process somewhere, but the question of whether a belief is justified or not is determined by the objective fact of whether or not it coheres with a total system of belief. Either it does cohere or it doesn't. If it doesn't, it isn't justified. If it does, it is justified.

To the alternative systems objection, which holds that there may be many mutually incompatible coherent systems that are equally coherent, Blanshard has offered a reply:

> The [coherence] theory does not hold that any and every system is true, no matter how abstract and limited; it holds that one system only is true, namely the system in which everything real and possible is coherently included.[7]

No doubt we would not always be able to distinguish between two apparently coherent incompatible systems, but in reality they would be *unequally* coherent. By close examination, we can usually discover which of two systems is closer to the truth.

One problem with such an idealized notion of truth and justification is that it removes the concepts from their normal use by fallible individuals. We may well believe that truth is ultimately one without also believing that our justified beliefs depend on their ultimate coherence in the true system. Note Blanshard's system involves coherent relations between *propositions*, but it is our beliefs that we are concerned about justifying. We may raise an objection: By making justification consist in a set of coherent propositions, rather than beliefs, Blanshard removes the subject of justification from the normal everyday world of our concern. How do we know whether any of our beliefs are about the correct propositions in the True Coherent System? As Kierkegaard said of Hegel's System, God may have such a System of Truth, but we mortals must live with more existential, partially justified beliefs. Justification would seem inaccessible to us. I won't pursue this criticism but leave it for your consideration.

Lehrer has sought to overcome the objections to Coherentism by defining the coherence of a statement p as p's being believed to have a better chance of being true than any of its competitors within a doxastic system containing only those beliefs held on truth-seeking grounds.

> (cj) S is completely justified in believing that p if and only if, within the corrected doxastic system of S, p is believed to have a better chance of being true than the denial of p or any other statement that competes with p.

The account of complete justification is a coherence theory in which the relation of coherence is explicated in terms of a statement being believed to have a better chance of truth than its competitors within a system of a specified sort. The system is a set of statements describing the beliefs a man would retain were he to purge his beliefs to bring them in

line with an impartial and disinterested search for truth, that is, the beliefs he would retain as a veracious man.[8]

Lehrer goes on to allow for a plurality of such systems. "Our epistemology, being doxastic, is at the same time pluralistic. It assumes
the competence of man in his quest for truth."[9] But, the question is,
What reason is there for supposing that our corrected systems are
true? Why should we believe that a person's belief that within the correct coherent system p is any more likely to be true than the rival's belief that not-p within an uncorrected system? In a later book Lehrer
develops his theory further by claiming that superior coherence entails *reasonableness*.

> p coheres with the acceptance system of S at t if and only if it is more
> reasonable for S to accept p than to accept any competing claim on the
> basis of the acceptance system of S at t.[10]

This might be helpful if Lehrer would only tell us what he means
by *reasonableness*, but unfortunately he doesn't (he regards it as a
primitive). On the face of it, what makes a belief reasonable for Lehrer
seems to be the fact that it *coheres* better with one's other beliefs! So
we have just gone around in circles. We seem to be assuming coherentism in order to justify it.

Another version of coherentism, one to which we have had occasion to refer, that has tried to meet these objections (especially the
isolation objection and no-input objection) is BonJour's moderate (or
impure) coherentism.[11] BonJour tries to show how observation beliefs get worked into a coherentist network. He appeals to a principle
of introspection (that introspective beliefs of the appropriate kind are
very likely to be true) and from there gets to spontaneous beliefs
about the physical world. If a system of beliefs that is coherent but
does not correspond with the world receives perceptual input from
the world, that system will either change, becoming more coherent,
or be regarded as incoherent.

But why must this be so? Why couldn't a person compartmentalize
his or her perceptual beliefs and his or her other beliefs? Or why
couldn't a person be led by certain observations to a false coherent
system? BonJour seems to assume that coherence tends toward truth,
but he owes us a better defense of this than he has given.

Overall, BonJour is vague on why coherence should require such
input. In fact, BonJour's system, with its strong empirical requirement
(he says it is a priori), turns out to be virtually indistinguishable from
a weak foundational system. (I'll discuss this later in this chapter.)

Additional Problems with Coherentism

Not only is coherence not *sufficient* for justification, but it may not be *necessary* either. In certain circumstances we may acquire beliefs that seem justified without cohering with the rest of our beliefs. Suppose that in 1493, Columbus's sister, upon hearing persuasive testimony of Columbus's discovery of America, suddenly came to believe that the world was not flat. Suppose that in her mind she still had a coherent flat earth picture. Perhaps in time the coherent picture would be corrected, but, meanwhile, wouldn't she be justified in accepting the evidence for a round earth with a new continent even though that belief did not cohere with her overall system? In fact, most of us have inaccurate pictures of world geography in our minds, but we may nevertheless be justified in believing that Burkina Faso borders Ghana, even though we have an inaccurate picture of where both countries are located in Africa, and even though our beliefs about the relative size and positions of African nations are incoherent.

Adherents of coherence theories hold that justification minimally requires logical consistency. But it may be the case that justification doesn't always require even this seemingly basic condition. Richard Foley argues that the lottery paradox shows that one can have inconsistent justified beliefs. Suppose you know that 1,000 lottery tickets have been sold to 1,000 different people and that only 1 person will win. You believe that person 1 (P1) will lose, that person 2 (P2) will lose, . . . , that person 1,000 (P1000) will lose, yet you also believe that 1 of these 1,000 persons will win. This is a contradiction, since you believe both that neither P1, P2, . . . , P1000 will win, but at the same time that either P1 or P2 or . . . P1000 will win. Yet, your belief seems justified.[12]

Several philosophers have tried to solve the lottery paradox. The coherentist Lehrer argues that we cannot be completely justified in believing of any particular person P1 through P1000 that he or she will lose the lottery, so the ideal believer will withhold assent. But, Lehrer also holds that the ideal rational believer will be interested in maximizing true beliefs and minimizing the number of false beliefs. Hence, it would make sense to believe that none of the 1,000 participants will win, since that way we will maximize the number of true beliefs (we will have 999 true beliefs and 1 false belief rather than 0 false beliefs and 0 true beliefs).[13] Furthermore, I don't see how we can help believing that each of the participants will lose the lottery. If there is a 99.9 percent chance that it will rain today, won't I automatically believe it? And won't I be justified in believing that it will rain?

I suppose the odds of dying when jumping off the Empire State Building are about 999 to 1. If I believe only what is completely justified (in Lehrer's sense), I won't believe that the person who jumps off the Empire State Building will die since there is an infinitesimal chance that he or she will survive the fall.

There is probably a .001 chance that I am wrong about virtually any empirical belief for which I have good evidence. So, Lehrer's coherentist defense against the lottery paradox would land us into a form of skepticism. Of course, skepticism may be true (what are the odds that it isn't?), but if we're justified in rejecting skepticism, we're probably also justified in believing propositions where the probability is less than .999.

Intuitions differ on these matters. For example, I once asked Gilbert Harman how he got around the evidence that there was a 99.9 percent probability that each of the lottery participants would lose. He replied that he didn't see any problem here. He didn't have any beliefs about the participants one way or the other.[14] If you can come up with a convincing way to solve the paradox, you won't accept it as a strike against coherentism. However, if you think that it shows that we can be justified in holding inconsistent beliefs, then it does provide an additional reason to reject coherentism. My own view is that the paradox can be solved by a fine-grained analysis of belief. In cases like lotteries we may be said not merely to believe of any given ticket that it will lose but that the likelihood of it losing has a certain probability. If you have 1 of 1,000 lottery tickets, I believe of you and every other holder of 1 ticket, not simply that you will lose (the coarse analysis), but that the probability of your losing is .999. But this view is controversial, so I leave it to you to work out your own views on the matter.[15]

Moderate Foundationalism

In light of these criticisms many philosophers, though by no means all, have given up coherentism. This is not to deny that coherentism can play an auxiliary role in the justification process or that coherence is important in providing internal consistency in our belief systems. A number of philosophers, including Robert Audi, William Alston, and Alan Goldman have attempted to incorporate coherentist elements into versions of foundationalism.[16] Audi accepts negative coherence as a constraint on foundational systems. That is, if one finds that his or her doxastic system is inconsistent, and hence incoherent, it is not warranted. Audi argues that in apparent counterexamples to consistency, such as the lottery paradox, we do not know that we won't win, since there is a chance that we will. We should only believe that we probably won't win the lottery. It also may be the case that coherentism provides a general framework for beliefs, which *contributes* to their justification.

Foundationalists like Audi and Alston who attempt to work the insights of coherentism into their epistemology provide a highly qualified, modest foundational theory. It consists of the following features:

1. An asymmetrical relationship exists between the foundations and the superstructure. Basic beliefs support inferential beliefs but need not derive support from those nonbasic beliefs. Of course, the basic beliefs *may* receive support from the nonbasic ones, but in such cases the justification is *overdetermined*. The additional justification is not essential.

2. Doubts about any psychological beliefs (beliefs about our mental states, e.g., our desires) being indubitable or incorrigible are allowed. Basic beliefs need not be infallible nor need they result in a system that is completely true. All that is required is that the basic beliefs be truth indicative, having a presumption of truth in their favor.

3. Basicality is person relative. Almost any belief can be basic for a person under certain circumstances. No particular type of content is required.

4. The primary foundational relationship is justification of belief rather than knowledge, although knowledge is the goal of believing and may also be conceived as foundational.

5. While classical foundationalism allowed only deductive inferences from the basic to the superstructure beliefs, moderate foundationalists allow superstructure beliefs to be only inductively based on basic beliefs. That is, the transmission of justification from the basic to the nonbasic beliefs is more flexible than allowed in classical foundationalism. This is related to feature 2. By relinquishing deductive certainty for the wider expanse of induction-induced beliefs, epistemic certainty is sacrificed for a belief system based on probabilities.

6. Coherence is allowed some scope in the justification process. It plays a negative role in foundational structures. If it is shown that our belief set is incoherent, it cannot be justified. For Audi and Alston, a justification of a belief can be overdetermined. That is, a belief may be justified by appeal to properly basic beliefs, but it

may, in addition, be justified by its cohering within a whole system of beliefs. The latter justification reinforces but does not replace the primary foundational justification.

7. One must distinguish between *having* a justification for a belief and being able to *show* that one has such. Moderate foundationalists argue that it is not necessary for a person to be able to show that he or she is justified in order for the justification to obtain. I may be justified in believing that Columbus discovered America in 1492 without being able at the moment of showing it.

Features 1, 2, and 4 seem self-explanatory and less controversial than the other points. What motivates feature 3 (the permissive latitude in counting almost any belief as a basic belief) is a fallibilist, person-relative notion of justification. For one person, empirical beliefs may be the only nonlogical posits allowed in the foundation, while for another person, beliefs originating in mystical experience may enter the foundations. Once we give up the requirement of infallibility of classical foundationalism, we are free to allow that different evidence can strike different individuals differently. This is perhaps because of a general coherentist feature in our noetic structure (feature 6). Things make sense as wholes, so that we cannot separate the content of our basic beliefs from the larger contexts. For example, a right-to-life advocate may hold the sanctity of all human life as a basic belief that justifies a general prohibition. But that basic belief also may cohere (though it need not) in a total worldview, perhaps in a religious belief system like Catholic theology. On the other hand, a secularist may hold as a basic belief that the moral principle not to kill innocent humans does not apply to fetuses, since his or her definition of humanity is based on a theory of human rights or personality, which requires that certain features be present (such as rational self-consciousness). This view of human personality may itself inhere within a wider worldview of evolution.

Again, turning to feature 5, which expands on what may count as a properly basic belief, the modest foundationalist allows for inductively derived beliefs in the superstructure. Statistical and probable beliefs are justified by being derived from observational beliefs, with the admission that what we are justified in believing may not yield truth.

Fallibilist foundationalism purports to get around the problem of the *given* (discussed in chapter 6) by dropping the need for an infallible foundation for our beliefs. Our basic beliefs are simply self-justified—innocent until proven guilty—or assumed to have been caused by *nondoxastic* states (that is, immediate experience, in which case the coherentist motto that only a belief can justify a belief would be false).

We need not insist on an infallible or incorrigible belief, let alone an empirically incorrigible one, to be justified in holding that a particular belief is basic for us at this point in time. Our memory belief that we made a promise yesterday to help our neighbor today justifies us in believing that today we have an obligation to help our neighbor. Our memory belief need not be incorrigible, let alone infallible. It still functions in a justificatory role.

Feature 7 is also important in the modest foundationalist theory. For one thing, it gets around the ascent argument discussed in the last chapter. Recall BonJour's objection that for the foundationalist to be justified in believing that belief *B* is properly justified, he or she must be able to justify that the given belief is of the relevant justifying type. Modest foundationalists distinguish between *having* a justification and *being able to show* that a given belief is justified. You might not be able to say exactly how your belief is justified—perhaps you don't understand the logic of justification, let alone foundationalism. Or, you may have forgotten the basic belief that grounds your derived belief; still justification is transferred from the forgotten belief to the derived one. In an externalist view of justification, one need not ever have been aware of the justifying ground for the derived belief (see chapter 8).

But as soon as we reach this point of accepting modest foundationalism (supposing we do), a problem arises. We must ask ourselves, "What is the justification for my accepting modest foundationalism?" When I ask myself that hypothetical question, I cannot find a foundational answer. Instead, I am forced to conclude that the meaning of justification is best explained by modest foundationalism. But why does it provide the best explanation of the meaning of a justified set of beliefs? Because it coheres better than other theories with our overall epistemological beliefs.

Sometimes I'm inclined to split the difference. Foundational processes seem to function on the level of logical, perceptual, memorial, and testimonial beliefs; but coherence processes seem to predominate with regard to theoretical beliefs, such as metaethical, religious, political, and metaphysical beliefs. Some perceptual beliefs seem to be based in nondoxastic states: Blue light causes me to believe that I am seeing blue. My memory belief just has the self-authenticating feel to it, and logical beliefs (e.g., of the form: that both p and not-p cannot be true) are indubitable. I find myself trusting the testimony of certain people without hesitation or by inferring the testimony reports from more basic premises.

On the other hand, my moral, political, metaphysical, and religious beliefs are generally based on complex considerations having to do with the best explanation of data and with coherence of relevant features. If there are foundational aspects to them, they probably have that appearance because I have forgotten how I justified them at an earlier point. A modest foundationalist would probably say that if I accepted these higher-order beliefs on the basis of testimony, then the original testimony belief (e.g., my mother told me God exists) is sufficient for proper basicality. Perhaps this is so for a child or a sheltered adult, but it is hard to see how a reflective young adult in our society can continue to hold to metaphysical beliefs simply on the testimony of others. We know too much about human fallibility to be content with that. So, contra Descartes and the classical foundationalists, we can lose our basic beliefs and change the structure of the justification of any particular belief. I will illustrate the way beliefs are justified in the last chapters of this book.

Nondoxastic Foundationalism and the Given

There is one further issue to discuss in this chapter: the second response to the coherentist criticism of foundationalism. Recall our discussion of the given from the last chapter. We noted that Sellars had argued that noninferential perceptual knowledge requires a cognitive aspect mediated through concepts, but all that foundationalists are able to come up with in the empirical foundations are noncognitive sense impressions. So foundationalism, relying as it does on the notion of the given, is a doctrine that lacks support.

We saw one attempt to meet this objection in the modest foundational efforts to defend the notion that basic beliefs are self-justifying (unmoved movers). Both coherentists and moderate foundationalists agree that only a belief can justify another belief, but they disagree on how that justification can occur. Some foundationalists admit that the meaning of a concept is derived from language learning and is not necessarily foundational, but the belief to which the conceptual meanings attach may be basic, even though their meaning rests on coherence-like features. This has a certain plausibility.

However, there is a criticism of requiring that what is basic in a foundational structure must be a *belief*. And here we come to the second way to ground foundationalism: the nondoxastic ploy. John Pollock, although he calls his system *direct realism* rather than nondoxastic foundationalism, argues that derived beliefs may be based on the nondoxastic. First, Pollock argues that we often perceive things without being aware of them. He gives the following example:

> Suppose . . . that you are driving on an icy road and your car begins to skid. While you are fighting to regain control of your careening automobile you pass a bright red billboard. Because you are concentrating on controlling the car you may not notice the billboard, and if you do not then it seems that you form no beliefs about how you are appeared to relative to the billboard. Later, when you have brought your car safely to rest at the side of the road you may *relive* your frightening experience. The whole series of events may pass before your mind again, and this time you may notice the billboard. It seems that this sort of thing really does happen. But in order for it to happen, it seems clear that you must have perceived the billboard when you passed it. Thus you can have perceptual experiences without being aware of them.[17]

I've had the experience, while driving on a freeway on which I had never driven before, of getting off at the right exit while talking to my partner. My partner questions me, "Did you see a sign telling us to exit? I didn't." "I must have," I say as I begin to see other markings, informing me that I have indeed gotten off at the right exit. We recognize features of people's faces without being able to state exactly what they are. We unconsciously notice the decorations in a room and surprise ourselves by being able to describe the room after leaving it.

Traditional classical and moderate foundationalism are doxastic, positing beliefs about appearances in the foundations of our noetic structure, but, argues Pollock, we rarely have beliefs about how things appear to us. Yet, these appearances are basic sensations from which we infer beliefs. For example, from my basic unconscious perception of the highway sign, I derive the belief that I am getting off at the right exit. If this is so, then nondoxastic states can serve as basic posits in the foundations of our belief systems. If this conclusion is valid, then Sellars's critique of the given is mistaken. We can have sensory experience that is not a belief, and this sensory experience can cause beliefs in the right ways.

The critics of the *myth of the given* would reject Pollock's analysis, insisting that there is still a cognitive element in the unconscious perception that derives its meaning from a coherent system. The issue, then, boils down to whether the foundationalist can succeed in arguing that coherence of meaning does not affect the structural feature of the basing relationship.

Summary

In this chapter and the last, we have examined different versions of the two major theories of the structure of justification: foundationalism and coherentism. We saw that classical foundationalism, with its bold claims of complete certainty, simply couldn't justify itself. The proposition that all and only infallibly certain beliefs are allowed to serve as foundations in a theory of justification and knowledge is self-referentially incoherent. The proposition is not justified by its own criterion. Fallibilism seems a more reasonable position. We also noted attacks on the idea of the given, on which classical foundationalism depends.

Next, we examined two forms of coherentism: linear and holistic; we judged that only the holistic had much chance of succeeding. But several arguments were leveled against it: the isolation objection, the input objection, and the infinite regress objection. Furthermore, we argued that coherence was not a necessary condition for justification.

Then, we explored modest foundationalism, the theory that while foundationalism provides the predominant structure for justification, coherentist features may serve as vital parts of the overall system. I suggested that the truth might be that both theories may contribute to an ideal or complete theory of justification. It seems difficult to do without the foundational notion that some beliefs are more privileged or basic than others. Yet, the structure of our theoretical beliefs seems significantly coherentist. The challenge is to explain in greater detail what exactly the relationship is in this complete theory of justification.

Finally, we examined a second version of moderate foundationalism, Pollock's nondoxastic thesis, wherein not merely beliefs, but sensory experiences form the basis of the foundational structure. We saw this as a second attempt to defeat the myth of the given.

QUESTIONS FOR DISCUSSION

1. What is the difference between coherence theories of truth and coherence theories of justification?
2. Explain the difference between linear and holistic coherentism.
3. Examine the three main criticisms of coherentism in this chapter. How might the coherentist respond to these objections?
4. Discuss the objection that coherence is not even a necessary condition to justification. Do you accept the analysis of the lottery paradox given in this chapter? Does it imply that sometimes it's all right to believe contradictions knowingly?

5. Alvin Plantinga offers the following as a counterexample to the thesis that coherence is a necessary condition for justification (what he calls *warrant;* see chapter 9).

> You are an eminent but idiosyncratic Oxford epistemologist; I am an unduly impressionable undergraduate. You offer me a battery of complex and subtly powerful arguments for the conclusion that no one is ever appeared to redly. I am unable to withstand the force of your argumentation and am utterly convinced. The next day I am walking along High Street, reflecting on the significance of what you have proved to me, when suddenly a great large double-deck red bus runs up on the sidewalk just behind me. I turn around in terror, see the bus, and am (violently) appeared to redly; since I have been re-flecting about these matters, I notice (that is, believe) that I am thus appeared to. Unless my noetic structure undergoes instant metamor-phosis (and we can stipulate that it does not), my belief that I am appeared to redly will be incoherent with my noetic structure; never-theless it will have a considerable degree of warrant.[18]

Is this a good counterexample to the thesis that coherence is a necessary condition for justification? How might a coherentist respond?

6. Explain modest foundationalism. What are its strengths and weak-nesses? Is it too weak to constitute an interesting epistemic theory?

7. What is nondoxastic justification? Is it a form of foundationalism or a different theory altogether?

8. Review the ascent argument (from chapter 6). How does the moderate foundationalist attempt to get around this argument against foundationalism? Do you think it is successful?

9. What is Pollock's nondoxastic foundationalism? How plausible is it? Does it defeat the critique of those who argue that the myth of the given undermines foundationalism?

10. At the end of this chapter I suggested that we split the difference between coherentism and foundationalism, drawing on founda-tionalist insights to justify logical, perceptual, memorial, and tes-timonial beliefs, and drawing on coherentist structures to justify theoretical beliefs. Do you think this is plausible? What are the problems with it? Could coherentist structures be used to justify foundational beliefs? Explain your answer.

11. Examine the quotation from Quine at the beginning of this chap-ter. Can you apply it to your belief system? Is every belief open to revision? Can any belief be saved in spite of the evidence, come what may?

NOTES

1. W. V. Quine, *Two Dogmas of Empiricism* (Cambridge, MA: Harvard University Press, 1956).
2. Georg W. F. Hegel, *Science of Logic* (1813); Francis H. Bradley, *Essays on Truth and Reality* (Oxford: Clarendon Press, 1914); and Brand Blanshard, *The Nature of Thought* vol. 2 (London: Allen & Unwin, 1939). See the appendix for a description of coherence theories of truth.
3. Keith Lehrer, *Knowledge* (Oxford: Clarendon Press, 1974); Gilbert Harman, *Thought* (Princeton: Princeton University Press, 1973); W. V. Quine, *From a Logical Point of View* (Cambridge, MA: Harvard University Press, 1953); and Laurence BonJour, *The Structure of Empirical Knowledge* (Cambridge, MA: Harvard University Press, 1985).
4. Bruce Russell, "Two Forms of Ethical Skepticism." In *Ethical Theory: Classical and Contemporary Readings,* ed. Louis P. Pojman (Belmont, CA: Wadsworth, 1989), 462.
5. Paul Moser, *Knowledge and Evidence* (Cambridge: Cambridge University Press, 1989), 173–176. Richard Fumerton makes the same criticism in "A Critique of Coherentism." In *The Theory of Knowledge: Classical and Contemporary Readings,* ed. Louis P. Pojman (Belmont, CA: Wadsworth, 1993), 242.
6. BonJour, *Structure,* 80.
7. Blanshard, *The Nature of Thought* vol. 2, 276.
8. Lehrer, *Knowledge,* 198.
9. Ibid., 198.
10. Keith Lehrer, *Theory of Knowledge* (Boulder, CO: Westview Press, 1990), 117. See pages 127ff for a discussion of reasonableness and probability. Since a full analysis of Lehrer's intricate theory is beyond the scope of this work, I must refer you to this brilliant, comprehensive but complicated work.
11. BonJour, *Structure,* especially chapters 5–7. An early accessible version of BonJour's theory, *Holistic Coherentism,* can be found reprinted in Pojman's *The Theory of Knowledge* (Belmont, CA: Wadsworth, 1993).
12. Richard Foley, "Justified Inconsistent Beliefs," *American Philosophical Quarterly* 16 (1970), 247–258.
13. Lehrer, *Knowledge,* 191–208. My discussion has been influenced by Richard Fumerton's "A Critique of Coherentism" in my anthology *The Theory of Knowledge.*
14. In the NEH Seminar on Naturalism at the University of Nebraska in early July 1993.
15. Richard Jeffries says that probabilities are all there is to the formation of rational beliefs ("Dracula Meets Wolfman: Acceptance vs. Partial Belief." In *Induction, Acceptance and Rational Belief,* ed. Marshall Swain (Boston: D. Reidel, 1970), 157–85. The concept of belief will be discussed at length in chapter 15.
16. Robert Audi, *Belief, Justification and Knowledge* (Belmont, CA: Wadsworth, 1988). Also, Audi, "Contemporary Foundationalism," in Pojman, *The Theory of Knowledge* 2nd ed. (Belmont, CA: Wadsworth, 1999); William Alston, *Epistemic Justification: Essays in the Theory of Knowledge* (Ithaca, NY: Cornell University Press, 1989); and Alan Goldman, *Empirical Knowledge* (Berkeley: University of

California Press, 1988). For a nondoxastic version of foundationalism (though he does not call it that), see John Pollock, *Contemporary Theories of Knowledge* (Totowa, NJ: Rowman & Littlefield, 1986).

17. Pollock, *Contemporary Theories of Knowledge*, 59. Pollock actually tries to distinguish his view from foundationalism, but I think this is a mistake. It is just a different variety of it. It has the same essential structure.

18. Alvin Plantinga, *Warrant: The Current Debate* (Oxford: Oxford University Press, 1993).

FOR FURTHER READING

Alston, William. *The Reliability of Sense Perception*. Ithaca, NY: Cornell University, 1993.

Blanshard, Brand. *The Nature of Thought*. 2 vols. Allen & Unwin, 1940.

BonJour, Laurence. *The Structure of Empirical Knowledge*. Cambridge, MA: Harvard University Press, 1985.

Goldman, Alan. *Empirical Knowledge*. Berkeley: University of California Press, 1988.

Haack, Susan, "A Foundherentist Theory of Empirical Justification" in Louis Pojman, ed., *The Theory of Knowledge* (see below). An illuminating attempt to combine foundationalism with coherentism.

Lehrer, Keith. *Knowledge*. Oxford: Clarendon Press, 1974.

––––––. *Theory of Knowledge*. Boulder, CO: Westview, 1990.

Plantinga, Alvin. *Warrant: The Current Debate*. Oxford: Oxford University Press, 1993.

Pojman, Louis, ed. *The Theory of Knowledge*. 2nd ed. Belmont, CA: Wadsworth, 1999. Part V contains several readings in this area.

Pollock, John L. *Contemporary Theories of Knowledge*. Totowa, NJ: Rowman & Littlefield, 1986.

Rescher, Nicholas. *The Coherence Theory of Truth*. Oxford: Clarendon Press, 1973.

Sellars, Wilfred. *Science, Perception and Reality*. London: Routledge & Kegan Paul, 1963.

In addition consult the For Further Reading section at the end of chapter 6.

CHAPTER 8

Theories of Justification (III): Internalism and Externalism

Bishop James Ussher (1581–1656), Primate of All Ireland, calculated the genealogies in the Bible and determined that the creation of the universe, including the heavens and earth as well as the first humans, took place in the year 4004 B.C. (during the week of October 23 to 30)—about 6,000 years ago. Modern science totally rejects Ussher's theory. The fossil record, the dating of stones (which posits that the earth is about 5 billion years old), the astronomical evidence that the universe is at least 15 billion years old, and our best evidence for evolutionary theory, all purport to refute Ussher's calculation.

But suppose that Ussher is right about the age of the universe and that his account of the creation is accurate, so that all our evidence for evolution and the longevity of the universe is systematically misleading. The carbon-14 test for dating organic materials does not function reliably after about 5,500 years. Dinosaur fossils were hidden in the earth to mislead unbelievers. Our evidence for an ancient universe is fraudulent, but such that finite minds like ours could never comprehend the truth unaided by revelation. If we had not sinned, our noetic devices would have processed all of this information reliably but, as it is, sin has corrupted our belief-forming mechanisms, so they are unreliable about such matters. Only through conversion, wherein divine grace sets our mechanisms back in proper working order, can we become knowledgeable of the hidden truth: The world was created in 4004 B.C.

Suppose that all this is the case and that our best scientific explanation is not just mistaken in certain details but comprehensively in error—a massive error theory. Would we, who are basing our beliefs on the evidence at our disposal, be justified in our false beliefs? According to internalists, as long as we are following the best evidence available to us, we are justified in believing the scientific account, and the creationists are unjustified in their lucky true belief. On the other hand, externalists argue that this is not the case. As long as a reliable process caused the creationists to believe the way that they did, they have knowledge, as well as justification. Internalists emphasize the *subject's* point of view, his or her actual possession of the reasons or grounds for one's beliefs, whereas externalists emphasize the *objective* factors: the point of view of an ideal observer, the evidence a fully informed observer would have, whether or not the believer has access to this evidence. Externalists are typically naturalists holding that whatever is justified or has positive epistemic status is determined by natural properties or processes.

Actually, there are two main types of externalists: reliabilists and substantive naturalists. The former, represented by Alvin Goldman, Marshall Swain, and Ernest Sosa, hold that reliable processes are necessary conditions for justified beliefs.[1] Beliefs are justified and yield knowledge when they are connected to what makes them true in the right way, that is, by a reliable process or mechanism. Unlike internalists, reliabilists deny that the cognizer needs to be in an inner state or be able to access the grounds for his or her beliefs. The second type of externalists, *substantive naturalists,* such as D. M. Armstrong, W. V. Quine, Fred Dretske, and Robert Nozick, reject the thesis that justification is necessary for knowledge.[2] Armstrong and Dretske hold that there must be a natural or lawlike connection between the truth of what is believed and the person's belief. Nozick, as we noted in chapter 2, holds that justification is not necessary for knowledge. True beliefs need only meet appropriate counterfactual conditions. Of late, Quine and Goldman, recommend that epistemology be delivered up to cognitive psychology. Normative epistemology, they contend, is an outmoded enterprise that should fall into place "as a chapter of psychology and hence of natural science. Normative epistemology studies a natural phenomenon, viz., a physical human subject."[3] That is, it studies the causal relations between sensory input and theoretical output. As descriptive modes replace evaluative, the notion of justification drops out of epistemology. Substantive naturalism is more radical than reliabilism, so an examination of it will be postponed until chapter 10.

One other approach to knowledge has recently arisen in epistemology, Alvin Plantinga's theory of "Warrant," or "Proper Epistemic Function," which focuses on the mechanisms of the cognizer. Warrant does the work of justification, but this concept claims to be free from the "deontological stable" of voluntarism, doxastic responsibility, and evidentialism, which, according to Plantinga, encumber positive epistemic states with a burden they cannot bear.[4] The question is whether Plantinga's theory is any more than a version of reliabilism. I will deal with Plantinga's views in the next chapter. First we want to survey the main debate between the reliabilists and internalists.

Internalism

Historically, from Plato to contemporary times, most epistemologists have been internalists of one sort or another. Thomas Aquinas was an internalist. René Descartes and John Locke, the twin pillars of modern epistemology, held to internalism, as did Bertrand Russell. Contemporary epistemologists Roderick Chisholm, Keith Lehrer, John Pollock, Laurence BonJour, William Alston, Robert Audi, Richard Foley, Earl Conee, and Richard Feldman all hold to one or another version of this theory. Conee and Feldman state it this way.

> A person has a justified belief only if the person has reflective access to evidence that the belief is true. . . . Such examples make it reasonable to conclude that there is epistemic justification for a belief only where the person has cognitive access to evidence that supports the truth of the belief. Justifying evidence must be internally available.[5]

Accessibility

Internalism stresses having reasons for one's beliefs that ground or justify those beliefs. As indicated by the preceding quotation, your "having reasons" for your belief is generally interpreted as your being able to *access* those reasons, being able to recall them from memory, to cite them when questioned, and to use them as premises in arguments. You are able to determine by reflection alone whether a given belief is justified for you. At first glance, in terms of intuition, there seems something right about this. We ask others for their reasons for holding positions that are not obvious, and when the positions are obvious, it is because we are aware of the grounds for those positions. If I believe that candidate X will make a better president than candidate Y and you believe the opposite, we offer each other our reasons and counterreasons for our beliefs. Normally, we suspect that people who can't give good reasons for their beliefs, who say that their side in a war is right, their religion is better than all others, or their political views are correct, are unjustified in holding those beliefs. Similarly, we tend to hold that those who give good reasons or show their evidence are justified, even if they are not right.

Being in possession of the grounds of our beliefs presumes that we have access to them. By introspection we can discover not only what we believe, but why we believe it. The belief may be justified on the basis of a perception, memory report, emotion, testimony, or inference from a set of other beliefs. We can become conscious of the grounds for our belief. In turn, they, or a significant number of them, can be said to be transparent to us.

While Descartes held that our basic beliefs had to be infallible, contemporary internalists require only that they be the best reasons available to us—either from a foundationalist or coherentist perspective. Because internalism is, first of all, a theory of justification, the justifying reasons need not be true. They need only be based on the best evidence available. Consider, when the *idiot savant* is asked the day of the week on which July 1, 2500, falls and gives the right answer, is he justified in his belief? Does he have knowledge or just information? Or suppose that Sherlock Holmes and his assistant Dr. Watson are investigating a murder. Holmes believes that Ken Keller did the deed because of the circumstantial evidence. Ken is a pipe smoker who smokes only Dunhill tobacco. The scent of Dunhill is in the air, and ashes are scattered on the floor. Ken wears a size 11 shoe and a footprint of that size is detected next to the body. Ken always stabs his victims with a dagger, and the one in the victim's breast may be Ken's. Plus, Ken, who is known to be in debt, was the prime beneficiary of the victim's will. So Sherlock Holmes is quite correct in reasoning that all the available evidence points to Ken Keller. He concludes that Ken did the dastardly deed. Watson, on the other hand, has an intuition that Moriarty did the deed, and has a strong conviction to that effect. Suppose that he's right, that Moriarty did kill the victim and placed all the misleading evidence in order to lead the brilliant Holmes astray. Watson has a true belief (by luck), but Holmes has a justified belief based on reasonable evidence. While we think that justification generally tends to connect with truth, it does not always do so. There's no guarantee that the best justified beliefs will turn out to be true, but over the long haul we discover that the best way to approximate or reach the truth is to have the best justified beliefs possible.

Responsibility

A second condition associated with internalism is *responsibility*. Accessibility is only a necessary condition for justification. The believer must have arrived at his or her beliefs through a process that seeks the truth. That is, even though I may have evidence for my belief (e.g., that God exists), if that evidence has not been obtained or is not sustained by truth-seeking dispositions, I am not justified in holding the belief. No one sets forth this position more clearly than BonJour. Addressing the question, Why is justification something to be sought and valued? he replies:

> What makes us cognitive beings at all is our capacity for belief, and the goal of our distinctly cognitive endeavors is *truth:* we want our beliefs to correctly and accurately depict the world. . . . [Unlike God or an ideal observer] we have no immediate and unproblematic access to truth, and it is for this reason that justification comes into the picture. The basic role of justification is that of a *means* to truth, a more directly attainable mediating link between our subjective starting point and our objective goal. We cannot, in most cases at least, bring it about directly that our beliefs are true, but we can presumably bring it about directly . . . that they are epistemically justified.
>
> It follows that one's cognitive endeavors are epistemically justified only if and to the extent that they are aimed at this goal, which means very roughly that one accepts all and only those beliefs which one has good reason to think are true. To accept a belief in the absence of such a reason, however appealing or even mandatory from some other stand-point, is to neglect the pursuit of truth; such acceptance is, one might say, *epistemically irresponsible.* My contention here is that the idea of avoiding such irresponsibility, of being epistemically responsible in one's believings, is the core of the notion of epistemic justification.[6]

Epistemic responsibility is analogous to moral responsibility. They both follow from duties. Just as I have a prima facie moral duty to tell the truth, I have a prima facie epistemic duty to seek the truth. Just as we morally ought to tell the truth, we epistemically ought to adjust our belief-forming mechanisms in such a way that we maximize the amount of our true beliefs and minimize the amount of our false beliefs. It is by using all the powers at my disposal to seek true beliefs (and avoid false ones) and to proportion the strength of my beliefs to the strength of the available evidence that I become justified in my beliefs. A question we will consider in chapters 9 and 16 is whether (and to what extent) I have voluntary control over my beliefs. Frequently, the internalist holds that epistemic responsibility entails that we must have voluntary control over our belief acquisitions (at least some of them). As John Pollock puts it, "I have taken the fundamental problem of epistemology to be that of deciding what to believe."[7]

The issue of the relationship between the will and belief is complex. The *major* controversy is whether we have *direct* control over some of our belief acquisitions. Can I will to believe that God exists even though I see that the evidence is balanced on either side? Can I get myself to believe that my friend is innocent of the crime he has been accused of, even though on balance the evidence is against him? There is a *minor* controversy over whether we can get ourselves to acquire beliefs *indirectly* by taking steps to procure those beliefs. For example, suppose I want to believe that candidate *X* is a better candidate than candidate *Y.* I concentrate on the evidence in favor of *X,* go to his or her political rallies, associate with *X*'s supporters, and avoid *Y*'s point of view until I finally form the desired belief.

Although internalists have been interpreted as holding both *direct* and *indirect volitionalism,* I think that they only need commit themselves to indirect volitionalism. Here they need only maintain that we have an epistemic duty to seek the truth and that we are responsible for paying attention to the evidence on both sides of issues. We are responsible for doing whatever is reasonable toward acquiring true beliefs. We are not responsible for actually obtaining the truth (bad luck may conspire against us), but we can be held accountable for the way in which we have acquired our beliefs. This interpretation of the responsibility requirement seems a reasonable requirement, which lends cogency to the internalist position. We will examine this issue more closely in chapter 15.

Criticisms of Internalism

But for all its initial plausibility, internalism is beset by problems that its opponents deem insuperable. The main difficulty has to do with the accessibility requirement.

Often, as with classical foundationalists (see chapter 6), it is alleged that the cognizer had infallible introspective access or a set of self-evident beliefs. Plato thought we had infallible knowledge of the Forms; Descartes, of the existence of God, the nature of the self, and the reality of the external world (though not perceptual knowledge). In more recent times, philosophers have defended such first-person reports as providing certainty or infallibility: "I know that I have a green sense datum," "I intuit that I am in pain," "I know by introspection and with certainty that I am angry," and "I know that I am sad." According to Chisholm, the proposition "I feel sad" believed by *S* at time *t* is self-presenting or self-evident. It is not possible that I believe that I am sad and be mistaken. Furthermore, it is not possible that I feel sad, consider whether I am, and fail to believe it.[8] Many of these claims of infallible knowledge or self-evidence have been called into question. Psychologists have shown that we are often wrong, or even self-deceived, about what seems to be certain knowledge.

We can construct counterexamples to virtually all of the preceding "self-evident" or "self-presenting" statements. For example, suppose Ruth is sad and considers whether she actually is. Her psychiatrist, being a pragmatist about truth and believing that it would be better for Ruth to overcome her depressive moods through positive thinking, assures her on the highest authority that the feelings she is having are really feelings of deep peace and well-being. Ruth, having a great deal of misplaced faith in her psychiatrist, believes him and consequently, whenever the "sad" feelings come over her, gets herself to believe that these are feelings of deep peace and well-being.

Or consider the following counterexample to the "self-presenting" belief, "I am in pain." Suppose Paul comes to his therapist, complaining of pains in his lower back, around the liver. The therapist, believing Paul to be a hypochondriac, assures him that he is mistaken. First, she gets Paul to do some aerobic exercises to relax him and convince him that he is mistaken about the location of the sensation. Sure enough, after twenty minutes of planned exercise, Paul no longer feels the pain around his liver but more in the middle of his back.

Next, the therapist informs Paul that he really doesn't have a pain in his back, only a peculiar type C tickle. "These kinds of tickles resemble pains superficially. But you must overcome your fixation with pains and get yourself to believe that these sensations are class C tickles." The therapist then goes through a lot of neurological explanation. Paul, convinced by the expertise of the therapist in showing him that he was mistaken about the location of the "pain" sensation, and impressed by her knowledge of neurology, accepts her word that what he is feeling is really a kind of tickle. So every time the pain comes on, he clenches his fists, and as the sensations wrench his back repeats to himself the mantra, "These sensations are tickles, not pain. These sensations are tickles, class C tickles," until he immediately and noninferentially believes that what he is feeling is a peculiar kind of tickle and not a pain.[9] Does Paul eventually come to feel the neurological state as a tickle?

Or consider the following experiment. Sally is brought into a room in which 10 of her peers are seated and asked to tell how many times a light flashes. Sally looks at the light and rightly reports that it flashed 11 times. Her peers express astonishment at that answer and reply, "No, Sally, it flashed 10 times. Look more carefully." The light flashes 11 times again, and Sally reports as much. Her friends repeat that she is mistaken and urge her to try harder. This process goes on until, typically, Sally comes "see" the light flashing 10 times, though it actually flashes 11 times. Indeed, the subjects report that they are absolutely sure they saw the light flash only 10 times. Does testimony of authorities—whether the media, educators, or our peers—influence what we see or think we see? Did Sally really come to see the light flashing 10 times, and was she justified in changing her mind on the issue?

Furthermore, the work of cognitive psychologists on introspective illusions has cast doubts on the reliability of our introspective reports. In one experiment, shoppers at a store were invited to evaluate articles of clothing. In two different studies, four different nightgowns or stockings were laid out. The shopper was told that the items were made by different manufacturers and asked to identify the garment of the best quality. The subjects typically surveyed the garments from left to right and the garment on the extreme right was "heavily overchosen." The extreme right-hand stocking was chosen by a ratio of almost 4 to 1, even though the garments were placed randomly in that position. When asked why they chose the way they did, none of the 430 subjects said that the position of the object had anything to do with their choice and, when it was suggested to them, they rejected the idea as ridiculous.[10] Experiments like this suggest that we do not always have conscious access to the causes of our beliefs and that we are often mistaken about the grounds for those beliefs.

The lesson of these experiments seems to be that what we consider self-presenting or self-evident may be false. They indicate that we may be wrong about the reliability of our introspective reports and that we may not even have access to the causes of our beliefs. Nisbett and Wilson sum up a large reservoir of research on introspective access this way.

> Evidence suggests that there may be little or no direct introspective access to higher order cognitive processes. Subjects are sometimes (a) unaware of the existence of a stimulus that importantly influences a response, (b) unaware of the existence of the response, and (c) unaware that the stimulus has affected the response. It is proposed that when people attempt to report on their cognitive processes, that is, on the processes mediating the effects of a stimulus on a response, they do not do so on the basis of any true introspection. Instead, their reports are based on a priori [knowledge], implicit causal theories, or judgments about the extent to which a particular stimulus is a plausible cause of a given response. This suggests that though people may not be able to observe directly their cognitive processes, they will sometimes be able to report accurately about them. Accurate reports will occur when influential stimuli are salient and are plausible causes of the responses they produce, and will not occur when stimuli are not salient or are not plausible causes.[11]

When the stimuli are salient and importantly noticeable, like pain or a bright color, we can make reliable discriminations and introspect reliably afterwards, but there is an enormous area where our unconscious mind does the major work of analyzing and deciding for us.

But we can go even further in undermining the accessibility thesis. Having evidence that is accessible isn't by itself even sufficient for justification. Consider the case of Dr. Watson, the companion of Sherlock Holmes, who has a string of evidence pointing to the fact that Moriarty committed the crime but has not put that evidence together in the right way to make the correct inference. On the other hand, he correctly believes that Moriarty committed the crime, but for the wrong reasons. Watson has reasons for his belief, but they don't support his belief in the right way, so he is not justified.[12]

Nor does evidence seem always necessary to justification. Take the case of forgotten evidence, which we discussed at the end of chapter 5. We often forget the reasons why we believe what we do. Still, we feel justified in our beliefs. For example, a mathematician may work out an elaborate proof, check it over, and use it successfully in solving problems. Later, he may forget the steps in the proof but still remember the conclusion. Isn't he still justified in his belief, even though he has forgotten how he arrived at it? Suppose my country goes to war with country X. I want to know whether I should oppose the war on moral grounds or support it as a just cause. I make a thorough study of the complicated issues and conclude that it is a just cause. I join the army and fight for my country. While in a foxhole one night my foxhole companion asks me whether our cause is just. I tell him "Yes," but I cannot recall the reasons. Am I still justified in believing our cause is just? I don't recall learning the capitals of the fifty states, but I can still name all of them and I believe that my recall is correct. Supposing that I am correct and I did learn the names of the capitals, is my belief about the fifty capitals justified?

Or suppose you do an experiment to prove a certain scientific theory *T*. You complete the experiment successfully and are certain you've proven the theory, but years later you forget your experiment. Do you then know that the theory is true? Are you even justified in holding that it is?

An observant reader may answer that I am justified in these cases because I have inductive evidence that, in cases where I recall having worked out a justification, it usually turns out that I did. But we may suppose that either I don't have such inductive evidence in these kinds of cases or that such inductive evidence is not strong enough to justify an affirmative answer.

We return to our question: Are we sometimes justified in cases of forgotten evidence, where we based our conclusions on evidence but cannot remember what it was? Is it the case that, as long as the belief was originally formed by being grounded in the right evidence (e.g., the relevant experiment regarding theory *T*) and was not defeated, it is still justified? If this is so, then having access to our evidence is neither necessary nor sufficient for justification or knowledge.

Reliabilism

The problems with the deontological account of epistemic responsibility and the fallibility with regard to cognitive accessibility plus the difficulties involved in solving the Gettier problem (see chapter 5), have led many philosophers to reject internalism in favor of an externalist account, especially the version called "reliabilism." What matters, according to reliabilism, is not being able to cite or access your justification, but whether the belief was produced (or is sustained) by a reliable process.[13] What counts is not whether you can give the correct account of your reasons for belief, but whether your belief-forming mechanisms (e.g., five senses, memory, introspection, testimony reports, and ability to make valid inferences) are functioning properly in a suitable context. Alvin Goldman, one of the early proponents of reliabilism, put it this way.

> Consider some faulty process of belief-formation, i.e., processes whose belief outputs would be classed as unjustified. Here are some examples: confused reasoning, wishful thinking, reliance on emotional attachment, mere hunch or guesswork, and hasty generalization. What do these faulty processes have in common? They share the feature of *unreliability:* they tend to produce *error* a large proportion of the time. By contrast, which species of belief-forming (or belief-sustaining) processes are intuitively justification-conferring? They include standard perceptual processes, remembering, good reasoning, and introspection. What these processes seem to have in common is *reliability:* the beliefs they produce are generally reliable.[14]

Reliabilists attempt to get around the Gettier counterexamples by dismissing or altering the third condition, stating that "Agent *A* is justified in believing that *p*" should be construed in terms of *being able to give reasons* for the belief that *p*. Reliabilists argue that we don't have to know or have access to the grounds for our beliefs in order to have knowledge. For example, unlike the amateur, the art critic knows that the painting before him is a counterfeit Picasso, but he need not be able to tell us how he knows, as long as the belief is formed in a proper way. I know that today is Tuesday although I don't remember how I found that out (I looked at my digital watch early this morning). We recognize the faces of friends, former classmates, and acquaintances, sometimes many years after seeing them, without being able to give our evidence for that recognition. We know that other minds exist, even though we can't give good arguments for that knowledge. Furthermore, reliabilism has the advantage that it attributes justified beliefs to animals and small children, who cannot give reasons for their beliefs.

Although Pollock's nondoxastic foundationalism, which is examined at the end of the last chapter, purports to be a version of internalism, it is compatible with the externalist's view. The processes that cause our beliefs need not themselves be beliefs.

Alvin Goldman sets forth three conditions for his reliablist theory of justification.

Agent A's belief that p (ABp) is justified, if

1. The belief that p is the result of a reliable process;

2. Given A's relevant alternatives, there was no perceptual equivalents that could lead A to have a false belief. For example, referring to our discussion of Ginet's example in Chapter 5, either Henry is able to distinguish the red barn he perceives in the countryside from the red barn facades surrounding it, or there are no such facades in the vicinity. Or, appealing to Dretske's example in chapter 3, there are no mules painted with black stripes in the vicinity which could be confused with the zebra you are seeing.

3. The *B*elief that p is true.

There is no need for cognitive access to the grounds of one's beliefs. Instead reliabilists emphasize the *causal* relationships, or *nomological* (i.e., lawlike) connections, between belief states (S believes that p) and the state of affairs that makes p true, such that given that S believes that p, it must be the case that p. D. M. Armstrong offers the metaphor of a thermometer as the proper model by which to understand knowledge. Some thermometers function better than others and under certain circumstances even a good thermometer can give a reading that fails to correspond to the temperature of the environment (e.g., when the temperature goes below 50 degrees Celsius). Such a reading is analogous to a noninferential false belief. At other times the reading will correspond to the actual temperature. Such a reading is like a noninferential true belief.

The correct readings may be further divided into two kinds: those that accidentally give the correct temperature and those that typically give the true temperature because they are functioning properly or are reliable. The first type is an inadequate thermometer that occasionally gets it right by chance—say, it is stuck at 74 degrees, which occasionally is the correct temperature. The second type gets it right a high percentage of the time, especially when functioning in standard conditions. Such accurate readings may be compared with noninferential knowledge. When a true belief unsupported by reasons stands to the state of affairs as a thermometer reading in a good thermometer stands to the actual temperature, we have noninferential knowledge.[15]

So not only are we justified in our belief by a reliable process, but we have knowledge as well. Knowledge is simply true belief that is justified by being caused by a reliable process.

Advantages of Externalism

Externalism has several advantages. It offers a solution to skepticism, dissolves the problems of induction and other minds, and makes sense of perceptual and memory knowledge. It claims to defeat some forms of skepticism. Since knowledge is defined as true beliefs caused in the proper manner, it doesn't matter whether the subject is able to give an account of his or her beliefs or is even conscious of those beliefs. In a similar vein, externalism dissolves the problems of induction and other minds, since these beliefs are seen as being caused by reliable processes. Let me elaborate these points.

Take the issue of skepticism. As we saw in our examination of Nozick's truth-tracking theory of knowledge, you can know that you have a head and are reading this book, even if you cannot know that you are not a brain in a vat or deceived by a mischievous demon. You do not need to know that the skeptical hypothesis is false in order to know the things you know. All that is necessary is that your beliefs are true and have arisen or are sustained in an appropriate manner. If I see a dog in front of me, I know that a dog is in front of me even if I can't refute the skeptic. Thus, even though reliabilism cannot disprove the skeptical hypothesis, it claims, contra the Cartesians, that the possibility of a deceiving demon does not show that I do not have knowledge of the external world.

With regard to perception, we often cannot give an account of our beliefs. We may not even know why we hold them. Suppose that you come to dinner at my home and after dinner I take you into another room and give you a quiz. "Do you know what color the walls were and what pictures were hanging on them?" I ask. You pause because you don't remember even noticing the walls or the pictures, but you correctly answer, "The walls were red, a couple of pictures of Oxford were on one wall, and a Renoir picture was on the other." "How did you know that?" I ask. You admit that you don't know how you knew. Your perceptual mechanisms picked up the information, stored it in your mind or brain, and allowed you to retrieve it at the appropriate moment. Were you justified in believing that the walls were red and that pictures of Oxford were on one wall? What if you thought that you were only guessing? What if you didn't really believe what you said but only said what came to your mind unbidden via the unconscious?

The reliabilist says that you knew the color of the walls and what pictures were hanging there, just as long as a reliable mechanism caused your beliefs. You could be wrong, of course. You can know without knowing that you know. The internalist has trouble with this sort of case and either says it is a borderline case of justification or is actually an unjustified true belief.

Similarly, for memory knowledge—say our forgetting our proof for theory *T*—reliabilism holds that one need not be able to give one's reasons for believing one's memory reports. Just as long as they were formed by reliable processes, one knows what one truly remembers.

With regard to the problem of other minds, the internalist has a difficult time offering a cogent argument. What justifies me in believing that there are other minds? I have never felt your pain, enjoyed your pleasures, experienced your desires, or possessed your particular beliefs. The only pains, pleasures, desires, and beliefs that I have experienced are my own. The standard argument from analogy, which holds that since others manifest the same behavior forms that I do when I am in pain, fails because it is an instance of hasty generalization to reason from one instance to many. By the argument from analogy I could just as well conclude that every pain in the world is a pain in my body. It would run like this:

1. Every pain that I have found in the world was in my body.
2. Therefore, probably every pain in the world took place in my body.

The reliabilist cuts the Gordian knot here by stating that it is not necessary that I be able to state the justification for why I believe in other minds in order to be justified in that belief. Just as long as the belief was caused by a reliable process, I am justified. I know that there are other minds. The reliabilist may say that we have natural belief-forming mechanisms that cause us to have these self-evident beliefs. We will discuss this topic further in chapter 14.

Similar difficulties exist with the problem of induction. The internalist has a difficult time giving noncircular reasons for believing in induction, but the reliabilist sweeps such a need aside and maintains that a reliable natural process (inherent in the inductive method itself) has caused us to have this belief.

A Critique of Reliabilism

Reliabilism, as a form of externalism, holds many attractions for epistemologists. It seems to bypass many of the perennial problems of epistemology and is scientifically respectable in that it explains its features in the light of natural processes determined by or reduced to psychological or physicalist characteristics. But there are weaknesses with externalism.

First, exactly what counts as a reliable belief-forming mechanism is vague. What percentage of true beliefs must the process be able to produce before it is to be admitted as reliable—80 percent, 95 percent, 99.9 percent? It would seem that the first time someone obtains a belief via what turns out to be a reliable process, the belief cannot justifiably be called justified, because a successful track record has not yet been established. If, with regard to one-time-only processes, the reliabilist appeals to subjunctive conditionals (how it would succeed if used a certain amount of times), we can raise the question, "Under what conditions would it work if tried many times and how many times is enough?"

Furthermore, it seems difficult to state the standard conditions that must obtain for a process to function reliably. How close must Henry be to a barn to be justified in believing that it is not a barn facade? At what speed does a rabbit or a rat have to be running before my belief-forming mechanism is deemed unreliable? At what distance does a given object have to be from me before it is not subject to reliable processes? Perhaps there are answers to these problems, but the reliabilist hasn't yet given clear solutions. They generally give us a promissory note that psychology will eventually solve these problems.

A second problem has to do with defeasibility, a notion we examined in chapter 5. Note Goldman's formula for reliabilism about justification.

> If S's belief in p results from a reliable cognitive process, and there is no reliable or conditionally reliable process available to S which, had it been used by S in addition to the process actually used, would have resulted in S's not believing p at t, then S's belief in p at t is justified.[16]

That is, if I could have used another normally reliable process that would have defeated my present belief that *p*, this belief, *Bp*, is not justified. Suppose, for example, that I have heard from normally reliable sources that the girl next door has been kidnapped. I am not justified in trusting that testimony in the event that there is another process available to me that would defeat that testimony, such as, I could go next door and see that she is playing in her sandbox.

Alvin Plantinga has pointed out that the notion of alternative reliable processes creates problems for Goldman's account.

> Still another problem here is the fact that there may be more than one reliable process available to *S;* perhaps there is a reliable process *P* such that if he were to use it, then he would not believe *p*, but another reliable process *P** such that if he were to use both *P* and *P** then he would believe *p*, and [a] reliable process *P*** such that if he were to use all of *P*, *P**, and *P*** he would not believe *p;* then perhaps Goldman would want to say that *S*'s belief would be justified after all, despite the fact that there is a reliable process available to him which is such that if he were to use it then he would not believe *p*.[17]

Let's put the point this way. I think that Goldman wants to say that a believer *S* is justified in the event that his or her belief has resulted from a reliable process and *S* has no defeater for his or her belief. To boil this down to a formula, let *Bsp* refer to *S*'s belief that *p* and *CRP* stand for "caused by a reliable process." Then *Bsp* is justified if:

1. *Bsp (CRP)*, and
2. there is no state of *S* that defeats *Bsp (CRP)*.[18]

The problem of defeaters is that we usually do possess other beliefs or considerations that counter our beliefs. Suppose I believe that I helped you with your homework last week. Even if my belief has been caused by a reliable belief-forming process, I may have counterevidence. I recall that I sometimes get my dates mixed up so that it was not last week but the day before yesterday, you deny that I helped you, saying it was someone else I helped, or I may be simply imagining that I helped you. All of these function as potential defeaters for my belief that I have helped you, but none is sufficient to override my belief that I helped you.

Perhaps one could say that only *relevant* or *undefeated* defeaters count. This may be correct, but the trouble is that the concepts of relevance and undefeatedness are very fuzzy. No one to my knowledge has given a clear analysis of these terms or their necessary and sufficient conditions that is nontrivial. However, I think that we do have a fairly good intuitive idea in concrete cases of what counts as a relevant defeater (e.g., going next door and checking on the girl would surely count as one). It seems then that the reliabilist has no greater difficulty here than any other epistemologist who uses the idea of a defeater or a relevant alternative or prima facie evidence. The intuitions play an ineliminable role in these cases.

Then there is the third problem—generality. How do we determine what is a natural process? Any instance of forming a belief will be an instance of many different process types. As Richard Feldman points out, "[T]he process taken leading to my current belief that it is sunny today is an instance of all the following types: the perceptual process, the visual process, processes that occur on Wednesday, processes that lead to true beliefs, etc."[19]

Goldman would appeal to the idea of relevance, holding that some types or processes are more relevant than others. But the generality problem persists. What is the relevant process type, and how does one distinguish it from other relevant types? If we define the process too narrowly, it turns out that every true belief is the product of a reliable process. If we define it too broadly, we get too many clearly unjustified belief acquisitions. For example, perception is usually seen as a reliable process but it yields unjustified beliefs as well as justified ones. Here the reliabilist offers a solution in terms of subprocesses, like vision, working under normal observation conditions in a suitable environment. But, as Feldman points out:

> No matter how observation conditions are specified, [Goldman's formula] is open to a devastating objection: numerous visual beliefs can be formed in the same observation conditions and some of these beliefs may be better justified than others. For example, when looking at the distant mountain-goat, I might believe both that I see an animal and that I see a mountain-goat. These beliefs are formed in exactly the same observation conditions, so, according to [Goldman's formula], they must either both be justified or both be unjustified. But surely that is mistaken. I might be entirely justified in believing that I see an animal, but not justified in thinking I see a mountain-goat.[20]

The reliabilist may respond by relativizing the reliability conditions to kinds of beliefs but then we have the difficult task of distinguishing the relevant types of beliefs. Broad and narrow construals of reliable processes vie with one another, and, to my knowledge, no one has successfully supplied a detailed account of how reliable processes work. Even by reliable criteria we should hesitate in accepting a reliabilism program.

Equally serious problems are that externalism in its paradigm forms seems to dissolve or seriously underemphasize the notions of (1) normativity and (2) accessibility.

Knowledge, it is argued by internalist opponents, is more than simply having true beliefs or properly caused beliefs. A long tradition, going back to Plato in the *Theaetetus,* holds that knowledge requires the ability to give reasons, a justification. The concept of justification is normative or evaluative. If you believe that you will get an A in your philosophy course because the astrology chart indicates as much, you don't have a good reason and aren't justified in believing this, even if it is true. On the other hand, if you believe that you will get an A because your average up until the final is an A+ and you understand all the material that is likely to be on the final, then you do have good reasons for your belief, even if it turns out to be false (for example, you get a mental block while taking the final and get a low grade, which leaves you with a B or C in the course).

Externalism either transfers normativity to the causes (Goldman), conditions (Nozick), belief-forming mechanisms (Plantinga), or else, as in the case of Quine, it reduces it to psychology (i.e., it gives a scientific account of belief formation that eliminates the need for or use of epistemic justification). Reliabilism transfers normativity to the causal or sustaining processes, while naturalism (or "substantive naturalism," see chapter 10) threatens to dissolve normativity altogether.

There are good and bad belief-forming processes, as the earlier quotation from Goldman makes clear, so the evaluative aspect seems irreducible. Both internalists and reliabilists agree on this point. What they disagree on is how normativity obtains. The internalist insists on an accessibility requirement that involves being able to cite the grounds of one's beliefs. The reliabilist insists that normativity has to do with the kinds of causal chains or external connections in belief production and maintenance. If your belief is produced by an appropriate cause, you have a justification for it whether you can access that cause or not.

But, internalists point out, there is a problem here. Internalists like Lehrer dispense with the idea of causation as a necessary condition for justification. At best, an internalist might concede, appropriate causation of a belief is necessary but not sufficient for justification. We can imagine counterexamples where a belief that p has been properly caused, but we would not want to say that the subject knew p. Laurence BonJour offers the following counterexample.

> Samantha believes herself to have the power of clairvoyance, though she has no reason for or against this belief. One day she comes to believe,

for no apparent reason, that the President is in New York City. She maintains this belief, appealing to her alleged clairvoyance power, even though she is at the same time aware of a massive amount of apparently cogent evidence, consisting of news reports, press releases, allegedly live television pictures, and so on, indicating that the President is at that time in Washington, D.C. Now the President is in fact in New York City, the evidence to the contrary being part of a massive official hoax mounted in the face of an assassination threat. Moreover, Samantha does in fact have completely reliable clairvoyant power under the conditions which were then satisfied, and her belief about the President did result from the operation of that power.[21]

In this case the reliability requirement is met, but would we not hesitate to say that Samantha knows that the President is in New York or is justified in her belief?[22]

Likewise, even if it turned out that Bishop Ussher was right in dating the creation of the heavens and the earth to the year 4004 B.C., and that present-day creationists had their correct beliefs formed in reliable ways (their belief-forming mechanisms were unconsciously tied into information patterns going back to creation, though they didn't have good reasons to believe this), as long as they weren't able to give good reasons for their beliefs, we would deny that they were epistemically justified in their beliefs.

Consider Keith Lehrer's example of Mr. Truetemp. Recall Armstrong's thesis that the properly functioning thermometer is the model for knowledge. Just as a reliable thermometer contains a lawlike relation to the temperature in recording accurate temperature readings, the knower's beliefs are caused in a lawlike manner by the external world. Lehrer argues that this model fails because the thermometer does not *know* the information it provides. He offers the story of Mr. Truetemp to convince us of this point.

Suppose a person, whom we shall name Mr. Truetemp, undergoes brain surgery by an experimental surgeon who invents a small device which is both a very accurate thermometer and a computational device capable of generating thoughts. The device, call it a tempucomp, is implanted in Truetemp's head so that the very tip of the device, no larger than the head of [a] pin, sits unnoticed on his scalp and acts as a sensor to transmit information about the temperature to the computational system in his brain. This device, in turn, sends a message to his brain causing him to think of the temperature recorded by the external sensor. Assume that the tempucomp is very reliable, and so his thoughts are correct temperature thoughts. All told, this is a reliable belief-forming process. Now imagine, finally, that he has no idea that the tempucomp has been inserted in his brain, is only slightly puzzled about why he thinks so obsessively about the temperature, but never checks a thermometer to determine whether these thoughts about the temperature are correct. He accepts them unreflectively, another effect of the tempucomp. Thus, he thinks and accepts that the temperature is 104 degrees. It is. Does he know that it is? Surely not. He has no idea whether he or his thoughts about the temperature are reliable. What he accepts, that the temperature is 104 degrees, is correct, but he does not know that his thought is correct. . . . Though he records the information because of the operations of the tempucomp, he is ignorant of the facts about the tempucomp and about his temperature telling reliability. Yet, the sort of causal, nomological, statistical, or counterfactual relationships required by externalism may all be present. Does he know that the temperature is 104 degrees, when the thought occurs to him while strolling in Pima Canyon? He has no idea why the thought occurred to him or that such thoughts are almost always correct.[23]

So Mr. Truetemp does not know that the temperature he records is correct. We are inclined to say that Truetemp is not justified in his beliefs about the weather in spite of the fact that they have been caused in the right way. Something more than correct information is needed for knowledge, and something more than a reliable process is required for justification. One must have a way of knowing or believing that the information is accurate.

If this is the case, reliability is not a sufficient condition for justification, let alone knowledge. Still, other counterexamples indicate that reliabilism is not even necessary for justification. A belief may be justified without being caused by a reliable process. Consider the following.

Suppose your twin (let's call him or her "I-2") on another planet or possible world were given experiences identical to yours—the same thoughts and beliefs—except that while your beliefs are true, I-2's are largely false. I-2 is completely wrong about his or her surroundings, makes wrong inferences, and is mistaken about his or her introspection reports. Although I-2's belief-forming mechanisms are, like yours, in perfectly good order and I-2 is as dedicated to seeking the truth as you are, a mischievous demon has brought about that I-2's beliefs are mostly erroneous. Can we maintain that your beliefs are justified but not I-2's? You are both in exactly the same internal state, only you have the good luck of not being deceived by the demon, whereas I-2 has the bad luck of being deceived by it. Unless we think that luck is important for justification, we seem forced to conclude that I-2 is as justified as you are in believing what he or she believes. But then reliabilism is not necessary for justification.

Naturally, reliabilists have responses to all of these criticisms, some of which will be considered in the next section. Sometimes they point out that the process of giving reasons is simply a sub-species of reliabilism. That is, internalism itself with its requirement for good reasons or arguments is a reliable process. The mistake of the internalist is to think that *only* the process of giving reasons is a valid justification process. Of course, the internalist regards this move as either an unwelcomed leverage buyout or epistemic imperialism.

Externalist–Internalist Reconciliation?

There seems to be truth in the reliabilist theory. We don't always know how or why we know what we know. As we have argued, perceptual beliefs seem to occur in noncognitive ways suitable to a reliabilist analysis, and memory beliefs may also be better analyzed via a reliabilist theory, though it includes accessibility. But when it comes to assessing religious, philosophical, and scientific theories (including reliabilism itself) or to giving an account of how we came to a decision in a complicated legal case, we want to be able to give a reasoned account of our decision. We are reason-giving creatures; we argue and rebut with arguments. This is a feature of the internalist's or justificationist's insight that must not be lost in our recognition of the limits of the internalist program. The two theories seem to complement each other, each applying to an aspect of the knowing or justifying process, but neither completely succeeding in explaining the meaning of knowledge or justification.

On the whole, reliabilism seems a better account of what it is to *know* a proposition, and internalism seems a better account of what it is to be justified in believing a proposition. Once you give up Cartesian infallibility, knowledge seems to take on an externalist dimension. Whether your true beliefs are actually cases of knowledge does not depend on you or your inner states alone, but on being fortunate. You are just epistemically lucky that it is not a demon but the actual world that is causing the belief states you are now in (at least I hope that's the case). Furthermore, one can know without knowing one knows, or being able to access one's reasons for belief, such as in the case of the art critic, the mother who has internal recognition processes of her almost indistinguishable twins, or the person who knows what color the walls of my dining room are.

On the other hand, internalism seems better suited to the concept of justification. Making inferences from basic beliefs is a conscious process, as is giving reasons for our beliefs, and both processes presuppose accessibility to the grounds of our beliefs. If this is correct, it is a mistake to treat internalism and reliabilist externalism as mutually exclusive. Both capture significant aspects of knowledge. The real task yet to be done is to sort out the ways in which reliabilism and internalism function on various levels and in various contexts of the epistemic process.

Strong vs. Weak Justification

This is in line with a recent distinction made by Alvin Goldman between strong and weak justification. Goldman asks us to consider a scientifically benighted culture that uses "highly unreliable methods for forming beliefs about the future and the unobserved."

> Their methods appeal to the doctrine of signatures, to astrology, and to oracles. Members of the culture have never thought of probability theory or statistics, never dreamt of anything that could be classed as "experimental method." Now suppose that on a particular occasion a member of this culture forms a belief about the outcome of an impending battle by using one of the aforementioned methods, say by consulting zodiacal signs in a culturally approved fashion. Call this method *M*. Is this person's belief justified, or warranted?[24]

Goldman notes that we are pulled into opposite directions on this question. On the one hand, we want to say, "No, justification is generated only by proper or adequate methods, and consulting zodiacal signs isn't anywhere near one of these." On the other hand, we feel some epistemic sympathy for the believer. Everyone else in his culture uses these methods, he is doing his epistemic best to have true beliefs and seems blameless. So in a sense he is justified.

Goldman thinks that we really have two different (but related) concepts of epistemic justification: (1) *strong justification* obtains when a justified belief is "(roughly) a well-formed belief, a belief formed (or sustained) by proper, suitable, or adequate methods, procedures, or processes."[25] The other concept, (2) *weak justification*, occurs when a false belief is a "faultless, blameless, or nonculpable belief." So our astrology adherent is justified in the weak sense, but not in the strong sense.

Goldman's suggestion of combining external and internal considerations is promising. It solves the problem of the demon hypothesis where your alter ego I-2 has the same true beliefs as you, but got them through unreliable methods. He or she is weakly justified, but not strongly so. The converse is true of Samantha in the clairvoyance case. She is strongly justified but not weakly so.

Now consider the story about Bishop Ussher at the beginning of this chapter in which the creationists luckily get the story right, whereas the scientists, using normally reliable belief-forming processes, have good reasons but get it wrong. Does the weak/strong distinction apply to this case?

One inclined to internalism might argue that the labels "strong" and "weak" bias the two types of justification, so that better labels should be substituted for "strong" and "weak"—say "objective" and "subjective," similar to the distinction made in ethics. Take abortion, an issue on which there is moral disagreement. Suppose for the sake of argument that abortion is really immoral and that there are good reasons for believing it to be so, only not everyone has access to the relevant assumptions or the argument is difficult to construct and follow. Further suppose that Christy has judiciously considered the arguments and has concluded that abortion is morally permissible. Having prima facie reasons for believing that abortion is permissible, she has an abortion in good faith. We could say that what Christy did was objectively wrong, but subjectively morally right or permissible.

Apply this distinction to the cases discussed in this chapter. The scientists who disbelieve Ussher's creation story would be subjectively justified, even though it turns out that they are wrong and the creationists are right. On the other hand, if creationism is false, as most biologists believe it is, then it could still be the case that any given creationist, having done his or her best, is subjectively but not objectively justified.

I propose that we substitute the notions "subjective" and "objective" justification for "weak" and "strong" justification, thus capturing a distinction already present in our conceptual scheme. Doing this will enable us to make another move in line with ethical assessment. In ethics the goal is to have both subjective and objective justification for one's acts. It is not enough to have objective justification—to have the right answer based on the right reasons—but one also must have a proper attitude, a good will, and a desire to do one's best. This may be called complete *ethical* justification. Likewise, complete *epistemic* justification consists in both having the right reasons for one's beliefs or having beliefs caused by reliable processes. However, one also must have his or her will formed in such a way that enables one to seek the truth or to have the best justified beliefs possible. If this is so, it turns out that epistemic justification is a combination of internalist and externalist factors.

Animal vs. Reflective Knowledge

There is another distinction that may be helpful in fully explicating the internalist-externalist debate—one that I owe to Ernest Sosa—a distinction between *animal* knowledge and *reflective* knowledge.[26] Animal knowledge is had by animals and small children, as well as ourselves, and includes our unconscious and immediate correct beliefs caused by reliable processes. Our unreflected true perceptual beliefs, memory beliefs, feelings of pain, facial recognitions, and immediate intuitions are all instances of animal knowledge. They have been caused by reliable processes or our faculties functioning in virtuous ways under favorable conditions. It is the paradigm of an external process or state, needing no reflective awareness. Reflective knowledge, on the other hand, in addition to being true belief caused by a reliable process or faculty functioning virtuously in proper circumstances, requires that the belief be justified. A belief is justified when it has its basis in its inference or coherent relationships to other beliefs in the believer's mind. Such justification could be foundational or coherentist. Examples of such justified, though not necessarily true, beliefs are your reflective religious, scientific, and political beliefs; your belief that skepticism is false (based on coherentist or foundational reasoning); or your belief that a mushroom will make you ill if you eat it, because the last ten mushrooms of that type eaten by your friends have made them ill and you are relevantly similar to them. Such beliefs seem to depend on language (or typically do) and are found in normal adult humans, but not in animals and small children.

So animal knowledge depends on reliability (of faculties and processes) and the truth of what is believed. It is wholly externalist. Reflective knowledge depends on reliability, truth, and justification, and as such it is both externalist and internalist, the justification aspect giving it its internalist component.

This distinction has the advantage of solving the puzzles that troubled other theories of justification and knowledge. Take for example Mr. Truetemp, who always gets the temperature correct but doesn't know why or how. Truetemp has correct beliefs, caused by a reliable process but not the kind we would call justified. With the animal knowledge–reflective knowledge distinction we can conclude that Truetemp has animal knowledge but not reflective knowledge.

Or take the problem of your twin I-2 in the demon world, who has the same internal reasons as you do for his or her beliefs, but no knowledge, because the reasons are all, unluckily, false. We saw that by applying Goldman's distinctions we could say that I-2 was weakly justified. Using our new distinction we can agree that I-2 is not functioning (intellectually) virtuously in his or her environment, but that I-2 is fully (reflectively) justified, not merely weakly so (which suggests that I-2 could do more, even if he or she is blameless).

Take Samantha, our clairvoyant. According to Sosa's distinction, she has a new (hitherto unrealized) type of animal knowledge because her true beliefs have been formed reliably, but she lacks justification and therefore reflective knowledge. Her case is similar to that of Truetemp's.

Does this schema apply to our creationists, who have special access, which they cannot articulate, for the truth of the thesis that the world was created in 4004 B.C.? It could be that God has implanted a causal process in us so that, if properly used, it would be a reliable process to enable all of us to believe this thesis, in which case we could call it "animal knowledge," although it would sound odd. Or it could be the case, as I initially described it, that this truth was a special insertion by God into the elect, so that it was not common to fallen humanity. Perhaps we should call this *supernatural knowledge,* that which is miraculously caused by a reliable supernatural process. If there is no God, of course, there is no supernatural knowledge. But if there is, I see no reason to deny the possibility of special access. In either case, the bizarre belief would be caused by a reliable process and mechanism, but the believers would still lack reflective knowledge, whereas our evolutionists would lack knowledge but be justified. As was the case with the demon world victim, the evolutionist is unlucky.

Reflective vs. Nonreflective Knowledge

This discussion leads us to modify Sosa's distinction of reflective knowledge and animal knowledge. We saw that supernatural knowledge cannot be accounted for by either of these types. Perhaps there are other types of knowing that do not fit his dichotomy. I suggest we divide the terrain into *reflective* and *nonreflective* knowledge, making no changes in Sosa's conception of reflective knowledge. But under nonreflective knowledge we might include: animal knowledge, supernatural knowledge, and, a third subtype, *fortuitous knowledge.*

Perhaps Truetemp's tempucomp and Samantha's clairvoyance are better described as fortuitous knowledge, since they do not normally occur to humans or animals. A clever neuroscientist has implanted the tempucomp device in Truetemp's brain, so that it has become a rare, reliable belief-forming mechanism. We may suppose that Samantha has contracted a rare disease—perhaps she is the first one ever to have contracted it—so that an utterly improbable combination of brain events has caused her to be sensitive to a part of the electromagnetic spectrum that causes clairvoyance waves to be transmitted to her. She has a reliable mechanism, which is neither typically animal nor supernatural. I suggest we call it a fortuitous reliable process and grant that Samantha has a type of nonreflective knowledge. If Samantha comes to understand the promptings of this process, sees inductive correlations between clairvoyant episodes, and integrates these deliverances into her total noetic structure, such processes may eventually become instances of reflective knowledge.

Furthermore, perhaps these reliable mechanisms are environment sensitive, so that Samantha only becomes clairvoyant on sunny days at latitudes between sea level and 500 feet. This would only mean that some of our reliable processes are relative to environmental features.

We see then that knowledge may be wholly externalist and depend in a certain way on luck or good fortune (that our belief-forming mechanisms are working properly and that the environment is cooperating with these processes), but that reflective knowledge contains an internalist component. One must be justified in order to know in this deeper sense, although one must also be lucky to have the world and one's belief-forming mechanisms cooperate.

Summary

In chapter 5, we examined the standard conception from Plato until the mid-twentieth century that knowledge is *true, justified belief.* Gettier's counterexamples show problems with this definition. Several theories have tried to meet Gettier's challenge. Internalist theories hold that justification depends on the reasons one possesses for one's belief. Internalists typically specify a fourth condition that defuses the problematic counterexamples. Externalist theories contend that the Gettier counterexamples point to fundamental problems in the internalist framework and opt for a process account of knowledge. What matters in knowledge, according to externalists like Alvin Goldman, is that the true belief is produced by a reliable process. Philosophers like Laurence BonJour, Richard Feldman, and Keith Lehrer have pointed to problems with reliabilism in terms of determining what counts as a reliable belief-forming mechanism or process, what counts as a defeasible process, how general the process must be, and what to make of the categories of normativity and accessibility of the grounds for one's beliefs.

Finally, we considered a reconciliation between reliabilism and internalism, distinguishing between weak and strong (or subjective and objective) justification and reflective and nonreflective knowledge. We will continue our examination of different externalist theories in the next two chapters.

QUESTIONS FOR DISCUSSION

1. What are the major strengths and weaknesses of internalism? What are the major strengths of reliabilism?

2. Examine the quotation by Laurence BonJour on why we should seek epistemic justification.

> What makes us cognitive beings at all is our capacity for belief, and the goal of our distinctly cognitive endeavors is *truth:* we want our beliefs to correctly and accurately depict the world. . . . [Unlike God or an ideal observer] We have no immediate and unproblematic access to truth, and it is for this reason that justification comes into the picture. The basic role of justification is that of a *means* to truth, a more directly attainable mediating link between our subjective starting point and our objective goal. We cannot, in most cases at least, bring it about directly that our beliefs are true, but we can presumably bring it about directly . . . that they are epistemically justified.
>
> It follows that one's cognitive endeavors are epistemically justified only if and to the extent that they are aimed at this goal, which means very roughly that one accepts all and only those beliefs which one has good reason to think are true. To accept a belief in the absence of such a reason, however appealing or even mandatory from some other standpoint, is to neglect the pursuit of truth; such acceptance is, one might say, *epistemically irresponsible.* My contention here is that the idea of avoiding such irresponsibility, of being epistemically responsible in one's believings, is the core of the notion of epistemic justification.[27]

Do you agree with BonJour that justification tends to promote truth? If so, why do you think this is so? Do you agree with BonJour that we have an epistemic duty to seek the truth and base our beliefs on the best evidence? What does he mean by "mandatory from some other standpoint"? Explain your answers.

3. Consider the counterexamples offered against "self-evident" and "self-presenting" statements. Are you convinced by them? Do you think that Ruth really believes that when she has a "sad" feeling she can get herself to believe that these are "feelings of peace and well-being"? Discuss the plausibility of these sorts of examples.

4. Stewart Cohen sets forth the following counterexample to reliabilism. Suppose in world *W,* René is a careful reasoner while George obtains a large number of his beliefs through wishful thinking, hasty generalization, and guessing. Suppose that both are deceived by a demon, so that they both are obtaining false beliefs. Wouldn't we still want to say that René's beliefs are justified, but that George's are not? If this is so, Cohen points out, the distinction between epistemic justification and nonjustification does not depend on the objective reliability of an epistemic process in a given world, but something more internal to the believer. How would a reliabilist respond to this problem?

5. Discuss Goldman's distinction of strong and weak justification. Is it a helpful compromise between externalism and internalism?

6. Internalists hold that externalism fails to satisfy our intuitions that inference is a conscious process. Michael Levin points out that some reliabilists argue that inference is a mechanical process. Our minds work like computers, calculating or making deductive inferences, and something similar seems to be going on when we engage in inductive reasoning. How would an internalist respond to this claim?

7. Hilary Putnam offers the following counterexample to reliabilism. Suppose that the Dalai Lama is infallible on matters of faith and morality. On reliabilist logic it would follow, claims Putnam, that anyone who believes in the Dalai Lama and who believes any of his statements on faith and morals uses a method that is absolutely reliable. Suppose that a true believer, Trudy, believes what the Dalai Lama says about euthanasia, abortion, and the existence of God, but her only reason for believing these things is "the Dalai Lama says so." Putnam says it is obvious that Trudy's beliefs are not justified, and so reliabilism is falsified. Is he right? How might a reliabilist respond to this counterexample? (See Putnam, "Why Reason Can't Be Naturalized," *Realism and Reason* [Cambridge: Cambridge University Press, 1983]. For a reliabilist response, see Alvin Goldman, *Epistemology and Cognition* [Cambridge, MA: Harvard University Press, 1986], 109–110.)

8. Examine the reliabilist claim to have defused skepticism. Is this true? Or do we still need to give reasons why skepticism is not to be taken seriously? For example, should the reliabilist be able to tell us why his "*reliably produced beliefs*" are true?

9. On balance which of the theories of justification discussed in this chapter seems most plausible? Or do you think they both are sound within a different range of epistemic phenomena? Explain your answer.

NOTES

1. See D. M. Armstrong, *A Materialist Theory of Mind* (London: Routledge & Kegan Paul, 1968); Alvin Goldman, "What Is Justified Belief?" in *Justification and Knowledge,* ed. G. S. Pappas. (Dordrecht, Holland: D. Reidel, 1979) and *Epistemology and Cognition* (Cambridge, MA: Harvard University Press, 1985); Marshall Swain, *Reasons and Knowledge* (Ithaca, NY: Cornell University Press, 1981); and Ernest Sosa, *Knowledge in Perspective* (Cambridge: Cambridge University Press, 1991).

2. D. M. Armstrong, *Belief, Truth, and Knowledge* (Cambridge: Cambridge University Press, 1973); W. V. Quine, *Ontological Relativity* (New York: Columbia University Press, 1969); Fred Dretske, *Knowledge and the Flow of Information* (Cambridge, MA: MIT Press, 1981); and Robert Nozick, *Philosophical Explorations* (Cambridge, MA: Harvard University Press, 1981). Armstrong is a borderline case between the two kinds of externalism. Knowledge is true belief where a lawlike necessity connects the proposition believed and the person's belief of the proposition, but it is the representation not the process that is reliable. Goldman's causal account of knowledge examined in chapter 5 is an example of externalism, which is not a version of reliabilism. Causal theories of knowledge may be considered a third form of externalism.

3. W. V. Quine, *Ontological Relativity and Other Essays* (New York: Columbia University Press, 1969), 82.

4. Alvin Plantinga, *Warrant: The Current Debate* and *Warrant and Proper Function* (Oxford: Oxford University Press, 1993).

5. Earl Conee and Richard Feldman, "Evidentialism," *Philosophical Studies* (1985), 15. Although the exact formulation of the internalist requirement is stated differently by different internalists, this quote captures most of the central elements. For a penetrating analysis of this subject see William Alston, "Internalism and Externalism in Epistemology" and "An Internalist Externalist." In his *Epistemic Justification* (Ithaca, NY: Cornell University Press, 1989), Alston states, "After I become aware of [the reliability of the process by which my belief is formed] I have an adequate reason for the conviction, and this should satisfy internalist scruples" (225).

6. Laurence BonJour, *The Structure of Empirical Knowledge* (Cambridge, MA: Harvard University Press, 1985), 7–8.

7. John Pollock, *Contemporary Theories of Knowledge* (Totowa, NJ: Rowman & Littlefield, 1986), 10. See also Roderick Chisholm, *Theory of Knowledge* (Englewood Cliffs, NJ: Prentice Hall, 1977), 6f, and Paul Moser, *Empirical Justification* (Dordrecht, Holland: D. Reidel, 1985), 126–127.

8. Roderick Chisholm, *Foundations of Knowing* (Minneapolis: University of Minnesota Press, 1982), 12. Here is Chisholm's formulation:

If the property of being *F* is self-presenting, then, for every *x*, if *x* has the property of being *F* and if *x* considers his having that property, then it is certain for *x* that he is then *F*.

As an instance of this principle, Chisholm writes,

If the property of being sad is self-presenting, then, for every *x*, if *x* has the property of being sad and if *x* considers his having that property, then it is certain for *x* that he is then sad.

9. This counterexample is an adaptation of Keith Lehrer's similar example in *Knowledge* (Oxford: Oxford University Press, 1974). See study question 3 for comments on this type of example.

10. Richard E. Nisbett and Timothy Decamp Wilson, "Telling More Than We Can Know: Verbal Reports on Mental Processes," *Psychological Review* 84, 3 (May 1977), 243–244.

11. Ibid., 231.

12. This example is based on a similar example by Roderick Firth, "Are Epistemic Concepts Reducible to Ethical Concepts?" In *Values and Morals,* ed. A. Goldman and J. Kim (Dordrecht, Holland: D. Reidel, 1978). Internalists may add a condition here—the agent must *appreciate* the evidence he or she has. That is, he or she must see how it is connected, but then it is not the evidence that is sufficient but the evidence properly appreciated.

13. My true belief may have been caused by an unreliable process but sustained by a reliable one, in which case it is nevertheless justified. Suppose that God exists, but I believe that God exists simply on the basis of wishful thinking or because my mother, who is not an authority, told me so. Later, I come to have adequate reasons for that belief so although my belief did not originate in the right way, it is sustained by the evidence.

14. Alvin Goldman, "What Is Justified Belief?" in *Justification and Knowledge,* ed. G. Pappas (Dordrecht, Holland: D. Reidel, 1979). Reprinted in *The Theory of Knowledge* 2nd ed., ed. Louis Pojman (Belmont, CA: Wadsworth, 1999).

15. D. M. Armstrong, *Belief, Truth and Knowledge,* 162–177.

16. Goldman, "What Is Justified Belief?"

17. Alvin Plantinga, "Positive Epistemic Status and Proper Function." In *Philosophical Perspectives, 2: Epistemology, 1988,* ed. James E. Tomberlin (Atascadero, CA: Ridgeview Publishing Co, 1988), 25.

18. Based on a handout and lecture, "Naturalistic Epistemology," given by Alvin Goldman at the National Endowment for the Humanities Institute on Naturalism held at the University of Nebraska, Lincoln, June 30, 1993.

19. See Richard Feldman, "Reliability and Justification," *The Monist* 68 (1985) for a development of this objection.

20. Ibid.

21. Laurence BonJour, *The Structure of Empirical Knowledge* (Cambridge, MA: Harvard University Press, 1985), 38.

22. Goldman has addressed examples like BonJour's in the following:

". . . [L]et the process be that of forming beliefs in accord with feelings of clairvoyance. Such a process presumably does not have a high truth ratio in the actual world; nor would it have a high truth ratio in normal worlds. But

suppose *W* contains clairvoyance waves, analogous to sound or light waves. By means of clairvoyance waves people in *W* accurately detect features of their environment just as we detect features of our environment by light and sound. Surely, the clairvoyance belief-forming processes of people in world *W* can yield justified beliefs." ("Strong and Weak Justification," in *Philosophical Perspectives*, 62)
Goldman seems correct here, but Samantha still would not be justified in believing that her clairvoyant practice was a reliable one, at least until a substantial track record or truth ratio were established.

23. Keith Lehrer, *Theory of Knowledge* (Boulder, CO: Westview, 1990), 163–164.

24. Alvin Goldman, "Strong and Weak Justification." In *Philosophical Perspectives, 2: Epistemology, 1988,* ed. James E. Tomberlin (Atascadero, CA: Ridgeview Publishing Co., 1988).

25. Ibid., 52.

26. See Ernest Sosa's "Reliabilism and Intellectual Virtue" and "Intellectual Virtues in Perspective." In *Knowledge in Perspective: Selected Essays in Epistemology* (Cambridge: Cambridge University Press, 1991). My rendition departs from, or at least is not dependent on, Sosa's virtue coherentism.

27. BonJour, 7–8.

FOR FURTHER READING

Alston, William. *Epistemic Justification*. Ithaca, NY: Cornell University Press, 1989.

Armstrong, David M. *Belief, Truth and Knowledge*. Cambridge: Cambridge University Press, 1973.

Chisholm, Roderick. *The Foundations of Knowing*. Minneapolis: University of Minnesota Press, 1957.

_____. *Theory of Knowledge,* 3d ed. Englewood Cliffs, NJ: Prentice Hall, 1989.

Cohen, Stewart. "Justification and Truth," *Philosophical Studies* 46 (1984).

Dretske, Fred. *Knowledge and the Flow of Information*. Cambridge, MA: MIT Press, 1981.

Feldman, Richard. "Reliabilism and Justification," *The Monist* 68 (1985).

Feldman, Richard, and Earl Conee. "Evidentialism," *Philosophical Studies* 48 (1985).

Goldman, Alvin I. *Epistemology and Cognition*. Cambridge, MA: Harvard University Press, 1985. Especially chapters 4 and 5.

Kornblith, Hilary, ed. *Naturalized Epistemology*. Cambridge, MA: MIT Press, 1985.

Moser, Paul. *Epistemic Justification*. Dordrecht, Holland: D. Reidel, 1985. Chapter 4.

Pappas, George, ed. *Justification and Knowledge*. Dordrecht, Holland: D. Reidel, 1979.

Pollock, John L. *Contemporary Theories of Knowledge*. Totowa, NJ: Rowman & Littlefield, 1986.

Swain, Marshall. *Reasons and Knowledge*. Ithaca, NY: Cornell University Press, 1981.

Tomberlin, James, ed. *Philosophical Perspectives, 2: Epistemology, 1988*. Atascadero, CA: Ridgeview Publishing Co., 1988. This volume contains several articles relevant to this section.

CHAPTER 9

The New Externalism: The Theory of Warrant and Proper Function

One of the most intricate, comprehensive, and challenging epistemic theories to appear this century is Alvin Plantinga's system of warrant and proper functioning, systematically set forth in his two volumes, *Warrant: The Current Debate* (1993) and *Warrant and Proper Function* (1993) (page references to these volumes are found in parentheses in the text). Purporting to go beyond reliabilism, Plantinga sets forth a version of naturalized epistemology, which, if it succeeds, solves most of the puzzles of a theory of knowledge and so wins out as the most comprehensive (though admittedly still incomplete) system available.

The key ideas are *warrant* and *proper function,* with the idea of warrant replacing that of *justification* in the analysis of knowledge. While Plantinga declines to submit a definition of the concept, warrant is characterized as the quality that when added to true belief yields knowledge. Plantinga also uses the generic term *positive epistemic status,* which is neutral between justification and warrant when discussing whatever "it" is that, when added to true belief, results in knowledge. The second idea, proper function, involves the notion of our cognitive faculties functioning according to a *design plan* in an environment for which it was intended, one that typically yields true beliefs. Let us examine the main features of this system in order to see how it works.

Rejection of Internalism

As we saw in the last chapter, internalist theories hold that justification of one's beliefs entails accessibility to the reasons for those beliefs. Plantinga defines *internalism* as the view that epistemic warrant and "the properties that confer it are internal in that they are states or conditions of which the cognizer is or can be *aware:* . . . the internalist holds that a person has some kind of special epistemic access to warrant and the properties that ground it."[1] Plantinga argues, in ways similar to our discussion in chapter 8, that the accessibility requirement is neither a necessary nor a sufficient condition for positive epistemic status. But Plantinga goes further than the typical reliabilist in rejecting the accessibility requirement. He rejects the entire concept of justification as misleading because it is bound to what he regards as a bankrupt system of epistemic volitions, duties, and responsibilities. Borrowing a term from ethical theory, Plantinga calls this a *deontological* system. Just as ethical deontologism holds that we have duties to act in certain specified ways and that we are responsible for our voluntary actions, epistemic deontologism also holds that we have duties to believe on the basis of evidence and that we are responsible for our beliefs, as though they were analogous to actions.

According to classical foundationalists like Descartes, Locke, Clifford, and, in our own time, Chisholm, we have some direct and even more indirect control over our belief states and are, thus, responsible for the beliefs with which we end up. We have duties to believe according to the evidence. As Clifford put it, "It is wrong always, everywhere and for anyone to believe anything upon insufficient evidence."[2]

Plantinga rejects both epistemic deontologism (he argues that we do not have duties to believe certain things because we do not have control over our beliefs) and the doctrine of evidentialism to which it is attached. First, let us examine his attack on evidentialism, the Cliffordian notion that having evidence is necessary and sufficient for warrant. Plantinga points out that evidence is not a sufficient condition for warrant (or positive epistemic status) because a person could have evidence but, due to cognitive malfunction, have no warrant for his or her belief. We have only to think of the Cartesian demon or brain-in-the-vat cases to see this.

To this end Plantinga tells of an incident his father had in meeting a man in a Grand Rapids psychiatric hospital. This man complained that he wasn't getting the credit he deserved for inventing a new form of human reproduction, "rotational reproduction," as the man called it. This novel method of reproduction eliminates the need for sex. How does it work? You suspend a woman from a ceiling with a rope and rotate her at a high speed. The result of the rotation process is a large number of children, enough to populate a city the size of Chicago. "As a matter of fact, he claimed, this is precisely how Chicago *was* populated. He realized, he said, that there is something churlish about insisting on getting all the credit due one, but he did think he really hadn't got enough recognition for this important discovery. After all, where would Chicago be without it?"[3]

Plantinga uses this case to argue that evidence doesn't imply epistemic warrant.

> Clearly this set of beliefs fit his evidence; they may fit perfectly. Perhaps it seems to him both that he remembers reading about how the method of rotational reproduction populated the whole city of Chicago, and also that he invented it, though he didn't get credit for it. Even if these beliefs do fit his evidence, however, it is clear that they have little or no warrant; they don't have the property . . . which is sufficient, together with true belief, for knowledge. The problem is not with a failure of fit between his beliefs and what is internally available to him: the problem is that his faculties are not functioning properly; he is insane.[4]

Plantinga downplays the role of epistemic duties, arguing that whatever epistemic duties we have, they are not "anywhere nearly sufficient for warrant."[5] He offers several counterexamples to the notion that epistemic duty fulfillment is necessary and/or sufficient for positive epistemic status.

1. Epistemic duty fulfillment is not sufficient for positive epistemic status. Consider Paul, who, when he is appeared to in one modality, forms a belief that he is appeared to in another modality. For instance,

> "When he is aurally appeared to in the way one is appeared to upon hearing church bells, the belief *he* forms is that there is something that is appearing to him in that way and that it is bright orange."

Paul is not aware of this quirk in his epistemic equipment, and it is not his fault.

> "Indeed, Paul is unusually dutiful, unusually concerned about fulfilling his epistemic duties; fulfilling these duties is the main passion of his life. . . . Then, surely, Paul is doing his epistemic duty *in excelsis* in believing as he does; but the proposition in question has little by way of positive epistemic status for him."(41–42)

Since Paul's epistemic faculties are defective, his belief lacks warrant.

2. But neither is epistemic duty fulfillment necessary for positive epistemic fulfillment. Suppose I nonculpably form the belief that our Alpha Centaurian conquerors hate my believing that I am perceiving something that is red.

> I also believe that they are monitoring my beliefs and, if I form the belief that I see something red, will bring it about that I have a set of beliefs most of which are absurdly false, thus depriving me of any chance

for epistemic excellence. I thereby acquire an epistemic duty to try to withhold the beliefs as that I see a red ball, or a red fire engine, or whatever. Of course I have the same epistemic inclinations everyone else has: when I am appeared to redly, I am powerfully inclined to believe that I see something that is red. By dint of heroic and unstinting effort, however, I am able to train myself to withhold the belief (on such occasions) that I see something red; naturally it takes enormous effort and requires great willpower. On a given morning I go for a walk in London; I am appeared to redly several times (postboxes, traffic signals, redcoats practicing for a reenactment of the American Revolution); each time I successfully resist the belief that I see something red, but only at the cost of prodigious effort. I become exhausted, and resentful. Finally I am appeared to redly in a particularly insistent and out-and-out fashion by a large red London bus. "Epistemic duty be hanged," I mutter, and relax blissfully into the belief that I am now perceiving something red. (45)

This would be a belief that was unjustified for me. But although I broke my epistemic duty in believing it, the belief has warrant for me. Indeed, I know, in spite of my dereliction to duty, that a something red has appeared to me.

Plantinga's conclusion is that since internalism is largely based on the idea of justification rooted in deontologism, and since deontologism with its panoply of epistemic duties is a false doctrine, internalism must be rejected.

The New Externalism

The rejection of the volitional normativity of deontological internalism with its notion of justification leads to externalism. If the external conditions yield the correct results, we are warranted and have knowledge. If the external conditions are not present, we lack warrant no matter how hard we are striving to do our epistemic duty.

Plantinga is attracted to reliabilism as a close approximation to the true theory but rejects it as not being able to solve the problem of generality (discussed in chapter 8) and as being subject to defeating counterexamples. The problem of generality, you will recall, has to do with belief-forming processes being either too specific or too generic. Reliabilism has a difficult time accounting for processes with only one output belief, for every true belief is the outcome of some specific cognitive process. It must also avoid processes that are too general, such as perception, which can produce both justified and nonjustified beliefs.

Plantinga also argues that reliabilism is not necessary or sufficient for positive epistemic status. Goldman's reliabilism states that a belief is justified as long as it is produced by a reliable process. "The justification status of a belief is a function of the reliability of the process or processes that cause it, where (at a first approximation) reliability consists in the tendency of a process to produce beliefs that are true rather than false." Plantinga argues that the outputs of many reliable processes are nonetheless unwarranted. Take, for example, the Case of the Epistemically Serendipitous Lesion.

> There is a rare but specific sort of brain lesion (we may suppose) that is always associated with a number of cognitive processes of the relevant degree of specificity, most of which cause its victim to hold absurdly false beliefs. One of the associate processes, however, causes the victim to believe that he has a brain lesion. Suppose, then, that S suffers from this sort of disorder and accordingly believes that he suffers from a brain lesion. Add that he has no evidence at all for this belief; no symptoms of which he is aware, no testimony on the part of physicians or other expert witnesses, nothing. (Add, if you like, that he has much evidence against it; but then add also that the malfunction induced by the lesion makes it impossible for him to take appropriate account of this evidence.) Then the relevant type . . . will certainly be highly reliable; but the resulting belief—that he has a brain lesion—will have little by way of warrant for S. (199)

In sum: Since the generality problem seems insuperable, and since we can have beliefs caused by reliable processes that are not warranted, reliabilism must be rejected, in spite of its approximation to the truth. In the place of reliable processes (or mechanisms), Plantinga focuses on cognitive faculties that function according to a design plan in a suitable environment. Here is a description of the theory.

> The notion of proper function . . . is crucial to the central paradigms of knowledge and warrant. But that notion is inextricably involved with another: that of the *design plan* of the organ or organism or system in question—the way the thing in question is supposed to work, the way it works when it works properly, when it is subject to no dysfunction. *Design plan* and *proper function* are interdefinable notions: a thing (organism, organ, system, artifact) is functioning properly when it functions in accord with its design plan, and the design plan of a thing is a specification of the way in which a thing functions when it is functioning properly. . . . The first condition for a belief's having warrant, as I see it, is that it be produced by faculties functioning properly. But this is by no means sufficient. A second condition is that the cognitive environment in which the belief is produced must be the one or like the one for

which it is designed. Your epistemic faculties may be functioning with perfect propriety; you may have passed your yearly cognitive examination at MIT with flying colors; but if you have been suddenly transported to a wholly different and alien cognitive environment, your beliefs may have little or no warrant. The basic picture, here, is that we have cognitive faculties that are adapted (by God or evolution or both) to our surroundings, our cognitive environment; and when a belief is produced by these faculties functioning properly, then we have warrant. (213–214)

We should notice in passing that the requirement of an appropriate cognitive environment allows Plantinga to get around Gettier-type counterexamples. The cognitive mechanism designed to select middle-sized objects wasn't meant to select facade barns at a distance. I leave you to consider how helpful this suggestion is and return to the main argument.

Having secured two conditions for warrant—a design plan and proper function—Plantinga now adds a third condition. Noting that some beliefs have pragmatic value (e.g., we believe that we will recover from an illness against the evidence and the belief actually creates the conditions for our recovery), he says, "to have warrant, a belief must also be such that the purpose of the module of the epistemic faculties, producing the belief is to produce true beliefs. Another way to put it: the belief has warrant only if the segment of the design plan governing its production is aimed at truth, at the production of true beliefs" (214). One final stipulation is added: the design plan of these faculties must be a *good* one.

> An angel might design my faculties, aiming at producing a rational creature whose beliefs were for the most part true. If this angel is one of Hume's lazy or incompetent or immature angels, however, then the fact that my beliefs are produced by faculties functioning properly . . . in the environment for which they were designed, and according to a design plan aimed at the truth—that fact will not be sufficient for warrant. It is also necessary that the design in question be a *good* design: that is, that there be a substantial objective probability that a belief of that sort produced under those conditions is true. We might call this *the presupposition of reliability;* it is the condition of warrant the reliabilist seizes upon. (214)

So Plantinga's system of proper functioning faculties according to a design plan incorporates the best of reliabilism but avoids its weaknesses. We may sum up the theory in this way—*S*'s belief *B* is warranted only if

1. *B* is produced in *S* by a properly functioning cognitive faculty;
2. *B* is produced in a cognitive environment that is fitting for this kind of cognitive faculty; that is, the environment must be the one or like the one for which it is designed;
3. the segment (module) of the design plan governing the production of that belief is aimed at production of true beliefs; and
4. there is a high statistical probability that beliefs so produced will be true.

A further word is needed on the notion of the design plan. Plantinga refers to it as the "specifications, or blueprint" of the organism, which causes the organism to work the way it does and defines the idea of proper function. It might seem that the idea that we are constructed according to a design plan requires a theistic interpretation (the design plan is the divine plan). Perhaps not, says Plantinga:

> This terminology does not commit us to supposing that human beings have been literally designed—by God, for example. Here I use "design" the way Daniel Dennett . . . does in speaking of a given organism as possessing a certain design, and evolution as producing optimal design: "In the end, we want to be able to explain the intelligence of man, or beast, in terms of his design; and this in turn in terms of the natural selection of this design." We take it that when the organs (or organic systems) of a human being . . . function properly, they function *in a particular way.* Such organs have a *function* or *purpose;* more exactly, they have several functions or purposes, including both proximate and more remote purposes. The ultimate purpose of the heart is to contribute to the health and proper function of the entire organism . . . But of course the heart also has a much more circumscribed and specific function: to pump blood. Such an organ, furthermore, normally functions in such a way as to fulfill its purpose; but it also functions to fulfill that purpose in just one of an indefinitely large number of possible ways.[6]

Our cognitive systems are similarly designed to function properly under the appropriate circumstances, in environments favorable to them. Either God or evolution (or both) designed us to function successfully in the world.

Finally, Plantinga considers his system to be a radical version of naturalized epistemology in some ways similar to Quine's (see chapter 10).

> So the view I propose is a radical naturalism: striking the naturalistic pose is all the rage these days, and it's a great pleasure to be able to join the

fun. The view I urge is indeed best thought of as an example of naturalistic epistemology; here I follow Quine (if only at some distance). Naturalistic epistemology, however, is ill-named. In the first place, it is quite compatible with, for example, supernaturalistic theism; indeed, the most plausible way to think of warrant, from a theistic perspective, is in terms of naturalistic epistemology. And second . . . , naturalism in epistemology flourishes best in the context of a theistic view of human beings: naturalism in epistemology requires supernaturalism in anthropology.[7]

In chapter 12 ("Naturalism versus Proper Function") of his book *Warrant and Proper Function,* the radical implications of Plantinga's theory of design plan, proper function, and warrant, are made explicit. Up until this point, the naturalist has been translating notions of "design plan" and "proper function" naturalistically, speaking of the fact that our "cognitive faculties are adapted (by God or evolution or both) to our surroundings, our cognitive environment," which when functioning properly produces warrant. The central thesis that knowledge entails warrant and that warrant entails proper function, which in turn entails a design plan has been allowed to exist in a metaphysically naturalist worldview.

But at this point, Plantinga pulls the rug out from under the metaphysical naturalist. He examines several attempts to provide a naturalist account of function and offers telling counterexamples to each of them. The notion of function, so important for science (especially biology and psychology), requires the notion of design, and design requires something non-natural, something or someone supernatural. Metaphysical naturalism, with its evolutionary account of the accidental development of conscious and rational beings, he concludes, lacks a coherent notion of function, let alone proper function. But if so, the argument goes, the naturalist cannot correctly claim to be warranted in any of his or her beliefs. Since warrant is necessary for knowledge, the naturalist is left entirely bereft of claims to knowledge. This includes, of course, the claim to know the truth of naturalism. In other words, Plantinga isn't just being rhetorical when he says early in his work that "naturalism in epistemology requires supernaturalism in anthropology." If we have knowledge, a supernatural being must have designed us.

Plantinga drives home the self-defeating character of naturalism in his final chapter, "Is Naturalism Irrational?" He argues not only that theism makes better sense of epistemic naturalism and proper functioning than secular naturalist theories, but in fact, if evolution is true and our cognitive faculties have merely evolved via a process of chance and necessity, then, while such processes may be survival selective, they are unlikely to have yielded mostly true beliefs. That is, evolution entails that our belief-forming mechanisms and resultant beliefs were produced in order to maximize survival, not truth. But evolutionary theory is one such belief. So if nontheistic evolution is true, we are not justified in believing it is.

In sum, Plantinga's system develops in three stages. In stage 1, he rejects internalism with its doctrines of justification, evidentialism, and deontologism. In stage 2, he embraces externalism with its emphasis on cognitive faculties functioning properly (as they were designed) in suitable environments. In stage 3, he ascends to metaphysical super-naturalism upon which to ground his epistemic naturalism. External-ist epistemologies require supernatural metaphysics. Plantinga's goal is to ground epistemology in Christian theism.

A Critique of Plantinga's New Externalism

Plantinga's critique of the main epistemic competitors and the development of his own system are powerful forces to be reckoned with. As with all the epistemic systems studied in this book, it has strengths and weaknesses. It seems more successful in dealing with the general-ity problem than are reliabilist theories. That is, by specifying whether a belief is formed by a properly functioning faculty in a suitable envi-ronment, we resolve the issues of specificity and generality (though we may invite the problem of specifying exactly which faculty is doing what—Plantinga admits that his inability to give a thorough account of this leaves his system incomplete). His new externalism promises to solve the Gettier problems. It also offers a more detailed analysis of positive epistemic status. In some ways it seems the most well worked-out system available. However, I think it has some serious difficulties that must be resolved before it is accepted as the correct theory. Let me briefly identify five of them.

Problem 1. Plantinga's theory holds that we have been designed in such a way that under appropriate conditions, our epistemic faculties function properly. But is it really clear that we do function properly, in Plantinga's sense? Or would it be more accurate to withhold judg-ment or even to suspect that our epistemic faculties' function gets a mixed evaluation? First of all, let us ask: Can a system be designed without functioning properly? Proper design does not seem sufficient for an efficient epistemic system. Plantinga recognizes this and admits that a Humean lesser angel could have designed us, so that we do not function well.

But what reason is there to suppose that we have been designed to function as well as possible or that our cognitive mechanisms have been designed to function in a way that produced a higher ratio of true to false beliefs? We can only discern a small part of the electromagnetic spectrum, but we would be better off if we were able to discern—and so avoid—gamma rays and ultraviolet rays. Our ears are crudely designed and fail to hear sounds in the upper and lower ranges. Compared with canines, we lack an acute sense of smell, which could save us in many situations. We could have been constructed with acute monitors to perceive deception in the auditory tones of the voices of enemies. Likewise, we could have been designed in such a way as to detect harmful gases, chemical toxicity, and harmful bacteria. Often our emotions get in the way of our judgment (neurologists say the limbic area of the brain overwhelms the cognitive area of our cerebral cortex), so that we fail to observe evidence clearly or to draw valid inferences. Our cognitive processes do not function optimally or even near optimally. They are fragile and break down because of disease and age, and it is unclear if our cognitive processes yield a sufficiently high proportion of true beliefs over false ones for us to conclude that this is *proper* functioning. Perhaps some of our epistemic processes work well in certain contexts, but they don't work well in many others.

These reflections have implications for Plantinga's theist account of proper functioning. If we are designed by a perfect being, shouldn't our cognitive processes function better? The fact that they are so imperfect may be construed as an argument against the perfection or omnipotence of whomever or whatever designed us or is responsible for our being. If an intelligent being designed our noetic faculties, this being seems to have had many limitations. Here, evolutionary theory with its nonteleological notion of adaptation and adequacy for survival and reproduction of genotypes rather than optimality, seems to have the advantage. I will not pursue this line of thought because it gets us beyond the structure of knowledge into philosophy of religion, but it is a problem with which to wrestle. I will return to the question of evolution and a divine design plan in problems 2 and 5.

Problem 2.   Our second criticism is of the relationship between design and proper function. Is a design plan a necessary condition for warrant? Can we function properly without being well designed or designed for a function? Plantinga defines warrant as properly functioning belief formation in an appropriate environment according to a design plan that is successfully aimed at truth. But, we can imagine situations where we are warranted in our beliefs in a way that does not presuppose a design plan.

Suppose that Al has been designed by God with properly functioning cognitive modules. Scientists have perfected the art of duplicating objects, and someone has accidentally left a duplicator on. Al accidentally falls in, producing Al-2. Al-2 is built exactly like Al; that is, Al-2 processes information in the same way, acquires the same beliefs in the same circumstances, and so forth. It would be highly counterintuitive to say that Al knows that a brown dog is in the room and that Al-2 does not, even though both can see the dog and both believe there is a dog in the room because they see the dog. Yet, Al-2's belief-producing faculties were not created with the intention of producing true beliefs.[8]

James Taylor invites us to imagine a person, Theodore, who acquires beliefs the way that we do. Unlike us, however, he has not been designed, either by a personal agent or by evolution. His coming to exist "was an unintended side-effect of an intentional action."[9] An angel botched another job, and somehow Theodore is the unintended result. He functions reliably and has warranted beliefs, but his cognitive faculties are not the result of a design plan.

Plantinga has responded to this putative counterexample. He argues that it is not clear that a being could originate as an unintended byproduct of another creation, so a Theodore creation may not be possible. Unless we have reason to think that it is broadly logically possible, it has little force as a counterexample.[10]

Is this a good response? Well, one might point out (*tu quoque*) that Plantinga's own counterexamples against the reliabilists (e.g., the Case of the Serendipitous Lesion) don't seem to happen to people either, but they may reveal a logical point, namely, that reliability may not be sufficient for warrant. Likewise, the Theodore case may show that proper design is not logically necessary for warrant. If Plantinga's science fiction counterexample is to be allowed, why isn't Taylor's? There seems no relevant difference.

Consider another type of counterexample. Imagine Samantha, discussed in chapter 8. A normal human without extraordinary powers, she is in a car accident in which her brain is put into a peculiar state so that she acquires clairvoyant powers. Clairvoyance was not part of the original design plan. It is not in the divine plan at all, but it becomes a feature of Samantha's cognitive apparatus. She regularly and reliably receives information via this process.

Plantinga rejects the Samantha-like cases too. He asks us to imagine a radio that accidentally falls off the roof, thereby improving the radio's reception, allowing it to receive radio waves from Eastern Europe and the like. In a sense it fulfills the purpose of the original design plan, so that if the radio loses these exotic qualities, we would still say that it is functioning properly. Or, we may say that when it falls, it receives a new design plan.

At first glance we might object that Plantinga is interpreting design plan so generously and broadly as to make it consistent with almost any functioning mechanism. A *properly* functioning faculty may simply be one that accomplishes some designated or identifiable goal.

Note that, at least in some of the passages already cited, Plantinga seems to want his theory to be acceptable to either naturalistic (non-supernaturalistic) evolutionary theory, theistic creationism, or theistic evolutionary theory. A worry immediately arises about whether the metaphor of design already begs the question in favor of theism. Strictly speaking, Darwinian evolutionary theory has no place for design or purpose. Artifacts, like knives and cars, are designed and have purposes, but products of evolutionary development do not.

According to naturalist evolutionary theory, the laws of nature and chance have caused a complex type of being, homo sapiens, to evolve from less complex life forms. Humans are survival selective; that is, we will tend to survive to the extent that we successfully adapt to our environment (individual survival) and reproduce (genotype survival). We have different mechanisms that play instrumental roles in these two survival processes, e.g., visual systems for seeing (discriminating a small segment of the electromagnetic spectrum), auditory systems (monitoring and manipulating sound waves for purposes of communication), a digestive system (enabling us to take in nourishment and excrete waste), a cardiovascular system (enabling us to circulate nourishment throughout the body), and a cognitive system (enabling us to take in information, process it, and make action-guiding inferences).

Some types of mechanisms or systems enable individuals to survive and flourish and reproduce better than others. Perfect or 20/20 vision is more fitness enhancing than 80/400 vision. An auditory range between 40 and 120 decibels is more fitness enhancing than a range between 60 and 90 decibels. Smelling with the acuity of a canine is more survival selective than smelling as weakly as we do. It would be better for survival purposes to have mechanisms that discerned harmful X rays, gamma rays, and ultraviolet waves or mechanisms that enabled us to perceive an enemy's intentions as we perceive colors or sounds.

According to evolutionary theory, obtaining true beliefs is of limited survival value. We need to navigate between hard objects and avoid predators and succeed in obtaining nourishment. To these ends we'd better have accurate beliefs, but it actually may help us to have some "higher-order" false beliefs or improbable beliefs. (William James describes the mountain climber who must get himself to believe against the evidence that he is able to leap a broad crevice in order to have even a small chance of succeeding.) All things being equal, a group of warriors who believe in a Jihad in which, if they die, they will go to heaven, will outlast or outfight warriors who have no such belief (and so are more likely to flee or surrender when the fight gets dangerous). Belief in invisible but nonexistent spiritual agencies who reward moral behavior and punish immoral behavior may likewise be fitness enhancing, in that such belief restrains socially harmful behavior and promotes socially helpful behavior.

But if Plantinga intends the notion of "design" to cover these kinds of cases, he seems simply to mean by design "any function whatsoever," or something like this. Then it would follow that Theodore and Samantha have design plans. It is only a matter of design plans that more or less successful. If the world only came into existence by chance five minutes ago, it would no doubt come into existence with design plans already built in.[11]

The issue is complex, but I leave it to you to decide whether the notion of a design plan comes to anything more than a broad type of functionalism. If it does reduce to functionalism, then it would seem that the theory of proper functioning reduces to a type of reliabilism—reliable functionalism. I will return to the issue of the metaphor of design in problem 5.

Problem 3. Plantinga may have rejected reliabilism too quickly. If the distinctions that we discussed in chapter 8 are correct (between animal knowledge, fortuitous knowledge, and reflective knowledge), the Case of the Serendipitous Lesion can be resolved in favor of reliabilism. It is a case of freak (or animal) knowledge rather than reflective knowledge. Alvin Goldman and Ernest Sosa have recently set forth companion versions of reliabilism that bypass the idea of proper functioning (and design) and focus instead on intellectual virtues.

According to Sosa, an intellectual virtue is a "competence in virtue of which one would mostly attain the truth and avoid error in a certain field of propositions *F,* when in certain condition *C.*"[12] A person *S* is warranted in believing some proposition within a class of propositions when *S* is in a suitable cognitive condition and in a suitable environment, so that *S* would most likely be right if *S* believed the proposition in question. Virtue Epistemology, as a form of reliabilism, claims to have the virtues of avoiding appeal to proper functioning and a design plan, so it does all the things that Plantinga's system does without the extra baggage. Of course, Virtue Epistemology is only in its incipient state and has yet to be fully developed, let alone scrutinized. We will examine it in chapter 11.

Problem 4.   An even more basic problem is Plantinga's rejection of internalism. He rejects internalism because of its deontologism, the idea that we have epistemic duties and that they are necessary and/or sufficient for justification. Plantinga argues such duties are neither necessary nor sufficient for positive epistemic status.

Here we must recur to a distinction I made in chapter 8 between objective and subjective justification. Fulfilling one's epistemic duties involves subjective justification, although it may not be enough for knowledge. Whether there is objective justification, beyond subjective justification, depends on whether we are internalists (who allow only subjective justification) or reliabilists (who sometimes allow both). The internalist never pretended that justification was sufficient for knowledge, and some internalists would concede that it is not necessary either. What the internalist insists on is that we have prima facie duties to check our evidence at appropriate times (e.g., when questioned by our epistemic peers), to cultivate our epistemic virtues, to pay attention to evidence over important matters, to learn to judge impartially, and so forth.

The theory is that there is a relevant causal relation between these epistemic duties, which form subjective justification, and knowledge. These duties can be overridden by other considerations, of course, as in the case of my confusedly believing that Alpha Centaurians are deluding me into seeing red. Such cases of deception are not the normal fare, however. Sometimes following the best evidence leads us astray, but this is a problem for the believer in warrant and proper function too. In unsuitable environments our belief-forming mechanisms don't function properly. Likewise, in unsuitable environments, commitment to following our epistemic duties may lead us astray.

Let me expand on this point by appealing to a distinction in utilitarian ethical theory. Following C. I. Lewis, utilitarians often distinguish between three types of moral rightness:

1. the subjective right act
2. the objective right act
3. the absolute right act

Consider Adolf Hitler's grandmother, Frau Schicklgruber, who is carrying the infant Adolf down the stairs of their home. She slips and little Adolf is about to smash his head against the step, which would bring about his death. But in the nick of time Frau Schicklgruber lunges forward and cushions the blow to Adolf's head by putting her own hand between his head and the lethal stair. She breaks her hand but saves his life.

Did Frau Schicklgruber do the morally right thing? Yes and no. From the perspective of subjective rightness she did; she acted out of goodwill, attempting to do a deed that she believed would prevent harm. The subjective right act is that act done out of good intentions, aiming at some utilitarian result.

But objective rightness goes beyond mere subjective intention and focuses on the evidence at one's disposal or reasons for action. An act is objectively right if and only if it is done according to the best evidence available, evidence that doing that act would maximize utility. Here, too, Frau Schicklgruber is justified. She had every reason to believe that it would be a good thing to save little Adolf from injury or death.

Absolute rightness is another matter, however, and here Frau Schicklgruber may well have done the wrong deed. The absolute right act is that act which *in fact* brings about the best utilitarian result. Perhaps we seldom or never can know for sure which act would have done that, but in hindsight we may have a good idea of what that would be. We have good reason to believe that it would have been better for humanity had Frau Schicklgruber let the infant die.

Apply this distinction to epistemic justification. Here, too, there is a subjective, objective, and absolute sense of justification. Subjective justification concerns an epistemic goodwill, doing one's best to bring it about that one has the best set of beliefs possible, a coherent set of mostly true beliefs. It is what the internalist's ideal of deontological justification is about.

Objective epistmic rightness or justification involves having one's beliefs based on the best evidence or having one's beliefs caused by a reliable process or belief-forming mechanism (or properly functioning faculty). It is on what reliabilism and externalism in general focus. But objective rightness does not guarantee knowledge or even true beliefs because a reliable belief-forming process or properly functioning faculty can occasionally yield false beliefs.

Absolute epistemic rightness or justification is the desideratum of both internalism and externalism, a case where warranted or justified belief yields knowledge. It is successful believing.

Plantinga and externalists in general emphasize the ideas of objective and absolute justification, but they tend to underrate the role of subjective justification, which internalists emphasize. Having good epistemic intentions, they rightly point out, is neither a necessary nor a sufficient condition for absolute justification (full knowledge), but it is highly relevant for knowledge. It plays an important causal role in getting us to focus on the available evidence, to critically evaluate the available evidence, and to develop our epistemic faculties to the point of precision, where it will be more likely that we will obtain more warranted beliefs.

To paraphrase Hamlet, subjective justification is better appreciated in the breach than in the observance. Consider cases where it is absent, such as in a case of prejudice, where the bigoted person holds his or her beliefs on a matter only by obstinate disregard and willful ignorance of the evidence that one could have if one only willed to see it. This individual has failed to develop the kind of virtuous belief-forming mechanisms that would cause him to become more objectively justified, which in turn would cause him to obtain a more verific set of beliefs.

If this is correct—if subjective justification is causally connected to absolute justification—then Plantinga has failed to see the intimate connection between internalist notions of justification and what he calls warrant. In the end all we can do is our epistemic best, and this is being subjectively justified.

Problem 5.   Recall Plantinga's radical claim that since knowledge entails warrant, and warrant entails proper functioning (according to a design plan in certain environments), and since the secularist cannot legitimately use the concept of function, the secularist cannot attribute warrant to any of his or her beliefs—or legitimately claim (or deny) that anyone knows anything. Several philosophers, including Larry Wright, John Pollock, Ruth Millikan, John Bigelow, and Robert Partgetter, have devised naturalistic accounts of proper functioning. Beginning with Pollock's definition that a thing's function is what it normally does, and moving on to more sophisticated definitions, Plantinga offers cogent counterexamples to many of the leading proponents of a naturalist account of function. He mentions, but omits analyzing, Wright's version of a naturalist account of function, which some philosophers believe to be the most promising version. Wright defines the function of a structure or process this way:

> The function of X is F means (a) X is there because it does F, (b) F is a consequence (or result) of X's being there.[13]

In other words, a function F of a structure or process X is both an effect of that structure and the cause of X's existence. Let us apply this formula to mechanical and biological processes. For example, the function of a knife is to cut things, which *means* (a) knives exist because they cut and (b) cutting is a consequence or result of a knife's being present. Applying the definition to biological entities, we would say "the function of the heart is to pump blood," which *means* (a) the heart is there because it does pump blood and (b) pumping blood is a consequence of the heart's being present.

This account of function seems superior to the ones Plantinga examines, but it may have problems of its own. Christopher Boorse offers one: A leak in a pipe releases gas, which knocks out a repair person intending to close the leak. We can apply Wright's definition to this situation: "the function of the pipe to leak gas *means* (a) the leak is there because it releases gas and (b) releasing gas is a consequence of the presence of the leak."[14] But surely something has gone awry here, for it seems absurd to say that the accident of a leak in a gas pipe has the function of releasing gas. Michael Levin has argued that Wright's account can survive Boorse's counterexamples, if we notice the difference

> between the role of the efficient cause of the leak—perhaps increasing gas pressure—and that of the efficient cause of hearts, the process that builds hearts out of protein. Not only do hearts exist because they circulate blood, heart-building processes *also* exist because they build hearts. These processes can be explained via their fitness effects, the advantage they confer on organisms by making (fitness-conferring) hearts. In contrast, the gas pressure did not increase because it was leading to a leak.[15]

I must leave the matter of whether Wright and Levin or Boorse and Plantinga are correct in their theses regarding the success of a naturalist account of function. Perhaps we should not expect exact definitions of biological concepts. After all, we don't have a watertight definition of most of the important biological concepts: "life," "species," and "gene." Perhaps the same goes for the concept "function." But I leave this suggestion for your consideration. Instead, I want to argue that even if Plantinga is correct and the naturalist's attempt at defining "function" fails, it does not matter. Or rather, it only shows that there is something wrong with Plantinga's basing the notion of warrant on a supernatural account of function.

Suppose we grant, as I am inclined to, that the idea of a design plan and epistemic *proper functioning* does presuppose a creationist or supernatural (theistic) view of human nature. As we noted earlier, especially in considering problem 2, the Darwinian evolution theory eschews the idea of design altogether. We have developed from lower forms of life through an accidental process of survival of the fittest in a struggle for survival. The process is one of chance and necessity, not purpose and design. Of course, we do speak of the heart having a function, implying purposiveness, but this is mainly either because we have a metaphysical (teleological) view of human nature or because we are treating the heart's workings metaphorically, as though it had an intrinsic function.

Plantinga argues that while science can theoretically get along without the idea of function, the price it will have to pay seems prohibitively high.

> For most of the disciplines falling under biology, psychology, sociology, economics, and the like essentially involve those functional generalizations of which we have spoken, and those generalizations, in turn, essentially involve the notions of proper function, damage, malfunction, purpose, design plan, and others of that family.

But what, precisely, is the problem? Can't anyone, theist or not, see that a horse, say, is suffering from a disease, is displaying a pathological condition? Can't anyone see that an injured bird has a wing that isn't working properly? That an arthritic hand does not function properly, or that a damaged rotator cuff doesn't work as it ought?[16]

The hypothesis of a Blind Watchmaker,[17] the mindless forces of natural selection, makes the full-blooded use of functional language unnecessary. Disease, pathology, insanity, and warrant itself, together with the concept of knowledge that requires functional notions, are no longer within the realm of our conceptual schemes.

But if this is true, "what's a poor naturalist to do?" (to quote Plantinga). My suggestion is that the metaphysical naturalist should admit that functionalist discourse is problematic and may need to be reinterpreted or used metaphorically and possibly abandoned for scientific purposes. Our functionalist language, accordingly, is metaphorical, a holdover from days when theology informed science. Strictly speaking, the naturalist contends, there are no natural functions, only purposive beings like us who impute functions to biological organs and systems in accordance with our interests.

But, if the secularist cannot use the notion of a function with regard to epistemology, neither can he or she buy into Plantinga's notion of design plan or warrant, which depends on the notion of function. But all is not lost. The evolutionist epistemologist can still speak of the adaptiveness of our cognitive faculties. Levin contends that "we could, indeed, retain Plantinga's definition of warrant by replacing 'cognitive faculties whose function it is to produce true belief' with 'cognitive faculties which exist because they produced true belief,' and 'working as they should in a cognitive environment for which they were designed' with 'working as they did in an environment in which they evolved.' Biology and epistemology would lose only a word."[18]

For those secularists who do not want to embrace internalism, there are, at least, two roads open. One is the sort of reliabilism examined in chapter 8, and the other is a more radical version of naturalist externalism more akin to evolutionary considerations. To this type of externalism, "Naturalized Epistemology," we now turn.

Summary

We have examined Plantinga's theory of warrant and proper function and noted its cogent critique of internalism, justificationism, deontologism, and other rival theories. In the end, it must be seen as a theistic or supernaturalist epistemology. If knowledge depends on warrant and warrant on proper function, then a supernatural entity must exist. The design plan is a divine plan; proper functioning is a functioning according to God's blueprint. As such Plantinga's theory does go beyond reliabilism and, for those who are inclined to a religious worldview, it marks itself as an original and plausible theory. But take away the theistic or supernatural foundation and what are we left with? The answer may be a version of reliabilism, what Tom Senor calls "teleological reliabilism," in recognition of its design aspect.

QUESTIONS FOR DISCUSSION

1. Examine Plantinga's critique of internalism. How strong is it? If you were inclined to internalism, would you give up this theory on the basis of Plantinga's attack? If not, how would you defend your position?

2. Some, such as Tom Senor, have suggested that Plantinga's theory is really another version of reliabilism (i.e., teleological reliabilism). Discuss this possibility.

3. Explain Plantinga's notion of a design plan. Does it suggest a supernatural designer? Is Plantinga's theory really a defense of theism?

4. Go over the five problems or criticisms leveled against Plantinga in this chapter. How strong are they? What might Plantinga say in response?

5. The discussion of problem 5 needs to be carried further than space permitted in this work. Look at the further discussion in note 16 (better yet, read chapter 11 of Plantinga's *Warrant and Proper Function* together with Wright's "Functions") and discuss

whether the idea of function can be dropped from biological and epistemological discussion. If it did, could we find a way to retain Plantinga's definition of warrant: "cognitive faculties whose function is to produce true belief"? Michael Levin has suggested that we could substitute the nonfunctionalist phrase "cognitive faculties which exist because they produce (d) true belief." He proposes replacing Plantinga's "working as they should in a cognitive environment for which they were designed" with "working as they did in an environment in which they evolved." ("Plantinga on Function and the Theory of Evolution," unpublished manuscript by Levin.) What would be the implications of making such substitutions? Would we lose more than a word?

NOTES

1. Alvin Plantinga, *Warrant: The Current Debate* (Oxford: Oxford University Press, 1993), 5.
2. W. K. Clifford, "The Ethics of Belief," *Lectures and Essays* (London: Macmillan, 1879), 183.
3. Alvin Plantinga, "Why We Need Proper Function," *Nous* (March 1993).
4. Ibid.
5. Plantinga, *Current Debate*, 45.
6. Plantinga, *Warrant and Proper Function* (Oxford: Oxford University Press, 1993), 13–14. I should point out that while the terminology itself may not commit one to a literal design by God, Plantinga later argues that a literal design is the only way to make sense of the ideas of a design plan and proper function. An interesting question is whether Plantinga deduces theism (or the creation by a lesser angel) from the idea of function.
7. Plantinga, ibid., 46.
8. I owe this example to Michael Levin who attributes it to Peter Unger.
9. James Taylor, "Plantinga's Proper Functioning Analysis of Epistemic Warrant," *Philosophical Studies* 64 (1991). My analysis is indebted to Taylor's article.
10. Alvin Plantinga, "Warrant and Designing Agents: A Reply to James Taylor," *Philosophical Studies* 64 (1991).
11. Plantinga writes:
    > Russell is right: it is surely possible, in the broadly logical sense, that the world should (sic) have popped into existence five minutes ago, complete with all its apparent traces of the past—all its dusty books, decaying buildings, mature oaks, crumbling mountains, and apparent memories. This is possible, more, it is compatible with my present experience's being as in fact it is. (*Proper Function,* 62)
12. Ernest Sosa, "Reliabilism and Intellectual Virtues," *Knowledge in Perspective* (Cambridge: Cambridge University Press, 1991), 138. See also his article "Proper Function and Virtue Epistemology," *Nous* 27, 1 (1993). Alvin Goldman,

"Epistemic Folkways and Scientific Epistemology," *Liaisons: Philosophy Meets Cognitive and Social Sciences* (Cambridge, MA: MIT Press/Bradford, 1991).

13. Larry Wright, "Functions," *Philosophical Review* 82 (1973).
14. Adapted from Christopher Boorse, "Wright on Functions," *Philosophical Review* 85 (1976).
15. Michael Levin, "Plantinga on Functions and the Theory of Evolution" (unpublished manuscript) for a defense of Wright. I am deeply indebted to Levin's discussion.
16. Plantinga, *Proper Function*, 197–198.
17. The term is Richard Dawkin's, who writes:
    All appearances to the contrary, the only watchmaker in nature is the blind forces of physics, albeit deployed in a very special way. A true watchmaker has foresight: he designs his cogs and springs, and plans their interconnections, with a future purpose in his mind's eye. Natural selection, the blind, unconscious automatic process which Darwin discovered, and which we now know is the explanation for the existence and apparently purposeful form of all life, has no purpose in mind. It has no mind and no mind's eye. It does not plan for the future. It has no vision, no foresight, no sight at all. If it can be said to play the role of watchmaker in nature, it is the *blind* watchmaker. (*The Blind Watchmaker* [New York: Norton, 1986], 5; quoted in Plantinga, *Proper Function*, 197)
18. Levin, op. cit.

FOR FURTHER READING

Feldman, Richard. "Proper Functionalism," *Nous* 27, 1 (1993).
Plantinga, Alvin. *Warrant and Proper Function*. Oxford: Oxford University Press, 1993.

CHAPTER 10

Naturalized Epistemology

We are like sailors who must repair their boat on the open sea, without being able to dismantle it in a dry-dock and reconstruct it there out of the best materials. (Otto Neurath)[1]

I see philosophy not as an a priori groundwork for science, but as continuous with science. I see philosophy and science as in the same boat—a boat which, to revert to Neurath's figure as I so often do, we can rebuild only at sea while staying afloat in it. There is no external vantage point, no first philosophy. All scientific findings, all scientific conjectures that are at present plausible, are therefore in my view as welcome for use in philosophy as elsewhere. For me then the problem of induction is a problem about the world: a problem of how we, as we now are (by our present scientific lights), in a world we never made, should stand better than random or coin-tossing chances of coming out right when we predict by inductions which are based on our innate, scientifically unjustified similarity standard. Darwin's natural selection is a plausible partial explanation. (W. V. Quine)[2]

Quine's Naturalism

In 1968 W. V. Quine, one of the premier philosophers of logic, gave a lecture, "Epistemology Naturalized," in which he sounded the death knell of classical epistemology centered in the normative notion of justification. Quine believes that, because classical foundationalism, from Descartes to Rudolf Carnap, has failed for three hundred years in its attempt to ground our knowledge claims, we should recognize that its method and goal are fundamentally flawed. As he says, the "Cartesian quest for certainty had been the remote motivation of epistemology, both on its conceptual and its doctrinal side; but that quest was seen as a lost cause."[3] We must give up traditional a priori epistemology, the method of setting forth conceptual criteria for knowledge and then applying them to science, and instead see empirical psychology as the successor to traditional epistemology.

Whereas "old epistemology aspired to contain natural science, epistemology in its new setting is contained in natural science, as a chapter of psychology." As cognitive psychology, the new epistemology is a descriptive examination of the relation "between the meagre input [of sensory stimulation] and the torrential output [our picture of the world.][4] The "meagre input" of our empirical observations now becomes the basis of a behaviorist naturalism, one centered in prediction and verification. We do not know the world as it is in itself (whatever that may mean), but only through sensory evidence, the reports of our activated sensory receptors. Thus, epistemology becomes empiricism. Quine called this new relationship of epistemology as the handmaiden of science, *epistemology naturalized.*

Although anticipated by the work of the American pragmatists, especially John Dewey, Quine's essay was the watershed expression of a pragmatic naturalistic attempt to understand the nature of knowledge. At this point, naturalistic epistemology still remains largely programmatic, and Quine's own work is subject to different interpretations. For our purposes we may note three central theses:

1. Traditional or classical epistemology, which claimed to ground our knowledge via a priori criteria, is a lost cause.

2. Skepticism, which motivated and undermined traditional epistemology, is a red herring, a pseudoproblem.

3. Science, as an extension of common sense and based on the method of verification, is our only guide to truth. As such, philosophy, especially epistemology, must be subsumed under its aegis.

We have already noted Quine's rejection of classical foundationalism. He sets forth the work of his mentor Rudolf Carnap as the culmination of three centuries of traditional epistemology. Carnap attempted a rational reductive reconstruction of experience in terms of sense experience, logic, and set theory. The reconstruction had two goals: a conceptual reduction, whereby physical terms are reduced to terms referring to phenomenal features of sensory experience, and a doctrinal reduction, whereby truths about the physical world are *correctly* obtained from sensory experience.

Along with most of Logical Positivism's grand design, the twofold reduction has generally been declared a failure. The conceptual reduction turned out to be an infinite labor, and the doctrinal reduction turned out to rest on an illicit idea of normativity or correctness. There is no single right way to characterize the world, but merely the relation between our different theories—a "meagre [sensory] input and the torrential output." It should be noted, however, that here Quine is not an antimodernist, equating all worldviews as equally justified. Science is the touchstone of truth, and observation statements are publicly verifiable, so that the range of acceptable theories is reduced to the range of acceptable practicing science.

Science and Skepticism

The second and third theses are related. Regarding the pseudoproblem of skepticism, Quine charges that we have been led astray by trying to solve an artificial problem. Because Quine is a pragmatist and is concerned with prediction and observation, he sees the skeptic as irrefutable but irrelevant. Rather than be preoccupied with the question of whether we have any knowledge, we must take science (as an extension of common sense) as our starting point. All philosophical questions occur within, not above, science. Science alone, with its ability to verify, explain, and predict, gives us an adequate understanding of the world. Regarding the confidence that we do have knowledge, Quine appeals to Darwin's theory of evolution. If most of our beliefs were not true, we probably would not be here.

> There is some encouragement in Darwin. If people's innate spacing of qualities is a gene-linked trait, then the spacing that has made for the most successful inductions will have tended to predominate through natural selection. Creatures inveterately wrong in their inductions have a pathetic but praiseworthy tendency to die before reproducing their kind.[5]

Quine bases his faith on science in its predictive success. It is the only game in town. Religion, intuition, and other rivals for knowing are either dismissed ("I do not believe in the Homeric gods") or left as unworthy of mention.

In replacing normative epistemology, which emphasizes justification, with psychology and biology, which are primarily descriptive, Quine seems to be rejecting the normative role of epistemology altogether. Jaegwon Kim, Hilary Putnam, Alvin Goldman, Barry Stroud, Morton White, and others interpreted Quine this way, and argued that normativity is necessary for both adjudicating the claims of science and the heart of traditional epistemology. Kim points out that the very notion of rationality to which Quine appeals is a normative one.[6] So, Quine has not shown that traditional epistemology was bankrupt. He simply has changed the subject.

Quine, however, has repudiated this interpretation. He does not reject the need for normativity. "Naturalization of epistemology does not jettison the normative and settle for the indiscriminate description of ongoing procedures." He calls epistemic normativity

> . . . a branch of engineering. It is the technology of truth-seeking. . . .
> There is no question here of ultimate value, as in morals; it is a matter of
> efficacy for an ulterior end, truth or prediction. The normative here, as
> elsewhere in engineering, becomes descriptive, when the terminal para-
> meter is expressed.[7]

Analysis of Quine's Naturalism

It is not entirely clear from these passages exactly how normativity relates to the descriptive role of science, but I interpret these and other passages in one of two ways:

1. They may be seen as pointing to a version of reliabilism. Induction and other science-validating methods yield a high ratio of true beliefs over false beliefs. In this case Quine's theory would reduce to a type of reliabilism (discussed in chapter 8). But then it is not clear that traditional epistemology, first kicked out the front door, has not snuck back through the back door. Conceptual analysis that characterizes knowledge as reliably produced true belief would still be the task of philosophers. Quine would probably say that he has not eliminated conceptual analysis altogether but only dethroned it, consigning it to the menial task of a doorman.

2. Quine may also be interpreted as giving a more pragmatic theory of normativity, one based on hypothetical goals. Given the normal human goals of survival, prospering, and having holistic world-views, scientific methods satisfy these desiderata better than any other set of methods. That is, science, as a human enterprise for explaining, predicting, and controlling, is normative or has normative criteria built into it. Because this kind of normativity depends on human values (the desires to explain, predict, and control), Quine's version of normativity will be hypothetical rather than categorical. It has the form: if you want success predicting behavior, you ought to do X rather than Y. If you want to predict the next appearance of a comet, use astronomical methods rather than astrological ones. Quine denies that there is any a priori or transcendent grounding of epistemic normativity.

Actually, these two interpretations are compatible. A process can be reliable and useful but not categorical or binding relative to our interests. Epistemology, qua the dimension of science, may offer us a reliable mechanism for approximating truth, but we may not always want the truth. We may be interested in aesthetic experience, hedonic pleasure, or some other kind of success. Therefore, the reliable aspect of epistemology may be subservient to the pragmatic. If we value truth, try science.[8]

Interpreted in this pragmatic manner, science is the sole adjudicator of justification and truth. Using the metaphor of Neurath, it is our only reliable raft at sea. We cannot jettison it without peril, nor can we take it apart all at once (hence, the rejection of skepticism). We may examine and replace one plank of the raft while being supported by the other parts, but we may never question the whole at once. We may improve our raft, but it is all we have to assure us of success of our needs and goals. As Quine asserts, "There is no external vantage point, no first philosophy. All scientific findings, all scientific conjectures that are at present plausible, are therefore in my view as welcome for use in philosophy as elsewhere." If this instrumentalist interpretation is accepted, then it is doubtful whether the notion of truth is doing traditional work. Quine's theory seems reduced to a pragmatic theory of truth—that which yields results that satisfy our concerns of predicting observations. This seems to conflate truth with justification, both of which have to do with satisfying instrumental requirements. But then we still have the traditional epistemic task of questioning whether the pragmatic theory itself is justified, let alone true.[9]

Either way, a prima facie case for the legitimacy of traditional epistemology is lurking between the lines of Quine's own arguments against traditional epistemology. If we accept the reliabilist explanation, we still have to determine what is a reliable process for truth conduciveness. If we accept the pragmatist interpretation, we have to ask exactly what we mean by that concept and why pragmatism is valid.

Furthermore, thesis 1 overlooks the possibility of fallibilist foundationalisms and versions of coherentism, such as BonJour and Lehrer's, which carry on the traditional tasks of epistemology in sophisticated ways. Not many philosophers hold to the strong infallibilist notions of Descartes or the radical reductivist programs of the logical positivists. Not many philosophers will deny the enormous contribution of cognitive psychology in helping us understand the way the mind forms beliefs. But it seems premature to move from these two premises— that infallibilist versions of foundationalism are bankrupt and that psychology has revealed much about the nature of human cognition—to the conclusion that epistemology must now be seen as a chapter within psychology. It is a non sequitur.

Regarding thesis 2—the idea that skepticism, which motivated traditional epistemology, is a pseudoproblem—Quine holds that the only place that the question "how is knowledge possible?" legitimately arises, is within science. But when it does arise within the scientific enterprise, the methods or conclusions of science are the only resources available to answer it. Therefore, the defeat of the skeptic is the defeat of the hegemony of epistemology.

But can't we doubt this? Quine himself admits that Hume's undermining of inductive knowledge leaves us with uncertainty ("The Humean predicament is the human predicament"). Elementally, Quine seems to accept skepticism as a starting point and places his faith in scientific method. Fair enough, but why deny the importance of coming to grips with the skeptic? As we have suggested in chapter 3, answering the skeptic illuminates the limits and legitimacy of our knowledge.

Quine does address the matter of skepticism via evolutionary theory. Darwin's theory answers the skeptic. "Creatures inveterately wrong in their inductions have a pathetic but praiseworthy tendency to die before reproducing their kind." As Hilary Kornblith puts it, "Since believing truths has survival value, the survival of the fittest guarantees that our innate intellectual endowment gives us a predisposition for believing truths. Knowledge is thus not only possible but a necessary by-product of natural selection."[10]

The argument goes like this:

1. If Nature does not cause us to have mostly true beliefs, we will not survive.
2. We have survived natural selection.
3. Therefore, Nature has caused us to have mostly true beliefs.

Psychology gives us an account of these belief-forming mechanisms and allows us to claim that we have knowledge.

There are problems with this argument. Survival might well have little to do with true beliefs but much to do with habits and behavior that have survival value. In fact, it could be that most of our beliefs are false, but adequate for survival.

Here are some examples. John Garcia and his co-workers performed experiments on rats in which the rats were fed distinctively flavored water or food and then given high doses of radiation, inducing radiation sickness. After a single exposure to radiation, the rats developed a strong aversion to their aforementioned distinctively flavored water or food. Even if the radiation is given as long as twelve hours after eating the food or water, the aversion pattern follows. As Stephen Stich puts it, "The rat behaves as though it believes that anything which tastes like the distinctive tasting stuff it had eaten will cause it to become deathly ill. Moreover, it is clear that this belief, if that is what it is, is the result of an innate belief (or aversion) forming strategy which is surely the result of natural selection."[11]

A similar phenomenon appears in humans. One of my earliest childhood memories is getting sick after eating greasy scrambled eggs at the age of three or four. I have detested eggs from that day until now. Since then, I have never been able to eat a scrambled egg, nor even the yoke of a hard-boiled egg (though I have unwittingly eaten plenty of cakes made with eggs). I've heard other people report similar tales of getting sick on mushrooms, purple grapes, or rancid meat and being unable to eat those kinds of items thereafter. We form false inductive generalizations from selective experiences. Perhaps Jewish kosher laws were formed in this way. But as long as adequate food is available, it really doesn't matter if we have such false beliefs. An animal could have such accidental false beliefs about the majority of food available and still survive as long as it had other sources of adequate nutrition.

What may be more important is whether a being errs in having false negatives rather than false positives. All things being equal, false negatives are more deleterious to survival than false positives. Better to avoid three harmless varieties of mushrooms than mistakenly eat one poisonous variety. If an animal, say an antelope, is supersensitive to predation, it may needlessly expend energy in reacting to rustling of the nearby bushes by fleeing the scene, but that is probably preferable to insensitivity to predation. Better to risk indigestion by eating on the run than risk being eaten by failing to run. One mistake could be fatal. So, false positives are preferable to false negatives. Better to be safe than sorry.

False beliefs may positively procure survival. Inducing beliefs that great spirits are protecting members of the tribe may enable these members to surmount dangerous obstacles that would otherwise destroy them. Consider two tribes, the Optimists and the Accuratists, who go to war. They are relevantly similar in every way except that the Optimists believe that if they die in battle (especially sacrificing themselves for their mates), they will be rewarded with an afterlife of unparalleled sensuous bliss, whereas the Accuratists, tailoring the strength of their beliefs to the strength of the available evidence, believe that in all likelihood this life is all they have, that death is the final cessation of consciousness. The Optimists are more likely to win; the Accuratists more likely to flee or submit to an inferior settlement.

Just as long as our beliefs enable us to move about in our environment and reproduce successfully, there may be no interesting correlation between survival and truth. As Pat Churchland says, "Boiled down to essentials, a nervous system enables the organism to succeed in the four F's: feeding, fleeing, fighting, and reproducing. The principal chore of nervous systems is to get the body parts where they should be in order that the organism may survive. . . . Truth, whatever that is, definitely takes the hindmost."[12]

Note Darwin's own doubts about the relation of true beliefs to survival:

> With me the horrid doubt always arises whether the convictions of man's mind, which has been developed from the mind of the lower animals, are of any value or at all trustworthy. Would any one trust in the conviction of a monkey's mind, if there are any convictions in such a mind?[13]

The issue is difficult, but naturalists like Quine must build a better case before they convince us that evolution solves the problem of skepticism. Perhaps a passage from *Word and Object* casts light on his view.

> We can investigate the world, and man as a part of it, and thus find out what cues he could have of what goes on around him. Subtracting his cues from his world view, we get man's net contribution as the difference. This difference marks the extent of man's conceptual sovereignty—the domain within which he can revise theory while saving the data.[14]

In other places Quine speaks of science as our "free creation," and the steps in developing theory as having an "arbitrary character of historical accident and cultural heritage," lacking any sense of inevitability.[15]

The force of these passages seems to be that the meagre sensory input results in a theoretical output that is mostly an arbitrary, free creation. But if this is all we have, how is it different from an illusion?

Quine has attempted to clarify his earlier work. In a reply to Barry Stroud, he writes:

> What then does our overall scientific theory really claim regarding the world? Only that it is somehow so structured as to assure the sequences of stimulation that our theory gives us to expect . . .
>
> In what way then do I see the Humean predicament as persisting? Only in the fallibility of prediction: the fallibility of induction and the hypothetico-deductive method in anticipating experience.

I have depicted a barren scene. The furniture of our world, the people and sticks and stones along with the electrons and molecules, have dwindled to manners of speaking. Any other purported objects would serve as well, and may as well be said already to be doing so.

So it would seem. Yet people, sticks, stones, electrons, and molecules are real indeed, on my view, and it is these and no dim proxies that science is all about. Now how is such robust realism to be reconciled with what we have just been through? The answer is naturalism: the recognition that it is within science itself, and not in some prior philosophy, that reality is properly to be identified and described.[16]

But if scientific objects are only "dim proxies of real entities," why should we believe in them? Ernest Sosa has characterized this passage, in the context of Quine's other work, in the following way:

The people, sticks, stones, and places of fiction are real indeed, on [Quine's] view, and it is these and no dim proxies that fiction is all about. Now how is such robust realism to be sustained? The answer is fictional realism: the recognition that it is within fiction itself, and not in some prior philosophy, that reality is properly to be identified and described.[17]

If this analysis is correct, Quine has left us without a world. He purports to reject skepticism in favor of science, but in reality it is a science within a general skepticism that he offers. In his own words, "The Humean predicament is the human predicament." Science, rather than being a solution to skepticism, is just sophisticated backgammon, a turning away from the disappointment that comes from the skeptic's sting. But the traditional problem of skepticism has not been banished from our intellectual lives. It reappears in Quine's efforts, more potent and disturbing than ever before.

Finally, Quine's Neurathian notion of knowledge (or *the Web of Belief*), constitutes a coherentist theory of justification. Here is his celebrated passage from "Two Dogmas of Empiricism."

The totality of our so-called knowledge or beliefs, from the most casual matters of geography and history to the profoundest laws of atomic physics or even of our mathematics and logic, is a man-made fabric which impinges on experience only along the edges. Or, to change the figure, total science is like a field of force whose boundary conditions are experience. A conflict with experience at the periphery occasions readjustments in the interior field. Truth values have to be redistributed over some of our statements. Reevaluation of some statements entails reevaluation of others, because of their logical interconnections—the logical laws being in turn simply certain further statements of the system, certain further elements of the field. Having reevaluated one statement we must reevaluate some others, which may be statements logically connected to the first or may be the statements of logical connections themselves. But the total field is so underdetermined by its boundary conditions, experience, that there is much latitude of choice as to what statements to reevaluate in the light of any single contrary experience. No particular experiences are linked with any particular statements in the interior of the field, except indirectly through considerations of equilibrium affecting the field as a whole.

If this view is right, it is misleading to speak of the empirical content of an individual statement—especially if it is a statement at all remote from the experiential periphery of the field. Furthermore, it becomes folly to seek a boundary between synthetic statements, which hold come what may. Any statement can be held true come what may, if we make drastic enough adjustments elsewhere in the system. Even a statement very close to the periphery can be held true in the face of recalcitrant evidence by pleading hallucination or by amending certain statements of the kind called logical laws. Conversely, by the same token, no statement is immune to revision. Revision even of the logical law of the excluded middle has been proposed as a means of simplifying quantum mechanics; and what difference is there in principle between such a shift and the shift whereby Kepler superceded Ptolmey, or Einstein Newton, or Darwin Aristotle?

Knowledge or justification of belief is relativized to human interest. Quine may be correct about our systems of belief being holistic but he may be wrong in rejecting a priori truth—at the core. The laws of logic seem to survive revision. Furthermore, we may question whether Quine is correct about the possibility of legitimately preserving any proposition "come what may," for some beliefs seem to stand up to scrutiny better than others. Even if we may never reach an absolute system of truth, we need to set forth criteria (norms) for deciding which systems are more adequate than others. That has been the traditional task of epistemology, a task that Quine takes for granted, even while denying that function.

Summary

Quine's Naturalized Epistemology, wherein the normative aspects of philosophical epistemology are turned over to science, is a bold and challenging proposal. Nevertheless, we have shown that at this early stage of development, he has not defeated contemporary fallibilist versions of foundationalism or justificationist coherentism. Examining his ideas on normativity, we note that either they reduce to a version of reliabiism (pragmatic reliabilism), discussed in chapters 8 and 9, or fail to address the challenge of skepticism satisfactorily. Note that even to assess Quine's system involves our engaging in normative analysis, for we want to determine whether he has good reasons for his theory.

With this said, it remains to be seen whether the Quinean program can meet these objections and eventually succeed in subsuming epistemology under cognitive psychology.

QUESTIONS FOR DISCUSSION

1. Describe Quine's program for naturalizing epistemology. Why does he reject traditional epistemology? What are the strengths and weaknesses of his proposal as you see it?

2. Examine the quotation from Otto Neurath at the beginning of this chapter. What is its significance for Quine's naturalized epistemology?

3. Has Quine rid himself of the problem of skepticism?

4. Compare Quine's adherence to evolution as an antidote to skepticism with Plantinga's use and rejection of evolutionary theory in chapter 9.

5. Quine speaks of the "meagre input [of sensory stimulation] and the torrential output [our picture of the world]." Jesse Hobbs has criticized Quine here, arguing that the truth is just the reverse. Our input is torrential, but our output is meagre by comparison.

   > When I evaluate my students at the end of the semester, I have to pick one of five grades to give them, based on three exams, fifteen homework assignments, classroom participation, and other interaction during the course of the semester. In writing this letter, I am drawing on my own thought and experience over many years of graduate school and work in analytic philosophy since graduate school. We forget many things, of course, and we are unaware of how much they still affect our behavior because the effect is subliminal, but the effect is there. (Correspondence, March 22, 1994)

   Is Hobbs correct and Quine mistaken? How might Quine respond to this criticism?

6. Discuss the problem of normativity. What role does it play in Quine's naturalized epistemology? What role does it play in traditional epistemology? What role do you think it should play in an adequate epistemic system?

7. Analyze Quine's statement on epistemic holism quoted at the end of this chapter. How sound is his reasoning?

NOTES

1. Otto Neurath, quoted in W. V. Quine's *Word and Object* (Cambridge, MA: MIT Press, 1960), frontpiece.
2. W. V. Quine, "Natural Kinds," *Ontological Relativity and Other Essays* (New York: Columbia University Press, 1969). Reprinted in *Naturalizing Epistemology*, ed. Hilary Kornblith (Cambridge, MA: MIT Press, 1985), 39.
3. W. V. Quine, "Epistemology Naturalized," *Ontological Relativity and Other Essays* (New York: Columbia University Press). Reprinted in *The Theory of Knowledge*, 2nd ed., ed. Louis Pojman (Belmont, CA: Wadsworth, 1999), 322.
4. Ibid., 325.
5. Quine, "Natural Kinds," 38–39.
6. Jaegwon Kim, "What is 'Naturalized Epistemology'?" *Philosophical Perspectives: Epistemology* (Atascadero, CA: Ridgeview Publishing Co., 1988). Reprinted in Pojman 1st ed., 329–340.
7. W. V. Quine, "Reply to Morton White." In *The Philosophy of W. V. Quine*, ed. L. E. Hahn and P. A. Schilpp (LaSalle, IL: Open Court, 1986), 664–665.
8. For a good discussion of this pragmatic naturalist normativity, see James Maffie, "Naturalism and the Normativity of Epistemology," *Philosophical Studies* 59 (1990).
9. Quine expresses himself loosely on the subject of truth. In *Pursuit of Truth* (Cambridge, MA: Harvard University Press, 1990) he sounds like a coherentist.
10. Hilary Kornblith, "Introduction: What Is Naturalistic Epistemology?" In *Naturalizing Epistemology*, ed. Hilary Kornblith (Cambridge, MA: MIT Press, 1985), 5.
11. Stephen Stich, "Could Man Be an Irrational Animal? Some Notes on the Epistemology of Rationality," *Synthese* (1984). Reprinted in Kornblith, 257.
12. Patricia Churchland, "Epistemology in an Age of Neuroscience," *Journal of Philosophy* 84 (October 1987), 548.
13. Letter to William Graham, July 3, 1881. In *The Life and Letters of Charles Darwin Including an Autobiographical Chapter*, ed. Francis Darwin (London: John Murray, Albermarle Street, 1887), vol. 1, 315–316. Quoted in Alvin Plantinga, *Warrant and Proper Function* (Oxford: Oxford University Press, 1993), 219.
14. W. V. Quine, *Word and Object* (Cambridge, MA: MIT Press, 1960). Quoted in Ernest Sosa, *Knowledge in Perspective* (Cambridge: Cambridge University Press, 1992), 101. This section has been influenced by Sosa's analysis.

15. W. V. Quine, *The Roots of Reference* (LaSalle, IL: Open Court, 1974). Also, "The Nature of Natural Knowledge." In *Mind and Language,* ed. Samuel Guttenplan (Oxford: Clarendon Press, 1975), 80.

16. W. V. Quine, "Reply to Stroud." In *Midwest Studies in Philosophy,* ed. Peter A. French, Theodore E. Uehling, Jr., and Howard Wettstein (Minneapolis: University of Minnesota Press, 1981), vol. 6, 474.

17. Ernest Sosa, *Knowledge,* p. 104.

FOR FURTHER READING

Almeder, Robert. "On Naturalizing Epistemology," *American Philosophical Quarterly,* 27, 4 (October 1990).

Dretske, Fred. *Knowledge and the Flow of Information.* Cambridge, MA: MIT Press, 1981.

Gibson, Roger. *Enlightened Empiricism.* Tampa, FL: University of South Florida Press, 1988.

Kim, Jaegwon. "What is 'Naturalized Epistemology'?" *Philosophical Perspectives 2.* Atascadero, CA: Ridgeview Publishing Co., 1988.

Kornblith, Hilary, ed. *Naturalized Epistemology.* Cambridge, MA: MIT Press, 1985.

Kornblith, Hilary. *Inductive Inference and Its Natural Ground: An Essay in Naturalistic Epistemology.* Cambridge, MA: MIT Press, 1993.

Maffie, James. "Recent Work on Naturalized Epistemology," *American Philosophical Quarterly,* 27, 4 (October 1990).

_____."Naturalism and the Normativity of Epistemology," *Philosophical Studies* 59 (1990).

Quine, W. V. *Ontological Relativity and Other Essays.* New York: Columbia University Press, 1969.

_____.*Pursuit of Truth.* Cambridge, MA: Harvard University Press, 1990.

Siegel, Harvey. "Empirical Psychology, Naturalized Epistemology, and First Philosophy." *Philosophy of Science* 51 (1985).

Sosa, Ernest. *Knowledge in Perspective.* Cambridge: Cambridge University Press, 1991. Especially Chapter 6.

Stich, Stephen. *The Fragmentation of Reason.* Cambridge: MA: MIT Press, 1990.

Stroud, Barry. *The Significance of Philosophical Skepticism.* Oxford: Clarendon Press, 1984. Chapter 6.

CHAPTER 11

Virtue Epistemology

Recently, several philosophers, including Alvin Goldman, Jonathan Kvanvig, James Montmarquet, and Ernest Sosa, have put forth separate versions of an epistemology based on virtue and vice.[1] Just as virtue ethics makes proper character traits, rather than moral principles or duties, the center of morality, virtue epistemology makes appropriate epistemic character traits, rather than epistemic principles or duties, the center of epistemology.

Virtue Utilitarianism

Ernest Sosa, one of the first to mark out the strategy for a virtue epistemology, likens it to virtue utilitarianism. Just as a virtue utilitarian highlights dispositions most likely to produce the highest aggregate good, the virtue reliabilist highlights dispositions likely to produce the highest aggregate of truth. Referring to the physician who is about to deliver the baby who will be named Adolf Hitler and who will wreak havoc on the earth, Sosa points out that by being a virtuous physician, one can unwittingly be instrumental in bringing about disutility. But, over all, the type of virtuous dispositions that operate here are likely to maximize utility. He applies this idea to the epistemic virtues.

> In what sense is the doctor attending Frau Hitler justified in performing an action that brings with it far less value than one of its accessible alternatives? According to one promising idea, the key is to be found in the rules that he embodies through stable dispositions. His action is the result of certain stable virtues, and there are no equally virtuous alternate

dispositions that, given his cognitive limitations, he might have embodied with equal or better total consequences. The important move for our purpose is the stratification of justification. Primary justification attaches to virtues and other dispositions, to stable dispositions to act, through their greater contribution of value when compared with alternatives. Secondary justification attaches to particular acts in virtue of their source in virtues or other such justified dispositions.

The same strategy may also prove fruitful in epistemology. Here primary justification would apply to *intellectual* virtues, to stable dispositions for belief acquisition, through their greater contribution towards getting us to the truth. Secondary justification would then attach to particular beliefs in virtue of their source in intellectual virtues or other justified dispositions.[2]

Virtue Reliabilism

Epistemic or intellectual virtues are the good ways, or habits, of forming and sustaining beliefs. They are truth conducive (or justification conducive). That is, they enable us to obtain and sustain important true beliefs and avoid false beliefs. Vices are the bad ways or habits of forming and sustaining beliefs. They are inimical to truth and do not help us avoid error. We arrive at the virtues by empirical observation based on the criterion of reliability. So, we may call this view Virtue Reliabilism. A target belief is justified if it is formed by virtuous properties and not by vicious properties.

Virtuous traits include proper perceptual practices, good memory, wisdom, clear reasoning, critical thinking, open-mindedness, impartiality, paying attention to evidence, epistemic conscientiousness, and discriminating and insightful observation. James Montmarquet also adds intellectual courage, "the willingness to conceive and examine alternatives to popularly held beliefs, perseverance in the face of opposition and even ridicule."[3] Vicious traits include guessing, hasty generalization, wishful thinking, prejudicial thinking, and hallucinating.

The virtues are truth conducive, but their goal is not deciphering just any truths, nor merely the largest number of truths, but truths that explain important aspects of thought and life.

The intellectual virtues can be thought of as either *powers of the mind* or *epistemic dispositions,* probably both. They *dispose* us to certain states, such as objective review of the evidence and critical review of our own beliefs. Intellectual conscientiousness, a central epistemic virtue, motivates us to seek truth and use the required methods to obtain the truth. But, one can be motivated to seek the truth and hold justified beliefs and still not succeed in obtaining these goals. One way to fail to attain truth is simply through bad luck. The environment misleads one, so using induction leads one astray. But, another way to fail is to lack the power of impartial review. I once tried to umpire a baseball game and, although I sought to call the pitches correctly, the players assured me I had failed miserably. I lacked the ability to discern when a pitch was within the strike zone. The inability to make relevant distinctions or see issues candidly may affect our perceptions, our metaphysical inferences, as well as our moral and political judgments—even though we may have the best will in the world. We need both the proper disposition, an epistemic goodwill, and the ability to judge impartially. I will discuss these twin aspects of epistemic virtue at further length in chapter 19.

Virtue Perspectivism

Sosa's version of Virtue Reliabilism ("Virtue Perspectivism"), the most developed virtue theory to date, defines an intellectual virtue as:

> a competence in virtue of which one would mostly attain the truth and avoid error in a certain field of propositions *F*, when in certain conditions *C*. Subject *S* believes proposition *P* at time *t* out of intellectual virtue only if there is a field of propositions *F*, and there are conditions *C*, such that: (a) *P* is in *F*; (b) *S* is in *C* with respect to *P*; and (c) *S* would most likely be right if *S* believed a proposition *X* in field *F* when in conditions *C* with respect to *X*.[4]

Sosa's theory seeks to distinguish itself from Goldman's Historical Reliabilism in two main respects: (1) by requiring not just that a cognitive process produce the target belief, but also that an intellectual virtue do so; and (2) by distinguishing between mere animal knowledge and knowledge that is "reflective," in that the knower enjoys an appropriate epistemic "perspective" on his or her first-level beliefs. This requirement of perspective is what makes the view one of virtue *perspectivism*. The view also distinguishes itself from Plantinga's proper functionalism in several ways, most notably by not using the controversial concepts of function or design.

I indicated that a strength of virtue epistemology is that it seems to yield answers closer to our intuitions than simple reliabilism. It identifies defective processes as vicious, even though they occasionally yield reliable subprocesses. Recall the thought experiment (in chapter 8) of the demon world where I-2 has all the beliefs that you do, fulfills his epistemic responsibilities, but, due to the demon, has all false beliefs. Reliabilism held that I-2 was not justified because the beliefs were formed by a deceptive practice, but Virtue Perspectivism states that I-2 is justified since he was in an epistemically virtuous state when he obtained the beliefs. It was simply bad luck that he didn't succeed in attaining true beliefs.

Conversely, in the Samantha case, reliabilism judged Samantha justified because she obtained her beliefs about the president being in New York by a reliable clairvoyant practice, but virtue epistemology would deny her that attribution, since she did not obtain her belief by a virtuous habit.

Likewise, Don, the dogmatist, who never doubts his political beliefs, who is prejudiced through and through, but who by luck arrives at a remarkable number of true beliefs, where impartial review of the evidence would have misled him, is not justified, since he lacks the virtues of impartiality and careful attention to evidence.

You may apply these virtues to the creationist/evolutionary controversy at the beginning of chapter 8. How does it come out?

Problems with Virtue Epistemology

But there are problems with virtue epistemology analogous to the problems of virtue ethics. It has been pointed out that moral virtues depend on moral principles for their validity as "good-making" qualities. Honesty is a virtue because it enables us to carry out the principle or duty to be honest. Greed is a vice because it causes us to act unjustly, take more than our share, and so forth. Likewise, the epistemic virtues seem to depend on good epistemic (deontic) principles: One ought to pay close attention to important data; one ought to reason carefully and logically; one ought not make hasty generalizations; one ought not form beliefs through wishful thinking; and so forth. It would seem then that epistemic virtues are dependent on the notion of justification and cannot be understood apart from it. One may say that the virtues are those enabling traits that make it more likely that we will carry out our epistemic duties, in which case it is the principles that are logically prior.

Specific problems have to do with determining exactly which epistemic traits are virtues and to what degree one must possess a trait before we can say it is a virtue. Sometimes virtue epistemologists speak as if possessing a capacity or power is to have a virtue. For example, John Greco lists "sight, hearing, introspection, memory, deduction and induction" as intellectual virtues.[5] But, surely this confuses a power with a virtue. Sight or hearing are capacities for seeing and hearing, but they are not necessarily *virtuous* ones. Our sight or hearing or any one of the traits that Greco lists can be defective. We need to distinguish between the person with excellent vision from the one with abysmal myopia or astigmatism. It is not sight but good vision that is the virtue, and likewise with all other epistemic traits.

But how good must a trait, say memory, be before it is a virtue? Simply better than average? But what about traits where average is really nearly perfect? For example, suppose the comparison group is made up of people with 20/20 vision or photographic memories? And must a virtue be relativized to context or should it be global? For example, suppose you have good inductive powers in generalizing from rural experience but fail miserably in urban settings. How should we describe your inductive ability? As defective? As virtuous relative to one set of circumstances but vicious relative to another?

Sosa, holding to a reliabilist virtue theory, argues that justification is relative to an environment E, so that a person S is justified in believing p relative to E, if and only if S's faculties would be reliable in E. So S need not actually be in E in order to be justified. The person who is a brain in a vat and who falsely believes that he or she is seeing a red tomato is justified relative to normal worlds but simply has the bad luck of being in an abnormal world where the virtuous trait is foiled by a mad scientist.

Jonathan Kvanvig's account of virtue epistemology differs from Virtue Perspectivism.[6] He argues that epistemology ought to focus on justification rather than knowledge or truth conduciveness. Rather, we should endeavor to define the virtues in terms of power for generating or supporting justified beliefs. Rather than rendering our beliefs probably true, the virtues "render it probable that our beliefs are probable. If so, however, there will be no argument to the claim that the virtues are truth-conducive, even if the concept of epistemic probability is itself truth-conducive. Since justified false beliefs are possible in general, we could be justified in thinking that a certain claim was justified and be wrong about it."[7]

Of course, there is nothing new in focusing on justification of belief rather than truth conduciveness. Internalists have emphasized this dimension for a long time. Most epistemologists have argued for or have had faith in the idea that epistemic justification tends toward truth, so that the best way to have true beliefs is to have well-justified ones. But there is no guarantee that our justified beliefs (especially those concerned with empirical and metaphysical matters) are true.

If the virtues were not emphasized in traditional epistemology, it may be because they were taken for granted. Just as we need powers and good habits in ethical living, so we need good intellectual powers and habits in our epistemic lives. So far there is nothing startling or antitraditional about epistemic virtues.

What is startling and antitraditional is the attempt to put the epistemic virtues at the center of epistemology, replacing or reducing evidential norms and modes of justification to a theory of doxastic virtues. Epistemologists like Kvanvig propose the possibility of such a revision, though they admit that all attempts to date have failed.

Whether such a radical proposal can be made plausible is one of the intriguing questions I leave you to work out. However, assessing the general role of the way the virtues work in epistemology is an exciting challenge with which every philosopher needs to come to grip.

QUESTIONS FOR DISCUSSION

1. Compare epistemic virtues to moral virtues. How are they analogous, and how are they different?

2. Go over the discussion of how virtue epistemology may yield answers closer to mere reliabilism. Do you agree with the diagnosis offered?

3. What are the general prospects for virtue epistemology? Should it be developed further than it has? Or is it largely just a complement to ordinary theoretical epistemology?

NOTES

1. Alvin Goldman, "The Internalist Conception of Justification." In *Midwest Studies in Philosophy,* ed. Peter French, Theodore Uehling, Jr., and Howard Wettstein (Minneapolis: University of Minnesota Press, 1980); Ernest Sosa, *Knowledge in Perspective* (Cambridge: Cambridge University Press, 1991), especially chapters 8, 13, and 16; Jonathan Kvanvig, *The Intellectual Virtues and the Life of the Mind* (Totowa, NJ: Rowman & Littlefield, 1992); James Montmarquet, *Epistemic Virtue and Doxastic Responsibility* (Totowa, NJ: Rowman & Littlefield, 1993). Alvin Plantinga, whose views we discussed in chapter 9, is sometimes considered a proponent of virtue epistemology. Epistemic virtues play a large

role in his system, but the dominant features are the notions of proper functioning and a design plan.

2. Sosa, *Knowledge in Perspective,* 139.
3. James Montmarquet, "Epistemic Virtue." In *A Companion to Epistemology,* ed. Ernest Sosa (London: Blackwell's, 1992), 116.
4. Sosa, *Knowledge in Perspective,* 139.
5. John Greco, "Virtue Epistemology." In *A Companion to Epistemology,* 520.
6. Jonathan Kvanvig, *The Intellectual Virtues.*
7. Jonathan Kvanvig. Personal correspondence with author, February 9, 1994.

FOR FURTHER READING

Goldman, Alvin I. "The Internalist Conception of Justification." In *Midwest Studies in Philosophy,* edited by Peter French, Theodore Uehling, Jr., and Howard Wettstein. Minneapolis: University of Minnesota Press, 1980.

――――. "Epistemic Folkways and Scientific Epistemology," *Liaisons.* Cambridge, MA: MIT/Bradford Press, 1992.

Kvanvig, Jonathan. *The Intellectual Virtues and the Life of the Mind.* Totowa, NJ: Rowman & Littlefield, 1991.

Montmarquet, James A. "Epistemic Virtue," *Mind* 96 (1987).

――――. *Epistemic Virtue and Doxastic Responsibility.* Totowa, NJ: Rowman & Littlefield, 1993.

Sosa, Ernest. *Knowledge in Perspective.* Cambridge: Cambridge University Press, 1991.

CHAPTER 12

A Priori Knowledge

Introduction: The Historical Debate

What kinds of knowledge are there? Most of this book has concentrated on one type of knowledge: perceptual or empirical knowledge. Almost everyone admits that if we know anything at all, we know truths about the world—that is, how it appears to us—as well as some truths about the way the world really is. For example, I know that some objects move and that I am now typing this paragraph. But the question is, Are there also other types of knowledge not dependent on our experience of the world? Do we have innate knowledge or ideas prior to experience? Can we know necessary truths apart from observation? Is it possible to have knowledge of what is beyond empirical reality—God, the soul, free will, moral truths?

The issue was first formulated in Plato's dialogue, *Meno*. Meno asks Socrates whether or not virtue can be taught. How do people come to know what virtue is? Socrates replies that he does not even know what virtue is. The following exchange takes place:

> Meno: How will you look for it, Socrates, when you do not know at all what it is? How will you aim to search for something you do not know at all? If you should meet with it, how will you know that this is the thing that you did not know?
>
> Socrates: I know what you want to say, Meno. Do you realize what a debater's argument you are bringing up, that a man cannot search either for what he knows or for what he does not know? He cannot search for what he knows—since he knows it, there is no need to search—nor for what he does not know, for he does not know what to look for.[1]

Socrates then calls Meno's uneducated slave and, drawing a square in the sand, asks the boy to try to double the area of the figure. Through a process of questions and answers in which the boy consults his own unschooled understanding, he eventually performs this feat. He seems to have "brought up knowledge from within."

> Socrates: Do you observe, Meno, that I am not teaching the boy anything, but only asking him questions; and now he fancies that he knows how long a line is necessary in order to produce a figure of eight square feet; does he not?
>
> Meno: Yes.
>
> Socrates: Do you see what advances he has made in his power of recollection? Were not all these answers given out of his own head? . . .
> Then he who does not know may still have true notions of what he does not know?
>
> Meno: He has.
>
> Socrates: And this spontaneous recovery of knowledge in him is recollection?
>
> Meno: True.[2]

Plato argues that the only explanation of how the boy was able to do geometry is that he already possessed knowledge of geometry in his soul. He must, then, have a soul that existed before his present life and that somehow learned geometry. One has to awaken the soul to the knowledge, which is already hidden in the soul, by putting questions to him, making what is implicit explicit. Socrates likens his method to that of a midwife who induces labor in a pregnant woman. He induces intellectual labor in a soul pregnant with knowledge. This is how Socrates answers Meno's question about how it is possible for virtue to be taught: We can teach virtue only by causing our auditors to recollect what they have forgotten about the Good.

According to Plato, the bridge between the World of Being and the World of Becoming is *Innate Ideas*. As we have seen, he held that learning is really a recollecting of what we learned in a previous existence. The soul, which is immortal, has been born many times and has had a single view of the truth:

> The soul having seen all things that exist, whether in this world or in the world below, has knowledge of them all; and it is no wonder that she should be able to remember all that she ever knew about virtue and about everything; for as all nature is akin, and the soul has learned all things, there is no difficulty in her eliciting, or as men say learning, out of a single recollection all the rest.[3]

In coming into existence, the soul has forgotten all the essential truths of reality that she had learned. The educator should be a spiritual midwife who stimulates the labors of the soul, enabling a person to recall what he or she really possesses but has forgotten.

Plato thought that all knowledge was *a priori* (literally "that which is prior or first") knowledge—knowledge one has independently of sense experience—as opposed to *a posteriori* ("that which is posterior") knowledge—contingent, empirical knowledge, which comes to us from experience through the five senses. According to Plato, unless ordinary empirical beliefs are related to the Forms they are not knowledge, since they are related to unstable appearances. An example of a priori knowledge is the mathematical equation "5 + 7 = 12." You don't need to appeal to experience in order to see that this equation is true. As in the case of Meno's slave, experience may be necessary in eliciting such knowledge, but once made active, the soul is able to recall it without aid of the senses.

The doctrine of Innate Ideas was held by a large number of philosophers after Plato, through the Middle Ages to René Descartes (1596–1650) and Gottfried Leibniz (1646–1716), who gave it a Christian interpretation. Unlike Plato, Descartes believed that the soul is not immortal. It does not have a previous existence, though it is eternal; it will live on forever once it is created by God. Descartes did not believe that the soul is born with knowledge of all essential truths, but only certain ones. The "natural light of reason" yields substantive metaphysical truths to those who used their faculties correctly. Even the Christian Existentialist Søren Kierkegaard (1813–1855) held that we have innate knowledge of God's existence, free will, and immortality.

In the first book of his *Essay Concerning Human Understanding* (1690), John Locke (1632–1704), set forth the classic critique of the doctrine of Innate Ideas, a critique which many philosophers have found "incontrovertible."[4] Locke argued that if the doctrine of innate ideas were true, everyone should be able to discover truths by accessing them. But innateness is not universal. Take even the most self-evident logical truths "Whatever is, is" and "It is impossible for the same thing to be and not to be." There are people who fail to assent to these truths: children, idiots, and savages. "Illiterate people and savages pass many years, even of their rational age, without ever thinking on this, and the like general propositions."[5] For Locke the mind was essentially a "tabula rasa," an empty tablet on which experience must write if we are to know anything. From simple experiences we learn simple ideas and from these we build complex ones, so that all of our knowledge is based on simple perceptions. All knowledge of the world was a posteriori knowledge.

The empiricist tradition, which eschews innate ideas, has dominated Western philosophy since Locke, so that not many epistemologists have endorsed innateness. But recently things have again been turning in the direction of innateness. I will return to this later in this chapter.

Leibniz divided propositions into *truths of reason* and *truths of fact*. The former are analytic propositions—truths demonstrable by the principle of contradiction (not ($p \& -p$)) or the principle of identity ($A = A$) alone—and the latter, synthetic propositions—the truth of which is discoverable by experience. All truths of reason are necessary truths, which the mind could discover without the aid of the senses.

Immanuel Kant developed these notions, making a posteriori knowledge refer to judgments that depend on empirical experience and a priori knowledge refer to those that do not. But he went further, taking the semantic notions—analytic and synthetic statements—and combining them with a priori and a posteriori knowledge. He defines *analytic statements* as those in which the predicate is already contained in the subject (e.g., "All mothers are women," in which the subject term *mother* already contains the idea of "woman," so we learn nothing new in our statement). The metaphor of "containment" was equivalent to logical entailment. *Synthetic statements* are just the opposite; the predicate term adds something new about the subject. "Mary is now a mother" is a sentence in which we learn something new about Mary. The following list summarizes these points.

EPISTEMOLOGICAL CATEGORIES

1. *A priori* knowledge does not depend on evidence from sense experience (Plato's Innate Ideas and Leibniz's "Truths of Reason"; e.g., mathematics and logic; Descartes's "cogito ergo sum").
2. *A posteriori* knowledge depends on evidence from sense experience (Plato's Appearance and Leibniz's "Truths of Fact"; e.g., empirical knowledge).

LOGICAL OR SEMANTIC CATEGORIES

1. *Analytic* The predicate is *contained* in the subject (explicative, not ampliative; e.g., "All mothers are women").
2. *Synthetic* The predicate is not contained in the subject but adds something to the subject (ampliative, not explicative; e.g., "Mary is now a mother").

Kant's innovation consisted in going beyond the two standard kinds of knowledge: a priori analytic and a posteriori synthetic knowledge.

Combining a priori knowledge with synthetic propositions, he argued that we had a third kind of knowledge, *synthetic a priori knowledge*—knowledge that may begin with experience but did not arise from experience, yet was nevertheless known directly. While the genesis of all knowledge may be empirical, not all judgments rest on empirical evidence.

> There can be no doubt that all our knowledge begins with experience. For how should our faculty of knowledge be awakened into action if objects affecting our senses did not produce representations and arouse the activity of our understanding to compare these representations, and, by combining or separating them, work up the raw material of the sensible impressions into that knowledge of objects which is entitled experience. In the order of time, therefore, we have no knowledge before experience, and with experience all our knowledge begins.
>
> But though all our knowledge begins with experience, it does not follow that it all arises out of experience. For it may well be that even our empirical knowledge is made up of what we receive through impressions and of what our own faculty of knowledge supplies from itself.[6]

Kant gives two criteria for a priori judgments: necessity and universality. These two criteria seem to coalesce into the concept of "necessity," in that by *universality* he simply means that a universal proposition has no *conceivable* exception. After all, an empirical judgment could be universally true but not true by necessity. As examples of synthetic a priori judgments, he offers $7 + 5 = 12$ and "everything occurs in time."

Although the idea of *analytic a posteriori* knowledge is not discussed in Kant's work, it seems clear that he rejected the idea because it was contradictory.[7] That is, the idea of an analytic judgment—which depends solely on the relations of the concepts involved—makes no essential reference to experience, whereas a posteriori knowledge depends on experience.

The essential claim of those who recognize synthetic a priori knowledge is that the mind is able to grasp connections between concepts that are not analytically related. For example, we simply know upon reflection that all events have causes: "For every change there is an antecedent event which is necessarily connected with it." Similarly, we need not consult our senses to tell us that space is something that exists independently of matter. "If we remove from our empirical concept of a body, one by one, every feature in it which is [merely] empirical, the color, the hardness or softness, the weight, even the impenetrability, there still remains the space which the body (now entirely vanished) occupied, and this cannot be removed."[8] Kant also thought our knowledge of mathematical truths was really *synthetic a priori,* rather than analytic.[9] The moral law—the judgment that we ought to act in such a way that we could will that the maxims of our actions would be universal laws—is known without appeal to experience.[10] Finally, he argues that the existence of substantial time is a synthetic a priori concept. In order to give you a sense of Kant's method and argument let's quote him at length.

1. Time is not an empirical concept that has been derived from any experience. For neither coexistence nor succession would ever come within our perception, if the representation of time were not presupposed as underlying them a priori.

2. Time is a necessary representation that underlies all intuitions. We cannot, in respect of appearances in general, remove time itself, though we can quite well think time as void of appearances. Time is, therefore, given *a priori.* In it alone is the actuality of appearances possible at all. Appearances may, one and all, vanish; but time (as the universal condition of their possibility) cannot itself be removed.

3. Time has only one dimension; different times are not simultaneous but successive (just as different spaces are not successive but simultaneous). These principles cannot be derived from experience, for experience would give neither strict universality nor necessary certainty. We should only be able to say that common experience teaches us that it is so; not that it must be so. These principles are valid as rules under which alone experiences are possible; and they instruct us in regard to the experiences, not by means of them.

4. Time is not a discursive, or what is called a general concept, but a pure form of sensible intuition. Different times are but parts of one and the same time. Moreover, the proposition that different times cannot be simultaneous is not to be derived from a general concept.

    Time is not something which exists of itself, or which inheres in things as an objective determination. . . . Time is nothing but the form of our inner sense, that is, of the intuition of ourselves and of our inner state. . . . Time is the formal a priori condition of all appearances whatsoever. . . . Time is therefore a purely subjective condition of our human intuition, and in itself, apart from the subject, is nothing.[11]

We can imagine a world with different physical laws—where Einstein's laws do not govern, where water is not wet nor fire hot, where mice are smarter than men, and human babies are born from elephants—but we cannot imagine a world without time. And yet we have no argument that establishes time's reality. It is a given in all our experience, a lens through which we see the world. It may not be real, but we cannot live without assuming its reality.

Like our judgment that all events occur in time, all synthetic a priori concepts are presupposed in all our experience. They are the conditions through which all experience gets filtered down to us as *appearances* of the world. That is, we are so constructed that we can have no knowledge of the world as it really is (the "thing in itself") but only as it comes in spatial-temporal-casual forms of intuitions. As red tinted glasses cause us to see the world in shades of red, so the constraints of synthetic a priori forms of intuitions determine us to experience the world causally, temporally, and spatially.

Although the exact description of what constitutes synthetic a priori judgments is controversial, philosophers, especially those of a rationalist cast, have included such propositions as "God exists," "I have a free will," "Every event has a cause," and "All things have sufficient reasons to explain them."

If we combine these categories, we arrive at the following table of how a rationalist or Kantian might classify judgments.

	Analytic	*Synthetic*
a priori	Identity Statements Entailments Tautologies Definitions "All bachelors 　are unmarried." "All bodies are 　extended."	Mathematics 　$5 + 7 = 12$ Exclusionary 　"Nothing red is green." Presuppositions of 　Experience 　space, time, and causality Moral Judgments 　the categorical 　imperative— 　"It's always wrong to 　torture for the fun of it." The Laws of Logic 　the principle of 　noncontradiction Metaphysical 　God's existence 　(ontological argument), 　freedom of the will
a posteriori	[None]	All Empirical Statements 　"All bodies are heavy." 　"All copper conducts 　electricity." 　"John is a bachelor."

Generally, rationalists assert (while empiricists deny) the existence of synthetic a priori knowledge. Empiricists believe that experience is the basis of all our knowledge except analytic truths. However, analytic truths are simply definitions or tautologies in disguise. Rationalists hold that reason can discover truths that are neither empirical nor analytic. For radical rationalists all knowledge is grounded in self-evident, a priori nonempirical knowledge. We now turn to a critical examination of the idea of a priori knowledge.

Is There A Priori Knowledge?

These propositions have been proposed by various philosophers (identified in parentheses) as examples of a priori knowledge.

1. If John is taller than Mary and Tom is taller than John, Tom is taller than Mary.
2. $5 + 7 = 12$ (Kant)
3. Nothing is both red and green (Chisholm).
4. Some sentences are not both true and false (Putnam).
5. If Socrates is a man and all men are mortal, Socrates is mortal.
6. Every event has a cause (Kant).
7. All bodies are extended (Descartes and Kant).
8. A greatest possible being necessarily exists (Anselm and Plantinga).
9. It is wrong to harm people just for the fun of it (Plantinga).
10. If I believe I exist, I exist (Descartes, Philip Kitcher).

"If John is taller than Mary and Tom is taller than John, Tom is taller than Mary." You do not have to know John, Tom, or Mary. You don't even have to know whether they exist or, if they do, how tall they are in order to know that this proposition is true. You need only whatever experience is necessary to understand the concepts involved, such as "being taller than."

To believe this proposition a priori, one need only consider it. No particular experience—perceptual, testimonial, memorial, or introspective—is necessary. Of course, such experience may occur. There is no reason why you can't know an a priori truth via an empirical process. Suppose as a child you were told by your father that John is taller than Mary and Tom is taller than John, so therefore Tom must be taller than Mary. You believed your father and so knew an a priori truth via an a posteriori process.

Contrast this with believing the categorical proposition, "John is taller than Mary and Tom is taller than John." To believe this you would need some empirical evidence (assuming that you can't just concoct empirical beliefs at will)—either perceptual, testimonial, or memorial (or possibly imaginary).

Leibniz spoke of a priori truths as "truths of reason." We just *see* that (2) 5 + 7 = 12 or that (3) nothing is both red and green. To see that such a proposition is true a priori is to apprehend not only that things are a certain way, but that they must be that way. Leibniz and Kant, as well as many others since them, have held that all a priori knowledge is necessarily true.

A contemporary proponent of this view, Alvin Plantinga holds that typical a priori knowledge, besides being true, must fulfill four conditions.[12]

1. The proposition p must be believed and believed to be necessarily true.

2. You must be able to form the belief immediately upon understanding it.

3. The proposition p must not be believed on the basis of perception, memory, or testimony (otherwise it would not be believed as necessary, but as contingent).

4. The belief must be accompanied with a certain phenomenal feel, what the rationalists called *intuition*.

When we say "nothing is both green and red," simply by knowing the meaning of the terms *green* and *red* we know both that this proposition is true and that it must be true. It cannot be false. It must be true in any world where there are colors—in all possible worlds. If you are like me, you feel certain that this is true. You cannot give a definition of colors. You just know that nothing that is green can be at the same time red.

Like Plantinga, most contemporary rationalists are fallibilists in that they admit that we could be mistaken about what we take to be the phenomenal feel of intuitive certainty. Such certainty is not infallible. You could believe with maximal certainty that p is necessarily true and still be wrong. And you could believe very weakly that a necessary truth is true and still have a priori knowledge, as when you believe that some nonimmediate arithmetical problem (e.g., 1,345 + 497.4 + 677.7 + 67.8 = 2,589.9) is a certain sum but aren't absolutely sure. A priori knowledge comes in degrees.

Not only is a priori belief fallible and a matter of degree, but there are necessary truths that no one knows—such as the truth regarding

Goldbach's Conjecture (an even number greater than 2 must be the sum of two prime numbers) or Fermat's Last Theorem (the equation $x^n + y^n = z^n$ has no solution for x, y, and z nonzero integers when n is greater than 2).

Typically, as with Leibniz, Kant, and Plantinga, the rationalists have asserted that all a priori knowledge must be of necessary truths. But there is reason to doubt this. Saul Kripke has argued that if someone stipulated that a bar in Paris was 1 meter long and defined the term *meter*, then we could know a priori that this bar was 1 meter long even though it was a contingent truth, not a necessary one.[13] Likewise, as Philip Kitcher and, interestingly, Alvin Plantinga[14] before him, have pointed out, I can know a priori that I exist. "If I believe that I exist, I exist" even though my existence is not necessary but contingent.

So, necessity is not a necessary condition for a priori knowledge. One may have a priori contingent knowledge. According to Kripke, any time we stipulate a definition of a term, we can know a priori the truth of the definition. For example, if we define "water" as the molecular structure H_2O, then we can know a priori that water is H_2O and if we define "pain" as any sensation that hurts, then we can know a priori when we have pain—even though there is nothing necessary either about pain or our having it. But this seems to reduce a prioricity to triviality.

So, what is so different about a priori knowledge? If it is fallible, comes in degrees of certainty, and need not be of necessary truth (but of contingent truth), how is it different from a posteriori knowledge?

We come back to Kant's simple point about dependency. We do not need any particular empirical knowledge in order to know a proposition is true a priori. Definitions, our existence, and mathematical and logical truths all have this property—they can be known a priori. Some a priori knowledge is trivial (definitions), but some could be profound—especially if there is such a thing as synthetic a priori knowledge. But before we turn to that we must consider one other attempt to define or characterize a priori knowledge—reducing it to analytic statements.

The A Priori as Analytic Truth

John Locke and David Hume, as well as all twentieth-century empiricists—most notably—Ludwig Wittgenstein, A. J. Ayer, and Richard Swinburne—hold that only analytic truth can be known a priori. All analytic truths that can be understood can be known a priori—this allows us to omit highly complicated truths. In general, empiricists deny any synthetic a priori truth but admit that analytic statements are known a priori. This is a rather meagre concession, since all analytic statements are ones in which the predicate adds nothing to the subject. For example, the analytic statement "All bachelors are unmarried" can be analyzed as "All men who are unmarried are unmarried"; as logical positivists like A. J. Ayer point out this is tautologous. These empiricists make the analytic-synthetic distinction a primary platform in their philosophy.

Such a distinction was challenged by W. V. O. Quine in his celebrated essay "Two Dogmas of Empiricism" (1953). Quine not only rejects the distinction but rejects the whole notion of necessary truths and the boundary between empirical and observation statements. All our statements are underdetermined by the evidence, so any statement can be retained if you are willing to make enough revisions elsewhere in your system, and at the same time any statement, including a law of logic, is subject to revision or rejection.

> The total field [of our so-called knowledge] is so underdetermined by its boundary conditions, experience, that there is much latitude of choice as to what statements to reevaluate in the light of any single contrary experience. No particular experiences are linked with any particular statements in the interior of the field, except indirectly through considerations of equilibrium affecting the field as a whole.
>
> If this view is right, it is misleading to speak of the empirical content of an individual statement—especially if it is a statement at all remote from the experiential periphery of the field. Furthermore it becomes folly to seek a boundary between synthetic statements, which hold contingently on experience, and analytic statements, which hold come what may. Any statement can be held true come what may, if we make drastic enough adjustments elsewhere in the system. Even a statement very close to the periphery can be held true in the face of recalcitrant experience by pleading hallucination or by amending certain statements of the kind called logical laws. Conversely, by the same token, no statement is immune to revision. Revision even of the logical laws of the excluded middle has been proposed as a means of simplifying quantum mechanics; and what difference is there in principle between such a shift and the shift whereby Kepler superseded Ptolemy, or Einstein Newton, or Darwin Aristotle?[15]

Specifically, Quine rejects the analytic-synthetic distinction because of its vagueness. The metaphorical character of the operative phrase "containment" spreads over the entire analytic-synthetic distinction. Furthermore, the concept of analyticity rests on the concept of "synonymy," or sameness of meaning. That is, if it is analytic that "A bachelor is an unmarried male," this is because the terms *bachelor* and *unmarried male* are already synonymous. But, Quine argues, the usual explanation of the synonymy of bachelor and unmarried male is that unmarried male is analytic. In other words the "explanation" is circular, and, Quine argues, other explanations of synonymy and analyticity are likewise circular. The upshot is that if all a priori statements are analytic statements, as the empiricists insist, and there are no analytic statements, then there are no a priori statements either.

Since Quine, the analytic-synthetic distinction has continued to be subject to sharp attack. Gilbert Harman has been one of the foremost critics of the doctrine. He doubts whether speakers of a language really make such a distinction, judging it to be the result of "training and indoctrination." He compares the concept of analyticity to that of witchery.

> Once upon a time, women with supernatural powers, so-called witches, were distinguished from other women. We can admit that there is a distinction between women who seemed to be witches and women who did not seem to be witches to someone who believed in witches. But we should not go on to suppose that there really is a distinction between some women and others, some who have supernatural powers and others who do not. Nor do we have to believe that the women who would be called witches by believers in witchcraft all shared some common characteristics that other women lacked. For it may be and indeed is probably true that they would seem to have something in common only to someone who attempted to look at them from the point of view of one who accepted the theory of witchcraft. For what they were thought to have in common was that they engaged in supernatural activities; various things could be taken to be evidence of that. E.g., perhaps one woman muttered in a strange way and then a cow died. Another seemed to prosper more than her neighbors. A third looked like some witches they burned at Easter. And so forth.
>
> The analytic-synthetic distinction is like the witch-nonwitch distinction in that it presupposes a false view. Just as there are no real witches, there are no really analytic truths. Just as the women called witches turn out not to have anything in common, so too the so-called analytic truths have nothing in common that would distinguish them from other truths. Nothing, that is, except their seeming to be analytic to someone who believes in the analytic-synthetic distinction.[16]

Harman goes on to point out that the various candidates for analyticity are so varied that they don't have much in common at all. Here are his candidates:

1. A brother is a male sibling.
2. Red is a color.
3. $5 + 7 = 12$.
4. If x is larger than y and y is larger than z, then x is larger than z.

He concludes that the only thing these four statements have in common is "that they have seemed analytic to someone who believed in analytic truth."[17]

Harman and Quine are right to point out that there are borderline cases and that some candidates for the classification of "analytic" don't have much in common with others. But a distinction need not be absolutely sharp to be valid. To think otherwise is to be in danger of committing the slippery slope fallacy. It seems to me the right way to think about this is to hold to the original Kantian insight that an analytic proposition is one in which the predicate is already "(covertly) contained" or implied in the subject, whereas in a synthetic statement the predicate does add some bit of information to the subject. Analytic statements should be viewed as conditional statements in the form of *modus ponens:* If (A & B), then A; or if (A & B & C), then A & B. Granted, it is sometimes hard to tell precisely when we have such conditionals, but it seems excessive to deny that seemingly analytic statements have *nothing* in common but "seeming analytic" to someone who believes a false theory.

If we apply this test to Harman's four examples, it looks like the first three are analytic, though the fourth is less clearly so. Take (1), "A brother is a male sibling." What is the meaning of "brother"? Well, a full brother is a male who has both parents in common with another person. A sibling is the child of a common set of parents. Therefore, we can say the idea of "male sibling" is what is meant by "brother." If we understand the meaning of the word *brother,* we don't learn anything new by being told that a brother is a male sibling.

Similarly with (2) and (3), if we understand the notion of "red," we understand that it just is a color and if we understand the notions 5 and 7, we see that together they make up 12. Break up the number 12 into its constituent parts, say 12 ones, and then separate these into 5 ones and 7 ones; or 3 ones and 9 ones; or 4 ones and 8 ones; and so forth.

Candidate (4) is a little more difficult, since it doesn't have a subject term. It may be a borderline case. It is a complex statement whose truth nonetheless seems guaranteed by the meaning of words. Whether one wants to call it a broadly logical truth or analytic depends on how one settles on a definition of analytic. It seems broadly analytic to me, since the antecedent logically implies the meaning of the consequent. If this is so, then the analytic-synthetic distinction seems to survive Quine and Harman's attack. Rather than the analytic-synthetic distinction being a case of superstition like witchcraft, the denial of it may be more like a case of mistakenly "seeing" superstition where reasonable rituals and genuine religion are occurring. Because the denial of the analytic-synthetic distinction has become so widespread in analytic philosophy, winning the adherence of some of the best philosophers in the Western world, I pause to wonder why I don't see it as a nondistinction. Perhaps you will see things otherwise.

But even if it turns out that there are no analytic statements, that would not necessarily be the end of all a priori statements. Mathematic and broadly logical truths might still survive as a priori truths by whatever classification we give them. Perhaps you would agree with Kant and classify them as synthetic a priori truths. We turn to the question of whether we can have a priori factual knowledge.

Is There Synthetic A Priori Knowledge?

Let us return to Kant's theory of the synthetic a priori. The primary task of the *Critique of Pure Reason* is to answer the question "How are synthetic a priori judgments possible?" A. C. Ewing has shown that Kant makes four claims about synthetic a priori judgments.

1. They are logically necessary (wholes determine their own parts).
2. They are not derivable from particular sensations, although empirical experience is the trigger to cause them to arise.
3. They are presupposed in all of our experience.
4. They are contributed by our minds.[18]

To these we should add a fifth claim.

5. They are not analytic propositions.

Our synthetic a priori "knowledge" is merely the presuppositions or conditions of experience, and therefore only of the *appearance* of the world to us, which is constructed as we are. We can have no a priori knowledge of reality (the *ding an sich*). As red tinted glasses cause us to see the world in shades of red, so the constraints of synthetic a priori categories cause us to experience the world causally, temporally, and spatially.

As mentioned earlier, all a priori knowledge is necessary and has universal application. It is true in all possible worlds, whereas a posteriori knowledge is contingent. It could have been different from the way it is.

For Kant, not only space, time, and causality were instances of a synthetic a priori knowledge, but mathematical truths were also. Kant gives the example of $5 + 7 = 12$ as an instance of a mathematical synthetic a priori judgment, since the concepts 5 and 7 taken separately do not have the meaning of 12. The concept $7 + 5$ is simply the thought of two numbers added together, which is not the same as the thought of the definite number 12. If 12 meant the same thing as 5 and 7, then one could not think of one without thinking of the other, but we can do this. This is more obvious in the case of larger numbers. Most of us do not readily think of $53,936 + 27,142$ as equaling $81,078$, although it does.

Kant's example of geometrical synthetic a priori is the statement "the straight line is the shortest distance between two points." He points out that the notion of "straight" is qualitative, whereas the notion of "shortest" is quantitative, assuming that a quantitative definition is never implicit in a qualitative notion. Kant simply thought it obvious that the truths of geometry gave us information about physical space—and so were synthetic or expansive rather than analytic.

Both of these examples have been challenged, especially by A. J. Ayer.[19] To many it seems that $5 + 7 = 12$ is an analytic statement. Just as "horse" and "steed" are synonyms, so the number 12 has many numerical synonyms, $5 + 7$ being one of them. The numbers 5 and 7 together just are 12 so that if you understand arithmetic, you'll see this as obviously true. According to Kant, analytic truths depend on the law of noncontradiction and it would be a contradiction to suppose that $5 + 7$ did not equal 12. In saying that we do not readily identify the addends with the sum, he does not prove that this constitutes a synthetic statement, just like forgetting that the statement "All bodies are extended" is an analytic statement proves that it isn't. Critics charge that Kant confuses a psychological relationship for a logical relationship. Presumably a perfectly rational being would upon hearing the equation immediately intuit that $7 + 5 = 12$. The same goes for every mathematical truth.

Similarly, Kant's geometrical example can be seen as an analytic statement. Given a Euclidian framework, we can define the term

straight line as the shortest distance between two points. The properties of geometry seem to be broadly analytic statements, deriving
from the initial axioms. As A. J. Ayer points out, Kant may be excused
for thinking that Euclidian geometry provided information about
physical space, since he lived before non-Euclidian geometries, which
disprove this. Geometries are purely logical systems that tell us that if
some situations can be brought under their definitions, these situations will also satisfy the theorems.[20]

But it is odd that Kant calls synthetic a priori judgments *knowledge*.
For it could be argued that Kant is actually a skeptic about the reality
of synthetic a priori propositions. While they are necessary conditions
for human understanding, they do not reflect reality (*ding an sich*)
but rather are the way our minds impose order on reality. These
propositions are not, strictly speaking, true, or nor do they constitute
knowledge for that matter. Space, time, and causality are contribu-
tions of the mind in perception, but are not themselves real. But if
causality is not a feature of reality, what sense does it make to say that
the ding an sich causes these categories to arise in the mind? What
sense does it make to say that we *know* every event has a cause?

Synthetic judgments about natural science or metaphysics are not
true, or we cannot know them to be so, so why should we believe
them? Shouldn't we remain skeptics about the matter? The ding an
sich looks a lot like Locke's notion of substance (a "something I know
not what").

Nevertheless, there may be reason to retain the idea of synthetic a
priori knowledge. Other philosophers, such as A. C. Ewing and Roderick Chisholm, have defended the notion on independent grounds.[21]
They don't tie synthetic a priori judgments to the mind's contribution
but contend that it reveals a dimension of reality. The following statements are examples of synthetic a priori propositions.

1. Nothing that is green can be red.
2. If there are more than 7 dogs, then there are more than 5 dogs.
3. If there are either dogs or cows but no cows, then there are dogs.
4. If all men are mortal and Socrates is a man, then Socrates is mortal.
5. There can be no synthetic a priori truths.
6. Not both p and not-p.

These are better candidates for synthetic a priori statements than
Kant's, but they may also be challenged. Take the first statement,
"Nothing green can be red." By understanding the notion of green as
a color, one understands that colors are exclusionary, so that one

color cannot be another any more than a human can be a rock. By simply analyzing the idea of green in the light of the appropriate background (which is included in the idea of green), one sees that this is a broadly analytic statement.

This is similar to the second statement, "If there are more than 7 dogs, then there are more than 5 dogs." If you understand the terms in the antecedent, you'll discover that the consequent is but one of many entailments of the antecedent. Likewise for the third and fourth statements.

But the last two statements may be more difficult. Take statement (5), "There can be no synthetic a priori truths." First of all, if this proposition is a synthetic a priori statement, then if it's true, it's also false. Therefore, it is false. Secondly, even if all other cases are doubtful, the laws of logic seem to function as synthetic a priori truths. The principle of noncontradiction is necessary for the very possibility of thought, including the thought of the principle itself. Its denial is self-refuting, since to deny the principle depends on the very principle it is denying. For if the principle of noncontradiction is not true, then the denial of its denial is just as valid as the denial itself.

Perhaps a convinced opponent of the synthetic a priori can find a way to reduce this statement to an analytic judgment but, on the face of it, it looks like what the proponent of the synthetic a priori wants. Statement (6), which states the law of noncontradiction, may be another example. Whether there are many other types is more controversial. Are our judgments about time, space, causality, the moral law, and other metaphysical propositions synthetic a priori truths? It would be a profound discovery if they were. The matter is one that makes philosophical inquiry deep and important.

Innate Ideas (Again)

Let us return to the Empiricist rejection of innate ideas. Locke and Hume, we noted, reject the idea that we are born with any substantive information or knowledge. Our minds are a tabula rasa on which experience writes its lessons. The Empiricists admit that our minds have capacities to learn—humans can, but dogs cannot, learn to speak a language and do mathematical equations. But, these capacities are left vague.

Recall Locke's two main arguments against innate ideas: (1) If there were innate ideas, everyone (including idiots, illiterates, madmen, and savages) would possess them. But idiots, illiterates, madmen, and savages do not possess them; so, innate ideas don't exist and (2) if there were innate ideas, they would be present from birth. But we see that babies and small children do not possess them. Therefore, innate ideas don't exist.

These arguments seem too narrow. It could be the case that all humans were born with innate ideas but that they were latent, needing the appropriate conditions to make what is implicit explicit—much like Socrates brought out the Meno's slave's geometrical ability. The nativist (i.e., one who believes in innate ideas) may argue that innate ideas are dispositions that manifest themselves only under certain conditions. Take the idea of brittleness in glass. Normally a piece of glass will break if dropped from a certain height. But if it is packed in a Styrofoam box and dropped, it probably won't break. Likewise, our innate ideas will not manifest themselves under certain conditions. Just as some people are born blind, some people may not be able to activate their latent knowledge. It may also be that children must be nurtured in certain appropriate ways if they are to have access to such knowledge. Consider Locke's second argument—children do not demonstrate knowledge of innate ideas. Why can't understanding of innate ideas be like our ability to walk or speak a language? We need to have the opportunity to activate these propensities.

Recent work in linguistics and the philosophy of language and mind by Noam Chomsky, Jerry Fodor, and others has proposed that we are born with a basic repertoire of ideas about grammar and language.[22] Chomsky argues that we are born with knowledge of the syntactical rules governing all natural languages. As support for his position, he points out that children learn languages in an incredibly short amount of time, form grammatically correct sentences, and form novel sentences. They have near perfect grasp of the grammar of their native dialect—though this may not be the same as the language they are taught in school. Furthermore, artificial languages with nonuniversal syntax do not procure the same results. Chomsky calls this nonconscious innate knowledge.

Chomsky's theory about innate ideas is controversial. Many philosophers argue that his work only shows a broad capacity to learn and that childhood is a time when this capacity is especially receptive. Furthermore, the idea of nonconscious knowledge is problematic, as it is ambiguous between the ideas (1) information one doesn't realize one has and (2) the proclivity to learn certain things. Only the former would support the Rationalist's theory against the Empiricist.

Likewise, Jerry Fodor has argued that the best explanation of our ability to understand a language is that the mind is born with a "language of thought," which possesses a primitive set of symbols, or concepts and processes, necessary for understanding language. These processes are computational in that they construct and organize sentences in a natural language. Like Chomsky's innate grammar, the knowledge of this language of thought is unconscious. In fact, Fodor says that these primordial concepts are indefinable but the basis for all other concepts. Our present concepts are simply the primordial (or prototypical) concepts triggered (rather than learned) by experience.

Like Chomsky's theory, Fodor's work has received a great deal of attention. Many philosophers accept Fodor's theory because it explains language ability better than any current rivals. Nevertheless, the majority of philosophers and cognitive psychologists in this field advise caution. We really don't know enough about the mind to be confident about any theory of the mind, whether it be nativist or empirical.

One final attempt to support a type of nativism is that of the British philosopher Peter Carruthers, who argues that evolution has programmed us with innate information useful for our survival.[23] The content of "folk psychology," those beliefs and desires that we intuitively take for granted, yields a basic set of beliefs that may be taken as innate. Examples of folk psychological beliefs are "Flee predators," "Better to flee unnecessarily sometimes than never to have time to flee at all," "Drink when thirsty," "It takes more energy to lift a heavy object than a light one," and "Cooperate for your common good." Folk psychological innate beliefs also include our pre-Humean acceptance of induction and other minds. The fact that these beliefs do not arise from philosophical argument but instead are survival selective lends support to the idea that we are programmed by God or Nature to accept them. Furthermore, Carruthers argues, these beliefs go beyond our perceptual mechanisms. Perception may tell us that a strange creature is approaching, but it is a belief that tells us to flee if we want to survive.

A complete critical analysis of Carruthers' thesis is beyond the scope of this book, but two things may be said in its favor. First, it reconciles Empiricism with nativism, showing that an Empiricist, who believes in evolution and is seeking the best explanation of our behavior, should adopt a form of nativism. Second, we do have basic folk psychological "beliefs"—in other minds, the inductive method, and the like—that are not obviously justified philosophically. Evolution would seem a reliable method for inducing true or survival adaptive beliefs beyond what reason can justify.

On the other hand, it could be that we don't have innate ideas at all but simply biological capacities and proclivities that dispose us to believe in the content of folk psychology. Babies are adverse to pain and falling, but this doesn't mean that they have beliefs about pain and falling. The beliefs are formed later. Likewise, animals display instinctive behavior that is adaptive but that we would hesitate to label beliefs. It could be that the basis of folk psychological beliefs is instinctive behavior, which later becomes cognized into beliefs. Again, the wise person should hesitate before adopting any substantive theory about innate beliefs at this point in history. Still, the prospects are exciting and such speculations as those by Chomsky, Fodor, and Carruthers are to be encouraged. They just might have hit on something amazing: the mind possesses innate ideas. If so, then Rationalism and Empiricism will have been reconciled. Evolutionary empirical philosophy, it would turn out, corroborates what rationalists have said since Plato, that our minds at birth are not a tabula rasa but are endowed with innate knowledge and reliable processes for forming true and useful beliefs.

QUESTIONS FOR DISCUSSION

1. What kinds of knowledge are there? Go over the various types of knowledge described in this chapter and discuss your conclusions on those that are the valid types of knowledge. Give your reasons for your choices.

2. Do we have innate ideas? Describe Plato's view and compare it with those of Chomsky, Fodor, and Carruthers.

3. Evaluate the Empiricist critique, especially Locke's, against innate ideas. How strong are his arguments?

4. Evaluate Kant's notion of synthetic a priori judgments. Note what is at issue in his formulations. Take his illustration of $5 + 7 = 12$. He claims it is one thing to consider the concepts 5 and 7 and another to conclude that they equal 12. This is even more obvious with regard to larger numbers. Do you agree with Kant that this is not simply an analytic truth, provable by definition?

5. Evaluate Quine and Harman's contention that the analytic-synthetic distinction is an invalid distinction. What are the arguments for and against their position?

6. Are there synthetic a priori truths? If so what are they? If not, why do you reject this category?

7. We spoke of evolution implanting innate ideas in humans for our survival. A theist might be inclined to say that ultimately God im-

planted these ideas in us. John Calvin says that the idea of God's existence is innate in us; only sin keeps us from acknowledging it. On the other hand, Peter Carruthers writes, "While classical rationalists held that the process [of producing innate knowledge] was divine intervention (our innate beliefs having been implanted in us by a veracious God), this idea is no longer taken seriously in scientific cultures."[24] Evaluate these claims.

NOTES

1. Plato, *Meno,* trans. G. M. A. Grube (Indianapolis: Hackett Publishing Co., 1976).
2. Ibid.
3. Ibid.
4. D. J. O'Connor and Brian Carr, *Introduction to the Theory of Knowledge* (Minneapolis: University of Minnesota, 1982), 150.
5. John Locke, *An Essay Concerning Human Understanding,* Book I.
6. Immanuel Kant, *Critique of Pure Reason,* trans. Norman Kemp Smith (New York: St. Martin's Press, 1969), 41. I have slightly edited the text in order to make it more readable.
7. An anonymous reviewer points out that Saul Kripke has given examples of allegedly a posteriori knowledge of analytic truths.

   If I believe some elaborate analytic claim because some expert is reliable, sincere, etc., [I would know the analytic truth a posteriori]. Or if we program a computer to spin out ever more complicated analytic truths from its theory of semantical markers and syntactical structures, then our acceptance of the analytic truths it generates will be based on our evidence that the program is a reliable one.

   Whether we accept these as cases of analytic a posteriori knowledge will depend on how we characterize knowledge.
8. Kant, 45.
9. Here is how Kant states his thesis:

   All mathematical judgments are synthetic. This proposition seems to have escaped the notice of the analysis of human reason up to date, indeed it seems to go against all of their opinions even though it is incontestably certain and of great consequence. For as they found that all the deductions made by mathematicians proceed in accordance with the principle of contradiction (which is required by the nature of apodeictic certainty), they supposed that the axioms themselves are known on the basis of the principle of contradiction; which is an error: for it is indeed possible to prove a synthetic proposition by the principle of contradiction but only by presupposing another synthetic proposition from which the former is deducible, yet never in itself (*Critique of Pure Reason,* Introduction, B-14).

   I have used Arthur Pap's translation here. For an important discussion of these matters see chapter 2 of Pap's *Semantics and Necessary Truth* (New Haven, CT: Yale University Press, 1958).

10. Technically, the categorical imperative is not a judgment about experience for Kant but a necessary and universal *command* of practical reason. However, it seems to me to have the same status as a synthetic a priori truth, being both universal and necessary.

11. Kant, 74–77.

12. Alvin Plantinga, *Warrant and Proper Function* (Oxford: Oxford University Press, 1993), 106.

13. Saul Kripke, "A Priori Knowledge, Necessity and Contingency." In *A Priori Knowledge,* ed. Paul Moser (Oxford: Oxford University Press, 1987), 151.

14. Philip Kitcher, "A Priori Knowledge," *The Philosophical Review* 76 (1980), 3–23; Alvin Plantinga, *The Nature of Necessity* (Oxford: Oxford University Press, 1973), chapter 1.

15. W. V. Quine, "Two Dogmas of Empiricism," *From a Logical Point of View* (New York: Harper & Row, 1953), 43.

16. Gilbert Harman, *Thought* (Princeton, NJ: Princeton University Press, 1973), 101–102.

17. Ibid., 103.

18. A. C. Ewing, *The Fundamental Problems of Philosophy* (London: Routledge & Kegan Paul, 1951), chapter 2.

19. A. J. Ayer, *Language, Truth and Logic* (London: Victor Gollancz, 1936), chapter 4. Reprinted in *The Theory of Knowledge,* ed. Louis Pojman (Belmont, CA: Wadsworth, 1992), VII.2.

20. Ibid.

21. A. C. Ewing, *Fundamental Problems;* Roderick Chisholm, *Theory of Knowledge* (Englewood Cliffs, NJ: Prentice Hall, 1989). Both reprinted in Pojman.

22. Noam Chomsky, *Language and Problems of Knowledge* (Cambridge, MA: MIT Press, 1988); J. Fodor, *Representations* (Brighton, England: Harvester, 1987).

23. Peter Carruthers, *Human Knowledge and Human Nature* (Oxford: Oxford University Press, 1992), especially chapter 8. This section of my work has profited from Carruthers' discussion.

24. Ibid., 110.

FOR FURTHER READING

Carruthers, Peter. *Human Knowledge and Human Nature.* Oxford: Oxford University Press, 1992.

Chomsky, Noam. *Language and Problems of Knowledge.* Cambridge, MA: MIT Press, 1988.

Fodor, Jerry. *Representations.* Cambridge, MA: MIT Press. 1987. Especially chapter 1.

Kitcher, Philip. "A Priori Knowledge," *Philosophical Review* 76 (1980).

Kripke, Saul. *Naming and Necessity.* Cambridge, MA: Harvard University Press, 1980.

Locke, John. *An Essay Concerning Human Understanding.* London: Awsham & John Churchill, 1690.

Moser, Paul K., ed. *A Priori Knowledge.* Oxford: Oxford University Press, 1987.

Pap, Arthur. *The A Priori in Physical Theory.* New York: King's Crown Press, 1946.

Plantinga, Alvin. *The Nature of Necessity.* Oxford: Clarendon Press, 1974.

_____. *Warrant and Proper Function*. Oxford: Oxford University Press, 1993.
Pojman, Louis, ed. *The Theory of Knowledge*. 2nd ed. Belmont, CA: Wadsworth, 1999. Part VII.
Quine, W. V. *From the Logical Point of View*. New York: Harper & Row, 1953.
Sleigh, R. C., ed. *Necessary Truths*. Englewood Cliffs, NJ: Prentice Hall, 1972.
Stich, Stephen, ed. *Innate Ideas*. Berkeley: University of California Press, 1975.

CHAPTER 13

Memory

For what is the memory but a faculty, by which we raise up the images of past perceptions. (David Hume)[1]

Hiking along an unmarked trail in the wilderness, you come to an intersection of trails. You are startled by a strange feeling. You look around and your eyes are attracted to a vista of the valley ahead; a little to your right, lies a lush forest and, in the distance, fascinating rock formations. The strange feeling turns into a feeling of familiarity.

"We've been here before," you tell your partner who is just coming up behind you.

She looks around. "Yes, that's the Y Valley below and that's Mt. X over there to the left."

"Oh yeah, we were here in June of '81," you respond. "Then this intersecting trail must be the Appalachian Trail. There should be a sign down the trail, about half a mile as I recall and then we should come to that village with the quaint green-colored grocery store where we resupplied last time."

In about ten minutes you reach the aforementioned sign, and in another ten minutes you are in the village where the quaint green-colored grocery store meets your eyes.

How did you know that you had been at the intersection of the trails before and how did you know that it was in June of 1981 that you were at this spot? What was the strange feeling that turned into a feeling of familiarity? How does the mind work to convey reliable information from our past?

The mind is surely a remarkable mechanism to call up memories as reliably as it usually does. We don't understand how it does so, but equally intriguing, it is doubtful whether we can even specify exact criteria for knowing when we have a veridical memory. Yet we have no doubts that many of our memory reports are veridical. We use them to make predictions as in the story just told ("There should be a sign down the trail about half a mile . . . and then we should come to that village with the quaint green-colored grocery store"). We corroborate them with others' reports (in this case your hiking partner's testimony, but written records are also used). Of course, we sometimes make mistakes and misremember or have hallucinatory experiences, and much memory is inexact, faint, and vague. But the fact that we seem to get it right so often and so spontaneously seems truly amazing.

Someone asks you how to get to a place with which you are familiar, and without hesitating you set forth accurate directions. You yourself regularly find your way back to your residence hall or home without thinking about it—unless you're drunk or your memory is impaired in some other way.

I've met people whom I haven't seen for years—since childhood—and recognized them. Apparently, one of the largest zones in the cerebral cortex is given to facial recognition. Last month I saw Sam for the first time. I only had a glance at the side of his face from about 20 feet away, yet when I met him last week, seeing his full face close up, I not only remembered seeing him a month earlier but recognized him at once as the man I had seen from the side. In speaking, you normally don't search for the right word but instead spontaneously utter your thoughts. Yet all the while, you are depending on memory of word meaning, syntax, and appropriate fit between word and situation. You begin to tell a joke without first thinking about the whole, confident that the words will fall into place. In typing, riding a bicycle, shooting a basketball, or playing a musical instrument, the memory habits spontaneously play themselves out. What are these habits but the memories of past exercises and training?

In this chapter we will inquire into the nature of memory as a way of knowing. How can we know that memory reports are veridical? How do we distinguish memory of the past from imagination? What, if any, are the criteria for adjudication in these matters? How do we know that there is a past? How do we justify our memory beliefs? What counts as a memory? That is, what is it to remember? Is memory a source of knowledge? Does remembering something entail that one knows it? Need a memory impression be something that happened to the person who possesses it? Must the access of information be internal—by introspection or by a memory spontaneously forcing itself upon you? What is the relationship between memorial knowledge and dispositional knowledge?

First, let's list some memory claims that we can refer to during our study.

1. I remember how to ride a bicycle.
2. I remember going to the circus with my grandfather when I was about four years old.
3. I remember eating cereal with a banana for breakfast this morning.
4. I remember that $13 \times 13 = 169$.
5. With great effort (lasting several minutes), I recall the name of the woman at the party across the room.
6. I remember that Abraham Lincoln was president of the United States during the Civil War.
7. I cannot recall the telephone number of the house where I grew up, even though we had that number for well over 15 years and I used it (I seem to recall) thousands of times. But a neuropsychologist might be able to cause me to access it through implanting electrodes in the cerebral cortex.

Memory as a Way of Knowing

Most of our beliefs are memories, and because knowledge is a type of justified belief, most of what we know we know via memorial knowledge. Memory is not an original source of knowledge but a preserver of knowledge. Nonetheless, it is a basic source *for the knower.* Most of our knowledge is based on memory (which represents perception or testimony) so a foundationalist is consistent in claiming that memory claims are basic beliefs that are prima facie warranted. To quote Hume,

> To believe is in this case to feel an immediate impression of the senses, or a repetition of that impression in the memory. It is merely the force and liveliness of the perception, which constitutes the first act of the judgment, and lays the *foundation* of that reasoning, which we build upon it, when we trace the relation of cause and effect.[2]

My remembering that I had cereal with a banana for breakfast is a *basic* belief for me. I may have it corroborated by another's testimony, but normally I don't need to do that. The memory impression conveys "the force and liveliness of the [original] perception." It is a justified belief, one that I can use to draw inferences (e.g., because I remember seeing the water on the streets and lawns earlier this morning, I infer that it must have rained last night). If my memory belief is a true belief, then I may be said to *know* that I had cereal with a banana for breakfast based on this memory report. So although not usually as forceful or certain as perception, memory may serve as a basic belief in the foundational theory of knowledge.

Yet there is a coherentist aspect to memory. Normally it fits in with most of my other beliefs, forming a holistic pattern and picture. I can check it against the testimony of other memories and other people's reports. If my trusted friends assure me that I didn't eat breakfast this morning ("It was yesterday that you ate cereal and a banana"), then I have cause to question my apparent memory posit. Memory beliefs only confer prima facie justification, that may be placed in doubt by conflicting evidence. For example, in (2)—"I remember going to the circus with my grandfather when I was about four years old"—I may later be told that it was my cousin who went to the circus with my grandfather. But over the years the report got the persons mixed up, and having been told so often about being taken to the circus, my imagination actually invented the scents of the circus (I did go to other circuses) within my mind. Perhaps my uncle explains to me how the myth of going to the circus with my grandfather got started. Once I discover that contrary evidence, I should doubt my memory report for it doesn't cohere with what else I know about my past.

Most of our knowledge is based on memory reports, not present perceptions. The present is fleeting, effervescent, uncatchable. Most of our perception is really a form of memory of the very recent past. Try reading the words in a paragraph without holding in your mind the words that went before. What do you find? Typically, you find that you don't understand what you've read. Understanding a text involves holding in the memory what went before so that meaning is conveyed to the mind. This is probably why we sometimes find that scanning, or reading a difficult text rapidly, surprisingly increases comprehension.

The actual present is fleeting and swift, impossible to catch before it is hurled into the past. William James pointed out that most of what we call the present is really our memory of the recent past. He called this phenomenon the "specious present. The practically cognized present is no knife-edge but a saddle-back with a certain breadth of its own on which we sit perched and from where we look in two directions in time."[3] Pain and Pleasure would be meaningless without memory—otherwise we wouldn't *remember* their hedonic (or doloric) tone. It is the fact that they endure for a while and are remembered as such that we feel them. All of our concepts, the vast majority of our beliefs (all but those caused in the immediate present), and the connections between them, which provide a more or less coherent framework for thought and action, are products of our memory.

Likewise, our knowledge of our native language, social conventions, and ways of relating to others are derived from memory.

Our personal identity, our sense of who we are, is connected to memory. We know ourselves in the context of a backdrop of memorial beliefs, having to do with family and personal history. We see ourselves as the person who did so and so and whose parents are such and such, and whose beliefs and desires and habits are this and that—all brought to mind through memory. Amnesia or loss of memory is terrible, not simply because it prevents us from using the knowledge of the past that we had, but because it robs us of the knowledge of who we are. Loss of memory is loss of self.

The Problem of Veridical Memory and Imagination

I claim to remember that you started the fight but you are just as sure that I did; memory seems to be playing a trick on at least one of us. Indeed there is psychological evidence that we edit our memories in line with expectations. R. A. Sulin and D. J. Dooling describe the following experiment. One group of subjects read the following passage:

> Carol Harris was a problem child from birth. She was wild, stubborn, and violent. By the time Carol turned eight, she was still unmanageable. Her parents were very concerned about her mental health. There was no good institution for her problem in her state. Her parents finally decided to take some action. They hired a private teacher for Carol.[4]

The passage was given to a second group of subjects, except that the name "Helen Keller" was substituted for "Carol Harris." A week after reading the passage subjects were tested for memory retention. They were presented with various sentences and asked to tell whether they remembered reading it in the passage. When they came to the sentence, "She was deaf, dumb, and blind," only 5 percent of the subjects who read the Carol Harris passage accepted this sentence, but 50 percent of the subjects who read the passage about Helen Keller thought (mistakenly) they had read this sentence. Apparently, these subjects read facts they previously knew about Helen Keller into the story they actually read.

Daniel Dennett describes neurological experiments indicating that the brain actually holds information back and inserts it in inaccurate sequence in the mind. For example, the subject is shown a red spot and then in quick succession a green spot in an adjacent location. The subject reports that he or she saw the red spot actually change into the green spot at an earlier time than the actual time when the green spot appeared. What may have happened is that the brain or mind took in the information of the two spots and interposed an intermediate change of a red spot to a green spot.[5]

Could it be that our brain frequently plays such tricks on us—as it were, "editing" the information that comes to it in accord with background beliefs, interests, and biases?[6] This might explain why I claim to remember you throwing the first punch, and you seeming to remember that I threw the first punch. Or why you remember that I insulted you first, whereas I clearly recall just the opposite. The brain or imagination may work in a way to keep from us any clear introspective criteria for distinguishing veridical from unveridical memories. On checking my diary or notes, I sometimes am surprised to find that I have gotten the sequence of two events reversed. I thought that I had taken chemistry before algebra, but, looking at my transcript, I see it is just the reverse.

Note the relationship between memory and perception in distinguishing veridical from unveridical memories. Take the perceptual claim that I see a white-haired bespectacled man cross my path. Here are the main possible relations between perception and memory in which error is possible.

1. I did see a white-haired, bespectacled man yesterday, but today I remember seeing the man as having blond hair and without glasses. My memory has failed me.

2. I misperceived a white-haired, bespectacled man yesterday (it was a woman who didn't have glasses), but today I remember that I saw a white-haired, bespectacled man yesterday. The fault lies in the perception, not the memory.

3. I misperceived a white-haired, bespectacled man yesterday (as in (2)) but today I recall that I saw a bald-headed man with glasses. The fault lies both in perception and memory.

4. I misperceived a white-haired, bespectacled man yesterday (as in (2)) but my memory causes me to recall that it was a woman who didn't have glasses, which is correct. Here, perception failed me, but memory, though failing to represent perception, somehow got it right.

Whether (4) is a case of a second-order memory overriding the conscious perceptual report or just a lucky mistake, I'm not sure. Either seems possible. At this point we don't know enough about the memory to decide the issue.

Normally, we believe that perception is more reliable than memory reports. As my wife said when I told her there were some conceptual difficulties in justifying memory reports, "Well, if you're not even sure that the tables and chairs that you're seeing are real, it's hardly surprising that you're having trouble with memory reports."

The point is that from an internal perspective there is no way to tell the difference between a veridical memory and an unveridical one. We can check our memories by consulting our diaries, notebooks, and the testimony of others, but sometimes this is not possible and sometimes our diaries, notebooks, and the testimony of others are erroneous. It may be that our diaries convey reports closer to the events in question, but they are still memory reports. It's fallibility all the way down—and this gives rise to skepticism about memory.

If there is reason to doubt our perceptions, how can we be sure that our memory reports are veridical or that the past exists? How do we know it does? Perhaps it is all an illusion. As Bertrand Russell pointed out,

> There is no logical impossibility in the hypothesis that the world sprang into being five minutes ago, exactly as it then was, with a population that "remembered" a wholly unreal past. There is no logically necessary connection between events at different times; therefore, nothing that is happening now or will ever happen in the future can disprove the hypothesis that the world began five minutes ago.[7]

It is a logical possibility that the remote past is an illusion but there is no reason to believe that it is. And there are reasons to believe that the past existed and that our memories are basically reliable. As I mentioned, we can check many of our memory reports by appealing to notes we have made or the testimony of others. We can make predictions based upon them. Because I remember that you paid me back the last time you borrowed money from me, I am willing to trust you with a loan today. Because I remember that San Francisco is west of Oakland, I will head west if I am in Oakland and desire to reach San Francisco.

Indeed, science itself rests on the assumption that there is a stable core in our memory reporting. The laws of motion and knowledge of the sun's position relative to the earth (all involving memorial knowledge of past observations) allow us to make predictions about a sunrise or a solar eclipse, and memory of these same factors allows us to make retrodictions about past sunrises and solar eclipses.

So while we cannot prove that the past exists, we cannot help but live as though it does. Science, commonsense inductive generalizations, together with a whole host of interlocking beliefs and practices, confirms its reality.

The Doctrine of Mental Images

Hume gave two criteria for distinguishing memory from imagination: vivacity and restraint. Here is the classic passage.

> We find, by experience, that when any impression has been present with the mind, it again makes its appearance there as an idea; and this it may do after two different ways: either when, in its new appearance, it retains a considerable degree of its first vivacity, and is somewhat intermediate between an impression and an idea; or when it entirely loses that vivacity, and is a perfect idea. The faculty by which we repeat our impressions in the first manner, is called the *memory,* and the other the *imagination.* It is evident, at first sight, that the ideas of the memory are much more lively and strong than those of the imagination, and that the former faculty paints its objects in more distinct colors than any which are employed by the latter. When we remember any past event, the idea of it flows in upon the mind in a forcible manner; whereas, in the imagination, the perception is faint and languid, and cannot, without difficulty, be perceived by the mind steady and uniform for any considerable time. Here, then, is a sensible difference between one species of ideas and another.
>
> There is another difference between these two kinds of ideas, which is no less evident, namely, that though neither the ideas of the memory nor imagination, neither the lively nor faint ideas, can make their appearance in the mind, unless their correspondent impressions have gone before to prepare the way for them, yet the imagination is not *restrained* to the same order and form with the original impressions; while the memory is in a manner tied down in that respect, without any power of variation.[8]

Memory images are generally more vivid, forceful, and lively than imagination reports and more constrained by reality. This statement needs a lot of qualification. First, there certainly are a lot of exceptions. The image of a particular enemy doing future or merely imagined violence to you can often be a lot more vivid, forceful, and lively than the faded impression of having breakfast last Thursday or having gone to church or school as a child. Vivid dreams and hallucinations, including drug-induced experiences, can often be exceedingly vivid, far more than memory impressions. If mystic experiences are not veridical, they would illustrate the power of the imagination in convincing us of metaphysical ideas, for the mystic is often absolutely convinced of the reality of his past experiences.

Secondly, contrary to Aristotle and Hume, not all remembering involves images.[9] Some people think in images more than others. My wife can report the colors, shapes, and even textures of scenes from our past hiking trips in remarkable detail, whereas I recall only faded blurs tinged with a sense of tranquillity. Some people claim not to remember in images at all. I cannot *picture* the faces of my friends and acquaintances very well, but I'm pretty good at facial recognition in spite of this. It's doubtful whether we have mental images of "13 × 13 = 169" or our names, yet we can easily recall these facts. I remember that the University of Notre Dame football team led by Joe Montana beat the University of Texas in the Cotton Bowl in January 1978, but I have no distinct images of the game. Mental images don't seem necessary or sufficient for memory, but memory seems more a matter of getting it right than having the right images.

Bertrand Russell sought to improve on the Humean scheme of mental images. Vivacity is not enough to constitute a memory. Two other features must be present: a feeling of familiarity and a feeling of pastness, which is really a collection of features within a remembered context that enables us to locate the memory in a correct period with fairly good accuracy.[10]

Russell's theory has been criticized as being too close to Hume's in holding a theory of mental images.[11] However, I think that his basic remarks are at least valid for a large segment of memory beliefs— what is called *event* or *episodic* memory as distinguished from *habit* (e.g., remembering how to swim) or *factual* memory (e.g., remembering the fact that Lincoln was president of the United States during the Civil War). When I introspect, something very much like Russell's two criteria seem close to what it means to remember something. Recall my story of coming upon an intersection of trails while hiking in the wilderness (page 228).

> Hiking along an unmarked trail in the wilderness you come to an intersection of trails. You are startled by a strange feeling. You look around and your eyes are attracted to a vista of the valley ahead; a little to your right, lies a lush forest and, in the distance, fascinating rock formations. The strange feeling turns into a feeling of familiarity.
>
> "We've been here before," you tell your partner who is just coming up behind you.
>
> She looks around. "Yes, that's the Y Valley below and that's Mt. X over there to the left."
>
> "Oh yeah, we were here in June of '81," you respond.

The feeling of familiarity that one gets in perceiving being there before, hearing a tune again, or smelling the scent of a perfume you smelled before seems basic and unanalyzable. Consider the following:

At a party I recognize a woman whom I remember meeting long ago but can't recall her name. I try to recall it. I go through the alphabet, "Ann, Amy, Arlene, Audrey, Alice, Betty, Beatrice, Barbara, Carol, Cathy, Carmine, Cindy, Celeste . . ." but nothing comes. I give up and rejoin the party. Then all of a sudden, it begins to come back, "Mary Baker—that's it, it's Mary Baker," I say to myself, feeling that this is close but not quite. "No, it's Marla . . . [pause] Brrrr . . . Barker!!! It's Marla Barker! That's her name. Met her at my cousin Abigail's wedding three years ago."

How do I know when I've got it right? That it's Marla Barker and not Mary Baker or some other name? It just feels right. It feels like a fit, a familiar ring accompanies the name "Marla Barker." The feeling I get when I am remembering an event or name is well described as one of "familiarity" with the image or thought. I don't choose to have this feeling, as I might choose to imagine the Chicago White Sox winning the World Series next year. I can't help having it. Memory (or reality) thrusts itself upon me. Sometimes I don't have this feeling, but those are usually times when I'm preoccupied or not paying attention, as though the feeling of familiarity is always potentially there but not necessarily enjoyed.

The second feature was the sense of pastness in a context of associated memories and images. This seems almost inexplicable as a feeling. It's hard to describe but one can "see" the difference for oneself. Compare the image of your eating breakfast tomorrow and your memory of having eaten it this morning. How can you distinguish one from the other? One feature will be, I think, this unanalysable sense of pastness attached to this morning's eating.

The senses of familiarity and pastness are similar and related to our concept of occurrent believing (to be discussed in chapter 14). How do you know when you believe something? Others may infer that you believe that *p* from your behavior, but you don't normally do that. You can look within and feel an assent, a feeling of "yesness." We just think that our belief represents reality in some sense of that word. Memory impressions are types of beliefs that purport to capture our past experiences. We sense they are true or verisimilar, but cannot say much more about these feelings. There is an inscrutability attached to memory, recognized by Thomas Reid long ago, but consistent with Russell's analysis.[12]

Look into your own memory, and see if something like this isn't the case with you. Phenomenological analysis is virtually impossible to prove because it rests on introspection. All the opponent has to say is "I don't see that when I look within" to make us hesitate in our account. So I must leave it to you to decide on what is the correct account.

What Is Remembering?

Can we define "memory"? First, we must note that there are different kinds of memory. Consider four of the examples of memory reports mentioned at the beginning of this chapter (page 230).

1. I remember how to ride a bicycle.

3. I remember eating cereal with a banana for breakfast this morning.

4. I remember that $13 \times 13 = 169$.

6. I remember that Abraham Lincoln was president of the United States during the Civil War.

These illustrate different kinds of memory. Memory (1) may be called *Habit Memory,* which includes all sorts of abilities and behavioral patterns: eating with a fork, driving a car, typing, speaking English and, to a lesser extent, Danish and German, and so forth. Memory (3) may be labeled *Episodic Memory,* some event or episode in my life which I can recall fairly easily. This kind typically has the characteristics described by Hume and Russell (pages 235–36). Normally, I can form images of these events. Memories (4) and (6) are instances of *Factual Memory,* (4) of an abstract mathematical fact and (6) of a historical fact. We may also call these *Impersonal Factual* memories and may distinguish them from *Personal Factual* memories such as:

8. I remember that I learned to swim as a very young child but cannot recall the events.

9. I remember that I spent my first two years of life in Chicago, Illinois, but I can't recall those years.

I remember these events either through the testimony of others or because they were caused by the original event (e.g., my learning to swim) or because I've inferred them (e.g., I infer that I must have learned to swim at a very early age, since I can recall swimming in Lake Michigan at the age of five or six).

Memory images typically only accompany Episodic Memory, and they are not necessary even there. There is no sharp line between Episodic Memory and Personal Factual Memory. Faint episodic memories merge with personal nonepisodic ones. Neither is there a sharp line between Habit Memory and other types of memory. As A. J. Ayer says,

In a case of habit-memory there may be an accompanying image, as when one is assisted to remember a quotation by visualizing it in print; and conversely, one can dispense with images in remembering an event. What is decisive in both cases is one's ability to give the appropriate performance, whether it be a matter of displaying some skill, stating a fact which may or may not have reference to the past, or describing, or, as it were, reliving a past experience. These performances may be stimulated by various means, including the presence of an image; but even in the case of the recollection of a past experience, these stimuli do not constitute the memory.[13]

While there is no very sharp line between different types of memory knowledge (or claims to remember), we intuitively recognize these differences.

Perhaps no one in contemporary philosophy sought to analyze the experience of memory more than Norman Malcolm (1911–1990). In his paper "A Definition of Factual Knowledge," Malcolm claims to give the necessary and sufficient conditions for factual memory.[14]

> Our definition of factual memory can now be stated in full as follows:
> A person *B* remembers that *p* from a time *t* if and only if
> *B* knows that *p and B* knew that *p* at *t, and* if *B* had not known at *t* that *p*, he would not know that *p*.[15]

Although Malcolm's surrounding discussion is very helpful, this definition seems inadequate. It is both too narrow and too broad. Let us see how it is too narrow. First, someone can remember a fact without believing it, and hence without *knowing* it—a point many epistemologists overlook.[16] For example, referring to (2), my memory of being taken to the circus by my grandfather when I was a child, suppose I have a veridical memory of that event but don't believe it because my Uncle Ed has mistakenly told me that it was not me but my cousin Al that was taken and that the family folklore simply got us mixed up. We were about the same age and looked alike. My uncle is an honest and reliable witness (this is an uncharacteristic lapse), so I believe him and discount my faint memory impression. Since I am justified in believing my uncle's report and don't believe my memory report, I don't know that I went to the circus, even though I remember doing so. But Malcolm says that I do know that I went to the circus, even though I don't believe it. Here, I submit, Malcolm's notion of memory is faulty.

But even if we give Malcolm this kind of case, other counterexamples are forthcoming to show that his definition is too narrow. For example, at an early age—at *t*—I learned my name. However, I heard it over and over again for many years, so that if I hadn't known it at *t* I would have subsequently learned it—at t_1 or t_2 or later. But according to Malcolm's definition, I don't remember my own name since, to paraphrase his final clause, "if I had not known it at t, I would not know that p." So, according to his definition, I don't remember my own name.

But Malcolm's definition is also too broad, because it would apply to cases that would not count as remembering. Suppose, for instance, when I was about six years old, one day before his fatal heart attack, my grandfather surreptitiously took me to the circus. No one else knew this at the time. After the outing, I came home and wrote the details down in my childhood diary. The next day after my grandfather was found dead of a heart attack, I told my parents that he had taken me to the circus and overindulged in beer and fatty hot dogs (against the doctor's strict orders, I discovered). The years go by and I have completely forgotten about the trip to the circus. Then, 40 years later, I discover my childhood diary, which gives the details of the trip. Not able to recall any of the images myself, I inquire of my parents and they assure me that my diary report is exactly what they remember me telling them the day after the outing. I have fulfilled all of the conditions in Malcolm's definition. I know that I went to the circus (based on my diary entry and my parents' corroboration)—and if I had not known at the original time that I went to the circus, I would not know it now—but I don't remember going to the circus. I only believe I went due to the testimony of my diary and parents.

Can necessary and sufficient conditions for factual memory be given? If I were to attempt a definition, I would first separate seeming to remember from actually remembering and then separate actually remembering from knowingly remembering. As in the first example of going to the circus, I can remember that p but not believe it, and therefore, not know it. Here is how a definition for a successful *episodic* remembering (achieving knowledge) might look:

Let S stand for the subject, R for successfully remembers, B for belief, and p for the proposition describing the episode in question. Then:

SRp iff

1. SBp.
2. SB that p happened in the past.
3. p did happen in the past roughly when and as S believes it did.
4. S's B that p was caused by the event of which it is a proposition.
5. SBp is, all things considered, justified.

I'm not at all sure that this can withstand counterexamples, but it's the best that I can come up with. Perhaps I need a *ceteris paribus* clause to save me from wayward causation. Of course, it only describes one type of personal or episodic memory. Whether there are many other types of memory not yet fully discussed is a problem that I wish to turn to in the next (and last) section of this chapter.

Internalism and Externalism Concerning Accessibility to Memory

Following are three questions regarding whether memory can be accessed internally (through introspection) or externally (e.g., via an electronic device).

1. Must I be able to access memories by my own will in order to have memorial knowledge? Or would I still have memorial knowledge if I could only have access to it through an external process (e.g., a neurologist's electrodes attached to appropriate locations in the cerebral cortex) that caused me to remember something long forgotten?
2. Is there a difference between dispositional knowledge and forgotten knowledge still resident in the neuronal structure of my brain?
3. Could one remember things one did not experience but happened to someone else, or must memory always be first person?

We will address these questions in this section.

There are many things that I used to know that I have forgotten. Take illustrations (5) and (7) listed on page 230.

5. With great effort (lasting several minutes), I recall the name of the woman at the party across the room.
7. I cannot recall the telephone number of the house where I grew up, even though we had that number for well over 15 years and I used it thousands of times. But a neuropsychologist might be able to cause me to access it through implanting electrodes in the cerebral cortex.

Look at (7) first. I used to know the phone number of the house where I grew up in Cicero, Illinois. We had the same number for at least 15 years (or so I seem to recall) and I used the phone, gave the number to friends, listed it on documents, and called home frequently. But, I no longer can remember what the number was. Nonetheless, it is probably still embedded in the neurons of my cerebral cortex—just inaccessible in its present form. Perhaps layers of other memory states cover it and prevent my internal access system from getting to it. Presumably, a neurologist could attach electrodes to my brain and locate the place where that lost information resides. Over thirty years ago, the Canadian neurosurgeon Wilder Penfield conducted a set of experiments in which he used such electrodes to stimulate the cerebral cortex of epilepsy patients. They began to recall memories from the past and even sang lullabies learned in early childhood, songs that they had forgotten.

Suppose that I went to a neurosurgeon who used the electrodes to trigger my neurons in such a way that I recalled my childhood telephone number. Wouldn't that count as re-remembering it? But could we say that as long as the datum was stored in my brain I *knew* the number all along—I just couldn't access it without help? What is it about the nature of accessibility that makes us want to say "No" to that question? How accessible must a memory posit be for us to say that we knew or remembered the fact even though we weren't directly aware of it?

Normally, we can recall memories by doing a mental search. Recall my tale of trying to remember the name of the woman at the party, Marla Barker. Sometimes, I am successful in recalling names within seconds or minutes, but sometimes the name just won't come. But in the middle of my sleep that night, I suddenly awaken. "It's Marla Barker!" I blurt out. My wife awakens. "What are you talking about?" I apologize and fall back to sleep.

How does this self-probing recall mechanism work? I have no idea. It seems analogous to calling up data from an old computer (after my first computer was about eight or nine years old it took an inordinately long time to boot up and access files).

Did I *know* Marla Barker's name before I had successfully accessed it? If you say no, then you need to explain why, since we agreed (I hope) that most of our knowledge is stored in our memory. Whether you can recall your phone number or fellow student's name in one second or one minute or one hour seems relative to several factors and seems not to disbar it from counting as knowledge. Could it be that all our knowledge of the past is relative knowledge in this temporal sense? Recall that in chapter 1 we distinguished between *occurrent* and *dispositional* knowledge (or beliefs) and said that most of our knowledge or beliefs were dispositional. If this is so, isn't this information about forgotten names and telephone numbers simply a form of dispositional knowledge? Is there a relevant difference?

If you say Yes, I did know Marla's name all the while, then the implications seem far reaching. Let me approach the matter indirectly.

Let us return to the neurologist who can cause us to access memory traces through probing electrodes in the cerebral cortex. Suppose that in the future neurophysiologists really do come to locate where different memories are stored and can cause us to become aware of them through the use of electrical devices. We might imagine a spy with a fabulous memory reading an enemy military document then taking an "amnesia drug" that causes him to be unable to access the memory of what he read. If and when he is captured and tortured by the enemy, he can't access the information and passes the most sophisticated of their lie detector tests. So the enemy releases him, convinced that he doesn't know their military secrets. Upon returning to his country, he goes into the government neurological department (located no doubt in the Pentagon), a military neurophysiologist attaches electrodes to the spy's brain and causes him to remember the enemy's military secrets.

Did the spy *know* these secrets all along since he memorized the enemy's military documents? Would it make any difference if instead of having a neurologist use external probes, the spy himself had used self-hypnosis to bring back this information? What if he could do that, but the neurologist's methods were faster and more efficient?

What's the difference between doing an internal search (by concentration or self-hypnosis) and having someone else help you jog your memory? We wouldn't say that just because you gave me hints or counseled me in order to help me recall Marla's name that I didn't remember it. But how is jogging my memory through the use of electronic devices any different in principle from jogging my memory through hints and counseling? Both are external tools and processes, and both result in my coming to remember (or re-remember) Marla's name. The internal feelings of familiarity, pastness, and fittingness accompany the experience. I know that the person I saw was named Marla Barker.

But now suppose that neurosurgeons are able to replace damaged brain tissue with either brain tissue from a child that recently died (but whose brain was not significantly damaged) or even that the new (prosthetic) tissue was designed and constructed from inorganic material (perhaps a type of silicon chip could be made to interact with the cerebral cortex). Whatever it is, it can hold memories. Well, suppose that it was a small child and that her memories are still intact in that tissue. When implanted into your brain, you presumably can access those memories. Would these memories now be your memories?

In one sense, they wouldn't, and in another sense they would be your memories. They wouldn't be yours because you were not the person who experienced the perceptions that are represented by the memories. They happened to the child. But in a sense, they would be yours in that you can recall them from the inside and use them in deliberations. Perhaps, following Oxford University philosopher Derek

Parfit, we could call these "Q-memories," memories that you inherit from the one who experienced the event represented by the memory.

Suppose that we checked out many of the Q-memories (e.g., we had them corroborated by the child's relatives) and found them highly reliable. We could say that they added to our knowledge base, since they seem to pass all the tests for appropriately justified true beliefs. Therefore, we could say that it is possible to *remember* what happened to someone else. Using this reasoning, the answer to question (3)—"Could one remember things one did not experience but happened to someone else or must memory always be first person?"—seems to be that we could remember someone else's memories. Is this reasoning correct? Would you be remembering or only Q-remembering?

Suppose that after physicist Stephen Hawking dies, a relevant section of his brain is attached to your brain. Using his memory knowledge, you begin to do innovative work in astronomy and physics. Wouldn't you have his knowledge without paying the price of studying in order to obtain it?

If you answered Yes (as I'm inclined to do), what if his brain part could be detached (it's a burden to carry about all the time and makes running, dancing, and playing basketball rather awkward). Do you still have this knowledge when the Hawking brain sector is removed? If it's nearby, you can quickly retrieve it—faster than you can recall some of the complicated knowledge you already have. Suppose that you are running a 20-kilometer marathon without your Hawking brain sector. How far would you have to run before it would be right to say that you no longer knew the knowledge that was in the brain-sector? 500 yards? 1,000 yards? 1 mile? Suppose we say it is one mile. If you can run back to it in five minutes, you still will access it quicker than I can access some of my memory knowledge. If you get into a sports car, you may be able to get to the brain sector in less than one minute.

Would it make any difference if you couldn't access these Q-memories directly but needed a neurologist to help you? He would attach the electrodes to the appropriate parts of the brain and cause you to remember the Q-memories. Is the ability to do it from the inside a necessary condition for authentic remembering? Which is closer to veridical remembering: internally accessing a Q-memory or externally (through something like a brain probe) being caused to remember an event in your life that you could not have accessed on your own?

These thought experiments can unsettle our cherished beliefs. If you don't like the idea that one can be said to *know* information in one's prosthetic or implanted brain sector, how is this different from knowing what is in your subconscious (a kind of dispositional knowledge), which a psychologist could help bring to consciousness? But if you admit that we can know the information in our prosthetic brain sectors, then how is this different from claiming to (dispositionally) know *now* things that I have written in my diary or notebook? or information that I've stored in my computer and can easily access? Is there a logical difference between information in my brain that I need some external help (e.g., a friend to jog my memory) to access and information stored in my computer that I may access through "jogging" my word processor?

If there is no essential difference between knowledge that I possess within and that which I possess without (both are a kind of memory knowledge), would you be justified in arguing with your teacher that she should allow you to bring your computer to class to take a test? After all, it's just a matter of external versus internal accessibility, and we saw that that is an epistemically irrelevant distinction. Why should educators get so hung up on internal accessing, especially when computers can beat us in accessing data?

These are intriguing questions for epistemology. Traditionally, in the precomputer, preneurological science age, we made knowledge, in particular memorial knowledge, totally a function of internal access. But perhaps we need to modify our thinking here in the light of current technology and philosophical psychology. You don't have to speculate about prosthetic brain sectors. You can just use your pocket calculator to add up your checkbook or use your computer to access the essay you've recently composed to see how these devices become extensions of our brain, an invaluable part of our memory and knowledge base.

Recently, a solution was submitted to Fermat's Last Theorem. More than 350 years ago Pierre de Fermat claimed to have found a proof of the proposition that for the equation $x^n + y^n = z^n$, there are no integral solutions for any value of n greater than 2. After hundreds of years of effort by the most brilliant mathematicians in the world, Andrew J. Wiles of Princeton University submitted a proof of this theorem. It is 200 pages long and, as I write this chapter, it is still being tested by mathematicians.[17] Suppose this theorem is correct. The question is does Andrew J. Wiles *know* the solution to Fermat's Last Theorem? If knowledge entails internal access, we should say that he doesn't know it, since without consulting his notes and going through what he has written, he couldn't reproduce the proof. But if we say that as long as he has access to the proof (in his notebook or in his computer) he *knows* the proof, then we are extending the idea of knowledge to what exists outside our minds, what we need to access our knowledge by external means.

If we grant all this, where do we stop? If we can be said to know what we don't internally remember but have written in this week's class notebook, couldn't we extend this to all the notebooks we've ever written in? I know a student who was a math-physics major in college, dropped out, and after six years is going back to college. He doesn't want to major in math and physics anymore because he has forgotten much of his higher-level math. But, supposing he still possesses his old notebooks, couldn't we argue that he still *knows* this math? Perhaps we could call this N-memory (for notebook memory).

But if we can be said to know or remember material long since forgotten but still in our books, why insist on those particular notebooks? Why not get the teacher's better notebooks and work from there? If we can be said to know material in our notebooks that is utterly foreign to us, why not say we know material in any book, as long as we can understand it?

Perhaps we need to expand our notion of memorial knowledge. We can use "I-Memory" (i.e., Internal Memory) to refer to that which we can easily access by ourselves. "E-Memory" (or External Memory) refers to knowledge that we need external prompting or electrode probes to access. "Q-Memory" refers to the memories of others that we might access internally (this is now not an option). "N-Memory" refers to all that material (including Andrew Wiles's 200-page proof of Fermat's Last Theorem) that we have set down in written form. And perhaps we can speak of "O-Memory" as that which is broadly available to us and which we could easily access if we had to—information in libraries, encyclopedias, dictionaries, and computers.

Is there something wrong with these arguments? Perhaps, but it's hard for me to say exactly what it is. I want to give pride and place to internally accessible memorial knowledge and don't want to let students bring in their notebooks or other aids when writing essays or taking exams. There is something special about conscious states of remembering and being able to recall information accurately and quickly from within. A sort of possessor-ship of understanding accompanies this kind of memory. It is connected in a holistic way with other background beliefs and associations that go to the depths of our being. The sort of indescribable feelings of familiarity and fittingness described earlier mark memories off from anything else—from mere true beliefs. Merely having this data in notebooks or computers leaves out this comprehensive and deep understanding. For a large segment of beliefs, at least ones that guide the deepest parts of our lives, we draw on an incredible reservoir of memories, values, and habits in order to understand who we are and how we ought to decide ordinary and difficult issues. Here the existentialists are correct to point out that the emotions and commitments, internal aspects of life, are necessary to being fully human. In this sense, memories play a crucial role in informing our lives in ways that merely consulting books can never do.

But still the question of whether we can be helped by electrodes and other external factors to remember is probably to be answered in the affirmative. We probably should extend our concept of memory to include what can only be accessed through external operations, but this doesn't mean that we will value the internal operations or savor those self-induced memory revelations any less. They will still enjoy pride of place, one necessary to the meaning of who we are.

QUESTIONS FOR DISCUSSION

1. Describe a case of your remembering. Break it down into component features; then analyze it. Then compare your description to the one given in this chapter.

2. How do we know that what we seem to be remembering is veridical and not merely or mainly a product of the imagination?

3. What are the foundational and coherentist components in memory beliefs? That is, how would a foundationalist see memory functioning and how would a coherentist differ in his or her account?

4. List and describe as many types of knowledge as you can. Can you find sharp distinctions between these various types? Explain your answer.

5. Look over my discussion of Malcolm's definition of factual knowledge. Can you discover a way to rescue Malcolm's definition? Can you find counterexamples to my attempt?

6. In the last section, we discussed whether memory could be external to the agent. Consider the difference between having a picture of your beloved in your wallet and having it on your desk. You can access it in either case—only in one case more easily than the other. What is the difference between having a memory image stored in your mind or in your wallet or computer, except ease of access? But sometimes we can access difficult information better via a computer or written record. Do you find this a plausible extended account of memory?

7. What is the difference between dispositional beliefs and memory beliefs?

NOTES

1. David Hume, *A Treatise of Human Nature* (Oxford: Clarendon Press, 1739), 86. My emphasis.
2. Ibid., 260.
3. William James, *Principles of Psychology* (London: Macmillan, 1890), vol. 1, 609.
4. R. A. Sulin and D. J. Dooling, "Intrusion of a Thematic Idea in Retention of Prose," *Journal of Experimental Psychology* 103 (1974): 255–262. Quoted in Alvin Goldman, *Epistemology and Cognition* (Cambridge, MA: Harvard University Press, 1986), 209.
5. Daniel Dennett, *Consciousness Explained* (Boston: Little, Brown and Co., 1991), 111–138.
6. Ibid.
7. Bertrand Russell, *Analysis of Knowledge* (London: Allen & Unwin, 1921), 159.
8. David Hume, *A Treatise of Human Nature*, I, I, III, 8–9 (my emphasis). Hume qualifies his views thusly:

   It is evident, that the memory preserves the original form, in which its objects were presented, and that wherever we depart from it in recollecting any thing, it proceeds from some defect or imperfection in that faculty. An historian may, perhaps, for the more convenient carrying on of his narration, relate an event before another to which it was in fact posterior; but then he takes notice of this disorder, if he be exact; and, by that means, replaces the idea in its due position. It is the same case in our recollection of those places and persons, with which we were formerly acquainted. The chief exercise of the memory is not to preserve the simple ideas, but their order and position. In short, this principle is supported by such a number of common and vulgar phenomena, that we may spare ourselves the trouble of insisting on it further. . . .

9. Aristotle, "Memory, even the memory of concepts cannot exist apart from imagery." *De Memoria* 450a13.
10. Bertrand Russell, *The Analysis of Mind* (London: Allen & Unwin, 1921), 162–168.
11. See Jonathan Dancy, *Contemporary Epistemology* (Oxford: Blackwells, 1985), chapter 12; D. J. O'Connor and Brian Carr, *Introduction to the Theory of Knowledge* (Minneapolis: University of Minnesota Press, 1982), chapter V.
12. Thomas Reid, *Essays on the Intellectual Powers of Man* (Edinburgh: Bell, 1785), 342. Here is Reid's criticism of Hume:

    All experience presupposes memory; and there can be no such thing as experience, without trusting our memory, or that of others: So that it appears from Mr. Hume's account of this matter, that he found himself to have that kind of memory which he acknowledges and defines, by exercising that kind which he rejects (349).

    Reid rejects the necessity of images and believes that it is impossible to give the necessary and sufficient conditions for memory. God simply gave us this mysterious gift. That's about all we can say about it.

13. A. J. Ayer, *The Problem of Knowledge* (Harmonsworth, England: Penguin, 1956), 142. Although Bertrand Russell is generally credited with the basic habit memory/event memory distinction, their fullest analysis is given by Ayer in chapter 4 of this book, which contains a fruitful discussion of memory knowledge in general.

14. Norman Malcolm, *Knowledge and Certainty* (Englewood Cliffs, NJ: Prentice Hall, 1963), 222–240.

15. Ibid., 236.

16. See for example the otherwise perceptive article of Jim Landesman, "Philosophical Problems of Memory," *Journal of Philosophy* LIX.3 (February 1, 1962) where he says "for to remember is not merely to have a true belief, but to know" (61). And again, "I contend, however, that in remembering something we are not acquainted with anything; we are simply exercising our knowledge that a certain event occurred. What we know in memory is that a certain proposition is true" (65).

17. John Horgan, "Trends in Mathematics: The Death of Proof," *Scientific American* (October 1993), 94.

FOR FURTHER READING

Ayer, A. J. *The Problems of Knowledge.* Harmonsworth, England: Penguin Books, 1956. Chapter 4.

Ginet, C. *Knowledge, Perception and Memory.* Dordrecht, Holland: D. Reidel, 1975.

—. "Memory." In *The Handbook of Western Philosophy,* edited by G. H. R. Parkinson. New York: Macmillan, 1988, 159–178.

Landesman, J. Charles. "Philosophical Problems of Memory," *Journal of Philosophy* LIX.3 (February 1, 1962).

Levensky, Mark, ed. *Human Factual Knowledge.* Englewood Cliffs, NJ: Prentice Hall, 1971. Contains three important articles on memory by R. F. Holland, William Earle, and E. J. Furlong.

Locke, Don. *Memory.* London: Macmillan, 1971.

Malcolm, Norman. *Knowledge and Certainty.* Englewood Cliffs, NJ: Prentice Hall, 1963. The last three chapters are important.

O'Connor, D. J., and B. Carr. *Introduction to the Theory of Knowledge.* Minneapolis: University of Minnesota Press, 1982. Chapter 5.

Russell, Bertrand. *The Analysis of Mind.* London: Macmillan, 1921.

CHAPTER 14

Other Minds

By what evidence do I know, or by what considerations am I led to believe, that there exist other sentient creatures; that the walking and speaking figures which I see and hear, have sensations and thoughts, or in other words, possess Minds? (John Stuart Mill)[1]

Some years back in the philosophy department at a midwestern university there was a faculty member, call him Harry, who claimed to be a solipsist. He said that only he existed and that everyone else, his colleagues, family, and students, was a figment of his imagination. The word around the department was "We must take good care of Harry, for when he goes, we all go!"[2]

Few, if any, of us are solipsists. The position seems ludicrous, sufficient for the verdict of "not quite with it." We are certain that other people have conscious states of mind and feelings like ourselves. We believe that people other than ourselves have beliefs and desires, hopes and fears, and that they feel pleasure and pain. Most of us are also certain that animals, such as dogs, cats, chimpanzees, apes, and gorillas, have feelings. We normally take these things for granted. But can we justify our certainty about conscious states and feelings in others? How do we know that there are other minds?

The Analogical Argument

The traditional view is that a form of the argument from analogy can be used to justify our belief in other minds. It was held by Bertrand

Russell, C. D. Broad, A. J. Ayer, and, among contemporary epistemologists, John Pollock.[3] The classic expression of this view is Mill's
brief discussion in *An Examination of William Hamilton's Philosophy*.
"I conclude it from certain things, which my experience of my own
states of feeling proves to me to be marks of it." These marks or evi-
dences are of two sorts: antecedent and subsequent bodily states. The
antecedent states are necessary for the feelings and the subsequent
states are effects of feelings.

> I conclude that other human beings have feelings like me, because, first,
> they have bodies like me, which I know, in my own case, to be the an-
> tecedent condition of feelings; and because, secondly, they exhibit the
> acts, and other outward signs, which in my own case I know by experi-
> ence to be caused by feelings. I am conscious in myself of a series of
> facts connected by an uniform sequence, of which the beginning is
> modification of my body, the middle is feelings, the end is outward de-
> meanor. In the case of other human beings I have the evidence of my
> senses for the first and last links of the series, but not for the intermedi-
> ate link. I find, however, that the sequence between the first and last is
> as regular and constant in those other cases as it is in mine. In my own
> case I know that the first link produces the last through the intermediate
> link, and could not produce it without. Experience, therefore, obliges
> me to conclude that there must be an intermediate link; which must ei-
> ther be the same in others as in myself, or a different one: I must either
> believe them to be alive, or to be automatons: and by believing them to
> be alive, that is, by supposing the link to be of the same nature as in the
> case of which I have experience, and which is in all other respects simi-
> lar, I bring other human beings, as phenomena, under the same general-
> izations which I know by experience to be the true theory of my own
> existence.[4]

The argument may be stated as follows: There are three causal
states in myself: (1) the initial modification in my body (e.g., when I
step on a nail); (2) my feeling (e.g., the pain) caused by (1); and (3)
my subsequent bodily change (e.g., a scream, the contorted facial expression, the sudden lifting of my foot). When other people step on
nails, I behold conditions (1) and (3), but not (2). I see the same kind
of physical states as I experience in myself, but I do not experience the
other person's feelings. But I can infer that he or she has feelings from
the fact that this person behaves in the same way that I behave in similar circumstances. While I cannot prove that the other being has feelings, this argument from analogy allows one to conclude that it is
highly probable that he or she has feelings.

There are problems with the argument from analogy. First, it is impossible to check up on the correctness of the conclusion that the other body is experiencing feelings like one's own. I can introspect into my own mind in order to see whether I am angry or fearful, but I can't introspect into my neighbor's mind to see whether he or she is angry or fearful. No matter how hard I try, I can't feel your pain or sense your tickle or experience your belief, doubt, or desire. Each of us is a closed book as far as checking up on another's mental states is concerned.

A second problem is that the analogical argument only gives us probability where what we need is certainty. We have no serious doubts about the fact that heteropsychological states exist. When you or I see our friend screaming after stepping on a nail or hitting his finger with a hammer, we instinctively know that he is in pain. In other words, we feel more confident in the conclusion of the argument from analogy than in the premises of that argument. So what good is the argument in the first place?

However, the main problem is that the argument from analogy seems to be a generalization from only one particular. Normally, inductive reasoning goes from many particular instances to an inductive generalization, but the argument from analogy regarding other minds proceeds from only one instance, my own, to a generalization about all other living animals and human beings. It is as though I discovered that I disliked eating eggs and generalize to the conclusion that therefore everyone in the world dislikes eating eggs (other people must be eating them under duress), or that having seen only one kind of tree, an apple tree, I infer that all trees are apple trees.

The analogical argument might even lead me to conclude that all the pains there are in the world are ones I alone suffer, since all the pains that I have felt—whether they were in my body or in someone else's—were in fact in my body. I have never experienced other people suffering any pains at all.[5] I am the scapegoat of the world's iniquities. Later, we'll consider a modified analogical argument by H. H. Price that attempts to overcome these difficulties.

Behaviorist Arguments

An opposite strategy, the behaviorist argument for other minds, is to discount consciousness altogether and concentrate on an organism's behavior. If a human or a dog engages in similar behavior as I do when stepping on a nail, we infer that it is in pain. The problem of other minds is solved by reducing mental states to physical states. Beliefs, not being inner states, are simply dispositions to act in appropriate ways under certain circumstances. Emotions are just bodily manifestations: anger-behavior, sadness-behavior, pain-behavior, belief behavior, and the like.

But the behaviorist argument has serious problems, one being the fact that we can feign behavior. I may be in pain and not exhibit it, as when I conceal that I have a headache, or I may pretend to be in pain in order to obtain sympathy from the school nurse as I ask for permission to leave school early, so I can get home in time to watch the World Series on TV. I may smile when I am sad, weep when I am happy, or pretend that I am angry or in agony in order to deceive someone. As Hamlet says, "I have that within which passeth show. These [tears] abut the trappings and the suits of woe." Good actors learn to affect emotions. Likewise, I may have a belief and not act it out. For example, I may believe that San Francisco is north of Los Angeles but do nothing about it. The behaviorist may demur, "That is because you don't *desire* to do anything about it. If you *desired* to go to Los Angeles, you'd act out that belief." True enough, but then how do you define "desire"? As a tendency to act as if you had the requisite belief? But this is to define terms in a circular way. We can know that we have both beliefs and desires even when we don't act them out. So behavior is neither a necessary nor a sufficient condition for mental states.

Furthermore, the statement "He has a pain" may seem to be about pain behavior when said by someone else about me but the statement "I have a pain" said by me is not about behavior but about a feeling. Nonetheless, the first statement refers to what I am avowing when I say "I have a pain." Hence, the apparent behavioral statement "He has a pain" in fact refers to a feeling, not merely behavior. Note, "He does not have a pain," when said by someone else of me, contradicts "I have a pain" said by me. First-person avowals like "I have a pain" are self-evidently primary here, so behaviorism is to be rejected. However, it may be, as modified behaviorists like Ludwig Wittgenstein and Norman Malcolm argue, that behavioral criteria are necessary requirements for our attributions of psychological phenomena. In Wittgenstein's words, "An 'inner process' stands in need of outward criteria."

Other attempts at solving the problem of other minds include the argument from inference to the best explanation, which states in effect that the best explanation of why we believe that other people have internal states like ourselves is that other people really do have internal states like ourselves. This is sometimes accompanied by an evolutionary or creationist account of human nature, whereby it is said that evolution or God (or both) caused us to believe in the existence of other minds. Opponents of this theory argue that it is more an evasion of the issue than a solution of the problem.

Let us consider versions of all three approaches.

Price's Revised Argument from Analogy

H. H. Price (1899–1984) sets forth a sophisticated version of the analogical argument, based not on bodily states but on *language understanding*.[6] It is by being able to understand and verify meaningful utterances that we infer that others have minds like our own. If I hear someone shout at me while I'm crossing the street "Watch out! There's a car coming!" I jump back to the curb and look to my left where a speeding car is quickly approaching. I understand the noises that came forth from the person and verified them. It is this ability for an entity to give new information, implying understanding and verification, that provides me with strong evidence for the hypothesis that it has inner states like my own.

Price's version of the analogical argument is stated thusly: "Situations *a* and *b* resemble each other in respect of a characteristic C_1; situation *a* also has the characteristic C_2; therefore, situation *b* probably has the characteristic C_2 likewise. The noises I am now aware of closely resemble certain ones which I have been aware of before . . . , and the resemblance covers both their qualities and their manner of combination."

Even if I cannot see the body from which the sounds come, I will infer that another mind is in the vicinity. The body from which these sounds proceed need not be a human body. "If the rustling of the leaves of an oak formed intelligible words conveying new information to me, and if gorse bushes made intelligible gestures, I should have evidence that the oak or gorse bush was animated by an intelligence like my own."[7] If it seems impossible that the sounds are coming from a body, I would be justified in concluding that they proceeded from a disembodied mind. Price's new version of the analogical argument blends with the argument from inference to the best explanation. Such reasoning to the existence of another mind from the new, verifiable information offers the explanation of another mind (embodied or disembodied) as the best and simplest "explanation of an otherwise mysterious occurrence" of the sounds. "It explains the curious fact that certain noises not originated by me nevertheless have for me a symbolic character, and moreover are combined in complexes which are symbolic for me as wholes."[8]

Malcolm's Neobehaviorist Critique

The classic critique of Price's new analogical argument was given by Norman Malcolm (1911–1990) in the article "Knowledge of Other Minds."[9] Under no circumstances would we or should we believe that just because meaningful utterances come from trees or gorse bushes these objects have minds. What would show that a tree or gorse bush *understands* the sounds that proceed from it? Malcolm rejects a pure behaviorist theory but contends that behavioral criteria are central to our belief in other minds.

For example, if a child says "red" when a red thing is in front of him or her, this is "indicative of a mastery of those words *only* in conjunction with the other activities of looking, pointing, trying to get, fetching and carrying." If the child says the right words but looks at or points to the wrong object, we would conclude that the child hasn't mastered the use of that word, for "the disparity between words and behavior would make us say that he does not understand the words." In the case of the tree or gorse bush, however, we cannot even say that there is a disparity between its words and *behavior* "because it is logically incapable of behavior of the relevant kind."

So, Price has the picture topsy-turvy. We do not learn about other minds from one's own case. That leads to solipsism, skepticism about other minds. But this is nonsense; we all know that there are other minds—that other people experience pleasures and pains, feel joy and anger, hope and fear. Rather, we learn about pain by noticing others crying, grimacing, limping, or holding their legs. These first-person psychological avowals such as "I'm in pain" are themselves primitive, natural behavioral expressions of pain.

So what is needed, according to the neobehaviorists, is a *criterion* by which we pick out the relevant mental state, since it is linked with the physical state. For example, my seeing the person next to me gyrating, her arm bleeding, with screams emitting from her mouth, makes it evident to me that this person is in pain. Sydney Shoemaker states the relation this way.

> If so and so's being the case is a criterion for the truth of a judgment of identity, the assertion that it is evidence in favor of the truth of the judgment is necessarily (logically) rather than contingently (empirically) true. We know that it is evidence, not by having observed correlations and discovered empirical generalizations, but by understanding the concept [in question]. . . . The search for the criteria for the truth of a judgment is the search for necessarily true propositions asserting that the existence of certain phenomena or states of affairs is evidence of the truth of that judgment.[10]

The connection between criterion and conclusion is not like the connection in a typical inductive argument in which dark clouds are contingently connected with rain or a fever connected with illness. The criteria of pain-behavior are noncontingently, or necessarily connected, to pain (and the same goes for every mental state-behavior). It's a logical truth that the behavior is evidence for the mental state. The behavior tends to make evident the truth of the mental state—though it can be overridden (people can feign).

Wittgenstein, Malcolm, and Shoemaker seem correct in saying that we should doubt whether trees and gorse bushes—or computers—uttering sounds could be evidence that they had mental states. Unless we had a lot more information, we should conclude that they didn't have inner feelings, though we might have to leave the mechanisms a mystery. The neobehaviorists are also correct to say that we learn about the existence of other minds from the behavior of others, but it's not clear that they have explained how this happens or why we are justified in accepting the conclusion. The most troubling aspect of their proposal is that it makes behavioral states a necessary (or "logical") condition for mental states. This would presumably exclude God or disembodied souls from having beliefs. Surely, religious believers may be justified in believing that nonphysical beings have mental states. At least I know of no disproof of disembodied spirits or deity. But it doesn't even seem right to say that it's a necessary truth for humans to have our mental states connect up with the present repertoire of behavioral states. We could have been made differently, so that when we are happy, we cry; when in pain, we turn deep green; when afraid, we levitate; and when angry, our heads swell in size. So it is doubtful whether the correlation of mental states with any given set of behavioral states is a necessary truth. Any given correlation seems contingent.

Neobehaviorism has another difficulty. It seems to place too much emphasis on the behavioral manifestations of mental states. In spite of occasional denials to the contrary, it still holds on to a notion of inference in explaining and justifying our belief in other minds. But it is inference from behavioral criteria, not analogy, that does the work. The behavioral argument, rejecting the primacy of the inner process, seems to take us further from the truth of our experience than the analogical argument. The fact is that we sometimes do use analogical thinking to infer the feelings of others and we do typically center our thinking about mental states in our own experience. We appeal to the older sibling to stop exploiting his or her younger sibling, saying "How would you like it if she did that to you?" The Golden Rule says "Do unto others as you would have them do unto you." People who have suffered deeply in life are generally more sympathetic to the sufferings of others. If you've been mugged or raped, you are much more likely to understand the feelings another person has than if you haven't. Furthermore, you feel your own pain with an intensity that goes beyond what you are normally able to empathize in others, and you experience beliefs, doubts, memories, desires, and fears in a self-referential way that is unlike understanding what these experiences must be like in others. Just as a person blind from birth cannot conceive what it's like to see a rainbow after a thunderstorm, anyone who has not had the requisite mental state cannot understand what it's like for someone else to have a similar state. These features are captured better by those who hold the analogical argument than the neobehaviorist, for the phenomenal experience is fundamental in giving an adequate description of mental states.

The Evolution Argument

Finally, we must look at a new approach to understanding the other minds problem, one which fits in with the argument from inference to the best explanation and is broadly within the reliabilist (externalist) camp. According to Michael Levin in "Why We Believe in Other Minds," we believe in other minds because evolution has selected this survival-oriented feature in us.[11]

Levin says that the problem of other minds is normally posed in this way: "On what basis do *I infer* that various organisms I observe are conscious, and is this inference *justified*?" Each stressed word contains an important assumption that is thought to be necessary for a solution. The first assumption presupposes that each individual is a sort of "information-processing atom" who goes from nonbelief to belief regarding other minds. The second assumption supposes that the process by which the conclusion is reached is inferential. The third assumption is that one must have an account of why one believes that the process is the correct one—why one is justified in his or her belief in other minds. All three assumptions are wrong: we don't *go* from nonbelief to belief on the matter of heteropsychological states; we don't normally use an inferential process in attributing mental states to others; and we don't need to be justified in the traditional sense of that notion in that we are able to give reasons why we believe that others are experiencing pain or pleasure or have beliefs or desires. But the second assumption is the main source of error. It holds the other two together.

It is rather unlikely that anyone *infers* the existence of other minds for the simple reason that creatures incapable of inference, at least of complicated inference, believe in them or hold beliefs that entail the existence of other minds. Mr. Lion surely believes that Mrs. Lion is amenable to mating, a belief triggered when Mrs. Lion nips him. When my wife scolds him, my 16-month-old believes that his mommy is angry, to the full extent to which he believes anything. Yet lions and babies are incapable of inference, certainly of sophisticated inference.[12]

Levin argues that since these noninferential beliefs about other minds in animals and babies are indistinguishable from beliefs about other minds in adults, the latter beliefs need not be inferential either. The argument can be stated this way.

1. Babies and animals' beliefs about other minds probably aren't inferential.
2. Babies and animals' beliefs about other minds probably are reliable.
3. Babies and animals' beliefs about other minds are similar to our own heteropsychological beliefs.
4. Therefore, our heteropsychological beliefs probably are reliable, but noninferential.

Next, Levin offers an argument from the best explanation accounting for our belief in other minds. It's a Darwinian story. Natural selection has caused human beings to believe in other minds.

Creatures who can detect the thoughts and feelings of human and non-human fellow creatures have an evolutionary advantage over those who cannot, because they can better predict what their fellow creatures are going to do. This is how, and why, belief in other minds got selected in. The same advantage would accrue to pre-human creatures, so this hypothesis predicts that pre-human creatures have heteropsychological beliefs implanted by natural selection. This coheres well with the fact, previously stressed, that dogs and other animals *seem* to hold beliefs about the attitudes of other creatures toward them. . . .

More specifically, I suggest that what natural selection has implanted is a tendency to form certain anticipations and undergo certain feelings when presented with certain characteristic facial expressions and bodily carriages. I *infer* nothing when I see you writhe; by so far ill-understood neural mechanisms your writhing *causes* me to think you are in pain. Moreover *I* infer nothing. The mechanisms themselves have been selected in because they helped my ancestors. My genes pre-wired these responses into my nervous system, so they are not my doing. Whether my belief is *knowledge* becomes a nearly uninteresting question, for the *warrant* for my heteropsychological beliefs is independent of my beliefs themselves and my continuing to hold them. I have not adopted such beliefs because I saw their epistemic merit, nor does continuing to hold them depend on my continuing to find meritorious the inference on which they are based. There is no inference. . . .

There is an obvious Humean twist to this hypothesis. Our belief in other minds is founded not on reason but instinct, today's surrogate for Hume's "human nature."[13]

Levin offers as evidence for his Darwinian hypothesis the fact that within a few weeks of life infants react to faces. They smile if presented with even a picture of a face. R. L. Fantz has shown that babies respond to human-facelike figures differently than to figures made of the same parts but scrambled.[14]

Babies soon react to the inner states of others. They sense their mother's depression, anger, or joy. "The signs of happiness make children happy, and the signs of anger frighten them." Animals who sense love and fear present similar evidence.

Secondly, Levin points out that his hypothesis is exactly what evolutionary theory would lead us to expect. Those who can understand another person's inner state have an advantage over those who cannot, for the former can make predictions about behavior that elude the latter.

> It is useful to know about the minds of others because what is on someone's mind is a good guide to what he will do, in particular if he will attack you. Any caveman ancestor unable to tell by looking if a visitor to his cave is spoiling for a fight is more likely than a more discriminating competitor to get into fights he would rather avoid. He will consequently be less fit than such a competitor—that is, less likely to have children who themselves will have children. Similarly, those able to read positive emotions with great difficulty at best (by induction from his own case) will waste much time approaching females whose disinterest would be evident to more discriminating competitors. Such obtuse strains are likely to have been selected out, if they ever existed.[15]

Levin acknowledges that there are difficulties with his hypothesis. First, one might take exception to the idea that animals and babies have beliefs. Here Levin suggests that a behavioral or *ascriptionalist* account of beliefs—one where outsiders ascribe beliefs to the subjects—is more consistent with evolutionary theory than the *literal* (or *occurrentist*) account which is more popular in philosophy. Animals and babies don't formulate sentences or propositions, but they act in such a way that an "outsider will find it advantageous to think of the subject as if he literally had heteropsychological sentences running through his mind."

I think that Levin is right about animals and babies having beliefs, although not sentences or propositions, but I think we can improve on his ascriptionalism. We may speak of propositional beliefs, *belief that,* and objectual belief, *belief of.* The former takes a proposition as its object, whereas the latter takes a thing or object as its content. Deer see a man with a gun in their neighborhood and believe that there's danger without forming a propositional belief. Likewise, while I jog along a road, thinking about how to save the world introducing epistemology in the United Nations, I avoid the cars, bicycles, people, and dogs all around me without forming the propositions: "A dog is crossing my path. If I don't slow down, I will bump into the dog. It is neither in my nor the dog's long-term interest to collide. Therefore, I ought to avoid hitting the dog." I subconsciously believe this practical argument, but I don't formulate it, nor do I have to. I instinctively know what course of action to take. If this is right, animals and babies have objectual beliefs sufficient for their survival.

A second problem Levin faces is that his account does not fit into the typical justificationist framework of giving arguments or reasons for why you believe something. He has given a causal explanation, but the question remains: How may I justify my particular belief that someone else is experiencing pain, pleasure, anger, or fear? Unless Levin can give an account for this, his evolutionary account may be dismissed as just another interesting hypothesis or even as begging the question.

Here Levin argues that justificationism (and the whole internalist way of looking at epistemology) is largely false and urges us to accept a reliabilist account of belief acquisition. What is important is that the belief in other minds has been formed in the right way, not whether animals, babies, or we can give a justification for our belief.

In the end, Levin concedes that his Darwinian account, while providing the best we can do, does not solve the problem of other minds. Why not? Because the question is tied to the metaphysical question: What *makes* an event a mental event?

> If an identity theorist says that brain event type or token *B* is mental event *M*, it is very natural to ask: what does *B* have that *B′*—the secretion of stomach acid, say—does not have. Why is *B* a *mental* event, and *B′* not? Once asked, no answer will be found adequate. If the materialist says, "*B* is an event involving the right kind of hardware," the original impulse will manifest itself again in the question, "What's so special about that hardware?" If we say that *B* is a conscious event because *B*

plays a certain functional role, it is still tempting to ask why *such* events are mental events, why *such* a role confers consciousness on an event. The impulse will not be allayed even by the assumption that one or another of these identifications is correct *de facto*. I feel the impulse in myself, and I daresay anyone who has thought about the mind-body problem feels it.[16]

I think Levin has signaled the salient point. Saying, as the materialist generally does, that mind is an emergent property of the right matter in the same way that water is an emergent property of H_2O won't do, for consciousness is like nothing else. We need consciousness in order to experience the emergent property of wetness, but what do we need to be the kind of being that experiences consciousness? We are tempted to say that consciousness is matter plus __?__. Until we understand the relationship between the mental and the physical better than we now do, philosophers will remain skeptical of all proposed solutions to the problem of other minds.

QUESTIONS FOR DISCUSSION

1. Why is there a problem of other minds? Is it a genuine problem? Explain your answer.

2. What are the strengths and weaknesses of the analogical argument for the existence of other minds? Consider H. H. Price's new version. Are the criticisms of it fair?

3. What are the strengths and weaknesses of the behavioral solution to the other minds problem? Evaluate Norman Malcolm's neobehavioral version of this theory.

4. What are the central features of Michael Levin's critique of standard solutions to the problem of other minds? Evaluate them.

5. Evaluate Levin's Darwinian hypothesis. What are its strengths and weaknesses? One criticism you might consider is based on the difference between the origination of a belief and its justification. Levin explains how beliefs in animals and humans might have originated, but what does that have to do with justifying my belief in other minds? For example, how does such an explanation justify my believing that the bleeding body lying on the street uttering screams is in pain?

6. Why does Levin think that the problem of other minds refuses to go away? Discuss his argument for the intractability of the problem.

NOTES

1. John Stuart Mill, *An Examination of William Hamilton's Philosophy* (London: Longmans, 1889), 243f.
2. I owe this story to Alvin Plantinga to whom you should write for further particulars. There is also the story of the woman who wrote Bertrand Russell, "I'm a convinced solipsist, and I don't understand why everyone isn't."
3. John Pollock, a contemporary adherent of the argument, puts it this way:
   Our knowledge of the mental states of others is based upon something like the traditional argument from analogy. . . . There can be no question of observing confirming instances of the correlation in the case of other people. The only basis I can have for extending the correlation to other people is that they are like me in many respects and hence it is reasonable to expect them to be like me in this respect as well. ("How to Build a Person." In *Philosophical Perspectives, I, Metaphysics,* ed. James Tomberlin (Atascadero, CA: Ridgeview Publishing Co., 1987), 137f.
4. Ibid.
5. I owe this consequence of the analogical argument to Alvin Plantinga. See his *Warrant and Proper Function* (Oxford: Oxford University Press, 1993), 70. He points out that there will be similar arguments for other mental states such as anger, belief, and the like.
6. H. H. Price, "Our Evidence for the Existence of Other Minds," *Philosophy* 13 (1938). Reprinted in *The Theory of Knowledge,* 2nd ed., Louis Pojman (Wadsworth, 1999), 516–527.
7. Ibid., 475.
8. Ibid., 479.
9. Norman Malcolm, "Knowledge of Other Minds," *Journal of Philosophy* 56 (1959). Reprinted in Pojman, 527–532.
10. Sydney Shoemaker, *Self-Knowledge and Self-Identity* (Ithaca, NY: Cornell University Press, 1963), 3–4.
11. Michael Levin, "Why We Believe in Other Minds," *Philosophy and Phenomenological Research* XLIV, 3 (March 1984). Reprinted in Pojman, 533–542.
12. Ibid., 489.
13. Ibid., 490f.
14. R. L. Fantz, "The Origin of Form Perception," *Scientific American* 204, 5 (1961), 66–72.
15. Levin, 491.
16. Ibid., 496.

FOR FURTHER READING

Ayer, A. J. *The Problem of Other Minds.* Baltimore: Penguin Books, 1956. Chapter 5.
Broad, C. D. *Mind and Its Place in Nature.* London: Littlefield, 1960.
Buford, Thomas O., ed. *Essays on Other Minds.* Champaign, IL: University of Illinois Press, 1970. Contains 16 important readings.

Dancy, Jonathan. *Contemporary Epistemology.* Oxford: Blackwell, 1985. Chapter 5.

Plantinga, Alvin. *God and Other Minds.* Ithaca, NY: Cornell University Press, 1967.

Pojman, Louis P., ed. *The Theory of Knowledge.* 2nd ed. Belmont, CA: Wadsworth, 1999. Contains the articles discussed in this chapter.

Russell, Bertrand. *Human Knowledge.* New York: Simon & Schuster, 1948.

Strawson, P. F. *Individuals.* London: Methuen, 1959.

CHAPTER 15

The Nature of Belief

This operation of the mind, which forms the belief of any matter of fact, seems hitherto to have been one of the greatest mysteries of philosophy: tho' no one has so much as suspected it, that there was any difficulty in explaining it. For my part I must own, that I find a considerable difficulty in the case; and that even when I think I understand the subject perfectly, I am at a loss for terms to express my meaning. . . . I confess, that 'tis impossible to explain perfectly this feeling or manner of conception (David Hume).[1]

Hume's Perplexity

Although the concept of belief was examined before David Hume in the history of philosophy, the concept was either set within a religious context, as *faith*, or, in the case of Plato and Descartes, differentiated from knowledge as an inferior cognitive state, mere opinion. Hume is the first philosopher to take the concept of belief seriously in its own right, to recognize the difficulty in analyzing it, and to offer a detailed description of it. In his youthful *magnum opus, A Treatise of Human Nature* (1739), written when he was in his early twenties, only one topic eludes Hume's self-confident mastery: belief. The section on belief was the only one that he felt compelled to amend in the Appendix of that work. Yet in the end, he had to admit that he still had not succeeded in articulating its meaning. This concept "one of the greatest mysteries of philosophy . . . I am at a loss for terms to express my meaning. . . . I confess that 'tis impossible to explain perfectly this feeling or manner of conception" (T, p. 628).

Hume's insight was to replace knowledge with belief as the central epistemological concept in human experience. Hume argues in *Treatise* (Book I, Part IV) that if we were strictly rational creatures, we would doubt every proposition by subjecting it to comprehensive scrutiny. But while such Pyrrhonic skepticism is theoretically possible, it is practically impossible. "Nature will always maintain her rights, and prevail in the end over any abstract reasoning whatsoever."[2] There is no danger that the valid arguments for skepticism, which defeat knowledge, will overthrow the experience of believing.

Whereas those before him, Plato, Aquinas, Descartes, and Locke, had seen belief mainly in terms of its inferior status to knowledge and had concentrated on deliberative beliefs, Hume focused for the first time on the psychology of believing, showing that it is more like a sensation than a cogitation. We are credulous animals who from childhood are inclined to believe whatever testimony reports. We have "a remarkable propensity to believe whatever is reported however contrary to daily experience and observation" (T, p. 113).

Hume asks, What is believing and "wherein consists the difference betwixt believing and disbelieving any proposition?" Believing, he answers, is either wholly possessing ideas or it is essentially a feeling. But if it were simply a combination of ideas, we could obtain beliefs at will simply by adding the idea of existence to our other ideas (e.g., we could come to believe that God exists simply by adding the idea of existence to the idea of God). Ideas are subject to the imagination, and there is nothing so free as the imagination. But it is obvious that we cannot produce beliefs simply by willing to have them. Hence, believing is not simply possessing ideas. So it must be a feeling (T, pp. 94, 123f).

Hume's next question is ". . . Wherein consists the difference between incredulity and belief?" He answers that the difference cannot lie in the content of what is believed but in the manner of apprehension. It is obvious, says Hume, that the only thing that distinguishes belief from disbelief or from not believing is an additional force and vivacity attached to the idea. "An opinion, therefore, or belief may be most accurately defined, A LIVELY IDEA RELATED TO OR ASSOCIATED WITH A PRESENT IMPRESSION" (T, p. 96, Hume's emphasis).

He defends this Vivacity View by appealing to our common experience in reading fiction. Two people read the same novel, but one mistakes it as history; the other correctly reads it as fiction. They will read it differently, says Hume, and the former will have a lively conception of all the incidents, which the latter lacks. The one who reads it as history "enters deeper into the concerns of the persons:

represents to himself their actions, and characters, and friendships, and enmities; He even goes so far as to form a notion of their features, and air, and person" while the other gives "no credit to the testimony of the author, has more faint and languid conception of all these particulars" (T, p. 97f).

The illustration says more about Hume and eighteenth-century Scotland's bias toward history over fiction than it does about the nature of our experience of believing. Yet he has a point, though it might better be put in terms of expectations and dispositions. When we turn from reading Dickens, we do not expect to see the casual effects of his characters in the world, but when we turn from reading the history of a war or some other events, we do. We have a sense of "this is real," even when we have finished reading history, a feeling that fails us when we put the novel down (or wake up from a dream).

Hume recognizes that he has not dealt adequately with the idea of believing and in the appendix of his *Treatise* tries to amend his definition.

> Belief is nothing but an idea, that is different from a fiction, not in nature, or the order of its parts, but in the *manner* of its being conceived. But when I would explain this *manner*, I scarce find any word that fully answers the case, but am obliged to have recourse to every one's feeling, in order to give him a perfect notion of this operation of the mind. An idea assented to *feels* different from a fictitious idea, that the fancy alone presents to us: And this different feeling I endeavor to explain by calling it a superior *force*, or *vivacity*, or *solidity*, or *firmness* or *steadiness*. This variety of terms, which may seem so unphilosophical, is intended only to express that act of the mind, which renders realities more present to us than fictions, causes them to weigh more in the thought, and gives them a superior influence on the passions and imagination. Provided we agree about the thing, 'tis needless to dispute about the terms. (T, p. 629)

This statement is significant, for it alters the definition of belief from being a mere occurrent feeling of vivacity into one involving dispositions and actions. A belief gives ideas more force and influence and "makes them appear of greater importance; infixes them in the mind; and renders them the governing principles of all our actions." Hume does not develop this insight, so that for the most part he is wedded to his earlier *occurrentist* model, wherein all believing is a conscious occurrence or feeling.

In his *Enquiry Concerning Human Understanding*, published nine years after the *Treatise*, Hume considers how beliefs are caused. How do beliefs arise in the mind? He rejects the rationalist account, that deliberate reasoning produces beliefs. He takes the notion of causality as a test case. If a person of the strongest rationality were brought suddenly into the world, he or she would not, at first, by any process of reasoning, be able to arrive at the idea of cause and effect "since the particular powers, by which all natural operations are performed, never appear to the senses; nor is it reasonable to conclude, merely because one event, in one instance, precedes another, that therefore the one is the cause, the other the effect" (E, p. 42).

The power in the mind that forces conclusions upon us is *custom* or *habit*, which operates through the experience of constant conjunction of two objects (e.g., heat and flame, snow and cold, weight and solidity). We are determined by custom to expect the one from the appearance of the other.

> All belief of matter of fact or real existence is derived merely from some object, present to the memory or senses, and a customary conjunction between that and some other object. . . . This belief is the necessary result of placing the mind in such circumstances. It is an operation of the soul, when we are so situated, as unavoidable as to feel the passion of love, when we receive benefits; or hatred, when we meet with injuries. All these operations are a species of natural instincts, which no reasoning or process of the thought and understanding is able either to produce or to prevent. (E, p. 46f)

What actually happens in an act of believing is that the observed constant conjunction of events creates a "union in the imagination" between two types of things, whereby the principle of transmission of vivacity and force causes the one to partake of the present force of the other. "I would willingly establish it as a general maxim in the science of human nature, that when any impression becomes present to us, it not only transports the mind to such ideas as are related to it, but likewise communicates to them a share of its force and vivacity" (T, p. 98).

We may sum up Hume's theory of belief with four theses.

1. **The Antirationalist Thesis.** Beliefs are not simply ideas in the mind, for then we could produce them at will simply by manipulating our imagination directly, adding the idea of existence to another idea and so producing a belief, which is impossible.

2. **The Occurrentist-Sentiment Thesis.** Beliefs are feelings or sentiments in the mind, depicted by the vivacity and forcefulness attached to ideas and thus separating them from what we regard as fiction. Like other feelings (e.g., gratitude, anger, pleasure) they are unbidden, spontaneous, and indefinable, but we all understand them, since they are common to human nature.

3. **The Causal Thesis.** Beliefs are caused by experiencing things in constant conjunction, whereby the feeling of vivacity and force of one thing becomes transmitted onto the other.

4. **The Antivolitional Thesis.** Beliefs, as spontaneous occurrences of vivid ideas in the mind, are passive occurrences, completely involuntary, beyond the pale of the will to effect. It makes no more sense to say that I choose to believe that *p* than to say I choose to feel anger or pain when someone punches me in the stomach.

Thesis 1 reflects Hume's radical empiricism, which we discussed in chapter 12. Thesis 3 is related to thesis 1 and to his general skepticism, discussed in chapter 3. If one accepts synthetic a priori knowledge, one will not be impressed by Hume's account here. In chapter 16 we will discuss thesis 4. Here we will briefly show that the second thesis is inadequate as it stands.

Hume's occurrentist-sentiment theory of belief is too narrow. Force and vivacity of feeling are neither necessary nor sufficient conditions for belief. We can believe without having occurrentist feelings at all. I may not feel anything at all when I tell you that I believe that $2 + 2 = 4$, or what my name is, nor need the belief in question be occurrent. When I am sleeping, I do not lose my belief that my name is Louis Pojman (and hopefully you don't lose your belief in your name either). If occurrentism were true, we would have to say things like: "When the Pope went to sleep last night, he lost his faith in the Catholic Church" or "When you were concentrating on your math problem, you ceased being conscious of who you were and who your parents were, so you didn't believe that your name was so-and-so or that your parents were so-and-so." So occurrent feelings are not necessary for believing.

Occurrent feelings are not sufficient for a belief either. You may have a strong imagination that overwhelms you, so that you vividly imagine yourself being murdered or winning the World Series with a home run in the bottom of the ninth inning of the seventh game, without believing that either of these things are happening.

Nevertheless, I think that Hume is close to the truth about belief in that something like a feeling is present in occurrent episodes of believing. Hume is correct in saying that we can distinguish the feeling of belief from a proposition that we don't believe or from mere imagination without being able to say exactly what the difference is. It does seem to be something mysterious, yet we all recognize it. It has to do with our sense of reality or expectations, so even if you don't normally have a feeling when you assert well-entrenched beliefs like your own name or simple equations, you do *feel* surprise at having them shown to be false (or denied by others). One of my relatives had absolute faith in former President Richard Nixon, so she presumably felt nothing in uttering "Nixon is an honest president," until someone challenged that statement. Then she felt emotion in asserting it. After the evidence of Watergate was revealed, she not only *felt* disbelief but shock in the fact that her former well-entrenched belief turned out to be false.

The Fall of Occurrentism and the Rise of Dispositional Theories of Belief

In the first half of the twentieth century the problem of belief was largely neglected. Idealists were concerned with knowledge, not belief, and from a different perspective. The Logical Atomists and Logical Positivists were concerned only with logical relations and strictly verifiable empirical knowledge. The general antimetaphysical attitude that dominated these schools tended to dismiss the concept of belief as tied to metaphysics (e.g., belief in God). In *Tractatus Logico-Philosophicus* (1921), Ludwig Wittgenstein reduced the scope of philosophy to logical analysis, dismissing the concept of belief as a psychological, rather than philosophical, issue.

What interest there was in belief was mainly in the Humean occurrentist camp. At Oxford University, John Cook Wilson (1849–1915) held that while knowledge is infallible, belief is fallible and wholly different from knowledge. His disciple H. H. Price (1899–1984) said that "it is impossible to know and to believe the same thing at the same time. If I know that *A* is *B*, I cannot at the same time believe that *A* is *B*, and if I believe it I cannot at the same time know it."[3]

Price was troubled by his own conclusions about the narrow scope of occurrentist notions of belief and knowledge, but it was Alexander Bain (1818–1903), Frank Ramsey (1903–1930), and R. B. Braithwaite (1900–) who caused the tide to turn toward dispositional accounts of belief. In the 1926 article "Truth and Probability," Ramsey minimized the feeling or occurrentist element in belief, reevaluating beliefs in terms of probabilities. According to Ramsey, there are no general beliefs, only habits based on singular beliefs. We do not believe that water is wet, but we have the habit of believing that each particular quantity of water is wet. Singular beliefs are maps of the mind by which we steer our way through life, and what we call general beliefs are only habits of forming new singular beliefs. While

Ramsey offered a causal account of belief in terms of degrees of probability, he did not embrace a wholly dispositional or behavioral account of belief. He thought that the difference between believing and not believing "could well be held to lie in the presence or absence of introspectible feelings."[4]

The most antioccurrentist philosopher of the period was the epistemological behaviorist Alexander Bain, who already in *The Emotions and the Will* (1859) wrote that "belief has no meaning except in reference to our actions. . . . An intellectual notion, or conception, is likewise indispensable to the act of believing, but no mere conception that does not directly or indirectly implicate our voluntary exertions, can ever amount to the state in question."[5] The only difference between imagining and believing was that in the latter case one was prepared to act if the occasion arose.

R. B. Braithwaite developed a more sophisticated version of behaviorism, call it *quasibehaviorism,* in which belief consists of two parts: (1) a subjective, cognitive attitude, "entertainment in thought" and (2) a behavioral disposition to act as if *p* were true.[6] The dispositional attitude is the *differentia* of actual belief, separating it from merely entertaining a proposition. This account is not wholly behavioral, since it recognizes conscious states: memory, the entertainment of propositions, and intentions. But it denies the Humean doctrine that beliefs are feelings and places the emphasis on "the readiness to act" or disposition to act feature of belief. Indeed, we only find out whether we believe propositions by observing our actions. It seems to me that my belief in the proposition that this is a pencil in my hand consists, apart from its entertainment, in appropriate actions (e.g., in trying to write with the pencil), and that my reasons for believing that I believe it are inductive. I have witnessed myself doing such things in the past and predict that I will do so again in the near future.

While quasibehaviorists like Braithwaite, and later Gilbert Ryle, made a significant contribution in pointing out that occurrentism is mistaken and that belief includes a dispositional feature, several problems attend their theory. First, it seems counterintuitive. We do seem to be directly aware of our beliefs without having to look at our behavior. I believe my memory reports (that I had orange juice and a banana for breakfast this morning) directly upon introspection without any observation of behavior. When asked whether I would like to go to the cinema, I report in the affirmative immediately and before I take any steps to go or evaluate the probabilities that I will go. Furthermore, on the strong dispositional account, the whole notion of weakness of will would not make any sense. If I said that it would be a good thing to stop smoking but continued to smoke, the assertion would be discounted by my behavior. Again, in the behavioral account, it would be impossible to hold contradictory beliefs (which most of us believe that we have discovered in ourselves and others—some philosophers make a living pointing them out in others), since this view reduces beliefs to actions that cannot be contradictory (e.g., I cannot *do* and *not-do* the exact same act, although I can believe in one part of my doxastic structure that I will fly to Chicago tomorrow and believe in another context that tomorrow I will stay home all day and read a book).

Finally, on the quasibehavioral account, intentions are given too scant attention. It is hard to see where they fit into the behavioral repertoire; since it is only the behavior that finally counts, intentions might just as well not exist. But intentions are not only causally important; no account of action (as distinguished from mere behavior) seems complete without them. Often we need to appeal to such subjective states to explain why someone did what he or she did, for any given behavior could have an infinite set of explanatory accounts. For example, I can take out a short-term life insurance policy either because I want to commit suicide and thereby help my family by making them rich, or because I want to harm them by spoiling them with material wealth when I die, or because I think that there is a finite chance that I will die this year, and I want to insure against a financial catastrophe to my family. Or perhaps I take out a policy simply because the insurance salesperson is a friend of mine who desperately needs to make a sale or lose her job. Strong dispositionalism fails to give us guidance on adjudicating these points. It seems to be an overreaction to an exaggerated occurrentism.

It was H. H. Price, Wilson's disciple, who changed his mind about occurrentism and brought a moderation into the debate. Having been converted from occurrentism to dispositionalism, Price nevertheless retained an occurrentist core. More than any other source, Price's 1960 Gifford lecture series, "Belief," is responsible for the kind of moderate dispositionalism that enjoys a hegemony in epistemological circles today.[7]

Price agrees with Braithwaite that to say that "*A* believes the proposition *p*" is to make a dispositional statement about *A,* and that this is equivalent to a series of conditional statements describing what *A* would be likely to say or do if such and such were to happen. But, Price emphasizes that belief is also tied up with emotions, so part of what it means to believe that *p* is to feel surprise when one finds that the proposition in question is false or to feel the strength of the belief when it is denied or challenged by others (B, pp. 20, 275–280). Furthermore, Price agrees that we need not have any feeling attached to belief as long as there is no "conflict situation" involved, but once there is, we may well feel the tension between doubt and belief or surprise. In modifying dispositionalism to include the occurrentist notion of feeling, Price gives the concept a wider sense than others. It is to be applied to:

> any mental state or process which is introspectible. What is felt, in this sense, is what can be (though it need not actually be) an object of introspection; what we feel is just something which we "live through." . . . Sureness is a state of mind in which conflict or tension is absent. But it might still be a state of mind which is lived through or "enjoyed" by the person who has it; and that, I suggest, is the sense which the word "feel" has when a person says "I feel sure." . . . Feeling sure *is* rather like feeling calm, or feeling tranquil. . . . But [Kneale] is mistaken in supposing that feeling tranquil is just the absence of uneasiness. It is a positive state that we sometimes "live through." Should we wish to say that when a man feels well, the truth is only that he does *not* feel at all ill? (B, pp. 288f)

Putting this all together, Price calls belief a "multiform disposition" in that it may manifest itself in many different ways.

> It should now be clear that if "*A* believes that *p*" is a dispositional statement about *A*, the disposition we attribute to him is a multiform disposition, which is manifest or actualized in many different ways: not only in his actions and his inactions, but also in emotional states such as hope and fear; in feeling of doubt, surprise, and confidence; and finally in his inferences, both those in which a belief just "spreads itself" from a proposition to some of its consequences (certain and probable) and those in which the inference is a self-conscious and self-critical operation. (B, p. 294)

While belief is not a mental occurrence, a residue of occurrentism persists. Belief is primarily a state of mind (including the subconscious mind), but belief acquisition, the realization of a belief, and the loss of a belief can all be mental occurrences.

Price also came to hold that there is a volitional aspect to believing. "There is indeed something voluntary about [acquiring a belief]. It is an exercise of our freedom. The initial suspension or inhibition is voluntary." Furthermore, the attention we give to the "logical connections between the proposition already believed and the other proposition to which our belief would have 'spread' if we had allowed it to" is also under our direct control. We will come back to the relation between belief and will in chapter 16.

An Analysis of Belief

What is it to believe? When someone comes to believe some statement, what precisely takes place? When Scott believes that there is a chair in the room, what is the state of Scott's mind? What happens to him in acquiring such a belief? In what ways may he acquire such a belief? Must he be conscious of the acquisition, by noticing the chair and then realizing that he notices it? Can Scott acquire the belief without realizing that he has done so? Or are our belief-forming mechanisms like border guards who first scrutinize all proposed luggage before allowing the traveler to pass through? Even if the border-entry model is true, it is clear that we have forgotten the origins of many of our beliefs.

Perhaps the clearest type of belief acquisition is occurrent believing, already noted in our study of Hume, where someone entertains a proposition and judges it to be true. Our occurrent beliefs are those that we are conscious of having now. We are conscious of some of our beliefs and can be said to believe them in varying degrees. I am now conscious that there is a computer in front of me and that I believe that it is a reliable machine. If suddenly it were to crash or break down, like my former computer once did, I would be mildly surprised, because I have a mild confidence in its reliability. The degree to which we believe a proposition can be measured by the degree of surprise that we would feel if we discovered that our belief was false. An occurrent belief is often accompanied by feeling. We have already criticized Hume for identifying belief with a feeling. A belief is often sustained even when you are not thinking about it, have no feeling about it at all, have gone to sleep, or have temporarily forgotten about it.

One might be tempted to react to the introspective model's weakness by taking a purely materialist view of the mind and shortcut the problem of believing by identifying belief states with brain states. But, one difficulty with this move is that we might have to say that permanently comatose people and dead people still have beliefs, as the brain states may remain long after the individual dies. Under this description many things we have "forgotten" would still be believed, since there is a brain state corresponding to the "forgotten belief." But such beliefs are not action guiding, so equating beliefs with brain states seems mistaken.

In the last section, we examined various attempts at providing a dispositional account of belief. The extreme dispositionalist is the behaviorist (e.g., Bain, Braithwaite, and Ryle), who rejects introspective reports and analyzes belief in terms of behavior. As we noted earlier, pure dispositionalism suffers from the weakness that it does not include intentions (or wants) in the assessment of actions and beliefs. But beliefs, wants, and actions form an interconnected web. In many cases, we cannot account for one of these without taking into consideration the other two. If we begin with belief and see Sue acting in a certain way, we are likely to infer that Sue must have some object or desire in mind. Of course, we may not be sure which action, belief, or desire is operative in any behavior. If we see Sue registering for college, we may infer that she has some belief about college being a means to some long-range goal, but we may be misled here. She may simply want to please her parents or get away from home; she may be registering under duress, or she may simply have nothing better to do. Actions are explained by beliefs and desires, and they are unintelligible apart from them. Likewise, desires are blind without beliefs, but beliefs need desires in order to motivate action.

Dispositional accounts help us understand belief behavior. If I want to get to goal G and believe that action A will be the best (or an adequate) means of getting G, then I will doubtless try to do A. But I may never have an opportunity to exercise my belief in action, or I may never want to act on my belief. Nonetheless, this is no reason for not attributing many beliefs that I "feel" that I have to myself.

Price may be right when he calls belief a multiform disposition, which manifests itself in many different ways, "not only in his actions, and his inactions, but also in emotional states such as hope and fear; in feelings of doubt, surprise and confidence; and finally in his inferences." This is true of both [those] in which a belief unconsciously "spreads itself" from a proposition to some of its implications and [those] that are self-conscious operations (B, p. 294). The statement recognizes the complexity of having a belief, including the Humean element of feeling, the essential dispositional aspect, and the tendency of beliefs to spread out, though connecting with other beliefs and drawing inferences.

In this respect, Frank Ramsey's metaphor of beliefs as maps by which we steer is helpful. D. M. Armstrong enlarges upon this description—particular beliefs are maps by which we steer, and general beliefs are dispositions to extend the original belief map according to rules.[8] Beliefs are by their nature causative of action, and the importance of having accurate beliefs can largely be explained in terms of the action-guiding aspect that the map metaphor brings out.

Beliefs are not all-or-nothing states in the way that John Henry Newman supposed.[9] We believe in degrees. As former President Ronald Reagan said in a Fourth of July speech, "I believed as a boy, and believe even more today, that [July fourth] is the birthday of the greatest nation on earth." I believe that my wife is an utterly honest person to a greater degree than I believe that my landlady is. I believe most of the propositions that are based on firsthand experience more than I do those based on testimony or the deliverances of memory. We each have our own peculiar noetic structure wherein evidence (even where it seems to be "the same") is believed to warrant conclusions in different ways and to different degrees. In your noetic structure the teleological argument for the existence of God may lend no support for the existence of a supreme being, whereas in your neighbor's it may lend weak support, and for someone like William Paley it supplies overwhelming proof.

It may be possible to classify many of our beliefs on a continuum of subjective probability. Each one of us will have his or her own belief system ranging on a scale from 0 to 1 with 0.5 being doxastic indifference, neither believing nor disbelieving. As long as we agree that there is a state of positively believing with utmost conviction that p, a state of withholding belief that p, and the notion of degrees of belief, we have all we need for a classified belief system. If we let the number 1 stand for the state of absolute conviction, 0 will represent its opposite (or complement), a conviction that p is false; 0.5 will stand for the state of uncertainty or withholding of belief; and between 0 and 0.5 and 0.5 and 1 will be all the rest of our belief states. We may not be sure of the exact numbers to give to these belief states, and our degree of conviction may fluctuate over time, but we may be able to quantify our beliefs roughly using this method. Most of us don't quantify our beliefs in this way, although I have tried it out on part of my own set of beliefs with some success.

One way to test the degree to which you believe a proposition is to imagine how surprised you would be if your belief turned out to be false. We might also imagine some future society with a highly developed lie detector type of machine for measuring the degree to which we believe a given proposition. We can imagine a Belief Meter that has two rubber balls wired to it, one which, when the balls are squeezed, measures the pressure of the squeezes. You hold a ball in each hand and are instructed to squeeze the ball in your right hand when you believe the proposition in question, to squeeze the ball in your left hand when you believe the contradiction of the proposition, and to refrain from squeezing either ball when you neither believe nor disbelieve the proposition or the contradiction. You would also be instructed to squeeze the appropriate ball with a pressure commensurate to the degree with which you believe the proposition. A certain amount of experience may be necessary to work out the correlations, but accuracy will be approximated by the help of a truth serum. In this way, we might be able to quantify our beliefs into a roughly ordered system. Such a system might do wonders to exhibit the actual degrees to which preachers, politicians, prognosticators, and patriots actually believe their assertions. For your enjoyment, I invite you to imagine a presidential campaign being run by such a method. On national television presidential nominee Senator Sly is hooked up to the Belief Meter and asked whether he really believes he can balance the budget without raising taxes and so on. Of course, we may still be self-deceived about our beliefs, especially our memory beliefs, but there is no reason to doubt that our introspective reports are generally reliable.

It may be objected that believing is too primitive and inexact a phenomenon for us to assign probability to in this way. Our beliefs are spontaneously formed, roughly hewn, inexact, vague, and even contradictory. It is doubtful whether we can use many of our beliefs as premises in arguments since we seldom bring them together consciously. So there seems little hope of getting the kind of cardinal ranking that I suggest.

Although there is truth in this objection—our beliefs are often rough and tumble, vague and even inconsistent—I am still hopeful. Reflection can bring greater order and clarity into our noetic structure, and rough measurings of the degrees to which we believe propositions seem to be possible. I've already mentioned some examples of this, but I must let you try it for yourself and be the final judge.

Not only do we believe propositions to varying degrees, but we have complex emotional or valuational attachments to our beliefs. We may call this feature "the depth of ingress" of our beliefs, a phrase I learned from Alvin Plantinga. Some of these emotional or valuational attachments are connected with our self-understanding or our sense of purpose in life. Normally, a belief that it will rain this afternoon or that the Toronto Blue Jays will win the pennant may be undermined without too much disturbance to our noetic structure (though these two can have existential importance for some people). But the defeat of your belief in your friend's loyalty, your spouse's fidelity, your child's innocence, your religious creed, or your hero's integrity may wreak havoc in your noetic system and send damaging tremors throughout your total personality. We value beliefs to varying degrees, even as we believe in varying degrees. If we would quantify these aspects, we might say that Sam's degree of belief that p is 0.6, whereas his depth of ingress index with regard to p is 0.9. The proposition plays a mightier role in Sam's life than many of the propositions that he never doubts but hardly cares about.

Belief is typically manifested in assertions, but an assertion is neither a necessary nor a sufficient condition for having a belief. One can believe without ever asserting, and one can assert insincerely. Still, one may argue that there is a conceptual connection between asserting and believing. We learn what believing means through assertions, and occurrent believings have the phenomenal feature of inward assertions, assentings, feelings of affirmation, or yesness.

While the clear cases of belief acquisition often involve entertaining a proposition, weighing the evidence, and making a conclusion, we may believe without any intermediate step of entertaining, as in normal perceptual beliefs where "seeing is believing." Furthermore, we probably are not aware of all our belief acquisitions, for we take in enormous amounts of information that seem to make up our noetic structure without our being conscious of ever acquiring the belief. If on being asked the color of the wall of the room I've just left, I give the right answer without ever consciously entertaining it, should it not be said that I believed all along it was that color, though I did not realize it? This seems right. Perceptual material is stored in our memory like consciously formed beliefs. What is more difficult is the question of whether one can be said to believe the obvious entailments of his or her explicit beliefs. Before this moment I have never thought of the proposition that 100 is more than 6.7781, but it is so obviously entailed by several other propositions that I feel sure about, that we may be tempted to say that I had a dispositional belief that 100 is more than 6.7781 before it ever came to consciousness. If this is so, then the border-entry model of believing is too rigid. I need never have first acquired a belief in order to have the belief.

On the other hand, Robert Audi argues that there is a difference between having a dispositional belief and a disposition to believe, and this kind of proposition fits the latter category. In this case, the tollbooth model of belief acquisition would be preserved. I only have a disposition to believe the obvious entailments of the beliefs. What do you think?

Belief is typically related to evidence that supports it, unless you accept the foundationalist model; then the belief in question is a basic belief or self-evident, in which case it provides evidence for other beliefs in an inverted-tree construction. Basic beliefs, as we noted in chapter 6, are generally self-evident or evident to the senses. Beliefs claim implicitly to be connected to the world, to represent the way the world is, and, hence, to imply a direct or indirect relation to the world. In memory beliefs, for example, there is the belief that what I am recalling at the moment is connected in a chainlike manner to what part of the world was like in some time past. In testimony belief there is the implied belief that what I am now accepting is causally connected with the world that my neighbor saw and is reporting to me.

Finally, we need to know what the relationship of the will to belief formation is and in what sense we can be held accountable for our beliefs. We will take up these questions in chapters 16 and 17.

QUESTIONS FOR DISCUSSION

1. How does Hume differ from Plato, Descartes, and others regarding the status of the concept of belief? Explain the significance of this shift.

2. Describe Hume's theory of belief. What are its main ideas? Compare and contrast his occurrentist view with dispositional accounts.

3. Explain the behavioral and quasibehavioral theories of belief. Evaluate them.

4. What is significant about Price's multiform dispositional account? Do you agree with it?

5. In discussing the *purely materialist* view of belief, I say that one of its implications would be that "permanently comatose people and dead people still have beliefs." Is this a fair criticism of materialism?

6. What do you make of the idea that we can give rough assessments of the degrees to which we believe various propositions? Some philosophers object that many of our beliefs are too rough hewn, primitive, and even inconsistent for us to assign probability to beliefs in this way. Does this criticism have merit? Can it be answered?

7. Continuing question 6, some students, as well as David Benfield, have objected to my use of the belief meter as "far-fetched." I have tried to defend it by likening it to a perfected lie detector test. Is that a good comparison?

NOTES

1. David Hume, *A Treatise of Human Nature* (Oxford: Clarendon Press, 1739), 628. Henceforth, abbreviated as "T" in the text.
2. David Hume, *Enquiry Concerning Human Understanding* (Oxford: Clarendon Press, 1748), 41. Henceforth, abbreviated as "E" in the text.
3. H. H. Price, "Some Considerations on Belief" (1934). Reprinted in *Knowledge and Belief,* ed. A. Phillips Griffiths (Oxford: Oxford University Press, 1967), 42.

4. Frank Ramsey, *The Foundation of Mathematics* (London: Routledge & Kegan Paul, 1931).

5. Alexander Bain, *The Emotions and the Will,* 1859.

6. R. B. Braithwaite, "The Nature of Belief," *Proceedings of the Aristotelian Society* 33 (1932–1933). Reprinted in Phillips Griffiths.

7. H. H. Price, *Belief* (London: Allen & Unwin, 1969). Henceforth, abbreviated as "B" in the text. See also his "Belief and Will." In *Belief, Knowledge and Truth,* ed. Robert Ammerman and Marcus Singer (New York: Scribner's Sons, 1970).

8. D. M. Armstrong, *Belief, Truth and Knowledge* (Cambridge: Cambridge University Press, 1973), 3–5.

9. John Henry Newman, *The Grammar of Assent* (London: Westminster Press, 1870), 232.

FOR FURTHER READING

Bogdan, Radu J. *Belief: Form, Content, and Function.* Oxford: Clarendon Press, 1986.

Goldman, Alvin. *Epistemology and Cognition.* Cambridge, MA: Harvard University Press, 1986.

Griffiths, A. Phillips, ed., *Knowledge and Belief.* Oxford: Oxford University Press, 1967. Contains classic articles by John Cook Wilson, R. B. Braithwaite, H. H. Price, and others.

Hume, David. *A Treatise of Human Nature.* Oxford: Clarendon Press, 1967.

Lehrer, Keith. *Theory of Knowledge.* Boulder, CO: Westview Press, 1990.

O'Connor, D. J., and Brian Carr. *Introduction to the Theory of Knowledge.* Minneapolis: University of Minnesota Press, 1982. Chapter 2.

Passmore, J. A. *A Hundred Years of Philosophy.* London: Macmillan, 1957.

Peirce, C. S. "The Fixation of Belief," *Charles S. Peirce: Selected Writings.* New York: Dover Publications, 1942.

Pojman, Louis. *Religious Belief and the Will.* London: Routledge & Kegan Paul, 1986.

Price, H. H. *Belief.* London: Allen & Unwin, 1967.

Stitch, S. P. *From Folk Psychology to Cognitive Science: The Case Against Belief.* Cambridge, MA: MIT/Bradford Press, 1983.

CHAPTER 16

Belief and Will

One can believe only if one wishes to. Perhaps the credibility of a given person will be revealed to me so persuasively that I cannot help but think: It is wrong not to believe him; I "must" believe him. But this last step can be taken only in complete freedom, and that means that it can also not be taken. There may be plenty of compelling arguments for a man's credibility; but no argument can force us to believe him. . . . A free assent of will must be performed. Belief rests upon volitions. (Josef Pieper)[1]

Introduction: Varieties of Volitionalism

It is a widely held view that we can obtain beliefs and withhold beliefs directly upon performing an act of the will. This thesis is sometimes identified with the view that believing is a basic act, one that is under our direct control. Descartes held a *global* version of this thesis: The will is limitless in relation to belief acquisition, and we must be directly responsible for our beliefs, especially our false beliefs; otherwise, we could draw the blasphemous conclusion that God is responsible for them.

> Whence, then, do my errors arise? Only from the fact that the will is much more ample and far-reaching than the understanding so that I do not restrain it within the same limits but extend it even to those things which I do not understand. Being by nature indifferent about such matters, it very easily is turned aside from the true and the good and chooses the false and the evil. And thus it happens that I make mistakes and I sin.[2]

The father of existentialism, Soren Kierkegaard, held this thesis: "Belief is not so much a conclusion as a resolution. . . . Belief is not a form of knowledge but a free act, an expression of the will."[3] Sometimes a less global, or *local,* version of this doctrine is held, asserting that only the beliefs that are not irresistible or forced upon us are under our direct control. Thomas Aquinas, John Locke, John Henry Newman, William James, Josef Pieper, C. I. Lewis, Roderick Chisholm, Jack Meiland, Robert Holyer, and Gilbert Harman are representatives of this position, holding that we may *volit* (i.e., obtain a belief directly upon willing it) when the evidence is not sufficient or irresistible in forming a belief.[4] I will call the thesis that some or all of our beliefs are basic acts of will "Direct Volitionalism." I will contrast this view with the thesis that some beliefs arise indirectly from basic acts of will and intentions. This thesis I will refer to as "Indirect Volitionalism."

Another distinction regarding the relation of believing to willing in belief acquisition is that between describing volitional acts and prescribing them. I will call *descriptive* those types of volitionalism that merely describe the process of coming to believe, through *voliting* (i.e., obtaining a belief directly upon willing to have it). I will call *prescriptive* those types of volitionalism that include a normative element. Direct Prescriptive Volitionalism states that it is permissible or obligatory to acquire certain beliefs directly by willing to have them. Indirect Prescriptive Volitionalism states that it is permissible or obligatory to take the necessary steps to acquire beliefs based on nonepistemic considerations. A schematic representation of the various theses I have in mind looks like this.

	Direct	*Indirect*
Descriptive	One can acquire beliefs directly simply by willing to believe certain propositions.	One can acquire beliefs indirectly by willing to believe propositions and then taking the necessary steps to bring about the belief in the propositions.
Prescriptive	One can acquire beliefs directly by willing to believe propositions, and one is justified in so doing.	One can acquire beliefs indirectly by willing to believe propositions as described above, and one is justified in purposefully bringing it about that one acquires beliefs in this way.

This schema is not meant to be an exhaustive set of relations between believing and willing but to capture the central theses regarding that relationship in the history of philosophy.

Descriptive Volitionalism has to do with the nature of believing and the type of control that we have over our belief states; Prescriptive Volitionalism has to do with the ethics of belief and our duties with regard to acquiring and sustaining beliefs. I will discuss these two types of volitionalism in both their direct and indirect forms, contrasting them with the standard mode of belief acquisition. In this chapter, I first set forth the criteria that a fully successful volitional belief acquisition would have to meet and show why we should be skeptical about whether any instances obtain. Then, I offer two arguments against Direct Descriptive Volitionalism: the Phenomenological Argument, which proceeds on the basis of an introspective account of the nature of belief acquisition, and the Logic of Belief Argument, which shows that there is a conceptual connection between believing and nonvolitional states. In chapter 17, I turn to Indirect Prescriptive Volitionalism and the ethics of belief and argue that we have a duty not to get ourselves to believe against the evidence.

Direct Descriptive Volitionalism

What role does the will play in forming a belief? Is belief formation in some sense within our direct control? Or does the judgment come naturally as a spontaneous response to the total evidence (including background information and assumptions)? If receiving evidence when entertaining propositions can be likened to placing weights on balanced scales, can the will enter in to influence the outcome? On the standard model of belief acquisition, judging is not a separate act but simply the result of the weighing process. It is as though the weighing process exhibited the state of evidence, and then the mind simply registered the state of the scales. On the volitional model, judging is a special action over and above the weighing process. It is as though the mind recognized the state of the scales but was allowed to choose whether to accept that state or to influence it by putting a mental finger on one side or the other, depending on desire. The nonvolitionalist need not deny that desire unconsciously influences our belief acquisitions, but he does resist the notion that beliefs can be formed by conscious acts of will. The volitionalist, on the other hand, need not maintain that such volits can occur any time one wants them to. There may be times when it is impossible to move the weights through any effort of the will. Here the analogy with freedom of the will is apposite. Just as the metaphysical libertarian need not claim that every act is within our control, just some significant acts; likewise, the doxastic libertarian need not claim that every belief is within our control, just some significant beliefs. It is sometimes possible to place the mental finger on the doxastic scales and influence the formation of a judgment or belief.

I will attempt to show that there are problems with the volitional notion of belief formation. Although it may not be possible to prove that no one ever volits or that it is impossible to do so (as Bernard Williams claims),[5] I will offer two arguments to undermine the thesis that we acquire beliefs through consciously willing to have them, but I will also indicate the legitimate role that the will does play in belief acquisition. My first argument is called the Phenomenological Argument Against Direct Descriptive Volitionalism. It involves an introspective analysis of the phenomenon of belief acquisition, showing that there is something psychologically aberrant about the notion of voliting. The second argument, the Logic of Belief Argument Against Direct Descriptive Volitionalism, attempts to demonstrate a conceptual connection between belief and truth, contending that there is something incoherent about holding that a particular belief is held decisively merely on the basis of *wanting* to have that belief.

The Phenomenological Argument Against Direct Descriptive Volitionalism

First, we must understand what is involved in direct volitionalism (in this section, *volitionalism* will stand for direct descriptive volitionalism, unless otherwise stated). The following features seem necessary and jointly sufficient conditions for a minimally interesting thesis of volitionalism.

1. Acquiring a belief is a basic act. That is, some of our beliefs are obtained by acts of will directly upon being willed. Believing itself need not be an action. It may be dispositional. The volitionalist need not assert that all belief acquisitions occur via the fiat of the will, only that some of them do.

2. Acquiring the belief must be done in full consciousness of what one is doing. The paradigm cases of acts of will are those in which the agent deliberates over two courses of action and decides on

one of them. However, acts of will may take place with greater or lesser awareness. Here our notion of will is ambiguous between "desiring" and "deciding." Sometimes by "act of will" we simply mean a desire that manifests itself in action, such as my being hungry and finding myself going to the refrigerator or being tired and finding myself heading for bed. We are not always aware of our desires or intentions. There is a difference between this type of willing and the sort in which we are fully aware of making a decision to perform an act. If we obtain beliefs via the will in the weaker sense of desiring (of which we are only dimly aware), how can we ever be sure that it was really an act of will that caused the belief directly, rather than the will simply being an accompaniment of the belief? That is, there is a difference between willing to believe and believing willingly. The latter case is not an instance of acquiring a belief by fiat of the will; only the former is. For the volitionalist to make her case, she must assert that the acts of will that produce beliefs are decisions of which we are fully aware.

3. The belief must be acquired independently of evidential considerations. That is, the evidence is not what is decisive in forming the belief. Perhaps the belief may be influenced by evidence (testimony, memory, inductive experience, and the like), so the leap of faith cannot occur just any time over any proposition, but only over propositions that have some evidence in their favor and are still inadequately supported by that evidence. Such propositions have an initial subjective probability of, or just under, 0.5. According to Descartes, we ought to withhold belief in such situations where the evidence is exactly equal, whereas Kierkegaard held that religious and existential considerations may justify leaps of believing, even when the evidence is weighted against the proposition in question. William James prescribed such leaps only when the option is forced, living, and momentous. It may not be possible to volit in the way Kierkegaard prescribed without a miracle of grace, but the volitionalist would have to assert that volitional belief goes beyond all evidence at one's disposal, and, hence, the believer must acquire the belief through an act of choice that goes beyond evidential considerations. Using our earlier metaphor of the weights, it is possible to place our volitional finger on the mental scales of evidence assessment, tipping them one way or the other.

In sum, then, a *volit* is an act of will whereby I acquire a belief directly upon willing to have the belief, and it is an act made in full consciousness and independently of evidential considerations. The act of acquiring a belief may itself not be a belief, but a way of moving from mere entertainment of a proposition to its acceptance.

There is much to be said in favor of volitionalism. It seems to extend the scope of human freedom to an important domain, and it seems to fit our experience of believing where we are conscious of having made a choice. The teacher who sees that the evidence against a pupil's honesty is great and yet decides to trust him, believing that somehow he is innocent in spite of the evidence, and the theist who believes in God in spite of insufficient evidence seem to be everyday examples that confirm our inclination to accept a volitional account of belief formation. At times we suspect that many of our beliefs, while not formed through *fully* conscious volits, have been formed through *half-aware* desires. On introspection we note that past beliefs have been acquired in ways that could not have taken the evidence seriously into consideration. Volitionalism seems a good explanatory theory to account for a great deal of our cognitive experience.

Nonetheless, there are considerations that may make us question whether on reflection, volitionalism is the correct account of our situation. I will argue that it is not the natural way in which we acquire beliefs and that while it may not be logically impossible that some people volit, the idea of going through such a process seems psychologically odd and even conceptually incoherent. In this section, we will look at the psychology of belief acquisition, and in the next, the logic of that experience. We turn then to the Phenomenological Argument Against Volitionalism, which schematically looks like this.

1. Phenomenologically speaking, acquiring a belief is a happening in which the world forces itself upon a subject.

2. A happening in which the world forces itself upon a subject is not a thing the subject does (i.e., is not a basic act) or chooses.

3. Therefore, phenomenologically speaking, acquiring a belief is not something a subject does or chooses.

This schema describes the standard mode of belief acquisition and, it will be urged, is the way all beliefs occur. The first premise appeals to our introspective data and assumes that acquiring a belief has a spontaneous, unbidden, involuntary, or forced aspect attached to it. The second premise merely points out the active/passive distinction; there is a difference between doing something and having something happen to oneself. Hence, the conclusion states that as a happening, believing is not something one does or chooses. The Phenomenological Argument asks us to look within ourselves to see if acquiring a belief is not different from entertaining a proposition, the latter of which can be done at will. The first premise is based on the view that beliefs are psychological states about states of affairs. They are, to use Ramsey's metaphor, mappings in the mind by which we steer our lives. As such, the states of affairs that beliefs represent exist independently of the mind; they exist independently of whether we want them to exist. Insofar as beliefs presume to represent the way the world is, and hence serve as effective guides to action, the will seems superfluous. Believing seems more like seeing than looking, falling than jumping, catching a cold than catching a ball, getting drunk than taking a drink, blushing than smiling, or getting a headache than giving one to someone else. Indeed, this involuntary, passive aspect seems true on introspection of most propositional attitudes—being angry, envying, fearing, suspecting, or doubting—though not necessarily of imagining or entertaining a proposition, where an active element may often be present.

The heart of the argument lies in the first premise. That premise can only be established by considering a number of different types of belief acquisition to see if they all exhibit this passive or nonvolitional feature: having the world force itself upon one. While such an investigation might never end, we can, at least, consider typical cases of belief formation of various types. Let us begin with perceptual beliefs. If I am in a normal physiological condition and open my eyes, I cannot help but see certain things, for example, this sheet of white paper in front of me. It seems intuitively obvious that I don't have to choose to have a belief that I see this sheet of white paper before I believe I see it. Here seeing *is* believing. This is not to deny a certain active element in perception. I can explore my environment, focus in on certain features, turn from others. I can direct my perceptual mechanism, but once I do this the perceptions I obtain come of themselves, whether or not I will to have them. I may even have an aversion to white paper and not want to have such a perception. Likewise, if I am in a normal physiological state and someone nearby turns on loud music, I hear it. I cannot help believing that I hear it. Belief is forced on me.

Consider, next, memorial beliefs. The typical instances of believing what I seem to remember require no special choosings. I may choose to search my memory for the name of my friend's spouse, but what I finally come up with, what I seem to remember, comes of itself and has its own weight attached to it. I do not choose to believe my memory report that my friend's spouse's name is Pam. Normally, I cannot help believing it. There may be times when we only faintly recollect, but the fact that we only weakly believe our memory reports does not imply a volitional element in the belief formation. Although there are times (especially when considering events in one's distant past or one's childhood) when we are not sure whether what we seem to remember actually occurred, even here it seems that it is typically the evidence of the memory that impresses us sufficiently to tip the scales of judgment one way or the other.

This analysis can be extended to abstract and logical beliefs. Very few volitionalists affirm that we choose to believe that the law of non-contradiction has universal application or that 2 + 2 = 4. These sorts of beliefs seem almost undeniably nonvolitional, and some volitionalists would even withhold the designation "belief" from them, classifying them as cases of knowledge *simpliciter*. In any case, all agree that in these cases, if one understands what is being asserted, one is compelled to believe (or know) these propositions. They are paradigms of doxastic happenings that force themselves upon us, regardless of whether we will to believe them.

A similar process is at work regarding theoretical beliefs, including scientific, religious, ideological, political, and moral beliefs. Given a whole network of background beliefs, some views or theories are simply going to win out in my noetic structure over others. We sometimes find ourselves forced to accept theories that conflict with and even overthrow our favorite explanations. Accepting a theory as the best explanation or as probably true doesn't entail that we must act on it. We may believe an explanation to be true but find it so unedifying or personally revulsive that we are at a loss over what action to take. Such might be the case when a libertarian finds herself forced by argument to accept the doctrine of determinism or when a person loses his religious faith. After "perestroika" and the recent anticommunist revolution in the former Soviet Union, I saw two bright Russian law students weeping. When asked why they were weeping, one student said, "We were taught that communism was the truth, which would win out over capitalism. We've been proved wrong, and we don't know what to do." When doxastic revolutions break out, chaos results, and we suddenly find ourselves without relied-upon anchors to stabilize us or maps to guide us.

We can also accept a theory as the best explanation among a set of weak hypotheses without believing it. We can accept a proposition and act on it as an experimental hypothesis, without assenting to its truth. A behavioral analysis would conflate such acceptance with belief, but there is no reason to accept behaviorism. Sometimes we accept a theory little by little as evidence from various parts of it makes sense to us. At other times, it is as though we suddenly see the world differently; what was once seen as a cosmic duck is now seen as a cosmic rabbit. The term *seeing* is appropriate—even as we do not choose what we see when we look at an object (though we can focus on part of it, neglect another part, and so forth), so we do not choose to be-lieve a theory and thereby come to believe it. Rather, we cannot do otherwise in these cases. Nothing I have said, of course, is meant to deny that the will plays an indirect role in acquiring such beliefs.

Finally, and most importantly, there is the matter of testimony be-liefs that arise on the basis of reports of others. This is the kind of be-lief that is emphasized by Josef Pieper and Jack Meiland. Certainly, this seems a more complex type of believing than perceptions or memory beliefs. Often we read reports in newspapers or hear rumors or predictions and hesitate before siding one way or the other. Some-times the news seems shocking or threatening to our whole noetic structure. Here one may have the phenomenal feel, at first glance, that a decision is being made by the agent. For example, I hear a re-port that someone I know well and esteem highly has cheated his company of $50,000. The evidence seems the sort that I normally credit as reliable, but I somehow resist accepting it. Have I willed to withhold belief or disbelief? I don't think so. Although I am stunned by the evidence, I have a great deal of background evidence that I cannot immediately express in detail but that I have subconsciously within my noetic structure. This evidence plays a role in putting the fresh data into a larger perspective.

Perhaps I find myself believing willingly that, in spite of the evi-dence, my friend is innocent. Does this "believing willingly" against the evidence constitute an act of will? I don't think so. Here the reader will recall the distinction between (1) willing to believe and thereby believing and (2) believing willingly, where one feels drawn toward a belief state and willingly goes along with it. One can identify with and feel good about what one comes to believe, but in neither case is the will directly causative. In addition, there is the experience of viewing the objective evidence as roughly counterbalanced but still feeling inclined one way or the other. Here something like our intu-itions or unconscious processes play a decisive role in belief formation, but these are not things over which we have direct control. Within our noetic structure are dispositional beliefs and dispositions to be-lieve that influence belief formation. There is no need to appeal to acts of will to explain instances of anomalous belief acquisition.

Normally, however, I find myself immediately and automatically assenting to testimony. If I am lost in a new neighborhood and look-ing for a supermarket, I may ask someone for directions. Under favor-able circumstances I will believe what he or she tells me because I have learned through experience that normally people will give reli-able directions if they can. Even if I have to deliberate about the tes-timony, wondering whether the witness is credible, I don't come to a conclusion on the basis of willing to believe one way or the other; rather I reach a conclusion because the complex factors in the situation incline me one way or the other. One of these factors may be my wants and wishes, which influence my focus. But once the belief comes, it is produced by the evidence and not by the choice.

It may be that, given enough time and resources, we can come to believe almost anything indirectly through willing the appropriate means and acting upon them. For example, we believe that the world is spherical and not flat, and no amount of effort seems sufficient to overturn this belief. But perhaps if we had good prudential reasons to do so (e.g., someone offered us $1 million if we could get ourselves to believe that the world was flat), we might go to a hypnotist, take drugs, or use elaborate autosuggestion until we actually acquired the belief.

Perhaps the volitionalist will respond that there is really little difference between a case of autosuggestion and a case of voliting. Consider the following cases, which progressively tend toward a state of successful autosuggestive belief acquisition.

1. It might be virtually impossible for anyone to use autosuggestion to come to believe that one does not exist.

2. It may take several days for the average person to get herself to believe through autosuggestion that the earth is flat.

3. It may take several hours to get oneself to believe that one's spouse is faithful where there is good evidence to the contrary.

4. It may only take several minutes for a garden-variety racist to get into a state of believing that people of another race are full human beings.

5. It may take some people only a few seconds to acquire the belief that the tossed coin will come up heads.

6. With practice, some people could get themselves to acquire the belief that the tossed coin will come up heads in an imperceptibly short amount of time.

7. Some masters at autosuggestion may be able to acquire beliefs about tossed coins without any time intervening between the volition and the belief formation.

Perhaps it is strange, stupid, or even perversely immoral to engage in such autosuggestive belief acquisition, but cases 2 and 5 seem psychologically possible (leave to the side for the moment the likely damage to our belief-forming mechanisms and our noetic structure as a whole). It is conceivable that 6 and 7 obtain. In throwing dice, one sometimes has the feeling that the lucky (unlucky) number will turn up in a way that resembles this sort of phenomenon. Perhaps there are some people who can believe some propositions at will, the way other people can blush, wiggle their ears, or sneeze as basic acts. If 7 is psychologically possible, then the first premise and the conclusion of the Phenomenological Argument must be altered to take into account these anomalies. The revised argument would read as follows:

1. Acquiring a belief is *typically* a happening in which the world forces itself upon a subject.
2. Happenings in which the world forces itself upon a subject are not things the subject does or chooses.
3. Therefore, acquiring a belief is not *typically* something a subject does or chooses.

However, while we can never entirely rule out such behavior, it seems dubious whether we actually do perform such acts. It is hard to know whether such a case would be one of imagining a state of affairs of believing a proposition; the distinction is blurred at this point. At some point, imagining *p* becomes believing that *p*. For most of us, most of the time, however, such belief acquisitions will not be possible. Consider the proposition that "this coin will land heads." Do you have any sense of yesness or noness, assent or dissent, regarding it? Or suppose that the local torturer holds out his two fists and says to you, "If you choose the fist with the penny in it, you will receive $100,000, but if you pick the empty fist, you will be tortured for the next week. The only stipulation on your choosing the correct fist is that when you choose it, you must not only point to it, but *believe* that the coin is in that hand and not in the other (a lie detector will monitor your reaction)." I take it that most of us would be in for some hard times.

The last illustration nicely brings out the difference between acting and believing. It is relatively easy to *do* crazy things if there are practical grounds for them. We can easily act when the evidence is equally balanced (e.g., call heads while the coin is in the air), but believing is typically more passive in nature—not a doing, but a guide to doing. The Phenomenological Argument shows that volitionalism is abnormal and bizarre, but it does not rule out the possibility of acquiring beliefs by voliting.

Another possible use of the will regarding belief acquisition is the *veto* phenomenon. Some philosophers (Locke and Holyer) hold that the will can act as a veto on belief inclinations, halting would-be beliefs in the process of formation. This is a negative type of volition; it does not claim that we can actually attain beliefs by the fiat of the will, only that we can prevent some from getting hold of us by putting up a doxastic roadblock in the nick of time. What seems to occur is this.

1. *S* entertains proposition *p* (this is sometimes under our direct control).
2. *S* is inclined to believe that *p*, or *S* suspects that *p* (this is not normally under our control).
3. The veto phenomenon occurs by raising doubts, suspending judgment, or "tabling" the proposition under focus.
4. *S* looks at further evidence or looks at the old evidence in a fresh light and forms a judgment (while the "looking" is under our direct control, the "seeing" or judgment is not).

Is the veto event under our direct control, or is it caused by a counterclaim, a sense that there is counterevidence, or a sense that there is something wrong with our first inclination? For example, I am interviewing candidate *A* for a vacant position in our department and have a strong inclination to believe her to be the right person for the job, but suddenly I remember that we still have two candidates to interview and realize that my inclination to believe "that *A* is *the* best candidate for the job" is founded on insufficient evidence. I must modify the proposition to state that she is a good candidate. Here it seems that another belief (namely, that there are other good candidates still to be interviewed) comes into play and forces the other belief aside. No act of will is present to my consciousness. But even if I do feel a will to believe or withhold judgment in these sorts of cases, it doesn't follow that the will causes the belief. It may well be an accompaniment.

Nevertheless, there are other types of vetoing in which I may clearly prevent a belief from forming on the basis of the evidence. Consider the situation in which John tells Joan that her father has embezzled some money from John's company, and before he is finished presenting the evidence Joan stops him, crying, "Stop it, please, I can't bear to hear any more!" It seems plausible to suppose that something analogous to her stopping John from providing the incriminating evidence, which would cause a belief to form, may also occur within us when we begin to consider evidence for a position we deplore. We may inwardly turn away from the evidence, focus on something else, and so fail to form a belief in the matter. This seems a case of self-deception, but in any case, the veto power seems to be sometimes under our direct control. Nevertheless, it does not show that we actually can acquire beliefs by voliting, only that the will has a negative role to play in preventing beliefs from fixing themselves in us.

Cartesia

Although our analysis hasn't ruled out the possibility of voliting, it does support the claim that there is something peculiar about the phenomenon. If voliters exist, they are like people who can wiggle their ears, blush, vomit, or regulate their heartbeat at will. But unlike these volitional phenomena, believing at will seems to involve a conceptual confusion. Typically, I take it that believing is representational in nature, purporting to mirror our world and our relations with the world, so that every instance of volitional-nonrepresentational believing deviates from that relationship in a fundamental way. To see this better, imagine a society, Cartesia, whose members all volit. They attain beliefs as we engage in coughing, both voluntarily and involuntarily. Regarding every proposition voliting will be a serious consideration. When a member of Cartesia hears that her spouse has been unfaithful, she must ask herself, not simply what the evidence is for this charge but whether she has an obligation to believe that her spouse is faithful in spite of sufficient evidence. Such people have no difficulty in making Kierkegaardian leaps of faith against sufficient evidence, let alone where the evidence is counterbalanced. For example, when these people throw coins up into the air, they form convictions about the way the coins will land. No doubt they will have a strong normative component regarding voliting in order to regulate the activity. There will have to be elaborate classification systems covering obligatory volits, permissible volits, little white volits, immoral volits, and illegal volits punishable by the state.

Such a society is hard to imagine, but in it there would have to be a distinction between voliting-type beliefs and nonvoliting-type beliefs. The latter alone would be treated as reliable for action guidance; voliting-type beliefs would be tolerated mainly in the private domain, where no public issue is at stake. In other words, the nonvoliting belief acquisitions would be treated very much the way beliefs are treated in our society, as action guides that, as such, should be reliable mirrors of the evidence.

Perhaps we can give an evolutionary account of the nonvolitional nature of belief acquisition. In order to survive, animals need a fairly accurate and spontaneous representation of the world. The cat's action of catching the mouse and the primitive human's running away from the bear would not be aided by intervening volits between the representations of the mouse and the bear and the beliefs that the representations were accurate, nor would it be helpful for us to have to decide to believe our perceptions under normal conditions. Basically, we are credulous creatures. For most believings, most of the time, *contra* Descartes and Kierkegaard, the will has nothing to do with the matter. Beliefs come naturally as that which purports to represent the way the world is so that our actions may have a reliable map by which to steer.

The Logic of Belief Argument Against Volitionalism

The Phenomenological Argument gets its force by attacking the second characteristic of an act of voliting: The act must be done in full consciousness. If my analysis is correct, voliting must be a highly abnormal phenomenon, if it exists in any positive form at all. However, I have not ruled out the possibility of some people voliting. In this sense, my analysis has resembled Hume's account in which it is a contingent matter that we do not obtain beliefs by fiat of the will.

A second argument will now be advanced that attacks volitionalism primarily on the basis of its third characteristic—that is, it must be done independently of evidential or truth considerations. (I use these terms synonymously to stand for evidence in the broad sense of the term, including the self-evidence of basic beliefs.) This argument, the Logic of Belief Argument, states that the notion of volitional believing involves a conceptual confusion; it is broadly a logical mistake. There is something incoherent in stating that one can obtain or sustain a belief in full consciousness *simply* by a basic act of the will, that is, by purposefully disregarding the evidence connection. This strategy does not altogether rule out the possibility of obtaining beliefs by voliting in less than full consciousness (not truly voliting), but it asserts that when full consciousness enters, the "belief" will wither from one's noetic structure. One cannot believe in full consciousness "that *p* and I believe that *p* for other than truth considerations." If you understand that to believe that *p* is to believe that *p* is true and that *wishing never makes it so,* then there is simply no epistemic reason for believing *p*. Suppose I say that I believe I have $1,000,000 in my checking account, and suppose that when you point out to me that there is no reason to believe this, I respond, "I know that there is not the slightest reason to suppose that there is $1,000,000 in my checking account, but I believe it anyway, simply because I want to." If you were convinced that I was not joking, you would probably conclude that I was insane or didn't know what I was talking about.

If I said that I somehow find myself believing that I have $1,000,000 but don't know why, we might suppose that there was a memory trace of having deposited $1,000,000 into my account or evidence to that effect in the guise of an intuition that caused my belief. But if I denied that and said, "No, I don't have any memory trace regarding placing $1,000,000 into my account. In fact, I'm sure that I never placed $1,000,000 into the account. I just find it good to believe that it's there, so I have chosen to believe it," you would be stumped.

The point is that because beliefs just are about the way the world is and are made true (or false) depending on the way the world is, it is a confusion to believe that any given belief is true simply on the basis of being willed. As soon as the believer, assuming that he understands these basic concepts, discovers the basis of his belief—as being caused by the will alone—he must drop the belief. In this regard, saying "I believe that *p*, but I believe it only because I want to believe it," has the same incoherence attached to it as Moore's paradoxical, "I believe *p* but it is false that *p*." Structurally, neither is a strictly logical contradiction, but both show an incoherence that might be called broadly contradictory.

Robert Audi has objected that my argument only has merit if one supposes that the believer is rational, for an irrational believer could continue to believe that *p* in some other sense. However, I think that there is something wrong with describing the irrational person as having a belief here at all. There is a fundamental confusion lurking in this person's noetic structure that disqualifies him from having that notion ascribed to him in the full sense of the word. That is, it is not necessarily the case that just because *S* believes that he believes that *p*, *S actually* believes that *p*, especially if consciously he also believes that not-*p* at the same time. While we can have contradictory beliefs without knowing that we do, it is hard to understand what a fully conscious contradictory belief would be. In like manner, the fully conscious voliter isn't believing anything when she believes that she has acquired a belief simply by voliting. It is as though she were saying: "To believe anything is to believe it because of some evidence (even self-evidence) *E*, but to believe what I am now believing is believed nonevidentially." What is it that is being believed?

My formulation builds minimal understanding of the concept of belief and truth or evidence into its premises, but if the reader is sympathetic to Audi's criticism, we can modify our formula to apply only to rational believing (leaving aside whether irrational believing *in this sense* is possible).

But, even if the believer can believe that it is his will that is caus-ing the belief in cases of doxastic incontinence, the argument would show that the believer could not believe that his belief was being caused or sustained in the right way. The rational believer, in full consciousness, would see that there must be a truth connection be-tween states of affairs and the belief (by virtue of which the belief is true), so the will is essentially unnecessary for the belief. It may, however, be necessary in order to get into a proper state of mind where he will be able to perceive the evidence clearly. Just as there is an instrumental relationship between opening one's eyes and seeing whatever one sees, but an intrinsic relationship between states of af-fairs in the world and what one sees, so likewise there is only an in-strumental relationship between willing to believe *p* and believing *p*, whereas there is an intrinsic relationship between state of affairs *S*, by virtue of which *p* is true, and my belief that *p*. Once the believer realizes that willing never makes it so, he must then give up the be-lief that it is the will that is decisively or intrinsically sustaining the belief that *p*, though one may believe that there is an instrumental relationship. At least, the believer will not be able to believe that the will *alone* is causing him or her to believe that *p*, but that the evi-dence is the deciding factor.

There is a clear difference between acting, which is volitional, and acquiring a belief, which is a nonvolitional event or happening. Be-lieving is evidential; to believe that *p*, is to presuppose that I have evi-dence for *p* or that *p* is self-evident or evident to the senses. I need not have a developed concept of evidence to believe this. Children do not have a full concept of belief, but they tacitly suppose something like this. On reflection, rational adults seem to recognize the connection between a belief and objective states of affairs. In a sense, belief that *p* seems to imply the thought of a casual chain stretching back from the belief to a primary relationship with the world, and so faithfully rep-resenting the world. We may have more or less confidence about the preciseness of the way our beliefs represent the world, but some de-gree seems implicit in every belief state.

Another way to make this same point about the evidentiality of be-lief is to define propositional belief in terms of a subjective probability index. As I argued in the last chapter, all believing is believing to a de-gree of confidence. You may test the approximate degree to which you believe in a proposition by imagining how surprised you would be if you found out that the particular belief in question turned out to be false. Recall my thought experiment with the Belief Meter, which enables us to quantify the strength of our beliefs. The meter has two rubber balls wired to it, which, when the balls are squeezed, measures the pressure of the squeezes. The subject holds a ball in each hand and is instructed to squeeze the ball in her right hand when she believes the proposition, to squeeze the ball in her left hand when she believes the proposition to be false, and to refrain from squeezing when she believes the proposition to be neither true nor false. In addition the subject is instructed to squeeze the appropriate ball with a pressure appropriate to the degree to which she believes the proposition in question. Accuracy will be approximated by the help of a truth serum. In this way we might be able to quantify our beliefs into a subjective probability index (e.g., it might turn out that Ann discovers that she only believes that God exists to a probability of 0.6, whereas she believes that it will rain today to a probability of 0.8). It might also turn out that Ann discovers that she had deceived herself into thinking that she had a deep conviction about God's existence, whereas she really only weakly believes in God's existence. (Of course, she could doubt the reliability of the Belief Meter, but we may suppose it has an excellent track record.)

In principle, I see no reason against the possibility of rough belief quantification as just described, but the point is that we already have a satisfactory notion of subjective probability in terms of the relative degrees with which we believe propositions. If believing were the result of our immediate willings, it would not be about the probability of states of affairs obtaining, but simply about our desires. It would be the case that I could come to a judgment that the probability of p, on the evidence E was 0.5 and via a volit conclude that it was 0.6. Could one in full consciousness make such a leap? It seems as possible as believing that $2 + 2 = 4$, and then deliberately believing at the same time that $2 + 2 = 5$.

It may be objected that this argument implies that one must have a concept of probability, but I think that we all do have a notion of degrees of belief that roughly incorporates subjective probability in the manner that I have described. If this argument is sound, the interesting thing is that not only can we not volit a belief, but we cannot even volit a change in the degree with which we believe a proposition. We cannot increase the strength of our belief that p from 0.6 to 0.65 simply by fiat of the will.

The Logic of Belief Argument has not ruled out the logical possibility of voliting; rather it rules out as logically odd (in the wider sense of the term) the possibility of acquiring a belief in full consciousness by a fiat of the will without regard to truth considerations. It does not rule out the possibility of obtaining the belief in less than full consciousness or indirectly. The phenomena in these cases seem similar to that of self-deception, where one is not fully aware of what one truly believes. Once one discovers that one has been self-deceived, the logic of the discovery seems to entail the giving up of the false "belief" (the one that the person thought he or she had on a conscious level). Likewise, once one realizes that the only basis for believing that *p* is one's wanting *p* to be true, the belief must wither. Hence, if one could come to have a belief through directly willing to have it, once he or she reflected on the acquisition and discovered its illegitimate origin, the person would give it up (unless, of course, there was now evidence for it). On reflection, he or she would see that the purported belief reflects only the content of the will. The belief has the same status as a product of the imagination.

Consider this similarity between imagining and willing to believe. Take for example, Vivid Imaginer Imogene, who gets so carried away with her imagination that she sometimes believes her imagination reports. While sitting bored to death in her logic class, she fantasizes that she is swimming in the Bahamas or is being embraced by Warren Beatty. She imagines these things so vividly that for the moment she believes that they are really happening, until the teacher rudely calls on her and breaks the spell of her daydream, thus shattering her transient "beliefs." Perhaps many of our beliefs, more subtle than this and which we never discover, are formed through the imagination. But, when we do discover that a belief has its basis in the imagination, we discard it as worthless—and we do so automatically, not by a volit. Voliting and imagining seem to display the very same logic regarding belief acquisition. Both are acquired independently of evidential considerations.

Of course, it is possible that a person regards his wants about reality as *evidence* for propositions. For example, someone might say, "I have found that whenever I want a proposition to be true, amazingly it generally turns out to be so." Here, wanting would indirectly cause belief, not by voliting, but rather by being regarded as reliable evidence, a type of credible testimony. It would still be the case that what causes the believer to believe is evidential, not simply the will's fiat.

If my analysis is correct, there is a deep conceptual confusion in self-consciously believing that any proposition has originated through a volit and/or that what sustains one's belief is one's will.

I conclude that voliting seems both psychologically aberrant and conceptually confused. It is psychologically problematic because of the feature of demanding that full consciousness attach to acts of will. It is conceptually confused because it neglects the evidential aspect of conscious belief acquisition and sustainment.[6]

QUESTIONS FOR DISCUSSION

1. Go over the various types of volitionalism. What are the main arguments for each type, and what are the main arguments against each type? You will be in a better place to answer this question after reading the next chapter, but you should get your thoughts in order now.

2. Discuss the Phenomenological Argument Against Direct Descriptive Volitionalism. What conditions must a fully volitional act meet? Are these conditions too strong? Is there a less-than-fully aware choice that is omitted from the discussion here? How would that affect the argument?

3. One problem (already pointed out by Hume) about phenomenological arguments is that they are based on what each of us finds in himself or herself through introspection. If you look within and find a process at work different from your neighbor's, how can you decide whether one of you is mistaken? How does this point bear on the Phenomenological Argument Against Direct Descriptive Volitionalism?

4. Consider the Veto Phenomenon discussed in this chapter. What are its implications for the relationship of the will to belief?

5. Analyze the Logic of Belief Argument Against Volitionalism. How strong is it? Does it depend too heavily on an implausible notion of subjective probability?

6. Consider the objection raised by William James in note 6 that there are self-creative or self-verifying beliefs, so that deciding to believe actually creates reality. Is this a good counterexample to the antivolitional arguments?

NOTES

1. Pieper, Josef, *Belief and Faith* (New York: Pantheon Books, 1953).

2. René Descartes, *Meditations,* trans. Elizabeth Haldane and G. Ross (Cambridge: Cambridge University Press, 1911), 175. Meditation IV and Replies.

3. Soren Kierkegaard, *Philosophical Fragments,* trans. D. Swenson (Princeton: Princeton University Press, 1962), 102f, 104. See also his *Concluding Unscientific Postscript* for evidence for this thesis.

4. Thomas Aquinas, *Summa Theologica* (London: Benziger Brothers, 1911) II, Q4, A.2; John Henry Newman, *An Essay in Aid of a Grammar of Assent* (Westminster, MD: Christian Classics, 1973), 232; William James, "The Will to Believe," *Essays in Pragmatism* (New York: Haefner, 1969); Josef Pieper, *Belief* *and Faith* (New York: Pantheon Books, 1953), 25f; Roderick Chisholm, "Lewis's Ethics of Belief," in *The Philosophy of C. I. Lewis,* ed. A. Schlipp (LaSalle, IL: Open Court, 1968); Jack Meiland, "What Ought We to Believe," *American Philosophical Quarterly* 17, 1 (January 1980); and Robert Hoyler, "Belief and Will Revisited," *Dialogue* (1983). Gilbert Harman, "Realism, Anti-realism, and Reasons for Belief" a paper circulated at the NEH Institute on Naturalism at the University of Nebraska, July 1, 1993. John Pollock writes, "I have taken the fundamental problem of epistemology to be that of deciding what to believe," in *Contemporary Theories of Knowledge* (Totowa, NJ: Rowman & Littlefield, 1986), 10.

5. Bernard Williams, "Deciding to Believe," *Problems of the Self* (Cambridge: Cambridge University Press, 1972).

6. There is one final objection to my thesis that we do not (normally) acquire beliefs by voliting. This objection centers on the phenomenon of self-creative or self-verifying beliefs, the activity described by James in his classic article, "The Will to Believe," whereby one's deciding to believe is causally operative in creating a state of affairs that makes the belief true. This, the objector claims, seems like a normal case of volitionalism.

   Suppose you are going to play a game of chess. Your using autosuggestion to get into a state of mind where you believe you will win actually plays a causal role in your winning. (It may, of course, have the reverse effect through causing overconfidence.) James's own example (with my filling out an interpretation) is of a person trapped at the edge of a crevasse, overlooking a yawning gorge. He calculates that a successful leap is improbable, but it will increase in probability in proportion to his convincing himself that he must get himself to believe what an impartial look at the evidence will not allow. So he volits the belief. Or consider a student who loves philosophy and whose self-identity is centered on the goal of being a good philosopher. She doubts whether she will ever become such, but believes that her chances of becoming good will be increased by believing that she will reach that goal. So she apparently volits and believes without sufficient evidence that she will become a good philosopher. Because of this confidence, she succeeds where she would have otherwise failed. These sorts of cases have been used as counterexamples to my arguments against volitionalism.

   There are two things to be said about these kinds of cases. The first is that they are not counterexamples to the thesis that we cannot acquire beliefs by fiat of the will. It seems reasonable to say that a deliberation process went on in each of these cases in which the will *indirectly* caused belief by refocusing the mind on favorable evidence rather than on the unfavorable evidence. No volit is necessary.

   For example, caught as I am before the yawning gorge, I ask myself, how in the world am I to attain the presumably necessary belief (which I don't have) that I can jump the gorge. I cannot just acquire it by a fiat, so I hit upon the idea of thinking of all the successful long jumps I made in grammar school. I then imagine myself a great Olympic track star. Perhaps a little hypnosis helps here. I focus on appropriate successes (real or imaginary), block out negative thoughts (if I can), and finally, self-deceive myself to the point where I believe that I believe that I can leap over the crevasse. But all this illustrates is a case of indirect volitional control, not direct control over believing. I have a goal, plan a policy of action, and indirectly come to attain that goal.

The second thing to say is that this example seems to be an instance where a form of self-deception has salutary effects.

FOR FURTHER READING

Alston, William, "The Deontological Conception of Epistemic Justification." *Epistemic Justification*. Ithaca, NY: Cornell University Press, 1989.

Chisholm, Roderick. *Perceiving*. Ithaca, NY: Cornell University Press, 1957.

Firth, Roderick, "Are Epistemic Concepts Reducible to Ethical Concepts?" In *Value and Morals,* edited by A. I. Goldman and J. Kim. Dordrecht, Holland: D. Reidel, 1978.

Heil, John, "Doxastic Agency," *Philosophical Studies* 43 (1983).

James, William. *The Will to Believe*. New York: Dover Publications, 1956.

O'Hear, Anthony. "Belief and Will," *Philosophy* (April 1972).

Newman, John Henry. *The Grammar of Assent*. London: Westminster, 1980.

Pieper, Josef. *Belief and Faith*. New York: Pantheon Books, 1953.

Pojman, Louis. *Religious Belief and the Will*. London: Routledge & Kegan Paul, 1986.

Price, H. H. *Belief*. London: Allen & Unwin, 1967.

Williams, Bernard. *Problems of the Self*. Cambridge: Cambridge University Press, 1972.

Winters, Barbara, "Believing at Will," *Journal of Philosophy* LXXVI (1979).

CHAPTER 17

The Ethics of Belief

. . . [B]ecause beliefs can have important consequences for the believer, it may be prudent to hold beliefs for which you have inadequate evidence. For instance, it is popularly alleged that lobsters do not feel pain when they are dunked alive into boiling water. It is extremely doubtful that anyone has good reason to believe that, but it may be prudentially rational to hold that belief because otherwise one would deprive oneself of the gustatory delight of eating boiled lobsters . . . . It is unclear whether moral considerations can be meaningfully applied to beliefs. (John Pollock)[1]

Indirect Volitionalism

In chapter 16 I argued that we cannot normally believe anything at all simply by willing to do so; believing aims at truth and is not a basic act or a direct product of the will. If we could believe whatever we chose to believe simply by willing to do so, belief would not be about reality but about our wants. Nevertheless, the will does play an important indirect role in believing. Many of the beliefs that we arrive at are finally the results of our policy decisions. Although believing itself is not an act, our acts determine the sorts of beliefs we end up with. It is primarily because we judge that our beliefs are to some significant degree the indirect results of our actions that we speak of being responsible for them. Although we cannot be said to be directly responsible for them as though they were actions, we can be said to be indirectly responsible for many of them. If we had chosen differently, if we had been better moral agents, paid attention to the evidence, and so forth, we would have different beliefs from what we do in fact have.

To be sure, we are not responsible for all our beliefs, and the degree of responsibility seems to vary in proportion to the amount of evidence available at different times and to our ability to attend properly to that evidence. For example, the person who pays attention regarding a certain matter often comes to have more accurate beliefs than the inattentive person. Attention is generally within our direct control. As long as we agree that the inattentive person could have acted differently, could have been attentive if he had really wanted to, we can conclude that the inattentive person is responsible for not having the true beliefs that he might have had. In the same way, we can conclude that the attentive person is responsible for the beliefs that she has.

Being (indirectly) responsible for our beliefs indicates that praise and blame attach indirectly to our epistemic states, that indirectly beliefs are morally assessable. It may be the case that I have many beliefs that I ought not to have. If I had been a better person, learned to investigate certain matters with the right categories, I might now be endowed with a more accurate system of beliefs and might believe many of my present beliefs in different degrees of confidence than I presently do.

Many philosophers reject the notion of an ethics of belief. Mill, James, and Meiland believe that there are no special doxastic moral duties. Hume and Price argue that there are only counsels of prudence. Price argues:

> But even if it were in our power to be wholly rational all of the time, it still would not follow that there is anything morally blameworthy about assenting unreasonably (against the evidence or without regard to the evidence) or that we ought to be chastised for doing so. There is nothing wicked about such assents. It is however true, and important, that unreasonable assent is contrary to our *long term interest*. It is to our long term interest to believe true propositions rather than false ones. And if we assent reasonably (i.e. in accordance with the evidence), it is likely that in the long run the propositions we believe will be more often true than false.[2]

The Libertarian View of Doxastic Responsibility

The only "ought" regarding belief acquisition is a prudential ought. A person is free to seek whatever goals he or she desires: happiness, salvation, convenience, aesthetic pleasure, and so forth. It is simply in one's long-term best interest generally to seek to have true beliefs. However, if you find yourself inclined to sacrifice truth for some other goal, you have every right to do so. We may call this the *Libertarian View of Doxastic Responsibility*. It affirms that believing is a purely private matter. Mill says that each person must be accorded "absolute freedom of opinion on all subjects practical and speculative."[3]

One may readily recognize the virtues of this position. Not many of us want to see government intervention into personal beliefs, totalitarian thought reforms, and brainwashing in order to help others acquire "true beliefs." The Libertarian position is right to emphasize human autonomy with regard to our private selves, and it may even be the case that it is a good thing to have a plurality of opinions in a society. Nevertheless, libertarian-prudentialist doctrine is false. *It sells the truth short.* It does so on two counts. It underestimates the significance of truth to the individual, and it ignores the social dimension of truth seeking. Personhood, involving a high degree of autonomy, entails respect for highly justified beliefs. Socially, truth seeking is important, for unless a society has accurate information, many of its goals are not likely to be reached. I will develop these ideas in the following analysis.

Perhaps the clearest account of a volitional stance on the ethics of belief is Jack Meiland's article "What Ought We to Believe? or the Ethics of Belief Revisited." Meiland argues that not only is it sometimes morally *permissible* to believe against the evidence but that it is sometimes morally *obligatory* to do so. In all cases of belief acquisition "extra-factual considerations are relevant."[4] After presenting Meiland's argument against a strict evidentialism and in favor of prescriptive volitional belief acquisition, I will attempt to show what is wrong with his position—what is new is not true and what is true is not new. Specifically, I will contend that there is a more moderate form of evidentialism, which escapes Meiland's criticisms and which provides a middle way between the two extremes of rigid evidentialism and volitionalism. I will outline what such a moderate evidentialism with regard to the ethics of belief looks like.

Following Meiland's interpretation, rigid evidentialism states that one ought to believe propositions if and only if they are backed by sufficient evidence. This position, which, according to Meiland, is found in Descartes, Locke, Clifford, and Chisholm, is largely impervious to subjective factors in belief formation. Chisholm's formulation is cited as a clear expression of this position.

1. Anyone having just the evidence in question is warranted in accepting the conclusion.

2. I am in a position of having that evidence.

3. Therefore, I am justified in accepting the conclusion.[5]

On this account, everyone is epistemically required to come to the same conclusion, given the same evidence. The argument for this position can be spelled out as follows. Suppose person *A* is justified on the evidence *E* in believing that *p*. Suppose further that person *B* has exactly the same evidence *A* has but believes that not-*p*. On the face of it, it seems contradictory to say that although *A* is justified in believing that *p* on *E*, *B* is justified in believing that not-*p* on *E*. This suggests that *E* both justifies belief that *p* and that not-*p*, but this defies our very notion of justification. Hence, the evidentialist concludes that not both *A* and *B* can be justified in believing what they believe on *E*. If *A* is justified in believing that *p* on *E*, then *B* is not, and vice versa. On the other hand, anyone who has the evidence *A* has is in the same state of being justified as *A* is, whether he or she knows it or not.

What this argument for evidentialism neglects is a notion of the larger context into which apparently similar evidence comes. Just as a farmer, a real estate dealer, and an artist, all looking at the "same" field, may not see the same field, so evidence is always relative to a person's individuating background beliefs, capacities to interpret data, and expectations. Meiland, rightly, points out that subjective factors play a strong role in our interpretation of evidence and in the formation of beliefs, but he oversteps the evidence when he interprets this subjectivism to include direct volitionalism, the acquisition of beliefs through conscious choices. Classical evidentialism may be too rigid in its notion of justification. It neglects psychological factors, which enter into every belief acquisition. All believing is believing from a perspective, and any type of evidentialism that neglects this perspectival element may be designated "rigid," in that it lacks a proper appreciation for the complexity of evidence gathering and assembling.

A second important feature of Meiland's position on the ethics of belief is his subsuming epistemic duties under the heading of general ethical duties. That is, we have no special epistemic duties that are not already covered by ethical principles *simpliciter.* If we claim that someone has a duty to believe some proposition, we must give moral reasons for that duty, not epistemic ones. Meiland argues on utilitarian grounds that it is often morally required that we act against so-called epistemic requirements of believing according to sufficient evidence. Here Meiland holds a stronger position than James, Chisholm, or Nathanson, who allow for voliting only when the evidence is insufficient, as a sort of a tiebreaker.[6] Meiland maintains that we are sometimes obligated to get ourselves to believe propositions even when we have sufficient evidence to the contrary. However, he does not go as far as Kierkegaard in allowing for believing against even conclusive evidence. When we have conclusive evidence, it is not in our power to believe against the evidence.

Consider a proposition against which we may believe, despite sufficient evidence. Suppose a wife finds lipstick on her husband's handkerchief, a blond strand of hair on his suit, and a crumpled piece of paper on which is written a telephone number in a woman's handwriting in his pocket. This would constitute sufficient evidence (on the rigid evidentialist account) that the husband is having an affair with another woman and would normally cause the wife to believe that her husband was being unfaithful.

However, the wife may have good reasons for rejecting the evidence, even though she admits that it is sufficient to justify belief in her husband's unfaithfulness. She rejects the belief for pragmatic reasons. Suppose that the wife closely examines the evidence and decides that if she comes to believe what it points to (or continues to believe that her husband is unfaithful), their marriage will be ruined and great unhappiness will ensue. If, on the other hand, she can get herself to believe that her husband is faithful, in spite of the evidence to the contrary, the marriage probably will be saved. She reasons that her husband will very likely get over his infatuation and return to his marital commitment.

Suppose that she has good evidence for this second belief. Should she not acquire the belief in her husband's faithfulness in hope of saving her marriage? Perhaps she also justifiably believes that undergoing this volitional process, somehow acquiring a belief by willing to have it despite the evidence, will do no permanent damage to her noetic structure. After acquiring the belief and letting the belief direct her actions, the marriage will be saved; and after the marriage is saved, she will recall the process that she underwent in order to save the marriage. Now, however, she will be in a position to live with the unwelcome evidence and even speak openly with her husband about it. Given these factors, isn't the wife morally obligated to take steps to obtain the belief in her husband's faithfulness?

Unlike the usual volitionalist strategy of advocating voluntary believing only in extreme cases, Meiland makes the rather daring claim that in every case of believing where there is insufficient evidence—or where there is sufficient evidence for an unwelcome proposition—extrafactual considerations are relevant considerations.[7] While Meiland believes that believing is within the direct control of our will (except where there is conclusive evidence), he is content to let his case rest on the possibility that we may indirectly cause ourselves to believe against the evidence.

A Critique of Meiland's Libertarianism

I want to outline four objections to Meiland's position on the ethics of belief:

1. His notion of evidentialism is overly rigid and ignores a broader form of evidentialism that obviates the need for a volitional alternative in most cases of believing.

2. A minor criticism is that Meiland fails to make clear why we may have an obligation to believe against the evidence when it is sufficient but may not have an obligation to believe against the evidence when it is conclusive.

3. His position undervalues the importance of having reliable belief-forming mechanisms and misconstrues the nature of belief acquisitions.

4. If Meiland's position is interpreted, by the principle of charity, as merely making the weak claim that sometimes we have a moral duty to override our duty to seek true, justified beliefs, then there is nothing new in his position. Let us look briefly at each of these criticisms.

Overly Rigid Evidentialism

Meiland is correct in criticizing the Clifford-Chisholm line of evidentialism, which focuses on a nonperspectival relationship between evidence and justification. This position seems to neglect or underemphasize the point that evidence is person-relative; each person views the data with a different noetic endowment. The Aristotelian and the Nominalist, hearing the argument from contingency for the existence of God, will each view its soundness differently. But, given their different worldviews, each may well be justified in coming to the belief she does. While there may be such a thing as *propositional warrant,* which provides objective evidence for a given proposition, justification has mainly to do with what is reasonable for a given person to believe, given his noetic structure, background beliefs, ability to pay attention, ability to weight evidence impartially, ability to interpret the evidence according to certain rules, and the like. A person living in the Middle Ages may well have been warranted in believing that the earth is flat, even though there may have been objective evidence—which anyone in an ideal situation would have had—to support the proposition that it is round.

Meiland posits an unnecessary dichotomy between objective (sufficient) evidence and subjective factors where the will determines the belief. Rigid evidentialism and volitionalism are not the only alternatives. Simply because objective evidence is not the only necessary factor in belief acquisition does not mean that the will can or should decide the matter. One must take into account such subjective factors as unconscious wants and past learning, which are internalized, so we are not aware of the information processing that our subconscious self is undertaking. For example, while failing the strong evidentialist's test of being able to give an account of his evidence, the chicken sexer nevertheless probably does have evidence for the reliable judgments he consistently makes. Given his high success rate in identifying the sex of chicks, it is more reasonable to say that he knows but cannot tell us (or even himself) how he knows the chick's sex than to attribute his success to acts of the will (or simply luck).

I am suggesting that a more moderate version of evidentialism recognizes subjective factors in belief acquisition without admitting that the will directly causes belief or that it should cause it indirectly. We don't need to bring in volitions to account for the subjective element in belief formation. An alternative interpretation of one of Meiland's examples will illustrate what I mean. Imagine a defense attorney who agrees with the prosecution and the jury that there is sufficient evidence against his client but nevertheless continues to believe in his client's innocence despite the evidence. His belief is vindicated years later. This is supposed to show that the attorney has a right to believe that his client is innocent, in spite of the evidence, where there are pragmatic grounds for doing so. I doubt that the will is directly involved here at all, and I believe that the attorney's belief can be accounted for through my modified version of evidentialism.

The attorney, Smith, hears and sees all the evidence *E* against his client, Brown. He concludes on the basis of *E* that Brown is probably guilty. But he pauses, introspects, and senses some resistance from within to that conclusion. He finds himself with a tendency to reject the first conclusion in favor of a belief that Brown is innocent. Perhaps he vacillates for a time between two belief tendencies, or he experiences undulating alternate belief states. When he is in court or looking at the evidence in private, he feels a subtle certainty that Brown is guilty, but when he faces Brown, looks him in the eye, and speaks to him, he senses that he must be wrong, even with the evidence that points to Brown's guilt. Perhaps we can say (following Price) that Smith half-believes that Brown is innocent and half-believes that he is guilty, the belief-states alternating so frequently that he cannot fully make up his mind. Perhaps the feeling that Brown is innocent finally wins out in the battle of Smith's mind.

Meiland would explain this alternation and conclusion by means of a decision to believe. I doubt whether this is the correct description of what is going on and suggest that it is more likely that Smith's previous experience with people, especially defendants, both innocent and guilty, has caused him to form reliable beliefs about characteristic features and behaviors of the guilty and innocent, including the "seemingly innocent" and the "seemingly guilty." He is unaware of this large repository of internalized evidence and cannot formulate it. Here we want to say that Smith's reliability at judging character and legal evidence warrants our saying that he has internalized skills and sets of inductive generalizations (e.g., judging from certain characteristic looks on innocent faces to a conclusion of particular innocence) that cause individual belief occurrences. Smith has data and skills that the jury does not, which a less competent attorney does not, and which the judge may not have.

One can generalize from this case and say with regard to any proposition p and for any person S that if S finds herself believing p, the belief that p is prima facie evidence for p itself relative to S; that is, S is prima facie justified in believing p. It may not be very strong justification, and S may be forced to weaken her hold on p when she cannot defend p, but it is some evidence, enough to start with. Furthermore, to the extent that S finds herself a reliable judge in a given area, to exactly that extent is she justified in holding on to a belief tenaciously in the light of evidence to the contrary. Modified evidentialism accepts intuitive judgments as playing an evidential role in believing. If my account of evidentialism is correct, then the motivation for much of Meiland's volitionalism is dissipated. Simply saying that subjective factors enter into our belief acquisitions is not sufficient to justify volitionalism, for in a sense all believing involves subjective factors that are causative in belief formation.

Conclusive Evidence

This leads to the second criticism of Meiland's position. This focuses on his distinction between insufficient evidence, sufficient evidence, and conclusive evidence in relation to the ability to volit. According to Meiland, it is only possible to volit (or indirectly get ourselves into a belief state through volitional means) when the evidence is not conclusive. Hence, it can only be morally required that we volit in those cases. But unless we reduce "conclusive evidence" to the trivially true definition "that which we cannot will ourselves not to believe," we seem to have a problem; if I have a moral obligation to believe (through volitional means) against sufficient evidence, why can I not have an obligation to believe (via those same means) against conclusive evidence? The answer cannot be simply that it is easier to do this in the first case. It may be that we must spend more time and effort getting ourselves to believe against conclusive evidence, going to a better hypnotist or whatever. But if our utilitarian cost–benefit analysis specifies that the psychic price is worth paying (e.g., we may be able to save our children's sanity or lives by believing that our spouse is faithful and keeping our marriage together, even though we catch him or her in bed committing adultery), then following Meiland's analysis, we should pay that price. I see no criterion to distinguish between believing against evidence where it is only sufficient and believing against the evidence where it is conclusive. If Meiland responds that there is a likelihood such manipulations would mess up the subject's mind, we should respond, "What makes you so confident this isn't what happens in every case of purposefully getting ourselves to believe against or in the absence of sufficient evidence?" This leads to the most serious criticism of volitional positions on the ethics of belief.

The Importance of Well-Justified Beliefs

My main criticism of positions like Meiland's (including William James's) has to do with the importance of having well-justified beliefs and truth seeking in general. We generally believe that these two concepts are closely related. Therefore, the best way to assure ourselves of having true beliefs is to seek to develop one's belief-forming mechanisms in ways that enable us to become good judges of various types of evidence, attaining the best possible justification of our beliefs. The value of having the best justified beliefs possible can be defended both on deontological grounds with regard to the individual and on teleological, or utilitarian, grounds regarding the society as a whole.

The deontological argument is connected with our notion of autonomy. Being an autonomous person includes, among other things, having a high degree of warranted beliefs at one's disposal upon which to base one's actions. There is a tendency to lower one's freedom of choice as one lowers the repertoire of well-justified beliefs regarding a plan of action, and since it is a generally accepted moral principle that it is wrong to lessen one's autonomy or personhood, it is wrong to lessen the degree of justification of one's beliefs on important matters. Hence, there is a general presumption against beliefs by willing to have them.

Cognitive voliting is a sort of lying or cheating in that it enjoins believing against what has the best guarantee of being the truth. When a friend or doctor lies to a terminally ill patient about her condition, the patient is deprived of the best evidence available for making decisions about her limited future. She is being treated less than fully autonomously. While a form of paternalism may sometimes be justified, there is always a presumption against it and in favor of truth telling. We even say that the patient has a right to know what the evidence points to. Cognitive voliting is a sort of lying to oneself that, as such, decreases one's own freedom and personhood. It is a type of doxastic suicide that may only be justified in extreme circumstances. If there is something intrinsically wrong about lying (making it prima facie wrong), there is something intrinsically wrong with cognitive voliting, either directly or indirectly. Whether it be Pascal, James, Meiland, Newman, or Kierkegaard, all prescriptive volitionalists (consciously or unconsciously) seem to undervalue the principle of truthfulness and its relationship to personal autonomy.

The utilitarian, or teleological, argument against cognitive voliting is fairly straightforward. General truthfulness is a desideratum without which society cannot function. Without truthfulness, language itself would not be possible, since it depends on faithful use of words and sentences to stand for appropriately similar objects and states of affairs. Communication depends on a general adherence to accurate reporting. More specifically, it is very important that a society have true beliefs with regard to important issues, so that actions based on beliefs have a firm basis.

The doctor who cheated her way through medical school and who, as a consequence, lacks appropriate beliefs about certain symptoms may endanger a patient's health. A politician who fails to take into consideration the amount of pollution being given off by large corporations that support his candidacy may endanger the lives and health of his constituents. Even the passerby who gives wrong information to a stranger who asks directions may seriously inconvenience the stranger. Here Clifford's point about believing against the evidence is well taken, despite its all too robustious tone. The shipowner who failed to make necessary repairs on his vessel and "chose" to believe that she was seaworthy is guilty of the deaths of the passengers. "He had no right to believe on such evidence as was before him."[8] It is because beliefs are action guiding maps by which we steer, and—as such, tend to cause actions—that society has a keen interest in our having the best justified beliefs possible regarding important matters.

Nevertheless, Meiland might reply, while there may be a general duty to seek to have well-justified beliefs, there may be many cases where other considerations override our duty to believe according to the evidence. In fact, these cases may be so numerous that one is tempted to conclude (as Meiland does) that "extra-factual considerations" are relevant to every case of belief acquisition (and, following this logic, relevant to every case of maintaining each of our beliefs). The trouble with this response is that it ignores the sort of intention skill entailed in truth seeking. It is dispositional, a habit. If it is to be effective at all, it must be deeply ingrained within us, so that it is not at all easy to dispense with. If the wife has been properly brought up as a truth seeker, she may simply not be able to believe against the evidence without going through elaborate conditioning processes that might seriously affect her personality and even her personal identity.

Furthermore, our beliefs do not exist in isolation from each other, so to overthrow one belief may have reverberations throughout our entire noetic structure, affecting many of our other beliefs. Getting oneself to believe against the evidence that supports a belief that p may upset our other justified beliefs q, r, and s, which in turn may affect still other beliefs. Bernard Williams has pointed out cognitive voliting

> is like a revolutionary movement trying to extirpate the last remains of the *ancien regime*. The man gets rid of this belief that his son is dead, and then there is some belief that strongly implies that his son is dead, and that has to be got rid of. It might be that a project of this kind tends in the end to involve total destruction of the world of reality, to lead to paranoia.[9]

After the wife succeeds in believing that her husband is innocent, what is the effect of this on her noetic structure? What happens every time she looks at the suit on which the strand of hair was found or sees a handkerchief? What happens every time she sees a strand of blond hair? or sees her husband talking to a blond? or sees a telephone number? Does she have to repress memories and deny that this is important evidence against her spouse's faithfulness? Do we have enough control over our knowledge about our unconscious selves to be able to predict the final result of volitional believing on our personality and character?

The utilitarian argument against volitional manipulation of our belief mechanisms might be stated this way.

1. Voliting is morally justified only if we have adequate evidence (acquired nonvolitionally) that it will result in better consequences than if we abstain from voliting.

2. But our noetic structure is such that we almost never do have adequate evidence that it will produce better consequences.

3. Therefore, voliting is almost never morally justified.

We almost never know how we will be affected by frustrating and manipulating our normal belief-forming mechanisms. Our subconscious realm, where normal beliefs are formed, seems very complex, so that in attempting to influence it over one matter, we may cause unpredictable chain reactions within our noetic structure (i.e., the set of our beliefs and belief-forming mechanisms).

Of course, Meiland might well reply that if, on reflection, the cost is going to be this great, we ought not believe against sufficient evidence in most cases. Perhaps this is a satisfactory reply and perhaps our main difference is merely one of emphasis: Meiland arguing against rigid evidentialism makes objective justification an absolute duty, and I arguing for a presumption of truth seeking, making it a very high moral duty. These are not incompatible views. However, I think that there is more to our difference than this. The difference is rooted in two different views of how evidence is processed and of the possibility of consciously willing to have certain beliefs against what is taken to be good evidence. Meiland simply believes that we have more control over our beliefs than I do, and this difference results in a difference about the relevancy of volitional strategies.

Meiland has a pragmatic justification of belief that goes like this.

1. *A* has sufficient evidence for *p* (i.e., there is a strong inclination on *A*'s part to believe that *p* or *A* does believe that *p*), but *A* also has nonevidential reasons for believing not-*p*.

2. After reflection, *A* decides that it is morally permissible or obligatory to get himself into a position where he believes not-*p*.

3. *A* takes whatever steps are necessary in order to get into that position, and, presumably, *A* comes to believe not-*p*.

There is something odd about this argument; it raises the fundamental question of whether a rational person can consciously carry out a cognitive volit or sustain a belief while knowing that one has obtained the belief solely through a fiat of the will. For example, what happens when the wife in Meiland's example reflects on her belief that her husband is innocent? She looks at her belief and looks at the way that it was brought about. Can she go on believing that her husband is innocent despite the sufficient evidence to the contrary? There seems to be something incoherent about the phenomena of consciously acquiring or sustaining a belief regardless of the perceived evidence against the belief. This brings us to our final criticism of Meiland's position.

What Is True Is not New

Meiland may escape all of my objections by arguing that while it is always relevant in principle to take pragmatic considerations into account in acquiring (and sustaining) beliefs, it may hardly ever be our actual duty. He may defend his flank by saying that he merely wants to show that truth seeking (as the rigid evidentialist conceives of it) is not an absolute moral duty, that it is overridable in some instances. But if this is all that he is saying, his position surely loses much of its brashness and excitement. It may be true, but it is hardly new. Most moral systems since that espoused by W. D. Ross, including those developed by such unlikely bedfellows as Richard Brandt, William Frankena, R. M. Hare, and J. L. Mackie, would agree that there are few, if any, moral absolutes, and that truth seeking is not a moral absolute (i.e., nonoverridable) but a strong prima facie duty. Meiland's position must be stronger than this in order to be interesting, but if it is stronger than this, it seems implausible.

Criteria for Morally Prescriptive Indirect Volitionalism

Let me conclude this chapter by offering a set of criteria by which to decide when it is morally permissible to indirectly volit. I side with Meiland against Clifford, Gale, and others who contend that we ought never under any circumstances get ourselves to believe anything where the evidence alone doesn't warrant it, simply because we have a need to believe it. Although I think that instances of justified voliting (indirectly) are probably exceedingly rare, there may be some. Meiland's example of the neurotic wife concerned with saving her marriage may indeed be such a case. Another may be the following.

Suppose that I gain some information about you that causes me to act in a way that you perceive as harmful to your interests. Further, I have obtained this information in a morally unacceptable way, say, by reading your diary or private correspondence, and that I would not have had this information had I not read this material. Further suppose that there is a competent psychiatrist who with minimum risk can make me forget the information that I possess about your private life. Or suppose that there is a psychologically harmless pill that will do this same thing. Is it obvious that you would not have a right to demand that I take the necessary steps to forget the memory belief that I have? Perhaps a certain type of forgiveness involves our using autosuggestion to forget in part the seriousness of the acts against us. Of course, self-creating beliefs seem the best examples of what may be morally permissible in this area. Suppose that you must swim two miles to shore in order to save your life. You have never swum that far and have good evidence that you can't do it. However, you reason that if you can get yourself to believe that you can swim the distance, the confidence will somehow produce a physiological state that will give you a better chance of swimming that far (thought not quite a 50 percent chance). Would you not be justified in getting yourself into that place?

If there are times when it is morally permissible or even obligatory to volit a belief against sufficient evidence, what conditions must be met? I suggest the following: a prudential condition and two utilitarian conditions (a general and a specific).

1. **A prudential requirement.** The justified volit would have to involve a nonvolitional cost—benefit analysis that might be undermined if the agent was not a dispositional evidentialist. The act must be seen as possible and worth doing on the evidence available. There must be some morally acceptable benefit that outweighs the cost involved in getting the new belief by voliting.

2. **A general utility requirement.** Others must not be significantly harmed by this act—or their harm must not outweigh the benefits that would accrue to the agent—and the benefits must be morally acceptable. Again, the leap is parasitical on evidentialism; a mistake may be dangerous. For example, if I get myself to believe that the world will end shortly (for religious reasons) and then become secretary of interior, I may treat the environment so poorly that I hasten the end of the world.

3. **The chain of deception requirement.** This is a special instance of the utility requirement. In getting yourself into a state S where you will believe that p, which you presently do not believe on the evidence, you will be responsible for a chain of unnecessary false reports. That is, if you were to tell others that p was the case, you would be lying. While the self that actually reports p will not be lying, that self is spreading a falsehood (or reporting falsely), becoming an unreliable witness, and starting a possible chain of false reports. In essence, in willing to deceive your future self (who will sincerely report to others) you are taking on the responsibility for

deceiving others. As the beginning of a chain of misinformation, only the most extreme grounds would seem to justify the volit.

If, however, you can make a cost–benefit analysis in the most rigorously evidentialist fashion and can determine that the volit is both psychologically possible and worth the cost of deceiving yourself and possibly others, then perhaps the volit is justified. If you are sure that you are not going to bring harm to others or lessen their autonomy significantly and that you will not harm your children by being an unreliable witness, then you might well be justified in acquiring a belief by willing to have it and doing what is necessary to bring it about.

But who can be so certain, given the uncertainty of how all these factors will work out in life? James's stranded mountain climber at the edge of the gorge certainly seems to be justified, since his options are limited. The person who read your diary may also be justified in trying to forget his belief. Perhaps the hermit who lives alone on an island is justified—though he may have an obligation to put a sign on the dock—warning people who approach that they trespass at their own risk, since the he has engaged regularly in voliting and may seriously misinform them on certain matters. For the rest of us, indirect voliting almost always will not be a relevant consideration but will be an imprudent and immoral act. Since truth matters, and we can take steps to acquire habits making true beliefs more likely, there is an ethics of belief.

QUESTIONS FOR DISCUSSION

1. Explain how the will plays an indirect role in believing.

2. Do we have an ethics of belief? That is, do we have moral duties to attempt to justify our beliefs? Or are our only duties to believe epistemic ones or counsels of prudence?

3. Go over my critique of Meiland's argument. How might Meiland respond to it?

4. Discuss the criteria for morally prescriptive indirect volitionalism given at the end of this chapter. What are their strengths and weaknesses?

5. John Pollock offers an illustration of how prudential justification can override epistemic justification:

> . . . because beliefs can have important consequences for the believer, it may be prudent to hold beliefs for which you have inadequate evidence. For instance, it is popularly alleged that lobsters do not feel

pain when they are dunked alive into boiling water. It is extremely doubtful that anyone has good reason to believe that, but it may be prudentially rational to hold that belief because otherwise one would deprive oneself of the gustatory delight of eating boiled lobsters . . . . It is unclear whether moral considerations can be meaningfully applied to beliefs.[10]

Pollock omits any discussion of the ethics of holding such beliefs. Is he correct? What is your view of this passage?

6. Can you think of specific beliefs about politics, religion, or ethics where we have moral duties to investigate the grounds for our belief? Give a concrete example of a situation where the ethics of belief would come into play.

NOTES

1. John Pollock, *Contemporary Theories of Knowledge* (Totowa, NJ: Rowman & Littlefield, 1986), 7–8.
2. H. H. Price, *Belief* (London: Allen & Unwin, 1967), 238.
3. John Stuart Mill, *On Liberty* (New York: Bobbs-Merrill, 1956). Mill continues, "the appropriate region of human liberty . . . comprises liberty of conscience in the most comprehensive sense: Liberty of thought and feeling, absolute freedom of opinion on all subjects practical and speculative, scientific, moral or theological." The statement is ambiguous, seeming to conflate the right to be protected from doxastic coercion and the right to manipulate our minds as we see fit.
4. Jack Meiland, "What Ought We to Believe? or the Ethics of Belief Revisited." *American Philosophical Quarterly,* 17 (January 1980). Reprinted in *The Theory of Knowledge,* 2nd ed., ed. Louis P. Pojman (Belmont, CA: Wadsworth, 1999).
5. Ibid., 19.
6. Roderick Chisholm, quoted in Meiland; Stephen Nathanson, "The Ethics of Belief" in *The Theory of Knowledge,* 2nd ed., ed. Louis P. Pojman (Belmont, CA: Wadsworth, 1999).
7. Meiland, 21.
8. W. K. Clifford. "The Ethics of Belief." Reprinted in Pojman, X.2.
9. Bernard Williams, "Deciding to Believe," *Problems of the Self* (Cambridge: Cambridge University Press, 1972).
10. Pollock, 7–8.

FOR FURTHER READING

Clifford, W. K. "The Ethics of Belief." Reprinted in *The Theory of Knowledge,* edited by Louis P. Pojman. Belmont, CA: Wadsworth, 1993.

Firth, Roderick. "Are Epistemic Concepts Reducible to Ethical Concepts?" In *Value and Morals,* edited by A. I. Goldman and J. Kim. Dordrecht, Holland: D. Reidel, 1978.

Gale, Richard. "William James and the Ethics of Belief," *American Philosophical Quarterly* 17 (1980).

James, William. *The Will to Believe.* New York: Dover Publications, 1956.

Kornblith, Hilary. "Justified Belief and Epistemically Responsible Action," *Philosophical Review* xcii, 1 (January 1983).

Livingston, James C. *The Ethics of Belief: An Essay on the Victorian Religious Consciousness.* Tallahassee, FL: American Academy of Religion, 1974.

Meiland, Jack. "What Ought We to Believe? or The Ethics of Belief Revisited," *American Philosophical Quarterly* 17 (1980).

Newman, John Henry. *The Grammar of Assent.* London: Westminster, 1980.

Pieper, Josef. *Belief and Faith.* New York: Pantheon Books, 1953.

Pojman, Louis. *Religious Belief and the Will.* London: Routledge & Kegan Paul, 1986.

Pojman, Louis, ed. *The Theory of Knowledge.* Belmont, CA: Wadsworth, 1993. Contains the classic articles by William James and W. K. Clifford plus articles by Jack Meiland and R. Feldman.

Price, H. H. *Belief.* London: Allen & Unwin, 1967.

CHAPTER 18

Belief and Acceptance

We have examined the nature of belief, the relationship of the will to belief, and the ethics of belief. One further relationship with belief remains to be explored, that between belief and acceptance. Is acceptance a special type of believing or a separate cognitive state altogether? This question, together with an analysis of the idea of acceptance, will occupy us in this chapter.

Keith Lehrer argues that knowledge requires not merely belief that a proposition is true, but a special type of belief, *acceptance*. Acceptance is assenting to a proposition when one's only purpose is to assent to what is true and to refuse to assent to what is false.

> There is a special kind of acceptance requisite to knowledge. It is accepting something for the purpose of attaining truth and avoiding error with respect to the very thing one accepts. More precisely, the purpose is to accept that p if and only if p. Sometimes we believe things that we do not accept for this epistemic purpose. We may believe something for the sake of felicity rather than from a regard for truth. We may believe that a loved one is safe because of the pleasure of so believing, though there is no evidence to justify accepting this out of regard for truth, indeed, even when there is evidence against it. So, there are cases in which we do not accept in the appropriate way what we believe. It is the acceptance of something in the quest for truth that is the required condition of knowledge.[1]

So acceptance is a species of the genus belief, the kind of belief that is solely truth directed. You can believe a proposition without accepting it, but you can't accept a proposition without believing it.

What are we to make of this? Note, first, that it presupposes an internalist view of knowledge. One must accept that *p* solely for the sake of having the truth. An externalist might say that as long as a reliable process caused you to have the true belief in the right way, you have knowledge. But internalists might balk at Lehrer's notion of acceptance as a criterion of knowledge. While you are cycling along a city street, a car door suddenly opens in front of you. You instantly believe that you must swerve to the left in order to avoid hitting the door or the driver. You don't form an intention about believing only for the sake of truth. Normally, beliefs are not within our direct control. They just happen. From an internalist perspective, what makes true beliefs knowledge is not their intentional aspect but whether they are justified. Surely, animals and children don't formulate second-order intentions to seek the truth, yet we would say that they have knowledge. My dog knows that food is before him, and my small daughter knows that her mother is holding her without having to form second-order intentions about believing these things only for the sake of possessing the truth. Knowledge is more natural than that.

Although Lehrer is correct to point to the notion of acceptance as a cognitive attitude, he is wrong to classify it as a special type of belief. One can accept a hypothesis that one does not believe. I may accept your hypothesis for the sake of argument without believing it. A scientist may accept a new hypothesis, although he or she is agnostic about it, but carry out a series of experiments in order to see what reactions will obtain or to see whether by some quirk it is true after all. The scientist accepts the hypothesis for the sake of finding the truth but does not believe it.

Furthermore, I can believe a proposition and yet not accept it. I see (and believe) that the evidence is against my hypothesis, yet I have a vested interest in the hypothesis, so I proceed as though the evidence didn't count significantly against it. I may even do this for the sake of truth. I believe that the evidence counts significantly against my hypothesis, but I also realize that although the chances are less than 50 percent, if my hypothesis is true and if I can perform other experiments to verify it, then the outcome will be a greater display of truth.

If this is correct, then Lehrer is wrong. Acceptance is a different cognitive attitude from believing. A given proposition may both be believed and accepted by a subject, but some propositions are believed without being accepted and others are accepted without being believed.

How do we distinguish belief from acceptance? Both are cognitive attitudes relating to propositions, but whereas belief is an involuntary attitude that a proposition is true, acceptance is a voluntary attitude. Beliefs force themselves on us, but we decide to accept premises in arguments or hypotheses in investigations to see what fruit they may bear. Beliefs occur spontaneously or after reflection without our deciding to believe, but acceptances are always deliberate. We speak of beliefs being *caused* but acceptances being determined by *reasons*. One may, of course, both believe and accept a proposition at the same time.

L. Jonathan Cohen in his recent *An Essay on Belief and Acceptance* argues for an even greater difference between these two cognitive attitudes. For Cohen, a belief is a disposition to *feel* that a proposition is true, whereas acceptance is the adoption of a policy or following through on a hypothesis. As Cohen puts it, "To accept that p is to adopt the policy of taking the proposition that p as a premiss in appropriate circumstances."[2] To accept that p is to include that proposition "among one's premises for deciding what to do or think in a particular context, whether or not one feels it to be true that p." Cohen finds an anticipation of his distinction in the work of C. S. Peirce, who distinguished between a judgment accompanied by "a peculiar feeling or conviction" and judgment "from which a man will act."[3]

Cohen thinks that a key difference between acceptance and belief is that acceptance is subjectively closed under deducibility, but belief isn't. That is, necessarily, if S accepts the conjunction of $p_1, p_2 \ldots p_n$ and the deducibility of q from that conjunction, S also accepts q. This is not true of belief, since it is a disposition to feel that p and feelings arise in one through involuntary processes of which one may be partly or wholly unconscious. According to Cohen, beliefs, unlike acceptances, carry no commitments and are neither intentional nor unintentional.

I doubt that this is correct. If I believe the conjunction of $p_1, p_2 \ldots p_n$ and the deducibility of q from that conjunction, I will also believe q—unless I am irrational. Subjective closure holds in both cases. What gives some initial plausibility to Cohen's thesis of difference here is that since acceptance is typically a conscious activity, I am often fully conscious of the entailment relations between premises, whereas believing is often simply dispositional (for Cohen it is virtually entirely so, though he offers very little argument here). As a result, I may not notice the implications of my beliefs. We all too often hold contradictory beliefs without realizing that we do, but rational beings cannot consciously accept contradictory beliefs. But then neither can they consciously believe contradictory beliefs.

Cohen argues that either belief or acceptance can function as the second condition in knowledge. Knowledge that p entails the subject either accepts that p or believes that p (where p is a justified true proposition). The scientist who accepts and acts on a hypothesis that he or she doubts can be said to know that the hypothesis is true if it is and if the evidence for it is good.

Again, I doubt this. Acceptance is too neutral a notion to bear the weight of knowledge. Suppose I truly believe that objectively there is a 1000:1 chance of my winning the $1 million lottery. But, because the ticket only costs $1, I accept the hypothesis that I will win and purchase a ticket. I also have evidence that my uncle is running the lottery and will rig it so that I will win. Nevertheless, I don't *believe* that he will be successful—though I may *accept* that he will. Suppose he is successful and I win the lottery. According to Cohen's logic of acceptance, I *knew* all along that I would win. This seems preposterous. Acceptance of a proposition may lead to knowledge and to right action, but it doesn't seem to be a condition for knowledge.

Cohen further claims that dividing the cognitive terrain between belief and acceptance offers the bonus of solving the problem of skepticism. The skeptic claims that you can never have conclusive reasons for any of your claims to know any given proposition *p*.

> You offer what seem to be veritable paradigms of warranted certainty, as when a person thinks he knows that his hand is in front of his face because he sees it there and touches it with his nose. But the sceptic comes up in each case with outlandish possibilities which refute your paradigm, such as the possibility that an evil neurologist is inducing illusions in you. So your confidence in your paradigms is shattered and you are tempted to admit that, even if you were in fact to know that *p*, you could never know that you knew. Hence it is apparently right to be sceptical about the existence of knowledge despite the fact that people often claim to have it.[4]

However, if we distinguish between belief and acceptance, we can cut the skeptic's Gordian knot.

> Your belief in the conclusive provability of the proposition that *p* may indeed be gravely weakened by your consideration of the sceptic's argument. . . . But loss of belief here does not entail cessation of acceptance. You may continue with the policy of premising that it is conclusively provable that *p* even if you no longer have the corresponding belief. And there may be good cognitive reasons for this continuance, such as that the counter-arguments are too outlandish to take seriously whereas the supporting arguments are solid and respectable.[5]

So while belief-based knowledge is undermined by the skeptic's sting, acceptance-based knowledge survives it. Based on our previous discussion, I will leave it to you to analyze Cohen's argument at this point.

There are clearer instances where acceptance does some epistemic work, such as clarifying issues. The scientist testing a hypothesis is one case. Consider the scrupulous scientist, for example, Einstein, who claims to have knowledge of some physical laws.

> In such cases having the knowledge that p, where the proposition that p states a physical law, implies that the scientist accepts that p and that the proposition that p deserves acceptance in the light of cognitively relevant considerations. The scientist must be willing to go along with that proposition, and anything it is seen to entail, as a premiss—one among many—for his predictions, explanations, further research, etc. And an involuntary belief that p would not be an adequate substitute for the scientist's voluntary acceptance that p since it would not entail this policy in the choice of premises. Nor would it deserve praise or blame in the way that a responsible act of acceptance deserves it. . . . There is a danger that possession of a belief that p might make him less ready to change his mind about accepting that p if new evidence crops up or a better theory becomes available. It might even make him less ready to look for new evidence or a better theory, when otherwise he would have done so. Also, in the establishment of a belief that p, some factors might be influential in the black box of the scientist's subconscious mind that he would reject as irrelevant or prejudicial if they came up for consideration before the tribunal of conscious acceptance.
>
> Ideally, therefore, a natural scientist would carry on without having any belief in the truth of his favored hypotheses. He could rest content with accepting them in the light of cognitively relevant considerations. And any other factual investigator, such as a historian, a detective, or an intelligence analyst, could treat his own favored hypotheses analogously.[6]

Of course, as Cohen admits, the scientist or investigator who actually believes his or her hypothesis may have advantages over the one who only accepts it. The believer may stubbornly persevere where the acceptor would give up the quest when the evidence turns against the hypothesis. Further, the believer's typically stronger commitment may afford insights into the nature of a hypothesis that are less likely to occur to one who only accepts the premise. Nonetheless, one can be impartial and passionate at the same time, so there is no reason in principle that the acceptor need be any less passionate about a hypothesis than a believer.

Perhaps a religious person who doubts his or her faith is another case in which the idea of acceptance functions as a good substitute for belief. Linda has just had her favorite arguments for the existence of God undermined by her philosophy professor. She feels confused and doubts the existence of God. But until she settles the issue more decisively one way or the other, she may be justified in living *as if* God exists or, in Cohen's terms, *accepting* the proposition that God exists, living in an experimental faith, much as a scientist commits himself or herself to the hypothesis until the counterevidence is overwhelming and completely undermines it.

Cohen shows that the notion of acceptance functions appropriately in legal contexts. A judge may instruct jury members to use certain rules of evidence that exclude certain types of considerations (e.g., past convictions and other inductive evidence) from their deliberation in finding the accused innocent or guilty. Part of the purpose of *exclusionary rules* is to prevent prejudice from entering into the jurors' verdict, so that false beliefs are kept out of the judicial process. Suppose that the jurors hear the evidence and on the basis of the total evidence believe that the accused is definitely guilty. In fact, there is no doubt in any of their minds, but the evidence on which their conviction is formed is that which the rules exclude. So in accepting the rules, they are committed to finding that there is insufficient evidence to convict the accused. They accept the proposition that the accused is innocent. Our legal system, which we'll presume is justified, sometimes demands that we go against our beliefs and accept a verdict based on limited evidence. Sometimes acceptance of a proposition is more appropriate than belief.

But let us ask the further question. Suppose the accused really is innocent. Do the jurors who accept the defendant's innocence on the basis of the (limited) evidence know that the accused is not guilty? I don't think so. As I argued earlier, acceptance isn't an adequate substitute for belief in the formulation of whatever it takes to characterize knowledge. Perhaps if the jurors also believed that the accused was innocent on that evidence, they'd have knowledge, but acceptance by itself is too weak an epistemic notion to bring us to the desideratum of knowing.

QUESTIONS FOR DISCUSSION

1. Go over Lehrer's argument for acceptance as a special type of belief that is necessary for knowledge. Do you see any reasons to accept Lehrer's position? What are the arguments against his formulation?

2. Describe Cohen's distinction between belief and acceptance. Explain where you agree and where you disagree with his position.

3. Review Cohen's argument that the belief-acceptance distinction overcomes the problem of skepticism. Do you agree with Cohen? Explain your answer.

4. Do you agree with Cohen that belief is "a disposition, not an oc-current feeling," that is, a disposition to feel that a proposition is true? Can you come up with counterexamples to that position? Consider the issue of acquiring a belief. How would Cohen account for that?

NOTES

1. Keith Lehrer, *Theory of Knowledge* (Boulder, CO: Westview, 1990), 11.
2. L. Jonathan Cohen, *An Essay on Belief and Acceptance* (Oxford: Oxford University Press, 1992), 115. See page 4 as well.
3. C. S. Peirce, *Collected Papers,* ed. C. Harshorne and P. Weiss (Cambridge, MA: Harvard University Press, 1934), 148. Quoted in a footnote in Cohen, *Essay,* 6.
4. Cohen, 106.
5. Ibid.
6. Cohen, 87–88.

FOR FURTHER READING

Bogdan, R. J., ed. *Belief: Form, Content and Function.* Oxford: Clarendon Press, 1986.
Cohen, L. Jonathan. *The Dialogue of Reason.* Oxford: Clarendon Press, 1986.
———. *An Essay on Belief and Acceptance.* Oxford: Oxford University Press, 1992.
Goldman, Alvin. *Epistemology and Cognition.* Cambridge, MA: Harvard University Press, 1986.
Lehrer, Keith. *Theory of Knowledge.* Boulder, CO: Westview, 1990.
O'Connor, D. J., and Brian Carr. *Introduction to the Theory of Knowledge.* Minneapolis: University of Minnesota Press, 1982. Chapter 2.
Pojman, Louis. *Religious Belief and the Will.* London: Routledge & Kegan Paul, 1986.
Price, H. H. *Belief.* London: Allen & Unwin, 1969.

CHAPTER 19

Epistemology and Religious Belief

We have examined the nature of knowledge as well as its components, belief, justification, and truth. We have considered the foundationalist-coherentist dispute and the internalist/externalist dispute regarding justification of beliefs and have concluded that both competitors in each of these paired dichotomies have something to be said in their behalf. We have indicated where one theory has an edge over another and have pointed out problems in every theory. If you are less satisfied with the result, if you would have preferred exact solutions to the questions considered, this may be due to the nature of philosophical problems themselves. Once a clear solution to a philosophical problem obtains, the question loses philosophical interest. Often it becomes a posit of science. Such has been the case with many questions of physics, biology, psychology, and neurology. For example, the puzzle of a bowl of water feeling warm to one hand and cold to the other was a philosophical problem in the Middle Ages because heat and cold were believed to be distinct substances. Indeed, physics, psychology, and biology once were part of philosophy, but as they developed decision procedures of their own, they separated themselves as distinct sciences.

Philosophical problems are those that defy scientific or algorithmic solutions, that disturb the mind without yielding clear and confirmable solutions. Epistemology attempts to understand the parameters of such problems and to show what is more reasonable and what is less reasonable in terms of solutions.

In this chapter I want to consider what has been one of the most perplexing problems in the history of philosophy: the epistemology of religious belief. I want to consider it partly because the topic has significance in its own right and partly because it serves as an example of how various aspects of the theory of knowledge can be applied to a topic. I will outline what I think is the best case for the justification of religious beliefs and will confine myself to theistic religions, especially Judaism, Christianity, and Islam, but my arguments will have implications for other types of belief as well—scientific (e.g., Darwinian evolution), political (e.g., conservatism, socialism, and feminism), and moral (e.g., utilitarianism, realism and antirealism, and abortion). I am not claiming this to be a complete account, let alone a completely successful account, but I do think it is instructive and plausible.

First, note that attempts at justification of theories, whether religious, political, moral, or scientific, involve coherentism: Our goal is to take account of an enormous amount of data and make sense of it. All theories, as W. V. Quine made us aware, are underdetermined by the evidence, so it is impossible for one theory to win out completely over all its competitors. What we want is the best explanation among rivals. Since there can be no final winner from an epistemic perspective, it is unlikely that we can be dogmatic about our religious beliefs. Yet religion is a very emotional subject, and typically believers believe passionately and with conviction. The epistemology of religious belief, it seems to me, has a moderating effect. It shows the antireligious that the case against religion is not as strong as they might have thought, but it shows the religious dogmatists (if they will study philosophy), that the case for religion is not as strong as they might imagine. This moderating effect carries over to all of our theoretical beliefs, or so it seems to me. Indeed, we need not even *believe* these theories but simply *accept* them as experimental hypotheses in the spirit of our discussion in chapter 18.

The Debate over Faith and Reason

In the debate over faith and reason two opposing positions have dominated the field. The first position asserts that faith and reason are commensurable, and the second denies that assertion. Those holding to the first position differ among themselves as to the extent of the compatibility between faith and reason, most adherents assigning the compatibility to the "preambles of faith" (e.g., the existence of God and his nature) rather than to the "articles of faith" (e.g., the doctrine of the Incarnation and the Trinity). Few have gone as far as Immanuel Kant and Richard Swinburne in maintaining a complete harmony between reason and faith (i.e., a religious belief within the realm of reason alone).

The second position, incommensurabilism, divides into two sub-positions: (1) one that asserts that faith is opposed to reason (which includes such unlikely bedfellows as Hume and Kierkegaard), placing faith in the area of irrationality; and (2) one that asserts that faith is higher than reason, is transrational. John Calvin (1509–1564), Karl Barth (1886–1968), Nicholas Wolterstorff, and Alvin Plantinga hold that a natural theology is inappropriate because it seeks to meet unbelief on its own ground (ordinary human reason). As Barth put it, to reason about faith is to assume the standpoint of unbelief; it "makes reason a judge over Christ." Revelation, according to these transrationalists, is "self-authenticating," "carrying with it its own evidence."[1] In his *Reason Within the Bounds of Religion* Wolterstorff advocates subjecting all our theoretical deliberations to the standard of our religion.[2] On this view, faith is not really against reason but above it and beyond its proper domain. Actually, Kierkegaard and the Jewish Existentialist Leon Shestov (1866–1938) show that the two subpositions are compatible. They hold both that faith is above reason and against reason, holding that reason has been corrupted by sin.

The irrationalist and the transrationalist positions are sometimes hard to separate in the incommensurabilist's arguments. At the very least, it seems that faith gets such a high value that reason comes off looking not simply inadequate but culpable. To use reason where faith claims the field is not only inappropriate but irreverent or even blasphemous.

In this chapter I will defend a strong commensurabilist position on faith and reason. My thesis is that a theistic religion such as Christianity, Judaism, or Islam is (among other things) an explanatory theory or hypothesis about the world, which as such is as much in need of rational justification as any other explanatory theory or hypothesis. That is, while a religion is also a form of life, a set of practices, it contains a cognitive aspect that claims to make sense out of one's experience. It answers questions about why we are here, why we suffer, and why the world is the way it is. These answers form a coherent network that requires reasons why they are to be preferred to other answers (or no answer at all). Here I will defend this thesis indirectly. I will try to clear some conceptual ground in order to bring support for a rationalist religious epistemology. If I can clear some of the major obstacles and arguments against the commensurabilist position, showing in the process the force of that position, I will have succeeded in my task. My assumption is that unless there is good reason to have a different method for evaluating religious claims, there is a presumption in favor of using the rational methods employed elsewhere here as well.

After a short section on conceptual frameworks and how they affect rationality, I will discuss three obstacles to the commensurabilist position:

1. My thesis implies a neutrality toward religion that is inconsistent with the attitude of *faith*.
2. The thesis subjects religious belief to totally inappropriate norms of formal (deductive and inductive) proofs.
3. The thesis ignores the fact that a necessary condition for faith is its very lack of justification.

Rationality and Conceptual Frameworks

Sometimes it is claimed that there is a clear-cut decision-making process, similar to the one used in mathematics and empirical science, when we arrive at justified belief or truth. A person has a duty to believe exactly according to the available evidence. Hence, there is no excuse for anyone to believe anything on insufficient evidence. Such is the case of Descartes and the logical positivists (especially A. J. Ayer), which is echoed in W. K. Clifford's classic formula, "It is wrong always, everywhere, and for anyone to believe anything on insufficient evidence." Laying aside the criticism that the statement itself is self-referentially incoherent (it doesn't give us sufficient evidence for believing itself), the problem is that different data will count as evidence to different degrees according to the background beliefs a person has. The contribution of Michael Polanyi, Karl Popper, N. R. Hanson, and Ludwig Wittgenstein has been to demonstrate the power of *perspectivism,* the thesis that the way we evaluate or even pick out evidence is determined by our prior picture of the world, which itself is made up of a loosely connected and mutually supporting network of propositions. Evidence is person-relative and context-sensitive. Do the farmer, the real estate dealer, and the landscape artist on looking at a field see the same field?[3]

The nonperspectivist position, seen in Plato, Aquinas, Descartes, Locke, Clifford, and most thinkers in the history of philosophy, seems dubious. However, the reaction (e.g., Friedrich Nietzsche, Norman Malcolm, Jacques Derrida, Richard Rorty, and the religious fideists)[4] has been to claim that since what is basic is the conceptual framework, no rational interchange between world views is possible. Our language or our conceptual systems determine validity. "Truth is what our peers will let us get away with" (Rorty). "Belief can only preach to unbelief" (Barth). No argument is possible. We may call this reaction to the postcritical critique of rationalism *hard-perspectivism*.

The nonperspectivist writes as though arriving at the truth were a matter of impartial evaluation of evidence, and the hard-perspectivist writes as though no meaningful communication were possible. The worldviews are discontinuous. As **fideists** say, "The believer and unbeliever live in different worlds."[5] There is an infinite qualitative gap existing between various forms of life that no amount of argument or discussion can bridge. For hard-perspectivists, including Wittgensteinian fideists, reason can only have intramural significance. There are no bridges between worldviews.

However, hard-perspectivism is not the only possible reaction to the postcritical revolution. One may accept the insight that our manner of evaluating evidence is strongly affected by our conceptual frameworks without opting for a view that precludes communication across worldviews. One may recognize the depth of a conceptual framework and still maintain that communication between frameworks is possible and that reason may have an intermural as well as intramural significance in the process. Such a view may be called *soft-perspectivism*. The soft-perspectivist is under no illusion regarding the difficulty of effecting a massive shift in the total evaluation of an immense range of data, producing new patterns of feeling and acting in persons, but he or she is confident that the program is viable.

One of the reasons given in support of this is that there is something like a core rationality common to every human culture, especially with regard to practical life. Certain rules of inference (deductive and inductive) have virtually universal application. Certain assumptions or basic beliefs seem common to every culture (e.g., that there are other minds, that there is time, that things move, that perceptions are generally reliable). Through sympathetic imagination one can attain some understanding of another's conceptual system; through disappointment one can begin to suspect weaknesses in one's own worldview and thus seek a more adequate explanation. It is not my purpose to produce a full defense of a soft-perspective position, only to indicate its plausibility. The assumption on which this chapter is written is that the case for soft-perspectivism can be made. And if it is true, then it is possible for reason to play a significant role in the examination, revision, and rejection of one's current beliefs and in the acquisition of new beliefs.

Does Rationality Imply a Neutrality That Is Incompatible with Religious Faith?

We may say that postcritical rationalists of the soft-perspectivist variety are individuals who seek to support all their beliefs (especially their convictions) with good reasons. They attempt to evaluate the evidence as impartially as possible, to accept the challenge of answering criticisms, and to remain open to the possibility that they might be wrong and may need to revise, reexamine, or reject any one of their beliefs. This character description of the rationalist is often interpreted to mean that rationalists must be *neutral* and detached with regard to their beliefs.[6] This is a mistake. It confuses *impartiality* with *neutrality*. Both concepts imply conflict situations (e.g., war, a competitive sport, a legal trial, an argument). But to be neutral signifies not taking sides, doing nothing to influence the outcome, remaining passive in the fray; whereas impartiality *involves* one in the conflict in that it calls for a judgment in favor of the party that is right. To the extent that one party is right or wrong (measured by objective criteria), neutrality and impartiality are incompatible concepts. To be neutral is to detach oneself from the struggle; to be impartial is to commit oneself to a position—though not partially (i.e., unfairly or arbitrarily) but in accordance with an objective standard.

The model of the neutral person is an atheist who is indifferent about football, watching a game between Notre Dame and Southern Methodist. The model of the partial or prejudiced person is the coach who, on any given dispute, predictably judges his team to be in the right and the other to be in the wrong and for whom it is an axiom that any judgment by the referee against his team is, at best, of dubious merit. The model of the impartial person is the referee in the game, who, knowing that his wife has just bet their life savings on the underdog, Southern Methodist, still manages to call what any reasonable spectator would judge to be a fair game. He does not let his wants or self-interest enter into the judgment he makes.

To be rational does not lessen the passion involved in religious beliefs. Rational believers, who believe that they have good grounds for believing that a perfect being exists, are not less likely to trust that being absolutely than believers who do not think that they have reasons. Likewise, doubters who live in hope of God's existence may be as passionate about their commitment as persons who entertain no doubts. In fact, the rational hoper or believer will probably judge it to be irrational not to be absolutely committed to such a being. Hence, the charge leveled against the rationalists by Kierkegaard and others that rational inquiry cools the passions seems unfounded.

However, nonrationalists have a slightly different, but related, argument at hand. They may argue that if there were sufficient evidence available, it might be the case that one might be both religious and rational. But there is not sufficient evidence; hence, the very search for evidence simply detracts believers from worship and passionate service, leading them on a wild-goose chase for evidence that does not exist. The believer is involved in cool calculation instead of passionate commitment, questioning instead of obeying.

There are at least two responses to this charge. First, how does the nonrationalist know that there is not sufficient evidence for a religious claim? How does the nonrationalist know that not merely a demonstrative proof but even a cumulative case with some force is impossible? It would seem reasonable to expect that a good God would not leave his creatures wholly in the dark about so important a matter. The nonrationalist's answer (that of Calvin and Kierkegaard, and suggested by Plantinga) that sin has destroyed the use of reason or our ability to see God seems unduly ad hoc and inadequate. It would seem that little children in nontheistic cultures should manifest some theistic tendencies on this view, for which there is no evidence. Second, why can't the search for truth itself be a way of worshiping God? a passionate act of service? Again, one would expect the possession of well-founded beliefs to be God's will for us. The Christian philosopher Gordon Clark once said that he would trust the Bible over all of his senses. The problem is how would he know what was recorded in the Bible except by using and trusting his senses?

What I have said about impartiality and religious belief is consistent with the idea that the claims of a religion cannot but move a person. Anyone who does not see the importance of religion's claims either does not have a sense of selfhood or does not understand what is being said, since a religion claims to make sense out of the world. For example, to entertain the proposition that a personal, loving Creator exists is to entertain a proposition whose implications affect every part of a person's understanding of self and the world. If the proposition is true, the world is personal rather than mechanistic, friendly rather than strange, purposeful rather than simply a vortex of chance and necessity. If it is not true, a different set of entailments follow that are likely to lead to different patterns of feeling and action. If Judeo-Islamic-Christian theism is accepted, the believer has an additional reason for being a moral person, for treating fellow humans with equal respect: God has created all people in his image, as infinitely precious, destined to enjoy his fellowship forever. Theism can provide a more adequate metaphysical basis for morality. Hence, it can be both descriptively and prescriptively significant.

Toward a Theory of Rationality

It is often said that rational persons tailor the strength of their beliefs to the strength of the evidence. The trouble with this remark is that it is notoriously difficult to give sense to any discussion of discovering objective criteria for what is to count as evidence and to what extent it is to count.

Deciding *what* is to count as evidence for something else in part depends on a whole network of considerations, and deciding *to what extent* something is to count as evidence involves weighing procedures that are subjective. Two judges may have the same evidence before them and come to different verdicts. Two equally rational persons may have the same evidence about the claims of a religion and still arrive at different conclusions in the matter. It would seem that the prescription to tailor one's beliefs according to the evidence is either empty or a shorthand for something more complex. I think it is the latter. Let me illustrate what I think it signifies.

Consider any situation in which our self-interest may conflict with the truth. Take the case of three German wives who are suddenly confronted with evidence that their husbands have been unfaithful. Their surnames are Uberglaubig, Misstrauish, and Wahrnehmen. Each is disturbed about the evidence and makes further inquiries. Mrs. Uberglaubig is soon finished and finds herself rejecting all the evidence, maintaining resolutely her husband's fidelity. Others, even relatives of Mr. Uberglaubig, are surprised by her credulity, for the evidence against Mr. Uberglaubig is the sort that would lead most people to conclude that he was unfaithful. No matter how much evidence is adduced, Mrs. Uberglaubig is unchanged in her judgment. She seems to have a fixation about her husband's fidelity.

Mrs. Misstrauish seems to suffer from an opposite weakness. If Mrs. Uberglaubig, as her name signifies, overbelieves, Mrs. Misstrauish, as her name signifies, underbelieves. She suspects the worst, and even though others who know Mr. Misstrauish deem the evidence against him weak (especially in comparison to the evidence presented against Mr. Uberglaubig), she is convinced that her husband is unfaithful. No evidence seems to be sufficient to reassure her. It is as though the very suggestion of infidelity were enough to stir up doubts and disbelief.

Mrs. Wahrnehmen also considers the evidence, which is considerable, and comes to a judgment, though with some reservations. Suppose she finds herself believing that her husband is faithful. Others may differ in their assessment of the situation, but Mrs. Wahrnehmen is willing and able to discuss the matter, give her grounds, and consider the objections of others. Perhaps we can say that she is more self-aware, more self-controlled, and more self-secure than the other women. She seems to have a capacity to separate her judgment from her hopes, wants, and fears in a way that the others do not.

This should provide some clue to what it means to be rational. It does not necessarily mean being intelligent or having true beliefs (though we would say that rationality tends toward truth); it might just turn out that by luck Mr. Wahrnehmen is indeed an adulterer and Mr. Uberglaubig is innocent. Still, we should want to say that Mrs. Wahrnehmen was justified in her beliefs but Mrs. Uberglaubig was not.

What does characterize rational judgment are two properties, one being *intentional* and the other being *capacity behavioral*. First, rationality involves an intention to seek the truth or the possession of a high regard for the truth, especially when there may be a conflict between it and one's wishes. It involves a healthy abhorrence of being deceived combined with a parallel desire to have knowledge in matters vital to one's life. Mrs. Wahrnehmen and Mrs. Misstrauish care about the truth in a way that Mrs. Uberglaubig does not. But second, rationality involves a skill or behavioral capacity to judge impartially, to examine the evidence objectively, and to know what sort of things count in coming to a considered judgment. It is as though Mrs. Wahrnehmen alone were able to see clearly through the fog of emotion and self-interest, focusing on some ideal standard of evidence. Of course, there is no such simple standard, any more than there is for the art critic in making a judgment on the authenticity of a work of art.

Still, the metaphor of an ideal standard is apt; it draws our attention to the objective features in rational judgment, a feature that is internalized in the person of the expert. Like learning to discriminate between works of art or with regard to criminal evidence, rationality is a learned trait that calls for a long apprenticeship (a lifetime?) under the cooperative tutelage of other rational persons. Some people with little formal education seem to learn this better than some "well-educated" people (even philosophers), but despite this uncomfortable observation, I would like to believe that it is the job of education to train people to judge impartially over a broad range of human experience.

As a discriminatory skill combined with an intention (or dispositional inclination), rationality may seem to be in a shaky situation. How do we decide who has the skill or who has the right combination of the two traits? There is no certain way, but judge we must in this life. The basis of our judgment will be manifestations of behavior that we classify as truth directed, noticing that persons with this skill seek out evidence and pay attention to criticism and counterclaims, that they usually support their judgment with recognizable good reasons, and that they revise and reject their beliefs in the light of new information. These criteria are not foolproof, and it seems impossible to give an exact account of the process involved in rational decision or belief, but this seems to be the case with any skill. In the end, rationality seems more like a set of trained intuitions than anything else.

Let us carry our parable a little further. Suppose now Mrs. Wahrnehmen receives some new information to the effect that her husband has been unfaithful. Suppose it becomes known to others who were previously convinced by her arguments acquitting her husband, and suppose that the new evidence confirms many of those arguments, so that the third parties now come to believe that Mr. Wahrnehmen is an adulterer. Should Mrs. Wahrnehmen give up her belief? Perhaps not. At least, it may not be a good thing to give it up at once. If she has worked out a theory to account for a great many of her husband's actions, she might better cling to her theory in spite of adverse evidence and work out some ad hoc hypotheses to account for this evidence.

This principle of clinging to one's theory in spite of adverse evidence is what C. S. Peirce, debunkingly, and Imre Lakatos, approvingly, call the principle of tenacity.[7] It receives special attention in Lakatos's treatment of a progressive research program. In science, theoretical change often comes about as a result of persevering with a rather vaguely formulated hypothesis (a core hypothesis), which the researcher will hold onto in spite of a good many setbacks. Scientists must be ready to persevere (at least for a time) even in the face of their own doubts and their recognition of the validity of their opponents' objections. If maximum fruitfulness of the experiment is to be attained, it must endure through many modifications as new evidence comes in. As Basil Mitchell has pointed out, a scientific thesis is like a growing infant, which "could be killed by premature antisepsis." The biographies of eminent scientists and scholars are replete with instances of going it alone in the face of massive intellectual opposition and finally overturning a general verdict. Hence, researchers cushion the core hypothesis against the blows and shocks that might otherwise force them to give it up. They invent ad hoc explanations in the hope of saving the core hypothesis. They surround the core hypothesis with a battery of such hypotheses, and as the ad hoc hypotheses fall, they invent new ones. Mitchell compares this process to a criminal network in which the mastermind (core hypothesis) always manages to escape detection and punishment "by sacrificing some of his less essential underlings, unless or until the final day of reckoning comes and his entire empire collapses."[8]

Admittedly, each ad hoc hypothesis weakens the system, but the core hypothesis may nevertheless turn out to approximate a true or adequate theory. But the more ad hoc hypotheses it becomes necessary to invent, the less plausibility attaches to the core hypothesis, until the time comes when the researcher is forced to give up the core hypothesis and conclude that the whole project has outlived its usefulness. In Lakatos's words, it has become a "degenerative research project."[9] No one can say exactly when that time comes in a particular project, but every experimental scientist fears it and, meanwhile, lives in hope that the current project will bear fruit.

Let us apply this paradigm to rational religious believers. Once they find themselves with a deep conviction, they have a precedent or model in science for clinging to it tenaciously, experimenting with it, drawing out all its implications, and surrounding it with tentative ad hoc or auxiliary explanations in order to cushion it from premature antisepsis. Nevertheless, if the analogy with the scientist holds, rational religious believers must recognize that the time may come when they are forced to abandon their conviction because of the enormous accumulation of counterevidence. Such rational persons probably cannot say exactly when and how this might happen, and they do not expect it to happen, but they acknowledge the possibility of its happening. There is no clear decision procedure that tells us when we have crossed over the fine line between plausibility and implausibility, but suddenly the realization hits us that we now disbelieve theory A and believe theory B, whereas up to this point the reverse was true. Conversion or paradigm switches occur every day in the minds of both the highly rational and the less rational. There is also a middle zone where a person considering two seemingly incompatible explanatory theories can find something plausible in each of them, so the person cannot be said to believe either one. Still, such individuals may place their hope in one theory and live by it in an experimental faith, keeping themselves open to new evidence and maintaining the dialogue with those who differ to avoid slipping into a state of self-deception.

The whole matter of double vision and experimental faith is quite complicated, but often we can see the world in more than one way and yet find our moral bearings. What I want to emphasize is the

Kierkegaardian point (used in an un-Kierkegaardian manner) that more important than *what* one believes is the manner in which one believes—the *how* of believing, the openness of mind, the willingness to discuss the reasons for one's belief, the carefulness of one's examination of new and conflicting evidence, one's commitment to follow the argument and not simply one's emotions—one's training as a rational person that enables one to recognize what is to count as a good argument.

This leads me to say a few things about the role and mode of argument in rationality. One problem that has plagued discussion in philosophy of religion through the ages is that the way philosophers have written has implied that unless one had a deductive proof for a religious thesis, one had no justification for it. The result of this narrow view of argument in religious matters has pushed those who believe in religion to the point of conceding too much, that is, that religion is not rational. This is one of the main reasons for the popularity of the incommensurabilist position. This is a mistake. Our concept of argument must be broadened from mere deductive and strict inductive argument to include nonrule-governed judgments. What I have in mind is the sort of intuitive judgment illustrated by the art critic in assessing an authentic work of art, the chicken sexer in identifying the sex of the baby chicks without knowing or being able to tell us how he knows the chick's sexual identity, the water diviner in discovering underground springs without knowing how he does so, or a child inventing new sentences. The child follows rules, which seem to be programmed into him or her, but he or she does not do it consciously and cannot tell us what the rules are. Later, however, he or she may be able to do so.

So "nonrule-governed reasoning" may indeed involve rules—only, we are not aware of what they are. In learning a skill we may or may not become conscious of the rules requisite for the performance of that skill. Michael Polanyi noted that while bicyclists tacitly follow rules in riding a bicycle, few know exactly what those rules are, let alone understand the basis in physics.

> I have come to the conclusion that the principle by which the bicyclist keeps his balance is not generally known. The rule observed by the cyclist is this. When he starts falling to the right he turns the handlebars to the right, so that the course of the bicycle is deflected along a curve towards the right. This results in a centrifugal force pushing the cyclist to the left and offsets the gravitational force dragging him down to the right. This maneuver presently throws the cyclist out of balance to the left, which he counteracts by turning the handlebars to the left; and so

he continues to keep himself in balance by winding along a series of appropriate curvatures. A simple analysis shows that for a given angle of unbalance the curvature of each winding is inversely proportional to the square of the speed at which the cyclist is proceeding.[10]

But this tells no one how to ride a bike. We have to learn on our own by trial and error—even though we are probably following rules such as described by Polanyi. We have *tacit* knowledge of these rules, but they seldom are articulated or come to consciousness. The phrase "nonrule-governed reasoning" refers to our conscious practice of trusting our trained intuitions and instincts, not to an actual absence of rules governing behavior.

Perhaps even more typical of everyday nonrule-governed reasoning is the process by which judges or juries make judgments when the evidence is ambiguous or there is considerable evidence on both sides of an issue. In weighing pros and cons and assessing conflicting evidence, the judge or jury does not normally go through standard logical procedures to arrive at a verdict. They rely on intangible and intuitive weighing procedures. It is hard to see how the deductive and strict inductive schemes of argument can account for our judgments when we have good reasons for and against a conclusion. Nor is it easy to see how deductive and strict inductive reasoning account for the decisions experts make in distinguishing the valuable from the mediocre. They cannot formalize their judgments, and we may not be able to offer an account of them, but we would still recognize them as valid and importantly rational.

Perhaps we ought generally to aim at formalizing our judgments as carefully as possible, using the traditional forms of reasoning, but it is not always necessary or possible to do this. We can be said to be rational because we typically arrive at decisions and judgments that other rational creatures would regard as a fair estimation of the evidence (this excuses the occasional idiosyncratic judgment—"Sue is perfectly rational except when it comes to assessing her children"), because we attempt to face the challenge of our opponent with the grounds of our beliefs, and because we are honest about the deficiencies of our positions. It is a whole family of considerations that leads us to an overall conclusion about whether or not the person is able to provide sound deductive or inductive arguments. Of course, induction plays a strong role in our relying on another's judgment (what we call *testimony*). It is because we have generally found that people of this sort usually make reliable judgments in cases of such-and-such a kind that we are ready to accept their intuitions.

A great deal more needs to be said about nonrule-governed judgments, but this discussion at least indicates that something broader than the standard moves is needed in an account of rational argument. Abduction is one type of this kind of reasoning, but what I am speaking of is broader than abduction, involving deeper qualities such as intuition. There is a need to recognize the important role that intuition plays in reasoning itself or, at least, in the reasoning or knowledge claims of the trained person. This is what the Greeks called *phronesis* ("wise insight") and *ortho logos* ("correct thinking"), and it should be given greater emphasis in contemporary philosophy.

Conclusion

As I said at the beginning of this chapter, I believe that this model for rational justification of religious belief (or acceptance) can be applied to scientific, political, and moral thinking. If what I said about the ethics of belief (chapter 17) is basically correct, we have not simply epistemic but moral obligations to seek truth and to justify our beliefs and acceptances. If soft-perspectivism is correct, then evidence is person-relative, yet we are able to reason with each other and become changed by rational discourse. If all theories are more or less underdetermined by the evidence, and it is not altogether clear in many cases how we are to compare evidence with evidence, criterion of excellence with criterion of excellence, then much of our debate must be done in a spirit of fallibility. None of us, it seems, knows enough to be dogmatic in theoretical matters. The theory of knowledge shows just how little knowledge we really have. While global skepticism has nothing to recommend it, the skeptical attitude, which leads to fallibilism, does. This is also an argument for Millian liberty in the marketplace of ideas.

> However unwillingly a person who has a strong opinion may admit the possibility that his opinion may be false, he ought to be moved by the consideration that, however true it may be, if it is not fully, frequently, and fearlessly discussed, it will be held as a dead dogma, not a living truth. . . . If opponents of all-important truths do not exist, it is indispensable to imagine them and supply them with the strongest arguments which the most skillful devil's advocate can conjure up.[11]

QUESTIONS FOR DISCUSSION

1. Examine the analysis of rationality in this chapter. What are its components? Does it leave anything important out?

2. Apply the discussion of rational justification in this chapter to political and moral beliefs. Does the application yield helpful conclusions, or do our moral and political beliefs have different aspects that call for a different type of analysis?

3. Does this chapter even do an adequate job of analyzing the relationship between reason and religious belief? Can the religious person hold his or her views as an "experimental hypothesis" as is suggested?

4. What do you make of the notion of nonrule-governed reasoning or argument? Is it valid? Can you do a better job than I have in explaining it? Can you provide other illustrations of this kind of reasoning?

5. Polanyi, in his magnum opus *Personal Knowledge,* spoke of *tacit knowledge* this way.

> We have seen how the urge to look out for clues and to make sense of them is ever alert in our eyes and ears, and in our fears and desires. The urge to understand experience, together with the language referring to experience, is clearly an extension of this primordial striving for intellectual control. The shaping of our conceptions is impelled to move from obscurity to clarity and from incoherence to comprehension, by an intellectual discomfort similar to that way which our eyes are impelled to make clear and coherent the things we see. In both cases we pick out clues which seem to suggest a context in which they make sense as its subsidiary particulars. . . .
>
> An illustration may exhibit this dual movement of comprehension in learning a language. Think of a medical student attending a course in the X-ray diagnosis of pulmonary diseases. He watches in a darkened room shadowy traces on a fluorescent screen placed against a patient's chest, and hears the radiologist commenting to his assistants, in technical language, on the significant features of these shadows. At first the student is completely puzzled. For he can see in the X-ray picture of a chest only the shadows of the heart and the ribs, with a few spidery blotches between them. The experts seem to be romancing about figments of their imagination: he can see nothing that they are talking about. Then as he goes on listening for a few weeks, looking carefully at ever new pictures of different cases, a tentative understanding will dawn on him; he will gradually forget

about the ribs and begin to see the lungs. And eventually, if he perseveres intelligently, a rich panorama of significant details will be revealed to him: of physiological variations and pathological changes, of scars, of chronic infections and signs of acute disease. He has entered a new world. . . .

Thus, at the very moment when he has learned the language of pulmonary radiology, the student will also have learned to understand pulmonary radiograms. The two can only happen together. Both halves of the problem set to us by an unintelligible text, referring to an unintelligible subject, jointly guide our efforts to solve them, and they are solved eventually together by discovering a conception which comprises a joint understanding of both the words and the things. (p. 100f)

Is this a good illustration of nonrule-governed reasoning?

NOTES

1. John Calvin, *Institutes of the Christian Religion* (1536), Book I, Chapter 7. See Alvin Plantinga, "Reason and Belief in God." In *Faith and Rationality,* ed. Alvin Plantinga and Nicholas Wolterstorff (Notre Dame, IN: University of Notre Dame Press, 1983) and Nicholas Wolterstorff, *Reason Within the Bounds of Religion* (Grand Rapids, MI: Eerdmans, 1976).

2. Nicholas Wolterstorff, *Reason Within the Bounds of Religion* (Grand Rapids, MI: Eerdmans, 1976).

   The religious beliefs of the Christian scholar ought to function as control beliefs within his devising and weighing of theories. . . . [He] ought to allow the belief-content of his authentic Christian commitment to function as control within his devising and weighing of theories. For he like everyone else ought to seek consistency, wholeness, and integrity in the body of his beliefs and commitments. Since his fundamental commitment to following Christ ought to be decisively ultimate in his life, the rest of his life ought to be brought into harmony with it. As control, the belief-content of his authentic commitment ought to function both negatively and positively. Negatively, the Christian scholar ought to reject certain theories on the ground that they conflict or do not comport well with the belief-content of his authentic commitment. (p. 72)

3. N. R. Hanson puts the point this way: "Let us consider Johannes Kepler: imagine him on a hill watching the dawn. With him is Tycho Brahe. Kepler regarded the sun as fixed: it was the earth that moved. But Tycho followed Ptolemy and Aristotle in this much at least: the earth was fixed and other celestial bodies moved around it." "Do Kepler and Tycho See the Same Thing in the East at Dawn?" *Patterns of Discovery* (Cambridge: Cambridge University Press, 1958), 5. Hanson goes on to argue that all seeing is theory laden. Seeing is "seeing as." See also Michael Polanyi, *Personal Knowledge* (Chicago: University of Chicago

Press, 1958) for the tacit dimension in perceiving. I have given a long quotation in the Questions section (question 5).

4. See Norman Malcolm, "The Groundlessness of Belief" (1977). Reprinted in *Philosophy of Religion,* 2d ed., ed. Louis Pojman (Wadsworth, 1994); Richard Rorty, *Contingency, Irony and Solidarity* (Cambridge: Cambridge University Press, 1989.)

5. Plantinga, 91.

6. J. McClendon and J. Smith make this mistake in *Understanding Religous Convictions* (Notre Dame, IN: University of Notre Dame Press, 1975), 108. But, I have heard many other philosophers do the same in discussion.

7. See Imre Lakatos, "Falsification and Metholdology of Scientific Research Programs." In *Criticism and the Growth of Knowledge,* ed. I. Lakatos and A. Musgrave (Cambridge: Cambridge University Press, 1970), 91–196. See also Basil Mitchell, "Faith and Reason: A False Antithesis," *Religious Studies* 16 (July 1980).

8. Mitchell.

9. Lakatos, 118.

10. Michael Polayni, *Personal Knowledge* (Chicago: University of Chicago Press, 1958), 49f.

11. John Stuart Mill, *On Liberty* (New York: Bobbs-Merrill, 1956).

FOR FURTHER READING

Alston, William P. *Perceiving God: The Epistemology of Religious Experience.* Ithaca, NY: Cornell University Press, 1991.

Crosson, Frederick, ed. *The Autonomy of Religious Belief.* Notre Dame, IN: University of Notre Dame Press, 1981.

Flew, Antony. *The Presumption of Atheism.* New York: Harper & Row, 1976.

Hanson, N. R. *Patterns of Discovery.* Cambridge: Cambridge University Press, 1958.

Mackie, J. L. *The Miracle of Theism: Arguments for and Against the Existence of God.* Oxford: Oxford University Press, 1982.

Martin, Michael. *Atheism.* Philadelphia: Temple University Press, 1990.

Phillips, D. Z. *Religion Without Explanation.* London: Basil Blackwell, 1976.

Plantinga, Alvin, and Nicholas Wolterstorff, eds. *Faith and Rationality.* Notre Dame, IN: University of Notre Dame Press, 1983.

Pojman, Louis. *Religious Belief and the Will.* London: Routledge & Kegan Paul, 1986.

————, ed. *Philosophy of Religion: An Anthology.* 3rd ed. Belmont, CA: Wadsworth, 1998.

Polanyi, Michael. *Personal Knowledge.* Chicago: University of Chicago Press, 1958.

Swinburne, Richard. *Faith and Reason.* Oxford: Clarendon Press, 1981.

GLOSSARY

Abduction. A form of nondeductive reasoning. Sometimes referred to as inference to the best explanation in which the proponent argues that this explanation beats all its rivals as a plausible account of the events in question.

Academic skepticism. The School of Skepticism that began in Plato's Academy and took as its motto Socrates' assertion that he knew one thing: that he didn't know anything. See *Pyrrhonian skepticism* and chapter 2.

Acceptance. To accept *p* is to adopt a policy of acting as though *p* were true, without necessarily believing that it is.

Ad hoc. A proposition added to a theory in order to save it from being considered logically impossible or implausible. As *ad hoc,* the proposition itself may have little or no support but simply serve to stave off rejection of the original theory.

Adverbial theory of perception. The theory that the grammatical object of a perceptual statement should be analyzed as an adverb. For example, the sentence "Mary is experiencing the sensation of a red square" should be analyzed as "Mary is being appeared to redly and squarely." The advantage of the theory is to bypass the debate enomenalism and indirect realism in perception. See chapter 4.

Agnosticism. The view that we do not know whether God exists. It is contrasted with theism, the belief in God, and atheism, the belief that there is no such being. Although the term is used loosely, a popular way of describing agnostics versus believers and atheists is to say that the believer in God holds that the probability of God's existence is greater than 50 percent; the atheist holds that it is less than 50 percent; and the agnostic holds that it is right at 50 percent. T. H. Huxley coined the phrase to describe an attitude that was less dogmatic than either theism or atheism.

A posteriori. From the Latin "the later." Knowledge that is obtained only from experience, such as sense perceptions or pain sensations.

A priori. From the Latin "preceding." Knowledge that is not based on sense experience, but is innate or known simply by the meaning of words or definitions. Hume limited the term to "relations of ideas," referring to analytic truths and mathematics.

Argument. A process of reasoning from a set of statements or premises to a conclusion. Arguments are either valid or invalid. They are valid if they have proper logical form and invalid if they do not.

Argument from illusion. The argument that claims that facts about illusions disprove *direct realism*. That is, direct realism claims that we perceive the world as it is, but if we cannot tell veridical perceptions from illusory ones, we should give up the idea that we have direct access to the world.

Belief. An attitude toward a proposition that assents to or holds that the proposition in question is true. Typically, belief is divided into two types: *occurrent* and *dispositional* beliefs. Occurrent beliefs are those we are presently conscious of, and dispositional beliefs are those that we hold in our total noetic structure that incline us to action. For example, I dispositionally believe that the earth is round even when I am sleeping. See chapters 13 through 16.

Coherence theory of truth. The theory that a proposition is true only if it coheres with a system of propositions that mutually entail and support each other.

Coherentist theory of justification. The theory that the justification of a belief involves the mutual support of a whole system of beliefs. See chapter 6 and *foundationalism.*

Contextual theory of knowledge. The theory that the ascription of knowledge regarding a true belief depends on the context in which the belief occurs. See *relevant alternatives* and chapter 6.

Contingent. A proposition is contingent if its denial is logically possible. Its denial is not contradictory. A being is contingent if it is not logically necessary.

Correspondence theory of truth. The theory that a proposition is true when it corresponds with the facts or states of affairs in reality. The theory goes back to Plato and, especially, Aristotle, who said that "To say of what is that it is not, or of what is not that it is, is false, while to say of what is that it is, or of what is not that it is not, is true."

Direct realism. The theory that we can perceive objects in the world directly, as opposed to indirect realism, which holds that there are nonphysical intermediaries (e.g., sense data or sense impressions). See chapter 4.

Disquotational theory of truth. The theory of truth set forth by Al-fre Tarski that seeks to simplify the notion to its bare bones. It says: Sentence S is true if and only if S is the case. For example, the sentence "Snow is white" is true if snow is white.

Doxastic. From the Greek *doxa,* for opinion or belief. It is sometimes used to distinguish a theory from an *epistemic* one, focusing not so much on knowledge but simply belief. See chapters 7, 15, and 16. See also *nondoxastic.*

Empiricism. The school of philosophy that asserts that the source of all knowledge is experience. John Locke stated that our minds were like blank slates (tabula rasa) on which experience writes her messages. There are no innate ideas. Empiricism is contrasted with rationalism, which holds that there are innate ideas, so the mind can discover important metaphysical truth through reason alone.

Epistemic Responsibility. The theory that we are responsible for many of the beliefs we acquire. We should proportion the strength of our beliefs to the strength of the evidence.

Epistemology. The study of the nature, origin, and validity of knowledge and belief.

Externalism. The epistemological view that knowledge is not to be understood in terms of reasons justifying a true belief but as beliefs produced by reliable processes, such as perception or deductive reasoning. See chapter 7 and *internalism.*

Fallibilism. The view, first articulated by C. S. Peirce and later developed by Karl Popper, that any of our beliefs or theories about the world could turn out to be false. Hence, we have no right to be dogmatic about any empirical or metaphysical belief. The theory generally allows that we can be certain about logical truths and beliefs about immediate experience.

Fideism. The doctrine that one does not need evidence for one's religious faith. Reason is inappropriate for religious belief. See chapter 19.

Foundationalism. The theory about the structure of justification and/or knowledge that divides beliefs into two categories: basic and nonbasic (or derived). It holds that basic beliefs are foundational and need no additional support, and that nonbasic beliefs are justified by their relationship to basic beliefs. A basic belief is immediately justified, whereas a nonbasic belief is mediately justified. See chapter 6 and *coherentist theory.*

Gettier problem. Traditionally, knowledge was defined as "true, justified belief." In a seminal paper, in 1963, Edmund Gettier provided two counterexamples to this definition, producing a search for alternate definitions of knowledge. See chapter 5.

The given. The idea that we have infallible or certain knowledge of immediate experience.

Global skepticism. The type of skepticism that doubts every type of proposition, except possibly logical truths. See *local skepticism.*

Incorrigibility. If someone incorrigibly believes some proposition *p,* it is impossible to show that person that he or she is mistaken. The person may be mistaken, but no one can demonstrate it. For example, if I believe that I am experiencing a red appearance, no one can prove that I am not experiencing it—even though the object that I am perceiving is some other color. *Incorrigible* does not mean *infallible.*

Indubitability. The term Descartes used for the state of being incapable of all doubt, since the belief in question was self-evident. Descartes used it as a synonym for "clear and distinct ideas." See *incorrigibility* and chapter 6.

Infallible. The idea that it is impossible that one can be mistaken about the belief in question, either because the belief is self-evidently true or logically necessary. The opposite of *fallibilism.* See *incorrigibility* and *indubitability.*

Innate ideas. The theory, first appearing in Plato's *Meno* and later in Descartes, that states that all humans are born with certain knowledge. Empiricists like John Locke rejected this doctrine, claiming that at birth each mind is a blank slate (tabula rasa). See chapter 10.

Internalism. The theory that knowledge is true belief justified in the appropriate manner as opposed to externalism where no reasons for belief are necessary for knowledge. See *externalism* and chapter 7.

Justification. The term signifies that one has sufficient grounds, reasons, or warrant for one's belief. Sometimes it is said that one is "in his or her epistemic rights to believe that *p.*" See chapters 5, 6, 7, and 17.

Local skepticism. That form of skepticism that doubts particular types of propositions (e.g., metaphysical propositions). See *global skepticism.*

Metaphysics. "Beyond physics." The study of ultimate reality, that which is not readily accessible through ordinary empirical experience. Metaphysics includes within its domain such topics as free will, causality, the nature of matter, immortality, and the existence of God.

Naturalism. The theory that epistemic explanations appeal only to the natural, physical order of reality as opposed to supernaturalism.

Necessary condition. A term denoting a special logical relationship. Condition *A* is a necessary condition for *B* means that if *B* is true, then *A* must be true. For example, being a female and having given birth are two necessary conditions for being a mother. So if *B*, Mary is a mother, is true, *A*, Mary is a female and has given birth to a child, is true. See *sufficient condition*. These concepts are used in chapter 5.

Necessary truth. A truth that cannot be false, such as an analytic proposition (e.g., "All bachelors are male").

Neutral monism. The view held by Benedictus de Spinoza and William James that reality was made up of one substance, neither matter nor mind, but something common to both of these.

Noetic structure. From the Greek *nous* (mind), having to do with an individual's system of beliefs, including one's belief-forming mechanisms. It sometimes includes desires too. See chapters 7, 15, and 17.

Nomological. Any law-like process. Externalists argue that so long as there is a law-like process that connects a belief with truth, it is justified. See chapter 8.

Nondoxastic. Meaning "not a belief state." Sometimes used regarding perceptual states. For example, John Pollock (in *Contemporary Theories of Knowledge*) holds that our empirical beliefs are justified at least in part by nondoxastic considerations. See chapter 7.

Normativity. From the noun *norm*, meaning proper standard or rule or principle used to evaluate or judge an epistemic or moral situation, the opposite of *description*. See chapter 10, W. V. Quine's naturalized epistemology, which seeks to eliminate or diminish the normative in favor of the natural processes of obtaining beliefs.

Occam's razor. Named after William of Occam (1290–1349). Sometimes called "the principle of parsimony," it states that "entities are not to be multiplied beyond necessity." The razor metaphor connotes that useless or unnecessary material should be cut away from any explanation and the simplest hypothesis accepted.

Ontology. The study of the essence of things and of what there is. What kinds of things are there in the universe? For example, the mind–body problem is in part a debate over whether mental events are of a separate substance or property from physical events or things. Descartes thought there were three different kinds of things: God, created souls, and created material things.

Phenomenalism. The theory that holds that propositions asserting the existence of physical objects are to be analyzed as propositions about sensations or perceptual reports. Berkeley's idealism, holding that material objects are simply ideas in the mind, is an extreme version of this theory. Mill's theory that material objects are "permanent possibilities of sensation" is a less radical version. See chapter 4.

Pragmatic theory of truth. The theory set forth by C. S. Peirce and William James, which interprets the meaning of a statement in terms of its practical consequences. They usually go on, as James does, to say that a proposition is true or false according to its results. Contemporary philosophers, such as Richard Rorty, hold variations of this theory. Rorty says that "truth" is what one can defend against one's peers. See chapter 1.

Prima facie. The Latin phrase that means "at first glance." It signifies an initial status of an idea or principle. In ethics, beginning with W. D. Ross, it stands for a duty that has a presumption in its favor, but may be overridden by another duty. Prima facie duties are contrasted with actual duties or "all things considered" duties. Similarly, we may speak of prima facie epistemic justification, as opposed to "all things considered" or actual justification.

Proposition. A sentence or statement that must either be true or false. Every statement that "states" how the world is a proposition. Questions and imperatives are not propositions. "Would you open the door" and "Please, open the door," are not propositions, but "The door is open" is since it claims to describe a situation.

Pyrrhonian skepticism. Founded by Pyrrho of Elis (ca. 360–270 B.C.). Whereas the academic skeptics held that we could be certain that we knew nothing, the Pyrrhonians denied even that. We cannot even know that we can't have knowledge. See *academic skepticism* and chapter 3.

Rationalism. The school of philosophy that holds that there are important truths that can be known by the mind even though we have never experienced them. The rationalist generally believes in innate knowledge (or ideas), so we can have certainty about metaphysical truth. Plato and Descartes are two classic examples of rationalists.

Regress problem. The epistemic "regress problem" signifies the problem of establishing justification or knowledge. If belief *B* needs to be justified by some other belief *C*, and *C* by *D*, and so on, we end up with an infinite regress or a circle. Coherentism solves the problem by explaining appropriately wide circles, whereas foundationalism seeks to ground all nonbasic beliefs in properly basic beliefs. See chapter 6.

Relevant alternatives. A form of the *contextual theory of knowledge* first set forth by Fred Dretske, which holds that one may have knowledge of an empirical proposition even if one cannot be absolutely certain of its truth, just as long as one can distinguish between it and the relevant alternatives. See chapter 6.

Reliabilism. The theory that knowledge consists in true beliefs that are produced by reliable processes or mechanisms. It is a version of externalism. See chapters 7 and 8.

Self-evidence. Self-evident propositions are those known independently of all others. They are evident in themselves. See chapter 6.

Sense data. The immediate objects of perception. The term was first set forth by G. E. Moore and Bertrand Russell to distinguish our awareness of physical objects from the objects themselves. See chapter 4.

Skepticism. The view that we can have no knowledge. Universal skepticism holds that we cannot know anything at all, whereas local or particular skepticism holds that there are important realms in which we are ignorant (e.g., Hume regarding metaphysics). See chapters 2 and 3.

Solipsism. The term is derived from the Latin "self alone" and signifies the thesis that I am the only conscious being in the universe. All other beings are properties of my mind. See the problems of other minds in chapter 12.

Sufficient condition. A term indicating a logical relationship. A is a sufficient condition for B means that if A is true, then B is true. Being a mother is a sufficient condition for being a woman who has given birth to an offspring. See *necessary condition*. This term is used in chapter 5.

Transmission. An epistemic category signifying how knowledge or justification can be extended, such as by deductive and inductive inferences. See chapter 6.

Volit. The act of acquiring a belief simply by willing to have it. See chapters 16 and 17.

Volitionalism. The theory that we can decide what to believe and successfully acquire beliefs by willing to have them. Direct volitionalism holds that we can acquire beliefs directly upon willing to have them; while indirect volitionalism holds that we can only acquire such beliefs by going through indirect processes. See chapters 16 and 17.

INDEX

349